The Mystery of Fascism

Other Books by David Ramsay Steele

Orwell Your Orwell: A Worldview on the Slab (2017)

Therapy Breakthrough: Why Some Psychotherapies Work Better than Others
(with Michael R. Edelstein and Richard K. Kujoth, 2013)

Atheism Explained: From Folly to Philosophy (2008)

Three Minute Therapy: Change Your Thinking, Change Your Life
(with Michael R. Edelstein, 1997)

From Marx to Mises: Post-Capitalist Society
and the Challenge of Economic Calculation (1992)

The Mystery of Fascism
David Ramsay Steele's
Greatest Hits

DAVID RAMSAY STEELE

ST. AUGUSTINE'S PRESS
South Bend, Indiana

Library of Congress Control Number: 2019945134

St. Augustine's Press
www.staugustine.net

To my wonderful, creative children:

Emma, Allan, Ursula, and Duncan

Cet animal est très méchant. Quand on l'attaque, il se défend.

Contents

Foreword by David R. Henderson

One thing I find annoying in much of my non-fiction reading is essays for which I don't know the point until almost the end. What I learned while writing for *Fortune* in the 1980s and 1990s and for the *Wall Street Journal* from the early 1990s to now is to tell the reader the main point up front. I give that advice to any budding writer who will listen. "Don't leave the reader in suspense," I tell them, "You're writing an op/ed or essay, not a detective novel. The easiest thing for a reader to do is stop reading."

I've almost never read essays that violate my rule and still keep me reading. And over the years, I've become more impatient, not less. Well, guess what? Many of David Ramsay Steele's essays and articles in this book violate my rule but every single one of them kept me reading with a keen desire to know where it was going. I'm not sure why. Maybe it's his biting humor that goes along with his keen powers of observation. Whatever the reason, it works.

David writes on a wide range of topics, and his writing is always interesting, well informed, and insightful. While the book is titled *The Mystery of Fascism*, and I highly recommend the title essay for its fascinating history and insights, there are so many more essays I recommend. I'll highlight a few.

In a piece that defends the idea that gambling is productive, David takes on one of the most important economists in the last half of the twentieth century, Paul Samuelson. He shows that in claiming that gambling is unproductive, Samuelson contradicts a pretty fundamental economic principle. Along the way, David argues with biting humor. An excerpt:

A footnote [in Samuelson's famous textbook] informs the reader that "in all professional gambling arrangements, the participants lose out on balance. The leakage comes from the fact that the odds are always rigged in favor of the 'house', so that even an 'honest' house will win in the long run." Notice the nasty quotes around "honest," and the use of the word "rigged" to represent the fact that these sneaky casino operators do not provide their services as a charity, but require to be recompensed for their efforts, just like college professors or writers of textbooks.

I'll never again argue against those who want to prohibit gambling without first rereading 'Yes, Gambling Is Productive and Rational'.

One of the most fascinating pieces is 'Life, Liberty, and the Treadmill', in which David discusses the literature on the connection between income and happiness. The books he reviews argue that there is little connection between income and happiness. Yet, writes David, the same evidence the authors discuss shows that poor people in rich countries are happier than poor people in poor countries. Moreover, although we so often hear that people are made unhappy when they are lower in the income scale than those around them, the evidence shows, writes David, that "people of moderate income are equally happy whether they live in predominantly poor or predominantly affluent areas." Also, of the three kinds of freedom one author discusses—economic, political, and private—the one most positively correlated with happiness is economic freedom. This should not be surprising, David notes, because economic freedom is the very substance of our lives:

> Compared to the option of living and working where you please, at whatever occupation you wish, doing what you choose to do without permission from anyone on high, the liberty to vote in elections or to pass out leaflets on the street is, for the great majority of folks, rather a minor consideration, especially in poor countries.

What happens to happiness when incomes fall rather than just rise slowly or stagnate? David notes that we don't have much evidence but that "thanks to the valiant efforts of helpful souls like Hugo Chavez, we will not run out of examples of countries with falling incomes, and perhaps this theory can be tested before long."

One of the most profound essays is 'What Follows from the Nonexistence of Mental Illness?' In that essay, David considers the thinking of psychiatrist Thomas Szasz who argued both that there is no such thing as mental illness and that people should not be forcibly treated for alleged mental illness. David pokes some important holes in Szasz's view that there is no such thing as mental illness, and also argues that even if people were mentally ill, this is scarcely justification for forcibly committing them to mental institutions or forcibly treating them for mental illness. The argument is nuanced and persuasive. It helped me square an intellectual circle that I had been struggling with for almost fifty years.

Not to be missed is 'The Bigotry of the New Atheism'. If you think that Christians and people of other religions are murderous, then wait until you see Steele's facts about the murders committed by atheists. I don't say this because of my love for Christianity: in fact, I'm an atheist.

I could easily name more than five additional essays that are insightful and informative. But why do so? Instead, I recommend that you read the book.

David R. Henderson is an emeritus professor of economics with the Naval Postgraduate School in Monterey, California, and a research fellow with the Hoover Institution at Stanford University. He is author of *The Joy of Freedom: An Economist's Odyssey* and editor of *The Concise Encyclopedia of Economics*.

Part I
More Popular than Scholarly

1
ALICE IN WONDERLAND (1987)

Walk into any decent bookshop in any part of the English-speaking world, and you are liable to find a shelf or two entirely taken up with the works of Ayn Rand. Week in, week out; year in, year out. If you're a bookseller, this is a sight better than Erich von Däniken or Leo Buscaglia.

Some of Rand's books are novels, some are on aesthetics, some on political philosophy, some on epistemology and metaphysics. These are books which, in the words of the old Sixties ads for *Catch-22*, "will change your life." They make converts. Typically, the future Randist begins with that bulky mega-seller, *The Fountainhead*. Reading *The Fountainhead* is an overpowering emotional experience. It is a spellbinding story with a certain amount of preaching sprinkled in. The reader may find the ideas, and even more, the hints of ideas, alluring.

The novice moves on to *Atlas Shrugged*, even bulkier (1,084 pages) but still phenomenally popular. The story is less spellbinding, indeed, less than spellbinding, and there is much, much more preaching sprinkled in, but by this time the reader has acquired a taste for Rand's distinctive form of rhetoric, and is ready to graduate to her nonfiction works, *For the New Intellectual*, *The Romantic Manifesto*, *The Virtue of Selfishness*, even *Introduction to Objectivist Epistemology*. Here the budding Randist finds, declaimed in strident, bad-tempered prose, a new gospel, a system of ideas, a creed applicable to all aspects of life. Among the articles of this creed are: that there is no God; that laissez-faire capitalism is the best possible economic system; that limited government is the only correct political order; that the United States of America is the best society in human history and virtually always entirely in the right in its conflicts with other powers; that cigarette-smoking is both harmless and morally virtuous; that Hume and Kant are loathsome villains, whilst Aristotle, Aquinas, and Ayn Rand are the great heroes of philosophy; that Rachmaninoff is a hero of music, while J.S. Bach and

{3}

Richard Wagner are among the villains, with their "malevolent sense of life"; that Dostoyevsky and Hugo are great novelists; that, in more recent times, Ian Fleming and Mickey Spillane are also outstanding writers—and of course, Ayn Rand; that a photograph can never be a work of art; that liking horror stories always indicates a mystical outlook and therefore mental sickness. And, most famously, that altruism or self-sacrifice is the great vice and source of all vices, whilst egoism or selfishness is the great virtue and source of all virtues.

There are many readers of Rand who graduate in this way, just by reading the books, without authoritative guidance, and they will perhaps tell you that the above is a caricature, that there is no creed, that some of these items are just Rand's personal opinions, with which they (the readers) happen to disagree. But in the old days there was an organized Randian church. It was called the Nathaniel Branden Institute. It lasted from 1958 until 1968, when it terminated due to the messy and spiteful falling out of Rand and Nathaniel, the rock upon which she had hoped to found her church.

When the Nathaniel Branden Institute (NBI) was in operation, there could never be any doubt in the minds of its apostles, adherents, apostates, or excommunicatees that Randism or Objectivism was indeed a creed. If you didn't smoke, you had better have a damned good reason—a certificate signed by several Objectivist physicians might be safest. If you were married to a theist, you had better get a divorce. If you were depraved enough to enjoy Bach, better change your musical tastes pronto.

Like many cults, the Randist network of NBI (which existed only in North America) used group pressure, scorn, and contempt to humiliate and degrade those individuals who betrayed wretchedness by signs of deviance—in this case, by liking Tolstoy, feeling a duty to help one's relatives, growing a mustache, entertaining the thought that there might be a God, feeling tolerant towards homosexuality, or being concerned about the disappearance of living species due to industrial pollution.

Ayn Rand is, on many counts, a remarkable figure. The mere sales of her books constitute an outstanding achievement, but I cannot think of any historical parallels for someone who used a popular art form to successfully promote an all-encompassing doctrine, especially one that was so eccentric a mix of disparate elements, and one that was so out of fashion when she began to propound it. We have to imagine something like Ferdinand

Lassalle writing Jack London's novels, but even this does not come near the prodigious strangeness and strange prodigiousness of Rand's accomplishments. She has had a significant impact upon the world, but there are unmistakable signs that the impact is only beginning. She has had a traceable influence upon the Reagan administration, which might have pleased her (she died in 1982) even though she fiercely opposed Reagan, because—and if you don't know already, shut your eyes and see if you can guess—he was anti-abortion, a clear demonstration that he was evil and sick, even though he might be posing as an anti-communist.

It's often claimed that Rand gave birth to the modern libertarian movement. This is an exaggeration, but it is true that the overwhelming majority of leading lights in the libertarian movement of the 1960s had earlier gone through a Randist phase, and even today the peculiar quirks of Randist jargon ("facts of reality," "whim-worshipper," "Robin Hood ethics," "blank out") pop up occasionally.

A Riveting Tale

The tale told by Barbara Branden is absolutely riveting.[1] It's considered high praise to say of a book that, having once begun it, you can't put it down, but for me the more significant accolade is that having *finished* it you can't put it down, and that is certainly true of this amazing and fascinating story. It recounts Rand's life, partly on the basis of personal recollection and partly on the basis of detailed research. The portrait of Rand is outrageously vivid, yet patchy. There was something abnormally potent and enthralling about Rand, and although those who never met her can hardly reconstruct exactly what it was, Branden's book is impressive testimony to its existence and approximate contours. Yet there are puzzling gaps and murky areas.

The organism which was later to denote itself as "Ayn Rand" was born in St Petersburg during the abortive Russian Revolution of 1905, and given the name Alyssa (Alice) Rosenbaum. The daughter of a self-made pharmacist, she emerged as a distant, precocious child. By the age of ten she was already making snap judgments about everything and everybody in the world,

---

1   *The Passion of Ayn Rand* by Barbara Branden. Garden City: Doubleday, 1986.

turning these judgments into unshakable dogmas, demanding as the price of non-belligerence that people accept these dogmas, and seething with violent indignation against anyone who denied, or for that matter, failed to personify, these dogmas. In one of the taped interviews which Rand gave Branden decades later, Rand says: "By fifteen, my sex theory was fully formed" (p. 34). As the context makes clear, the fifteen-year-old's theory of sex incorporated views she had held passionately since at least the age of ten.

Alice and her family suffered hardships during the civil war following the Bolshevik *putsch*. Bolshevik repression served only to encourage in her breast precisely those counter-revolutionary feelings the persecution was designed to extirpate. By chance, Alice avoided the liquidation which the heroine of her first novel, *We the Living*, could not escape, and in 1926 she contrived to visit relatives in Chicago. Like droves of others before and since, Alice had to lie to get into the US, pretending her visit was intended to be temporary. Despite this, immigration controls were not prominent among the state interventions later denounced by Rand.

On the boat over, Alice changed her name to Ayn (rhymes with MINE!). In one of Branden's many infuriating omissions, she explains that "Ayn" was taken from the name of a Finnish writer whom Alice had not read, but says nothing more about this writer, or whether Rand subsequently read her—or him. It goes without saying that the Finnish Ayn was a ferociously evil, mentally sick, whim-worshipping mystic, like everyone else, but readers need to be told how this discovery was made, and any little details associated with it. Some years later, Ayn Rosenbaum selected the name "Rand" from her Remington-Rand typewriter. As Rand remarked, criminals and writers usually keep their initials when they change their names.

From Chicago, Rand moved to Hollywood in search of fame as a screen writer. Awkward, pathetic, and still far from fluent in English, she seems to have aroused feelings of warm altruism and Christian charity in many people, who went to great lengths to help her. In Russia she had admired Cecil B. De Mille's pictures, so she went to the De Mille studio, to be given the usual polite brush-off. In the street she spotted De Mille in the flesh, and stood gawping at him, provoking his curiosity. De Mille got her a job, and the De Milles took the little Russian waif under their protective wings.

Working as an extra on *King of Kings*, she instantly fell in love with, and later married, another extra, Frank O'Connor, who was to spend most of his life boozing and living off her books, the epitome of the "mooching bum" she was always cursing in her apoplectic writings. With De Mille's help again, she got a job summarizing and adapting screenplay proposals. During the thirties she became aware of the strong Bolshevik sympathies of Western intellectuals, and worked on her first novel and her play, *Penthouse Legend* (better known as *Night of January 16th*) which introduced the gimmick, since imitated several times, of having more than one ending, with the choice made by the audience or, as in this case, by a jury selected from the audience. Both novel and play were modest successes, and Rand became known as that then freakish creature, a writer and intellectual who was a strong anti-Communist and in no way sympathetic to socialism.

In the late thirties and early forties she worked on her second novel, *The Fountainhead*, and worked for the Willkie campaign against the re-election of Roosevelt. She met many of the leading figures of American conservatism, which in those pre-Buckley days still contained strong elements of classical liberalism. She was later to fall out with all these conservative acquaintances. With the sale of the movie rights to *The Fountainhead* for fifty thousand dollars, Rand moved from obscurity to fame and from poverty to comfort. In 1947 she appeared as a 'friendly witness' before the House Un-American Activities Committee, investigating Communist infiltration of Hollywood. Branden makes some gestures towards defending Rand for this discreditable activity.

As *The Fountainhead* was beginning its delayed success, and while working on *Atlas Shrugged*, Rand heard from two young admirers, who were to change their names to Nathaniel and Barbara Branden. (It has been contended that the name "Branden" is derived from "ben-Rand," but Branden doesn't confirm this.) They both became worshippers of Rand, and introduced her to other acolytes. In 1958, NBI was formed to indoctrinate enquirers and followers into the complete system of Ayn Rand: her opinions on art, politics, and metaphysics were presented to the "students of Objectivism" as sacred truths. But even before the formation of NBI, Nathaniel had first married Barbara on Rand's recommendation, then commenced a once-a-week sexual arrangement with Rand, twenty years his senior, with the full knowledge and consent of his and Rand's spouses. This "rational" affair continued for a decade, as NBI expanded, Rand's fame grew, and Rand and Nathaniel lectured together to the unsuspecting flock.

The great break between Rand and Nathaniel came after an interregnum in the affair, following which Nathaniel refused to recommence it because of his involvement with another woman, an involvement which he had kept from Rand's knowledge. Rand's discovery of how she had been deceived led to the expulsion and anathematizing of Nathaniel, the breakup of NBI, and the demand that all true followers of Objectivism should join Rand in pouring scorn, hatred, and lies upon the Brandens. Apparently, Rand's theory was that since Nathaniel had behaved so immorally, he had forfeited any right to decent treatment, so any kind of stories could be fabricated about him—including the charge that he had misappropriated the funds of NBI. The question was even raised at an Objectivist discussion of whether it would be moral to have Nathaniel assassinated. (Bear in mind that these "rational" people were kept in the dark about what Nathaniel was supposed to have done, and were expected to follow Rand blindly in attacking Nathaniel.)

Much, one supposes, to Rand's vast annoyance, her denunciations of Nathaniel and intrigues against him did not halt his extraordinary success as a pop psychologist. His fame as both writer and therapist has grown remarkably. His *Psychology of Self Esteem* (twenty-one impressions since 1969) deals at length with problems of insufficient self-esteem, but says nothing about the problem of excessive self-esteem.

The soap opera continues. Some of it you can catch up on by reading *The Passion of Ayn Rand*. The orthodox Randists, led by Leonard Peikoff, have put it about that anyone who utters a word in praise of the book is to be shunned, boycotted, and cut off root and branch. Outside the ranks of the Elect, voices have been raised that Branden's omissions and misleading emphases call for correction, and we can expect numerous further memoirs and polemical commentaries. I very much doubt that any of them will be half as well-written or gripping as this one.

A Selective Picture

I am not one of those blessed by past personal contact with any of the original Randist apostles. I cannot pronounce on the numerous allegations and counter-allegations which Branden's book has stirred up. But it's clear from a modest amount of background knowledge, plus a careful examination of

The Passion of Ayn Rand, that it is a piece of special pleading. The author is, I am sure, telling the truth and nothing but the truth, as she remembers it, but she is not telling the whole truth. She places facts in that light which best suits her purposes.

On my first reading, I concluded that Rand had treated Branden very badly, and Branden had responded with continuing adoration, despite some criticisms. On my second reading, I concluded that the author was all the time working very hard to give me exactly that impression—which by no means implies that it is untrue, but does put it in a different perspective. The attitude Branden has towards Rand is one that individuals generally hold only towards their parents: a burning anger, a rage for self-justification, contained by a rigid insistence that the parent is good and worthy. In Branden's case, this seems to be bound up with her urgent need to deny the patent fact that Rand had a blighting effect upon her (Branden's) life, as Rand did on the lives of most of those she knew.

This book contains many statements describing Rand as an extraordinary intellect—"the brilliance and intricacy of her mind" (p. 173), "her astonishing intellectual powers . . . vast intelligence" (p. 303)—yet it contains no evidence for these statements. It is asserted that Rand's conversation was tremendously high-powered and persuasive, but no attempt is made, by this veteran of hundreds of these conversations, to reproduce any of the searing insights or masterly analyses. I conclude, on the evidence of Rand's writings, that this is because there were none: undoubtedly Rand possessed an uncommon personal magnetism, especially for docile souls who craved for someone to tell them what was what, but she was no great thinker in any field. (There are two or three isolated witticisms. Asked who, in her proposed kind of society, would "look after the janitors," Rand replied: ". . . the janitors.")

Branden does mention Rand's "series of angry ruptures with people who had been her friends" (p. 153) but somewhat plays this down. Rand fell out nastily with almost everyone, a propensity which some Randists have inherited. There is no mention here, for instance, of Rand's breaks with Rose Wilder Lane or Edith Efron.

Branden's angry worship of Rand is revealed in her constant desire to catch Rand out in mistakes, and yet defend Rand strenuously against the unpleasant inferences which might be drawn from these mistakes, though such inferences are often all too obviously warranted. Branden's apology for Rand's behavior over the alterations to *We the Living* (pp. 114–15) is noteworthy. The first edition of *We the Living* reflects Rand's political ideas shortly after her arrival in the US, including her Nietzschean contempt for the fate of the common herd. Some time later, Rand brought her views more into conformity with Anglo-Saxon liberalism. She removed from later editions the passages praising ruthless elitism, but stated in her foreword: "I have not added or eliminated to or from [*sic*] the content of the novel . . . all the changes are merely editorial line-changes." Branden tries to defend this by a soft-focus exegesis of the shrill anti-common man message of the first edition. This not only glosses over Rand's lack of candor about the changes; it leaves unexamined the broader question, Rand's reticence about her own change of views and therefore about the sources of that change of views. For any non-Randist with an interest in fiction there is also something quaint about the assumption, undoubtedly made by Rand and shared by Branden, that a speech by a "good" character must coincide with the author's own opinions.

Rand had a very poorly developed sense of humor, which she defended by being almost opposed on principle to humor. She had great scorn for the notion that one should be able to laugh at oneself. By taking up this position, she deprived herself of many long hours of rich amusement. Rand and all her circle were people who took themselves too seriously. Her laissez-faire liberal views aside, she is typical of a certain kind of left-wing intellectual who tries to subject her whole life, including her sexual relationships, to "rationality." Rand's affair with Nathaniel was supposed to be rational. According to Rand, the person one loves represents one's highest values. Since Rand was the noblest person Nathaniel knew, as well as being the most rational person in human history, it was right and proper for them to go to bed once a week. When it came out that Nathaniel no longer wanted an intimate physical involvement with his intellectual mentor, because she was too old and he had found someone else, Rand's sexual jealousy was rationalized in the verdict that Nathaniel was morally depraved. This sort of thing would be merely comical, if it were not that the personal misery was magnified by everyone's determination to be, as they thought, rational.

Human sexual impulses are largely the outcome of past competition among genes. Human feelings and responses are those which have tended in the past to cause some genes to reproduce themselves more rapidly than others. Our endowment of sexual emotions did not come about in order to enhance the happiness of individuals or the well-being of society, but in order (as it were) to enhance the copyability of little bits of DNA. If you try to make something rational out of that, you make a fool of yourself. Behavior may be legitimately described as "rational" or "irrational" insofar as the means chosen are well or badly suited to achieve the ends sought. It makes no sense to speak of ultimate ends (like whether or not you wish to stay alive or to avoid suffering) as rational or irrational.

The Randist Legacy

Branden tries to defend Rand's humorlessness by relating it to her singularly logical mind (p. 172), but this must be wrong because Rand did not possess a singularly logical mind. She was inclined to sloppy thinking. She took herself too seriously, partly because she was humored by the likes of the Brandens, who tolerated her cantankerousness on the mistaken grounds that she was a great thinker—though even great thinkers should not be humored when they take themselves too seriously. This did a disservice to Rand, as such humoring generally does, because it enabled her to live increasingly within her own world of fantasy, unchallenged by effective criticism. Perhaps she was too set by her twenties for any criticism to be effective. Be that as it may, gullible followers are never scarce.

Branden's desire to place Rand's tantrums in a favorable light often leads her to make dubious judgments. Branden remarks upon "how rare it had been in her life that a hand was held out to her in simple human kindness" (p. 169). On the evidence of Branden's own book, this is far from the case. In her 1957 autobiographical note to *Atlas Shrugged* ("About the Author"), Rand asserts: "I had a difficult struggle . . . No one helped me . . ." It appears from Branden's account that Rand was a constant beneficiary of charity and kindness until she started making big money from *The Fountainhead*.

When she arrived in Chicago, she was looked after by the relatives who had made it possible for her to get out of Russia. She declared then that when she became rich, she would buy her aunt a Rolls-Royce. When she did become rich, she didn't even reply to these relatives' letters. On arrival in Los Angeles, Rand stayed at the Studio Club, a philanthropically-subsidized home for young women seeking their fortunes in Hollywood. She was often behind with her rent, but was not evicted. After *We the Living* was published, Rand gratefully sent an autographed copy to the Studio Club's director. The Studio Club subsequently had to close for lack of funds. At every turn, people went out of their ways to help Rand by recommending her writings and finding her jobs and contracts. She habitually repaid kindness with indifference or with venom.

The most unsuccessful part of Branden's book is the final chapter, a listing of numerous people of prominence in many fields who have been influenced by Rand. Many of these people are prominent and avowed libertarians. Surely Branden should have mentioned the fact that Rand despised and detested libertarianism? (She does mention Rand's hostility specifically to the Libertarian Party, attributing this to the fact that some LP members were anarchists.) Rand always denounced the libertarian movement, its philosophy, its methods, its goals, and its personalities. Among other things, she castigated it for "plagiarism" of her ideas, an instance of her colossal presumptuousness, since a political movement is free to be influenced by any published writer, libertarians have always been frank or over-generous about what they owed to Rand, and Rand herself took the ideas from others.

Although Rand's influence is indeed enormous and still growing, Branden overstates it. This is part and parcel of the *ostinato* "rooting for Rand" theme in Branden's book. It only spoils the absorbing account of an intrinsically fascinating figure to keep insisting implausibly that she is a world-shaking genius.

The method of listing people prepared to say "Rand changed my life" is not convincing. The majority of confirmed meat-caters in the US had some early contact with McDonald's, but this doesn't mean we can confidently attribute the prevalence of meat-eating to the influence of McDonald's. People with an appetite for certain kinds of ideas will gravitate to the purveyors of those ideas. Alan Greenspan does not appear to owe any of his economic ideas to Rand—economic theory was apparently the one area where she did not personally hand down the total truth. Murray Rothbard was a libertarian before he met Rand, and would have been an effective free market propagandist aside from his brief association with Rand. The fact that Billie Jean King was inspired by reading *Atlas Shrugged* is not of great consequence for anyone else. Some of the most effective proponents of libertarian ideas, like Ludwig von Mises and Milton Friedman, do not show evidence of the slightest Randist influence. (Mises met and admired Rand, but there is no taint of Randism in his writings.) As for the relationship between Randism and Reaganite conservatism, it should be obvious which is the flea and which is the dog.

The major effect of Rand upon libertarians has been to favor the doctrine of natural rights, though most libertarian writers who do accept natural rights (Rothbard, Nozick, David Friedman, for example) adhere to forms of the doctrine which aren't particularly close to Rand's, and to date this preoccupation with natural rights has not borne any fruit in the shape of a coherent explanation or defense of the doctrine (that is any advance upon Herbert Spencer). I doubt that Randism will ever have any appreciable direct impact on philosophy or politics, though it may perhaps have some small impact on literature, by helping to rehabilitate the supreme importance of a good story.

The Randist influence on the libertarian movement has slumped in the past ten years, a thoroughly healthy development, but also an inevitable one, as young people first captivated by Rand find the dogmas beginning to chafe. Randism will never have any influence on *National Review/American Spectator* conservatism, enmired as that is in its own equally threadbare, but more popular and more intelligently-argued dogmas, associated with religion, traditionalism, and state-worship. Randism's influence within the libertarian movement will continue to dwindle away: Rand is becoming to libertarianism something like Fourier to socialism.

The only home for born-again Randists will be in the narrow church of Peikoff and Schwartz, The Ayn Rand Institute and *The Intellectual Activist*. While pouring abuse on libertarianism (mainly because it permits a wide range of philosophical and strategic views, encompassing approval of God, anarchy, sexual and chemical deviation, and the natural rights of dispossessed Palestinians) the Objectivist cult offers a warm embrace only to those who swallow the Randist creed in every detail. After all, how could a rational person co-operate politically with anyone who didn't like Rachmaninoff?

Given the vast readership of Rand's writings, and the dazzling appeal of a creed which offers a solution to all intellectual, personal, and social problems by learning to mouth a few catch-phrases, I expect that the cult will achieve a very large membership during the next few years, comparable to Scientology or La Rouchism—with about the same intellectual level, the same deleterious effects on the minds and lives of the cult members, and the same, absolutely negligible amount of influence on political thought.

Atlas Winced

Rand's best work by far is *The Fountainhead*, an extraordinarily gripping story based on the idea that a person who knows what he wants and strives for it without being afraid of other people's reactions is admirable, while a person who is continually taking his bearings from other people's evaluations is sadly warped. Rand's original title was *Second-Hand Lives*. The characters are stylized, diagrammatic representations of notions from Rand's ethical and psychological theories, but she has taken some pains to make them different from each other, internally consistent, and believable. The book is especially attractive for readers who know nothing of Rand's ideas, for the characters' bizarre motivations then seem to be sometimes inexplicable. and this adds an intriguing air of mystery to an otherwise cut-and-dried narrative. Judging from Branden's account, it's an enormous pity that Rand was made to shorten the novel by eliminating one major character. Inclusion of Roark's first cohabitee, the film star Vesta Dunning. would have made Roark less conventionally well-behaved and his egoism more of a challenge. (Rand. who never fully mastered English, mistakenly used the term 'egotism' in *The Foutainhead*. Instead of correcting this in later editions, she attached a note explaining that she had been misled by a faulty dictionary—and. to prove it, citing the dictionary in question!) In this work Rand displays an extremely astute dramatic sense—inclined to run to crude melodrama, but there is a welcome niche in fiction for crude melodrama. Somehow this talent of Rand's was lost when she came to perpetrate that crashing failure, *Atlas Shrugged*.

In *The Fountainhead*, the preaching is kept within bounds, and is generally not too jarringly inauthentic. The one bad lapse is the long speech in which Ellsworth Toohey lays bare his own motivations—but Rand had put herself in an impossible position with her ethical theory. For Rand, a villain must be a completely self-sacrificing person. Toohey is an intelligent villain who wants power. but somehow it has to come across that in wanting power he is not being selfish—which would be virtuous! If Toohey had been dedicated to a mistaken ideal—based on the theory that everyone would be happier in a world of self-sacrifice—it would be convincing, but we would have no reason to hate him. If Toohey had known that universal self-sacrifice would lead to universal misery, but wanted it for the selfish motive of getting power for himself, this would have been detestable, but dangerous to Rand's egoistic message. Toohey has to want to do his bit towards a goal which (it is made clear) can arrive only after his death, to know that the goal will make everyone completely wretched, and to want it for that reason. But this just makes him an unbelievable loony, bereft of any plausible link to real persons like Lewis Mumford and Harold Laski (who were among Rand's models for Toohey).

The movie of *The Fountainhead* retains enough of the book that it must deeply puzzle any reflective person who sees it, unaware of the ethical and political baggage. Gary Cooper is a disaster as Roark. Branden claims that the movie was shot nearly unchanged from Rand's script, but surely this must be wrong. As I recall, the film plays down or conceals altogether the crucial fact that the building dynamited by Roark is a government housing project. Surely Rand would never have willingly permitted that.

The Fountainhead illustrates Rand's disgust for people she called "second-handers." There is a strange oversight in the treatment of this subject by Rand and her followers. The second-hander is someone who thinks relationships are more important than ideas. The heroic or independent person is someone who thinks ideas are valuable in themselves and that relationships are merely instrumental. Neither Rand nor Branden ever seem to have noticed that the first is virtually a definition of a woman's personality, and the second, of a man's personality. Branden does note that Rand had problems with her own femininity, that when she was young she had a fierce crush on a beautiful female tennis-player, that Rand wore short hair and a cape, chain-smoked. and for a while even carried a cane, that she was always strangely drawn to beautiful women. Naively or wisely, Branden who psychologizes a lot on other matters, does not speculate about this. Perhaps subconscious perception of Rand's gender ambiguity helps to account for her otherwise inexplicable spell, as, according to W.W. Bartley III, was the case with Wittgenstein.

The Fountainhead continues to be a huge commercial success, but Branden cannot resist her usual extravagant overstatement. She refers to "the odyssey of *The Fountainhead*, unique in publishing history . . ." (p. 180). Literally this is correct: the career of every book published is unique. But Branden makes clear that what she means is that Rand's novels are unmatched in their contrast between a slow start and subsequent multi-million sales. There have actually been much more extreme contrasts, for example *The Great Gatsby*, *Steppenwolf*, and *Lord of the Rings*.

In *Atlas Shrugged* a future United States is sinking into interventionist chaos, with more and more government controls causing more and more disorganization. The rest of the world has long since collapsed into the barbarism of starving "peoples' states." One by one, all the most brilliant intellects in the US—businessmen, artists, scientists, businessmen, philosophers, businessmen, businessmen, and businessmen—mysteriously disappear. The heroine, who manages a large railroad corporation. becomes aware that there is a conspiracy behind the disappearances. The plot is that of a mystery story, but there is no mystery: the solution is obvious before page 50, and is hammered into the reader's head on each of the next few hundred pages. The great achievers are going on strike, because they are fed up with the way everyone else is living off their achievements whilst maligning and persecuting them. The achievers have disappeared into obscurity. and every year they all take a holiday together at Galt's Gulch, a utopian haven in the mountains, based on gold coinage and the mutual respect born of rational greed.

The book has many virtues, including a fundamentally sound plot and a lucid, unpretentious narrative style. It was the first major work I read connected with twentieth-century free market ideas, and I was at first dazzled by its seeming audacity and its eerie, anachronistic, dreamlike quality. I was also inspired by its hints of a fully-worked out theoretical system, a metaphysical, epistemological, and ethical structure which somehow supported the author's political conclusions. It was a great disappointment to find later that this system did not exist. The various speeches and allusions in *Atlas Shrugged*—so obviously far-fetched and logically slipshod, but perhaps defensible as rhetoric within a novel—are themselves quoted at length in Rand's fiction essays on philosophy, art and politics. The horrible, pitiful truth finally dawned: *this is all there is to Rand*. She really believes that this mouth-frothing sloganeering is philosophy, is reasoning, is the way to persuade rational people.

All the faults of *The Fountainhead* have become horribly magnified, and most of its saving features have been lost. *Atlas Shrugged* doesn't contain any convincing characters, only cardboard cut-outs which move jerkily this way and that, while the ventriloquist-author has them spouting her doctrines. The good characters all agree exactly with the author's views on sex, business, music, philosophy, politics, and architecture—the only exception is that sometimes one of the good characters hasn't quite grasped a significant point, and when the penny drops and he comes into full conformity with Rand's opinions, this is a highly dramatic development. The bad guys all agree with what the author says all her ideological opponents must believe (almost entirely different from what these opponents actually do believe, outside fiction). Both goodies and baddies continually expound their incredibly shallow *Weltanschauungen* in Rand's stilted jargon. None of them is authentic or has a personal voice. Unlike Toohey in *The Fountainhead*, none of the villains is intelligent or effective. (Stadler doesn't count; he is stated to be a genius, but this never affects his described behavior.)

Just as in real life Rand surrounded herself with yes-persons, hanging on her words and reciting them anxiously back to her, so in *Atlas Shrugged* she creates a world of zombies mouthing her patented terminology and going into the zombie equivalent of convulsions of delight whenever they hit upon another of her conceptual gems. Galt's Gulch is indeed Rand's Utopia: a society where everyone makes speeches all the time expounding Rand's opinions, the listeners all blissfully nodding their heads in agreement The true plot of *Atlas Shrugged* is: how some good-looking individuals were saved by coming to agree in every particular with Rand, and how everyone else was eternally damned. The book has often been described as nightmarish; it has something of the unnerving quality of a delusional system made real which we find in some Philip K. Dick novels, notably *Eye in the Sky*. (But Dick could really write, and he was doing it on purpose.)

Of all modern tendencies in fiction, Rand's novels are closest in spirit to the socialist realist works favored by the Stalinist regime. Stalin said: "Artists are engineers of the soul." Rand said: "Art is the technology of the soul."

One of the climactic points of *Atlas Shrugged* is Galt's long speech. which explains Rand's theories, in Rand's language, over all radio and TV channels simultaneously, and helps to bring about the downfall of "the looters." Actually, airing this tedious drivel over all stations would speedily lead to a revolutionary overthrow of the government which permitted such lax regulation of the airwaves, followed by the guillotining of Galt. With cretins like Rand's villains running the US, I reckon I could take over within a week, given a handful of marines and a few rock'n'roll tapes, except that plenty of others would get in ahead of me. Galt's speech is fifty-eight pages long, and I suppose ninety percent of readers skip most of it, as I did on my first reading. Branden claims that it took Rand "two full years" to write (p. 266). It feels like two full years reading it.

In Branden's judgement, part of Gait's speech takes "a major step toward solving the problem that haunted philosophers since the time of Aristotle and Plato: the relationship of 'ought' and 'is'—the question of in what manner moral values can be derived from facts." No such problem has haunted philosophers since the times of Plato or Aristotle. In the eighteenth century, David Hume raised a different question: whether values could be derived from facts (alone) at all, but this attracted no attention at the time, and didn't haunt anyone until the twentieth century.

According to Galt's speech, in a passage singled out by Branden, "There is only one fundamental alternative in the universe: existence or non-existence—and it pertains to a single class of entities: to living organisms." This is false. Any class of matter (atoms, crystals, stars, and so forth), not just living organisms, may exist or not exist. Galt (Rand) also emphasizes that: "to think is an act of choice . . . *man is a being of volitional consciousness*." This too is false. Thinking is involuntary, like digestion or blood clotting. If you don't believe this, try to stop thinking for a few seconds. Galt (Rand) also keeps insisting that "existence exists." This seems to be of momentous importance to Galt (Rand), but in the only sense I can make of it (that 'existence' is something which exists in addition to all the things which exist) it is not evident, and I believe it is false. (If what is meant is that "Things which exist exist"—existents exist—then that is trite and has never been denied by anyone.) And so it goes on, fifty-eight pages of it, one pompous vacuity after another.

There is the possibility that Atlas Shrugged may be produced as a TV mini-series. This would probably be its most favorable incarnation. The characterization is not up to the level of *Falcon Crest*, but the plot is a lot more interesting, and thankfully most of the pedantic dialogue would have to be cut. Galt's speech could be eliminated altogether and something should be done about the fact that Rand's 'future' is now impossible, since she did not forsee such developments as the eclipse of rail by air travel. Maybe Dagny Taggart should run an airline instead of a railroad.

Some of Branden's misjudgments are astounding. In *Atlas Shrugged,* she refers to "the faint sadomasochistic overtones of its love scenes, the troubling violence of the sexual encounters" (p. 299). Nearly all of Rand's romantic scenes in all her works are loudly and obviously sadistic. She was into domination. There is much grabbing of wrists, yanking of arms, ripping of cloth, and brusque insertion. Both *Penthouse Legend* and *The Fountainhead* contain rapes, performed by the heroes and presented as entirely admirable. (It's true that in both cases it is made clear that the rapees 'really want it'.)

Randolatry

The disciples of Ayn Rand were second-handers *par excellence.* They quavered at the thought of her disapproval. They humored her outbursts and reverently went along with the make-believe that she was a towering intellect. Mrs. Branden, for example, could have walked away from it all. Potentially, she seems to have been a better writer than Rand, but she gave that up for the sake of her submission before the cult. All this was done in the name of reason and self-interest. It is a familiar spectacle to see individuals suffering the cruel and vindictive humiliation reserved for sinners within a religious cult, but it is appallingly ironic when this deliberate humiliation is done in the name of that person's self-interest. Rand and her circle—including the Brandens—helped to introduce a lot of entirely pointless misery into the lives of their followers, and I am afraid Branden is insufficiently clear about expressing her regrets for the harm that she participated in doing, even though she was also one of the victims.

Randism was and is a religious cult. ('Religion' is 'a system of faith and worship'.) Branden has often described Objectivism as a cult, but in this book she withdraws this label. She now states that although Objectivism has some of the features of a cult, it cannot be a cult because of its commitment to reason and individualism (p. 352). Well, there is a lot of talk about reason and individualism, just as among Bolsheviks there is a lot of talk about science. But reason does not consist in shrieking the word 'reason' all the time. It consists in subjecting one's ideas to rational criticism, holding every position tentatively, and being prepared to abandon any position if it is successfully criticized. Reason consists, as Socrates put it, in 'following the argument wherever it leads', especially, of course, if it leads where you don't want to go. There is no evidence that the Randists understood the most elementary requirements of rational discourse.

Branden quotes Sidney Hook, from his review of Rand's *For the New Intellectual*: "Despite the great play with the word 'reason', one is struck by the absence of any serious argument in this unique combination of tautology and extravagant absurdity" (p. 321). That is exactly right. The Objectivists, no less than the devotees of a theistic sect, are engaged in abusing their minds by reiterating articles of faith. As for their individualism, it reminds me of the individualism of the mob in *The Life of Brian*. Trying to get the crowd to stop worshipping him, Brian shouts: "You are all individuals." The crowd drones back ecstatically. "We are all individuals." Unlike Brian, Rand was addicted to the idolatry of her besotted admirers.

Rand wrote an article called 'The Argument from Intimidation' (included in *The Virtue of Selfishness*) in which she describes the kind of *ad hominem* argument which says that only those who are in some way deficient can hold a particular point of view. In the heyday of socialism, this kind of argument was commonly employed against any voices dissenting from the socialist dogma. However, there is one writer who resorts to this kind of argument more frequently than any other, and that writer is Ayn Rand. The Argument from Intimidation is her stock-in-trade. (For example, the essay 'Collectivized Ethics', in *The Virtue of Selfishness*, opens: "Certain questions, which one frequently hears, are not philosophical queries, but psychological confessions . . ." Again, on the first page of the introduction to that book, we are told that to raise doubts about the advisability of Rand's use of the word 'selfishness' implies "moral cowardice.")

As Branden points out, although Rand in principle conceded the possibility of honest disagreement or honest error, in practice she tended always to conclude that disagreement with her opinions was a symptom of sickness and therefore of evil. Rand herself announces that she had "long ago" lost interest in debates with critics.

Egoistic Ethics

Rand asserts that ethics is entirely based on reason, and that the supreme moral virtue is selfishness. or rational self-interest. This is developed at times (See 'The Objectivist Ethics' in *The Virtue of Selfishness*) by biological, or biological-sounding, arguments. What is good for an organism is what contributes to that organism's survival and well-being. This seems clear enough: it is moral to do what is to one's advantage, and immoral to do what is against one's advantage. It follows that it is moral to cheat, murder, and steal, on those occasions where a rational analysis shows this to be to one's advantage. But no such conclusion is drawn by Rand.

Respecting other people's lives and property, even when this hurts one's bank balance or survival prospects, is stated to be in one's rational self-interest. From a biological point of view—maximizing one's chances of survival, good health, or reproduction—this is obviously not always the case. Rand explains that the standard of ethics is not the individual's bodily or biological survival, but the survival of man *qua* man," or man as a rational being. Thus, all Rand's biological-sounding arguments go by the board: it may even be 'selfish', in her redefinition of the term, to court death for the sake of a 'cherished value'. But there is no clear stipulation of how the nature of man as a rational being, or the values which it is permissible for a rational egoist to cherish. are to be determined. The outcome is that Rand appears to be urging egoism. but is actually urging unselfish sacrifice of one's interests to what she tells us is the life proper to a rational being. All this terrible confusion and double-talk arises because Rand cannot stomach the manifest truth that it can be to a person's advantage to violate the rights of another person. If ethics is to tell us that people's rights may not he violated, it must tell us that we ought sometimes to do things against our own interests.

Rand's main weapon against the above point is to imply (Argument from Intimidation) that anyone who makes it must believe that "man is a sacrificial animal". Here she overlooks two points: 1. that it is generally held that many decisions are morally neutral: ethically, you may do one thing or the other; and 2. that moralists have focused on cases where individuals ought to sacrifice their interests, not because sacrifice of one's interests *per se* is held to be necessarily good, but because it is assumed that there is comparatively little problem about getting individuals to do what is right when that happens to be also to their advantage.

In talking to various Randists, I have been offered two sorts of elaborations of Rand's argument. 1. It is claimed that to violate someone's rights when this appears to be to one's benefit will always be to one's net disadvantage because of the psychological repercussions to wit, the loss of one's self-respect.

This, however, throws the justification of morality onto something which is either an 'irrational whim', or some other principle of morality (what forms one's standards of self-respect) which in turn requires justification. It is not true that everyone's self-respect will suffer if they violate someone else's rights (or suffer enough to outweigh the gains). I have met people who would never be able to live with themselves if they passed up the chance to gyp some poor sucker, especially by violating his rights, the more violations the better. One might say that they ought not to be like this, but in that case one is appealing to a moral standard not derivable from that person's self-interest. (Rand holds that all morality is rational self-interest alone.)

2. It is claimed that violations of rights wouldn't work out well for everyone in the long run. One version of this is to claim that, for instance, if everyone were a thief, wealth would be greatly reduced, and there would be a lot less to steal—which is no doubt true. However, this is not an argument from self-interest. It is an argument from the welfare of society. A rational-minded person will weigh the consequences of his actions—if he is a pure egoist the consequences for just his welfare. Any one act of theft or even any one person dedicating his life to theft is not going to make the difference between a society in which rights are generally respected and a society of interminable pillage. A rational egoist will scoff at appeals to the long-term consequences for society, especially if he is getting on in years. The rational egoist will be a free rider on other people's unselfish respect for rights. (It's even perfectly reasonable for an egoist to support laws against theft whilst himself practicing theft: there is nothing contradictory about this position.)

The Gospel of Spleen

In one respect, the tragedy of Rand is like the tragedy of the Beatles: because she could do one or two things very well, she became surrounded by a lot of admirers who were prepared to encourage her to believe she could do any number of things superbly. By sticking to fiction, she could have become a sort of minor rightwing Jack London. As it was, she didn't write much fiction, and most of it is not outstanding.

But the tragedy, in Rand's case, begins earlier. If Branden's reconstruction of Alice's early life is at all reliable, it seems that she had the makings of a good mind, but lacked any training in critical thought. She was more intelligent than almost everyone she met, and soon formed the theory that other people's inane and unsystematic defenses of conventional thinking were the only alternatives to her own half-baked notions. Since she was quick-witted, she was always able to improvise new elaborations to these notions, without ever wondering whether some of them might be radically mistaken. By the time she was able to read arguments by people cleverer than she was, it was too late for her to learn the elements of rational enquiry: she was a messiah who announced the truth and cursed all who rejected it.

Recalling what she said to Nathaniel after their first meeting with Rand, Branden reports: "I feel as if, intellectually, I've always stood on a leaking life raft in the ocean. and as I jump to cover one leak with my foot, another spurts forth—and I leap to cover it—and then there's another. . . . But now I have the sense that it might be possible to stand on solid ground . . . as if for the first time the earth is firm beneath my feet" (p. 236). Rand fed the appetite for certainty. She spoke as if she had a fully worked-out system which accounted for everything. Such a system, if it could exist at all, would be a vast structure made up of minutely-reasoned segments. Rand's theories. such as they are, do not form a vast structure, and she had no talent for minute reasoning. The impression of all-encompassing explanation is given by bold, broad, sweeping, imprecise assertions. An unrelenting covering fire of vituperation and demeaning is maintained against anyone who might point to any of the difficulties with these assertions. Presumably some of the brighter disciples are able to keep the faith by telling themselves that these assertions can he interpreted as gestures indicating the general lines upon which a more rigorous argument might one day be built—but this is an unwarranted attitude—a kind of faith, because (apart from Randism's demonstrable errors at the broadest level) surprising refutations often spring from fine details. The doctrinal structure of Randism is bluff, buttressed by abuse of all critics.

In every sect there is an official and an unofficial doctrine. The official doctrine is formulated, written down, and recited. The unofficial doctrine is conveyed more indirectly. It is a set of attitudes and responses. It may even he denied if an outsider detects it and tries to formulate it. In the case of Randism, part of the unofficial doctrine is that rational people can discern the truth about things at a glance, by a swift act of 'integration'. (Enemies of Randism are described as 'unfocused': correct thinking is characterized as 'focusing'. The impression conveyed by this questionable metaphor is that the more rational you are, the more you will focus, and if you are very rational, you will be able to discern the truth just by looking because, you see, everything will be sharply in focus.)

Another part of the unofficial doctrine is that it is fine and laudable to be a spiteful person, to nurse spiteful feelings and express spiteful sentiments against everything evil and sick—everything that is not Randist. Three-quarters of Rand's essays are exercises in unremitting spitefulness. (In a review of Barbara Branden's book. Peter Schwartz declares: "Ayn Rand does not need me to defend her against lice" (Circular letter to readers of *The Intellectual Activist*, 20th August 1986). To appreciate that sort of remark, you need to understand not merely that Schwartz doesn't feel ashamed of having written it, and not merely that he pats himself on the head for having written it, but that he pats himself on the head because it is such a very rational thing to write. He abandons all intelligent discrimination to let loose his infantile rage, and is able to feel that this is a worthy and heroic, because supremely rational, way to behave.)

"The virtue of selfishness" sounds like a serious challenge to conventional thinking, or at least an echo of Stirner, but because 'selfishness' is redefined, most of traditional bourgeois morality comes out unscathed. What Randism adds is the denigration of common decencies. Randism excoriates 'whims', but since the reasoning performed by Randists is so slovenly, it amounts to a rationalization of whims, usually nasty ones. Randism is a Gospel of Spleen.

Free Life, 1987

2
PARTIAL RECALL (1994)

On September 22nd, 1969, eight-year-old Susan Mason was raped and murdered near her home in Foster City, California. Over twenty-one years later, on November 29th, 1990, George Franklin was found guilty of the crime.

Franklin was convicted because of the eyewitness testimony of his daughter Eileen, who claimed that she had seen her father kill little Susie, and then forgotten about it for over twenty years, after which the memory of that old event had come back to her in flashes until it was full and detailed. Eileen also remembered that her father had sexually molested her and her siblings.

Eileen's memory of the killing did not contain anything verifiable that could have been known only to an eyewitness. The murder had been reported in the press in 1969, and the account given by Eileen could have been put together from easily available facts, plus added elements that are impossible to check. Eileen's account had been adapted with successive retellings, to remove conflicts with facts known to the prosecution, and to incorporate details as she learned them from the prosecution.

Because of a judge's ruling, the defense was unable to explain to the jury that there was no independent corroboration of Eileen's memory of the murder. But Harry MacLean, who interviewed jurors as part of the research for his detailed account of the trial, considers that allowing the excluded evidence would probably not have changed the verdict. So a man was convicted of murder purely on the testimony of a witness who claimed that she had seen the murder at age eight (Eileen was the same age as her friend the murdered girl), forgotten the whole thing for over twenty years, then recollected it in detail. Evidently the jury considered that an eyewitness testimony, delivered with an assured air and filled with graphic detail, by a self-assured and articulate person, did not lose much credibility through having been lost in oblivion for two decades.

Intimations of Immorality

Though it is an extreme example, the Franklin case is no isolated curiosity. Over the past six years it has become fashionable to suppose that child sex abuse is extremely common, that its memory is frequently "repressed" by its victims, that these "repressed memories" cause problems for the victims years later, and that the way to cure the problems is to resurrect the repressed memories and publicly humiliate the perpetrators—frequently the victims' parents.

A person consults a therapist, complaining of eating disorders, panic attacks, gloomy feelings, low self-esteem, or other very common afflictions. The therapist tells the client that the root of the problem is a repressed memory of childhood sexual abuse. If the client protests that she can remember nothing of this, the therapist insists that the absence of memory is a symptom of "denial," itself evidence of the abuse trauma. The therapist urges the client to conjure up mental images of abusive incidents and dwell upon them. A few clients obligingly create such images pretty quickly and readily accept them as genuine memories. But most have to work hard and long to produce images which they at first find difficult to accept as true recollections.

The therapist explains that a quality of dreamlike unreality is a common characteristic of true memories under the influence of "denial," and that these fragmentary images must represent actual occurences—as proved by the fact that the client is still depressed, or anxious, or overeating, or whatever. The therapist toils for months to persuade the client that the apparent fantasies are true memories. The therapist's air of confident certainty impresses the client, who assumes that therapists know something other people don't about the human mind. The therapist exhorts the client to work on the fragmentary images, and every new detail is greeted by the therapist with warm approval, as a sign that the client is making progress and may be curable. An increasing number of therapists now use this approach with virtually every client.

After months of such treatment, many clients will have crystal-clear "memories" of their childhood abuse. They are then ready to spurn, shun, and sue the perpetrators, often their flabbergasted and agonized parents.

Legal safeguards built up over centuries, in recognition of the fact that memories become distorted with the passage of time, are now being dismantled. Statutes of limitation and other laws have been modified to permit and encourage suits for damages on the basis of decades-old incidents supposedly recalled in therapy. The state of Washington changed its laws in 1989 to permit recovery of damages for injuries resulting from child sexual abuse at any time within three years of *remembering* the abuse. Many other states have followed suit, and most states have by now at least begun the process of similarly changing the law.

Legislators, police, and other influential people have swallowed without a qualm the theory that there are such things as "repressed memories" which can "come back" after years of being forgotten. During the Clarence Thomas confirmation hearings, one senator asked Anita Hill about the discrepancies between her earlier and more recent accounts of her sexual harassment, and helpfully offered the suggestion that she had "repressed" some of the memories. Professor Hill immediately concurred that, yes, she must have repressed them.

In the jury selection for the Franklin trial, those prospective jurors who were skeptical about the possibility that memories could be repressed and then recovered, or even about psychiatry generally, were excused from the jury, whereas no move was made to excuse those who thought that recovery of repressed memories is feasible, and it was known that at least one juror was a zealous proponent of this theory. This is just as though, in a trial for murder by casting evil spells, prospective jurors were interrogated about their theological views, and only those committed to a belief in the efficacy of witchcraft were permitted to serve.

In Hollywood, the discovery of one's sexual abuse in childhood has rapidly taken its hallowed place alongside crystals, channeling, and politics in the style of Kim Il Sung. To those who can remember their past lives in the Neolithic epoch, or that even more remote era when Bolshevism was the future that worked, remembering that your parents abused you in infancy is a piece of cake.

The Quran of this psychotherapeutic jihad is *The Courage to Heal* by Bass and Davis, a manual for producing whole new memories of long-forgotten childhood molestation. Among this book's confident assertions: "If you think you were abused and your life shows the symptoms, then [even though you don't recollect it] you were" (p. 22). The authors maintain that "demands for proof are unreasonable," and strongly encourage the deliberate whipping up of hatred against the supposed perpetrators: "You may dream of murder or castration. . . . Let yourself imagine it to your heart's content" (p. 128). With evident regret, they counsel against actual killing or maiming, and recommend clients to "get strong by suing," then provide a list of lawyers eager to take up such cases. There is a chapter entirely devoted to conjuring up lost memories and a chapter entirely devoted to convincing yourself that these conjured-up memories are true. In all this book's 528 pages, there is not a word of caution that the memories produced may not be authentic.

Last Year in Manhattan Beach

The vogue for adults to recover memories of childhood molestation coincides with an enormous proliferation of accusations and prosecutions for recent sexual molestation of children. Frequently, as in the notorious McMartin and Edenton cases, alleged child victims are handed over to dedicated psychotherapists, who browbeat the children for hours on end, often to the point of physical exhaustion, demanding that the children say that the accused molested them. The theory is that the children are "in denial" and need to be helped to remember. Even so, it generally takes weeks or months of unremitting interrogation, in which the therapists work hand in glove with prosecutors, before the children produce the story the prosecutors want.

These two phenomena—the intensive interrogation of children to get them to "disclose" incidents of molestation and the intensive interrogation of an adult client's memory to get that client to "remember" incidents of molestation—have their similarities and their differences. The most obvious difference is that in cases involving adult clients, it is usually undisputed that, throughout the years immediately before consulting a therapist, the client has no knowledge of any past molestation. This is explained by saying that the client has repressed the memory. By contrast, in the case of recent sex abuse allegations, the therapists need not take the view that the children have forgotten the molestation. The children could remember it, but be too embarrassed, scared, or cautious to mention it. Obviously, this sometimes happens in genuine cases of child molestation.

To many psychotherapists, the distinction between forgetting and being afraid to talk is unimportant. Both are covered by the label "denial," which obscures everything and explains nothing, since in plain English a denial can be true and most commonly is. This is typical of the way in which people are persuaded to believe in repressed memories because of something quite different (in this case, being ashamed or scared to talk) that is made to sound similar.

Pressuring children to say that something happened recently and pressuring adults to remember that something happened long ago are alike in this respect: either method may result in the creation of a belief, in the child's or the adult client's mind, that something happened when in fact it did not. Although psychotherapy of small children may not begin with any claim that a genuine memory has been lost, it may, just like psychotherapy of an adult client, result in the manufacture of a counterfeit memory.

Memory à la Mode

A significant proportion of these stories, both from children and from adults, involve accounts of Satanic cults. Belief in the existence of such cults has been proliferating since the early 1970s, but was boosted by the publication in 1980 of the influential yet wildly implausible "survivor story," *Michelle Remembers*. Such real or imagined phenomena as ritual killing of animals and of blonde virgins, desecration of cemeteries, backward-masking of messages in heavy metal ditties, Goth make-up, drug-dealing, pornography, Dungeons & Dragons, missing children, and witches in children's literature are now routinely attributed to Satanic cults.

Intensive investigation of many incidents attributed to Satanic cults has always failed to find corroborative evidence, and in most cases has demonstrated the reports to be false. There are rare, isolated murderers who avow that Satan is giving them instructions to kill people, just as there are similar murderers who get their orders from God, the FBI, or Martians. There are groups of teenage daredevils, as ignorant of Satanism as of any doctrinal system, who daub signs in public places. There are associations of violent criminals who use torture as a means of persuasion, and are sometimes also superstitious. There are avowedly Satanist groups totaling a few hundred members in the US, most notably Anton LaVey's Church of Satan, which appear to be thoroughly bourgeois and law-abiding. The Satanic cults which keep popping up in recovered memories, vast networks of outwardly respectable people who secretly practice the ritual rape, torture, and sacrifice of animals and children, can be distinguished from all of the above.

One example, Gail Feldman's *Lessons in Evil, Lessons from the Light*, must suffice here to give the flavor of the kind of thing that has recently become respectable. Feldman's book, bearing effulgent blurbs from prominent writers and doctors, was published by a prestigious house and launched with a lavishly funded nationwide author tour. It is an account by a psychotherapist of one client, "Barbara," whose initial symptoms are that she feels tense during sex and sometimes gets angry with her daughter.

Dr. Feldman immediately understands that these symptoms can only have arisen from childhood sex abuse. Barbara has vague feelings, which she may have picked up from previous therapists, that she might have been sexually abused in childhood, but no memories. Using hypnosis, the therapist takes the patient back to the age of five, and the five-year-old reports the ritual killing of a cat by her grandfather, who makes her eat the cat's heart and drink its blood. Though Barbara is at first disinclined to accept that this scene is a real memory, the therapist knows better and reassures the patient that it really happened.

Feldman reads *Michelle Remembers* to find out what Satanic cults are all about, and then elicits many more macabre disclosures. It turns out that Barbara's childhood was crowded with incident. It's chop, chop, saw, saw, and scream, scream, with corpses both whole and in pieces, both freshly cropped and nicely matured, liberally bestrewn around the family hearth. Snakes in bodily orifices and drinking of urine are among the more prosaic of the everyday occurrences of Barbara's exciting home life.

Déjà Vu

Toward the end of the story, the patient is regressed to a prior existence, and learns that her daughter is the reincarnation of her father in that previous life. Told this by Barbara, Dr Feldman responds "'Whew.' I gripped the sides of my chair. 'That is really something. . .'" This finding, naturally, explains Barbara's anger towards her daughter, and the anger then goes away. We also learn that Feldman herself regressed to a previous life as an

American Indian woman, and on one of these regressions is spotted by one of her current friends, also regressing—there are more things in heaven and earth, Horatio—to the same eighteenth-century Amerindian village. Informed of this by the friend, Dr. Feldman reports: "My mouth fell open"—but not, it's clear, with incredulity. In that previous life, Feldman died in childbirth, and this explains her hostility to her husband (the one in her current life), which also evaporates immediately upon the discovery of its centuries-old cause.

Soon the recovered memory therapists will begin to be called to account for the misery that they and their infinitely gullible clients have unleashed upon this society. They will undoubtedly jettison memories of previous lives pretty quickly, and will denounce these stories as the work of a tiny minority of incompetents. Then, more hesitantly, they will dissociate themselves from the Satanic cult fables. It is therefore helpful to understand right now that the quality of all evidence for recovered memories of childhood sexual molestation is precisely the same in every respect as the quality of the evidence for recovered memories of past lives or Satanic rituals.

Why do so many therapists' clients produce memories of being raped and sodomized, while a substantial minority (some say one in five) also produce memories of Satanic rituals, and a smaller number produce memories of previous lives? The answer is simplicity itself. Memories recovered conform to the views of the therapist. Many therapists believe in Satanic cults, and all their clients produce memories of Satanic cults. Comparatively few believe in reincarnation, but all their clients produce memories of past lives. (Bass and Davis view any past-life recollections as symptoms of denial, and keep the clients working on these memories to move the recalled incidents into this life.)

Since reincarnation is absurd, and since there are no Satanic cults, as the controversy flares and the recovered memory therapists start to feel the heat, these stories will probably melt away. Child molestation actually does occur, so this more banal story is difficult to dismiss out of hand in any particular case, and this kind of false accusation is harder to combat. And parallel with all the great witch-hunts of history, anyone who comes to the defense of those accused of sex abuse can be defeated by the simple ploy of accusing them of sex abuse.

You Must Remember This

The juggernaut of ill-founded accusations against innocent people is still accelerating, and can be expected to gather momentum for years to come. Resistance is growing too. The False Memory Syndrome Foundation was founded in February 1992, to assist victims of unsubstantiated accusations arising from allegedly recovered memories, and to promote research into the whole question of manufactured memories. By mid-1993, FMSF had more than five thousand families on file, and cases continue to flood in week by week.

Unfortunately, one of the first fruits of this resistance has been escalating demands for stiffer licensing requirements for psychotherapists. Aside from the inefficiency engendered by government licensing—as well as the sheer insolence of a government telling me whom I can pay to give me advice—such demands are misconceived in a more specific way. It's assumed that psychotherapists can do things which are so important that insufficiently qualified people ought not to be allowed to try to do them. The truth is that psychotherapists cannot do these things at all, or cannot do them any better than priests, rabbis, clairvoyants, bank loan officers, or radio talk-show hosts.

If a person says that something happened to him last night, or twenty years ago, he may be telling the truth, or lying, or mistaken. Psychologists, psychiatrists, and other psychotherapists are no better able than you or I to determine which is the case. Research has shown that therapists are actually rather poor at discriminating truth from falsehood (and they are often not very truthful themselves, when describing what occurs in their therapy sessions). However, there simply does not exist a body of technique which permits anybody to discern whether what someone says is the truth—beyond the well-known methods we may all adopt, such as trying to find independent corroboration, examining the story for plausibility and consistency, noticing whether related statements by the same person appear to be true, and so forth.

If a child says that Mr X took her to the Moon in a spaceship and raped her, a psychotherapist may tell us that the trip to the Moon is false and the rape a reality. But the psychotherapist is no better placed to make this judgment than you or I. The psychotherapist's statement adds nothing to the child's testimony.

Memories We've Been Sharing

According to a popular theory, the mind has an unconscious as well as a conscious part. All kinds of strange things may lurk in the unconscious, unknown to the individual, but capable of influencing his feelings and behavior. All our experiences are recorded accurately in the unconscious—as though we contained a perfect videotape record of everything that ever happened to us. If we have any emotional troubles, it's probably due to terrible memories of what befell us in childhood—memories of which we're entirely unaware, because we have "repressed" them as too horrible to contemplate. The cure lies in remembering them again. In one way or another, the thing to do is to explore those terrible things that happened to us in childhood. The exact technique recommended for accomplishing this varies widely, but the general theoretical framework usually goes unquestioned.

Where did this theory come from and how was it conveyed from a small group of intellectuals to the masses? A careful historical investigation would be necessary to ascertain the complete answer, but a great boost undoubtedly came from the activities of Sigmund Freud. I'm not sure just how many elements of the currently popular theory of the mind were widely believed before Freud, though all of them were accepted by some psychiatrists, and the belief that all experiences are stored somewhere in the mind has ancient roots.

Freud's doctrine, known as psychoanalysis, was launched upon the world with evangelical zeal. The new faith found some disciples in Europe, but more critics. It encountered less opposition in the United States, where it rapidly infiltrated popular culture and made a living for thousands of psychoanalysts. Today we live in a post-Freudian culture, in which many questionable tenets of Freudism are taken for gospel by the public and the media.

These Foolish Things

Freud's specific theories include the famous Oedipus Complex, the theory that every little boy wants to kill his father and make love to his mother. To get the hang of Freudian dream interpretation it's enough to bear in mind that a bunch of flowers or a gate always means the female genitals, anything pointed or cylindrical always means the penis, gold coins always mean feces, and so forth.

Although such specific details had many adherents for a while, and figures like Dr Bird in *The Caine Mutiny* became very thick upon the ground, the Freudian movement has always generated numerous heterodox offshoots which abandon or dilute these picturesque flights of fancy, while retaining the fundamental Freudian model of the mind, in which present neurotic problems are caused by disguised memories. Like Judaism, psychoanalysis has affected the world most profoundly through the intermediation of its apostasies and heresies.

For many years Freudians gave a standard account of the manner in which Freud came up with the fundamentals of psychoanalysis. According to this tale, Freud had a number of patients who told him they had been sexually molested in childhood. At first, Freud naively concluded that real incidents of molestation were the root of their troubles. Later, Freud decided that these childhood molestations were indeed the source of the problem, but were in fact imaginary—they were fantasies of the patients.

A few years ago, various feminist writers announced that they had uncovered a scandal about Freud: the stories Freud's patients had told him were actually true, and Freud had lacked the courage to offend the parents or other grown-ups who were the perpetrators. Allegations that Freud had "suppressed the truth" harmonized well with the galloping frenzy anent alleged child molestation, and a hurricane of enraged name-calling blew up.

This argy-bargy was all beside the point. Freud did indeed suppress the truth—by claiming that his patients had recounted stories of childhood molestation. As we now know from the researches of several writers, especially Allen Esterson, Freud's patients did not tell him any such thing. The episodes of child seduction were invented by Freud to explain his patients' symptoms, and then recounted by Freud to the bemused patients. Childhood "seduction" was a fantasy, not in the unconscious minds of the "patients," but in the conscious mind of the "doctor."

Early in his career, Freud was struck by the problem that he knew of no way to determine which of his patients' recollections were true and which were fantasies. Freud never did find a way, and neither has anyone else, but Freud cut the Gordian knot by postulating that fantasized traumas were just as important as real traumas, and this became the keystone of psychoanalysis.

This comedy is even more richly droll because the "recollections" were not what the "patients" claimed to remember, but were all made up by Dr. Freud in the first place. Verily, a prince among mountebanks!

Don't Forget to Forget?

Is there such a thing as a repressed memory? Recent accounts of research and theory are sometimes worded in a conciliatory and eclectic fashion, to give the impression that repression may be supported by the evidence. But on closer reading, such accounts merely note that some findings are compatible with parts of the repressed memories theory. For instance, people often forget things, and sometimes later recall what they have forgotten. People tend to remember pleasant occurrences in preference to unpleasant ones. Extreme shocks may cause forgetfulness of the events surrounding the shock. Adults have an almost complete amnesia covering their first few years of life, and this includes any traumatic events.

Such conclusions do not substantiate the distinctive features of the repression theory: that we forget events because they are too horrible to contemplate; that we cannot remember these forgotten events by any normal process of casting our minds back but can reliably retrieve them by special techniques; that these forgotten events, banished from consciousness, strive to enter it in disguised forms; that forgotten events have the power to cause apparently unrelated problems in our lives, which can be cured by excavating and reliving the forgotten events.

The repressed memories story is part of our folklore. It simultaneously appeals to self-pity, self-exculpation, and self-importance. It is particularly relished by literary people, whose standards of argument are frequently undemanding, and who often find the post-Freudian mythology of symbols and childhood influences wonderfully stimulating. But as for the story's relation to the available evidence, it is in part refuted, in part seriously in doubt, in part untested, and in part untestable. There is no evidence that an upsetting early experience, remembered or forgotten, real or imagined, has any great bearing on the course of one's subsequent life.

We tend to forget those experiences that made little impression because they seemed unimportant at the time. Though most of us remember pleasant experiences in preference to unpleasant ones, this is because we prefer to think about pleasant experiences, not because we can't bear to think about unpleasant ones. We also remember important experiences in preference to unimportant ones. Consequently, we will probably remember an important unpleasant experience. Gloomy people, prone to depression, tend to think gloomy thoughts and have better recall for unpleasant events—the opposite of what we would expect if their problems were due to repressing memories of unpleasant occurrences.

Individuals who have been interned in concentration camps, tortured, caught up in some natural disaster, or accidentally trapped for hours in a terrifying situation have no trouble remembering that these ordeals occurred. One study followed up adults who, as children aged five to ten, had witnessed the murder of their parents. Not one of them had the slightest difficulty in clearly remembering the event. There is a strand of folklore which acknowledges that harrowing experiences are difficult to forget—an account of the *Titanic* disaster was appropriately entitled *A Night to Remember*—and this is the strand that matches observable facts.

Those few studies cited to show that people forget major traumatic episodes are at best inconclusive. It proves little, for instance, to ask people whether they now remember something they had once forgotten for a while, since we have no assurance that their present memory is accurate. Furthermore, we often don't give some incident a thought for years, and in this sense "forget it," but are able to recall it if the occasion arises. Even if we forget something in the sense of being unable to recall it, this doesn't prove that the memory was repressed. We forget things all the time because we attach little importance to continuing to think about them.

We forget most of what happens in the first three or four years of our lives, including being sexually abused if that happened, but although it can't be ruled out that some recollections of early events may pop up after years of having been forgotten, there are no reliable techniques for recovering accurate memories of these forgotten years. This amnesia is perhaps due to the physiology of brain development; as far as we know, it is more or less the same for almost everyone, no matter how idyllic or distressing their childhoods.

There is also a conceptual problem with the repression scenario. If a memory is stored but willfully not retrieved, consciousness has to recognize the memory in order to know not to retrieve it. But if that memory is recognizable, it must, one would think, be retrievable.

Thanks for the Memory

Our tendency to forget what is unpleasant more readily than what is pleasant is generally harmless and sometimes beneficial. If you dwell on a past traumatic event, you will probably remember it better. You may also make yourself miserable.

There is no evidence for the popular idea that in order to make your peace with some disturbing event you must vividly relive it, work through it, or "come to terms with it." Your past experiences are powerless to cause you any pain or problem; only your willful and morbid dwelling on them can hurt you. Reports of concentration camp survivors show that many of them have no long-term emotional ill-effects—these are the ones who "put it out of their minds" as an irrelevant distraction and focus on their current and future projects.

Similarly, it is of no great moment whether people believe you or not. If you were actually molested and other people are now skeptical, you may feel that insult has been piled upon injury. It would be nicer if they believed you, but if they disbelieve you, that's one of many disappointments of the kind that life has in store for all of us. Neither the fact that you were molested nor the fact that other people won't believe you were molested is any excuse for snarfing that extra slice of pizza.

If you don't dwell on a past traumatic event, the memory will slowly fade. With each year that passes, your recollection of the event (in the event that you hypothetically choose to make an effort to recall it) will become less and less reliable. If you don't think about it, the memory is not doing anything to you. It is not going to make you lose your sleep, or overeat, or work too hard, or become anxious—such everyday hazards are the normal lot of human beings, have nothing to do with repressed memories, and are usually not symptoms of any illness.

The Shock of Non-Recognition

People are sometimes inclined to believe in memory repression because of the well-known phenomenon of traumatic (or post-traumatic) amnesia. Individuals involved in serious accidents occasionally have a complete memory blank for the accident, and sometimes for a period preceding the accident as well. Or they may remember something of the event, but forget important details. Bouts of extreme pain are sometimes forgotten. The most common and clearly identifiable cases involve a physical assault upon the brain, as in electroshock therapy, alcoholic intoxication, or a head injury. In other cases, the same result seems to be produced by an emotional shock such as intense pain or fear.

These examples don't support the repressed memory theory. It's fairly clear that amnesia due to a physical interference with the brain arises because of the shock itself, and not because the shocking event would be too horrific to think about. It seems quite reasonable to extend this to cases of pure emotional shock: the amnesia could, for example, be due to interference with attention. You cannot remember anything unless you pay attention to it—this is why more than ninety percent of Americans cannot accurately describe either face of a US penny, and most cannot even pick out the correct penny in a multiple-choice test. Extreme pain or fear may interfere with the capacity to pay attention.

The superb thriller *Mirage* (1965), starring Gregory Peck, illustrates the conventional wisdom, with a psychiatrist and others telling the hero that he can't remember because he doesn't want to. Whether by accident or design, the action of the movie does not require this interpretation.

The idea that we forget things because we find them too horrible to think about appeals to the primitive theory that remembering is reliving. In fact, a memory of a harrowing experience need not be a harrowing memory, and normally, if the original experience were distressing, the memory of it would be much less so, if distressing at all. Nothing is ever too terrible to contemplate. Would you rather have another root canal or remember twenty times that occasion when you had a root canal?

I can remember such episodes as the time I was attacked and robbed by three ruffians in a subway station. This perturbed me while it was occurring, but subsequently I could go through the incident in my mind with no flicker of alarm. Yet if I think carefully about a story I once read in which, following a rock collapse in a mineshaft, a man squirmed for miles through a pipeline about eighteen inches in diameter, I will break out in the proverbial cold sweat, though nothing like this has ever happened to me. Despite such evidence from introspection, many therapists believe that deep emotion accompanying the "recovery" of a "memory" confirms its authenticity. The truth is just the opposite: any powerful emotional display is fair grounds for suspecting the memory to be counterfeit.

In traumatic amnesia, there is generally an awareness of a memory gap, and this gap is in itself often worrying. Although the individual loses all recollection for a certain span of time, he recalls the end of the period before the amnesia and the beginning of the period after the amnesia, and is usually in no doubt that something is wrong, something is missing.

It could be argued that awareness of a gap arises from the fact that other people talk about the traumatic occurrence, or talk about the unexplained circumstances in which the individual is discovered after the traumatic occurrence. If the trauma were a secret rape, the victim might therefore not become aware of the gap. I don't think that this is convincing; however, many of the recovered memory cases concern recollections of repeated episodes of abuse over several years. The victim would therefore have to forget each incident singly, or at some point forget several incidents collectively. Many of these incidents are supposed to involve the most bizarre concomitants (repeated ritual killings of babies are standard issue) and are supposed to have occurred in a day-to-day context where family discussion of the atrocities is quite frequent. The victim must therefore forget very numerous chunks of time over a long period without any awareness that there is a gap in memory. In cases of atrocities against several siblings simultaneously, each of the siblings has to have the same lack of recall without any suspicion of a gap. There is absolutely no evidence that anything remotely like this has ever occurred or ever could occur.

Down Memory Lane

When I say "no evidence," I mean no evidence apart from the memories themselves—memories supposedly recovered by alleged victims under the spell of psychotherapists who passionately believe in the recovered memory theory. These therapists will indeed often say that there is "abundant clinical evidence" for recovery of repressed memories, but whenever they say anything like this, they mean only the ever-proliferating examples of clients who produce uncorroborated stories, usually after intensive persuasion by therapists. In the same way, a professional astrologer can honestly say that he has abundant clinical evidence that people's destinies conform to their birth signs. What could conceivably happen in consultations that would count as evidence against the psychotherapist's or the astrologer's theories?

Recovered memory therapists usually maintain that the accuracy of the recovered memories is beyond question, and react with indignation to any suggestion that they might be artifacts of therapy. They cite the clarity and detail of the memories, the emotional display that accompanies their recovery, the similarity of different clients' experiences, and the absence of any motive to concoct false stories. Exactly these arguments are advanced by defenders of other tall tales, including sightings of ghosts, conversations with the dead, religious visions, recollections of past or future lives, and UFO abductions.

I have not been able to find a publicly recorded example of an indubitably repressed memory which has been recovered and then proved correct (Wakefield and Underwager review and criticize all the stock anecdotes). In order to qualify, the memory would have to be of a post-infancy event of such a dramatic nature that common-or-garden forgetting would be ruled out. Given the hundreds of thousands of recovered memory cases, we would expect to find some cases that could be independently corroborated. In other child molestation cases, where recovery of repressed memory is not involved, pretty clear proof capable of lasting for years does occasionally turn up—for example, a pornographic movie featuring the victim and the perpetrator. And the bizarre quality of many of the current spate of recovered memories makes independent proof quite likely. If babies have been dispatched by the dozen, like Thanksgiving turkeys, we might expect once in a while to turn up the infant remains that would confirm a recovered memory, but this has never happened.

Professor Lenore Terr, a vocal advocate of repressed memories who testified eloquently at the Franklin trial, maintains that isolated instances of trauma will be remembered, but numerous repeated instances may be repressed. This surmise, which has not been corroborated by any research, is arresting because of its conflict with common sense: one would think that the greater the number of incidents, the more likely they would be remembered. Terr's proposal can be seen as an attempt to reconcile the repressed memories theory with the everyday observation that individuals generally do recall any uniquely horrible experience they have had since their fifth birthday. Cases of repeated trauma are rarer and more difficult to pin down, but casual reading and conversation suggest that people beaten by their parents for years, or trapped in wars or the worst kinds of prisons, can indeed recall the kinds of unpleasant things that happened, though they may be hazy as to details. Speculations like Terr's will be tested many times by research studies in the next few years, and they will be reclassified from unsubstantiated to disproven, or I will eat my hat. It is already noticeable that, among psychologists, researchers tend to be skeptical about repression, while the believers tend to be clinicians. Clinicians who pay no heed to controlled studies always run the risk of reading their own theories into their clients' histories, and thus repeatedly finding worthless confirmation of those theories.

Among My Souvenirs

One of the reasons for ready public acceptance of the colorful yarns spun by recovered memory clients is that people generally overrate the reliability of memory, and one of the reasons for this overrating is the representation of memory in narrative works.

The novelist always strives to convince the reader of the story's authenticity, and many readers would regard the depiction of memories as fallible as people's memories actually are as a cheap trick, like wild coincidences or supernatural intervention. This is especially so with murder mysteries: the reader would feel cheated if recollections related in the story were dismissed as erroneous at the end, unless misperception of the conjuring-trick type were employed. Mysteries frequently involve elaborate and detailed memories of events years before the capable detective begins to ask questions, but these memories, as memories, are virtually always impeccable.

An outstanding exception is the corpus of eighty-two Perry Mason novels by Erle Stanley Gardner, which frequently focus on the fallibility of eyewitness testimony. In his own experience as a defense attorney, Gardner became well-versed in police trickery. Mason remarks that the worst kind of evidence is eyewitness testimony, and the best kind is circumstantial. At first blush this may seem paradoxical, because juries must rely on somebody's eyewitness observations of the circumstantial evidence. But there is no paradox. Circumstantial evidence usually endures in physical objects, and can be looked at by many different people with different prejudices on repeated occasions, whereas eyewitness testimony often relies on a few people's rapid interpretations of an unexpected, evanescent episode.

Gardner fully understood what has now been experimentally demonstrated: that it is easy to get someone to identify the police's nominee by suggestion and by letting the witness see the suspect, for example in a mugshot. The witness will then confuse the recollection of the photograph with a recollection of the crime. The witness will be hesitant at first, but will become more convinced as time passes. Note that, once the process is complete, the witness does not sense that the suspect is familiar and carelessly infer that this familiarity arises from seeing the suspect commit the crime. To the contrary, the witness distinctly "remembers" the suspect committing the crime. A bogus memory has been implanted.

The outstanding treatment of memory in literature is Proust's marvelous *À la Recherche du Temps Perdu*. Proust believed that it is only when remembered that events take on their full emotional resonance. Of course! Once the memories have been suitably remodeled they are much more satisfying than when they were merely accurate. There would be no excuse for fiction if it did not improve upon real life.

Nowhere in Proust have I found an unambiguous declaration that departures from accuracy give memories their magical potency, much less that the lucidity of a recollection is insufficient grounds for supposing it to be true. There is no dispute that Proust's account of memory from a subjective standpoint, and the architectural lyricism of his writing, make this work one of the wonders of the world. But for what it's worth, Proust's memory was terrible. *À la Recherche du Temps Perdu* contains many quotations, for example, and they are nearly all wrong. Many writers have invested too much faith in memory, with suspicious results. To mention only one conspicuous case, Wordsworth's "Ode on Intimations of Immortality" is a beautiful exercise in self-deception. The "glory and the freshness of a dream" don't characterize infantile perceptions of the world, but sentimental adult reconstructions of those perceptions.

False memory occurs in classic works only in the form of some evil potion or spell. In Wagner's *Götterdämmerung*, Siegfried downs a draft which makes him forget all about Brünhilde and therefore feel virtuously free to marry Gudrun. His true memory returns, wholly intact, when he is dosed with the appropriate potion. Such stories reinforce the popular view that there has to be an altogether exceptional explanation for any major mistakes of memory, that the true memory is always "there," and that it can be brought to consciousness by some arcane means, whereupon its truth is self-evident.

In science fiction, false memory was brought to the fore by A.E. Van Vogt in *The World of Null-A* (1945). This stupendous work of imagination stimulated one of the divine voices of this century, Philip K. Dick, who began to explore false memory and other systematically fallacious forms of awareness in such stories as *Time Out of Joint* (1959). Dick's most brilliant employment of the false memory theme is his little gem, "We Can Remember It for You Wholesale" (1966), the point of departure for the Schwarzenegger movie *Total Recall*. For all its artistic perfection, "We Can Remember It for You Wholesale" endorses the popular view that all our experiences are accurately stored somewhere in the mind and that there is some intrinsic difference between a false memory and a true one. Dick's story freely uses the terms "false memory" and "extra-factual memory." It's interesting to speculate whether such terms were ever employed in this sense any earlier, but we can be sure that they are going to become familiar to everyone over the next few decades—one of many cases where the future is more certain than the past.

The movie *L'année dernière à Marienbad* (1961), an essay on the flashback, shows how someone can be in acute doubt as to what happened a year ago, and, in such scenes as the "crumbling balustrade," how fantasy can become confounded with memory. No doubt many other examples can be found, but outside science fiction and stories with an amnesia or hypnosis gimmick, little attention has been paid to the false memory phenomenon. That is about to change.

Memories Are Made of This

According to recent psychological research, *memory is imagination*. In remembering, we don't consult a videotape recording somewhere in our brains—no such recording exists. Even though we remember some events accurately, we do so by reconstructing images of those events from incomplete traces, and we rely heavily on our interpretive theories, which change over time, modifying the memories themselves. If our theory tells us that something had to have happened, we may well distinctly remember that this very thing did happen, and picture it happening in our mind's eye just as though we had witnessed it. Of course, some people are more fanciful than others, and it has been claimed that about five percent of the population, because of the way their brains are wired, have daydreams of such vividness that they can be mistaken for genuine occurrences in the physical world.

The popular view that we store every experience somewhere in our minds, but require special and difficult techniques to retrieve those experiences, has not been borne out by research. We fail to remember, or subsequently forget, most of our experiences, and no techniques exist for reliably recovering memories that have been lost.

When we recollect something that seemed significant to us at the time, and has seemed significant ever since, and when we do so in a spontaneous, unpressured situation, our memories are overwhelmingly accurate for the main points, and somewhat less so for details. But when we have difficulty remembering, and rack our brains in an effort to remember, the accuracy of recall drops sharply—the racking of our brains will eventually turn up "memories," and these may possess a compelling verisimilitude, but they will be largely false.

What often saves us from manufacturing counterfeit memories is that when we can't remember something, we sensibly accept that the memory is lost, and give up trying. If for some reason we don't give up, we will eventually generate images, and if we are somehow convinced that these images are veridical, *we will* eventually turn them into lifelike memories.

Hypnosis has often been employed in an attempt to elicit memories of the details of incidents. Occasionally, an accurate detail will be produced, but more often, a "convincing" (that's to say, vivid) detail will be elicited that is later shown to be false. For example, hypnosis may get a witness to "remember" a car registration number, but it will most often turn out to be wrong. Hypnotic regression is employed to recover memories of past lives and abductions by aliens in UFOs. It can also be used to "progress" people into the future—it's easy for the subject to recall himself rich and healthy in retirement, or commanding intergalactic battleships a thousand years hence, but alas, a little more tricky to remember next month's commodity prices or Derby winner.

As far as accuracy goes, hypnosis is no different from trying hard to remember something you can't remember; the rigmarole of hypnosis merely encourages you to keep trying. The same applies to "truth drugs" like sodium amytal and sodium pentothal. They will increase the output of apparent memories, but many of these will be false. The folklore tenet that all our experiences are tucked away somewhere in our minds, if only we could get at them, is upheld by the belief that some people have "photographic memories." Certainly there are rare individuals whose memories are much better than other people's, but the record of the most spectacular and most famous of these—"S," studied by Luria—shows that his memory feats were accomplished by an extraordinary facility with mnemonics. "S" was essentially doing what you and I do when we refer to the word "HOMES" to recall the names of the Great Lakes, only the stories he made up to help memorize his material were sometimes far more complex than the material itself.

Ah, Yes, I Remember It Well

We habitually assume that our memories are dependable, but occasionally we reminisce with friends over something that happened years ago, or we are called upon in a court hearing to give a detailed account of precisely what occurred. On such occasions we find to our disgust that other people's recollections are pitifully erroneous, and often spectacularly so.

In a series of experiments, Elizabeth Loftus and her colleagues reduced the creation of false memories to a practical technique. The experiments began modestly, as investigations of the reliability of eyewitness testimony. Subjects would be shown a movie of an auto accident, then their accuracy of recall would be tested. If a false assumption were put into one of the questions ("How fast was the car going when it passed the barn?" when there had been no barn), a high percentage of subjects would later recall a barn. Attempts by other researchers to show that the true memories are there all the time—that the leading questions merely influence what subjects report, not what they "really remember"—have been neatly refuted by several elegant experiments.

From these unambitious beginnings, which merely demonstrate more rigorously what has long been known, and do not transcend what was familiar to Erle Stanley Gardner, the implantation of false memories has ascended to greater heights. Memories of entirely bogus events have been put into the minds of experimental subjects. A man was encouraged to recall childhood occurrences, with the help of close family, under the direction of experimenters. One of these events—that of being lost in a supermarket—was made up by the psychologists. Once the subject had recalled this fictitious event, he continued to work on it for more details, which obligingly came. At the end of the experiment, the subject was asked to guess which of his recollections was false, and picked one of the true memories. Told of the implantation of the false memory of being lost, the subject at first refused to believe it, citing the clarity, detail, and emotionally upsetting quality of the recollection as proof that it must have happened.

A striking instance of implantation of false memories involved Paul Ingram, chair of the county Republican committee in Olympia, Washington, who was arrested for child abuse in 1988. He at first denied everything and was told he was "in denial." A psychologist and a Christian minister worked with detectives by suggesting to Ingram some incident and having the concerned and compliant Ingram ponder and visualize that incident. After five months of interrogation, Ingram began to "remember" and confess to numerous bizarre sexual crimes, including his involvement in—ho, hum—a Satanic cult which had polished off twenty-five babies.

Richard Ofshe, a social psychologist employed by the prosecution, smelled a rat, and tested the accuracy of Ingram's confessions by fabricating an incident and suggesting this to Ingram in exactly the same manner. Sure enough, Ingram at first couldn't remember it, but after a while increasingly elaborate memories began to appear, and eventually Ingram wrote a detailed statement confessing, with telling and authentic touches, to the story that Ofshe had made up.

There are well-documented cases where evidently sincere confessions have been subsequently refuted. Most juries don't grasp how malleable is memory, and hence how worthless as evidence is a confession to a crime, if made after considerable pressure and absent verifiable details which the confessor could have known only if he were the culprit. In general, it's a good rule of thumb that any conflict between a person's memory at one date and his memory at a later date should be resolved in favor of the earlier recollection—and this includes those cases where the memory is absent at the earlier date.

If Memory Serves

Induced, implanted, or artificially created memories are now called "false memories," but they might—for example, by sheer coincidence—correspond to fact, just as a false clue left at the scene of a crime by a meddlesome person might happen to point to the real criminal. However, these memories are still false *as memories*.

On the other hand, a true memory may be quite false. This can occur because people's perceptions of events depend upon fallible interpretations. It was long ago demonstrated, in experiments which have been repeated many times, that if a dramatic event is staged unexpectedly for a roomfull of people, who are then immediately requested to record what they have witnessed, the accounts are filled with errors, often quite bizarre ones. A false perception may be truly remembered—this possibility should be distinguished from false memory. The well-known contradictions in different individuals' interpretations of the same event, most famously depicted in Kurosawa's *Rashomon* (1951), seem to owe more to false perceptions than to false memories.

A false memory may be a slight inaccuracy in a recollection of a real event, a major misinterpretation of an event, or a completely bogus event. Such memories are not experientially much different from genuine memories—there is no way for a putative rememberer to be sure, purely by inspecting his memory, whether it really happened that way, nor is there any way in which another person can tell, purely by interviewing the putative rememberer. (There is some evidence that false memories may be subtly distinctive, but no method is known for reliably discriminating them.)

Some false memories are more vivid, detailed, and powerful than true memories of comparable age could be. Minute details of color, scent, and texture may be recollected as though the scene had been witnessed only moments ago—which, of course, may be the precise truth of the matter. The vividness, detail, and sometimes highly distressing qualities of these images are often taken as evidence of their truth, when in fact these features suggest the opposite. Any genuine memory of years ago has a faded, ill-formed character. If you remember talking to someone ten years ago you may well be right, but if you consult your memory of that conversation to determine on which side his hair was parted, you are deluded.

Lest We Forget

There's no dispute that we may forget something for a while, in the sense of having no occasion to call it to mind, and then one day remember it— though it is likely that if the period of "forgetting" is many years, an accurate recall will have been helped by some refreshing of the memory during those years. For instance, we may recall an incident from thirty years ago, aided by the fact that it has several times been mentioned in conversation within that period.

There's equally no dispute that our memories may play us false. The greater the effort to remember something we have difficulty remembering, the greater the likelihood that the memory eventually reconstructed will be partly or entirely false. If we battle for months to recall something of which we have no recollection, and then battle for more months to convince ourselves that the images produced in our minds are true, the memory thus constructed is almost sure to be false.

Recovered memory therapy, this latter-day exorcism, is an audacious folly which already rivals the cruelties of the Inquisition and appears set to catch up with some of Stalin's purges. As the sheer scale of this malevolent credulity becomes a scandal, we shall no doubt hear that there are a few irresponsible therapists who exercise insufficient caution. Yet any introduction of rational standards immediately disqualifies all recovered memory cases. This follows from three salient facts: that these cases are not independently corroborated, that the subjective quality of a putative memory cannot guarantee its veracity, and that there is no scientific evidence that anyone has ever repressed a memory.

If recovered memory therapists are induced to be less aggressive in their suggestions to clients, they will be "successful" in fewer cases, and only the more fanciful of clients will "remember" the imaginary enormities. The sheer volume of bogus accusations will be reduced, but every one of them will be just as bogus. There is now talk about establishing "guidelines" for evaluating recovered memories, but as with guidelines for burning witches at the stake, such legitimizing fictions ought to be resisted.

Here is the only guideline we need: The fact that a memory has been recovered after a period of alleged repression is sufficient to show that the so-called memory is worthless as evidence of any actual occurrence outside that person's mind or brain. A tale supported only by a recovered memory merits exactly the same credence as we would accord to a story whispered in someone's ear by Wotan or Jupiter.

Select List of Sources

Baker, Robert A. 1990. *They Call It Hypnosis*. Buffalo: Prometheus.

———. 1992. *Hidden Memories: Voices and Visions Within*. Buffalo: Prometheus.

Bass, Ellen, and Laura Davis. 1988. *The Courage to Heal: A Guide for Women Survivors of Child Sexual Abuse*. New York: Harper and Row.

Bolles, Edmund Blair. 1988. *Remembering and Forgetting: Inquiries into the Nature of Memory*. New York: Walker.

Bower, Bruce. 1993. Sudden Recall. *Science News* 144:12–13.

Cohen, Gillian. 1989. *Memory in the Real World*. Hove: Erlbaum.

Coleman, Lee. 1990. False Accusations of Sexual Abuse: Psychiatry's Latest Reign of Error. *Journal of Mind and Behavior* 11:3–4.

Davis, Laura. 1990. *The Courage to Heal Workbook*. New York: Harper and Row.

Eberle, Paul, and Shirley Eberle. 1993. *The Abuse of Innocence: The McMartin Preschool Trial*. Buffalo: Prometheus.

Esterson, Allen. 1993. *Seductive Mirage: An Exploration of the Work of Sigmund Freud*. Chicago: Open Court.

FMS Foundation Newsletter. Ten issues a year, available by $20 subscription from The False Memory Syndrome Foundation, 3401 Market St., Philadelphia, PA 19104.

Faust, David, and Jay Ziskin. 1988. The Expert Witness in Psychology and Psychiatry. *Science* 241:312.

Feldman, Gail Carr. 1993. *Lessons in Evil, Lessons from the Light: A True Story of Satanic Abuse and Spiritual Healing*. New York: Crown.

Franklin, Eileen, and William Wright. 1991. *Sins of the Father: The Landmark Franklin Case—A Daughter, A Memory, and a Murder*. New York: Fawcett.

Goldstein, Eleanor. 1992. *Confabulations: Creating False Memories, Destroying Families*. Boca Raton: Social Issues Resource Series.

Loftus, Elizabeth E. 1979. *Eyewitness Testimony*. Cambridge: Harvard University Press.

———. 1980. *Memory: Surprising New Insights into How We Remember and Why We Forget*. Reading: Addison-Wesley.

———. 1993. The Reality of Repressed Memories. *American Psychologist* 48:5 (May).

Loftus, Elizabeth E., and Katherine Ketcham. 1991. *Witness for the Defense: The Accused, the Eyewitness, and the Expert Who Puts Memory on Trial*. New York: St. Martin's.

Luria, A.R., 1968. *The Mind of a Mnemonist*. New York, Basic Books.

MacLean, Harry N. 1993. *Once Upon a Time: A True Story of Memory, Murder, and the Law*. New York: Harper Collins.

Ofshe, Richard, and Ethan Watters. 1993. Making Monsters. *Society* 30:3 (March–April). Parkin, Alan J. 1987. *Memory and Amnesia: An Introduction*. Oxford: Blackwell.

———. 1993. *Memory: Phenomena, Experiment, and Theory*. Oxford: Blackwell.

Raschke, Carl A. 1990. *Painted Black: From Drug Killings to Heavy Metal, The Alarming True Story of How Satanism Is Terrorizing Our Communities*. San Francisco: Harper and Row.

Richardson, James T., Joel Best, and David G. Bromley, eds. 1991. *The Satanism Scare*. New York: Aleline.

Sauer, Mark, and Jim Okerblom. 1993. Trial by Therapy. *National Review* (September 5th).

Schumaker, ed., John F. 1991. *Human Suggestibility: Advances in Theory, Research, and Application*. New York: Routledge.

Smith, Michelle, and Lawrence Pazder. 1980. *Michelle Remembers*. New York: Congdon and Latte (Pocket Books, 1981).

Victor, Jeffrey S. 1993. *Satanic Panic: The Creation of a Contemporary Legend*. Chicago: Open Court.

Wakefield, Hollida, and Ralph Underwager. 1992. Uncovering Memories of Alleged Sexual Abuse: The Therapists Who Do It. *Issues in Child Abuse Accusations* 4:4.

Watters, Ethan. 1991. The Devil in Mr. Ingram. *Mother Jones* (July–August).

Wexler, Richard. 1990. *Wounded Innocents: The Real Victims of the War Against Child Abuse*. Buffalo: Prometheus.

I thank Dr. Michael Edelstein and Dr. Jeffrey Victor for their helpful comments on a draft of this article.

Liberty, March 1994

3
WHY STOP AT TERM LIMITS? (1995)

The worldwide triumph of democracy has been breathtakingly swift and thorough. We now confidently wait for the last few beleaguered outposts of one-party rule to run up the white flag and announce their dates for open parliamentary elections.

Yet, even as democracy is on the point of subjugating the entire planet, there are many indications of a profound alienation from actually existing democracy, especially in those countries which have long endured it. The more politicians fawn on the voters, the more the voters feel that politicians are unrepresentative, out of touch, and inaccessible. The term-limits movement is one response to this deep-seated frustration.

Most people now think of democracy as a system where a high proportion of adults are able to vote periodically, their votes are counted, and control of the government goes to those individuals who manage to attract a majority of the voters. This is *not* what democracy meant to the Athenians who invented the concept. It is not what democracy meant to political thinkers (mostly unfriendly to democracy, of course) from Plato to Montesquieu.

The classical conception of democracy leans heavily on the procedure known as election by lot, technically called *sortition*. Under this procedure, holders of political offices are chosen by a purely random method from a list comparable to the present voters' roll. Any of us might find himself picked for a seat in Congress or on the local board of assessors, just as any of us might find himself picked for a seat on a jury.

With our increasing reliance upon pre-election opinion polls, several writers have suggested—some with their tongues thrust more firmly into their cheeks than others—that we cut out the elections and simply use sample polls to decide which candidate wins. But election by lot goes further: we cut out the opinion polls too, and pick the winners directly from the eligible population.

Election by lot could exist in piecemeal, supplementary form but, for the sake of clarity, let's think about it in a sweeping, wholesale fashion. There would cease to be any voting for seats in the Senate and House of Representatives. The people to fill those positions would be picked by lot from a list of all those eligible. This list could be similar to the present voters' roll, or it could be the sum of all present jury lists, or a list of all adult citizens.

The President could also be chosen in this way, directly by lottery (as occurs in the classic science-fiction novel *Solar Lottery* by Philip K. Dick) but the specter of a demented psychopath taking control would doubtless be raised to scare people off this proposal. Actually I think that the chance of such an outcome would be more remote than the chance of the same kind of malevolent prodigy clawing his way to the top through vote-catching and political trading. But as a safeguard the lottery could select the delegates to the Electoral College; in that case there would still be rival presidential candidates who would compete for office by attempting to attract Electoral College votes.

Election by lot shares some of the advantages of majority voting. Like voting, election by lot provides a system for removing our current rulers without violence, in a way that reflects evolving public opinion and is demonstrably even-handed and above-board.

Because of well-known statistical characteristics of large numbers, the views of members of Congress would correspond much more accurately with the views of the whole population than those of our present congressmen do. A new meaning would accrue to the statistical term "representative sample." The range of popular opinions would be represented with fine accuracy, though these opinions would still have to be hammered out in congressional debate in order to forge policies. Once in Congress, members would be free, as they are today, to "vote their consciences." But these consciences would be typical, average consciences, rather than the atrophied consciences of dedicated power-seekers.

At one stroke, the electoral lottery would solve all the problems perceived as arising from the under-representation of various groups. The laws of statistics would guarantee that Congress would both "look like America" and think like America. While there might be anomalies at any given time, normally slightly more than half the members in each chamber would be women, thirteen percent would be blacks, and so forth, without gerrymandering. There would also be far fewer lawyers in Congress, which offers advantages as well as disadvantages.

A Congress elected by lot would be far more lively intellectually. The members would no longer be constricted by the present necessity of making their public mouthings correspond to the safe middle ground for the sake of re-election. There would be more eccentrics, more loose cannons, more independent voices in public life, in place of today's grey mediocrity and wheedling insincerity. Voting alliances would form in Congress, but these would be looser than today's shepherded flocks.

Moreover, a government chosen by lot would be more willing to do what its members perceived to be in the general interest—just as we recognize that Supreme Court justices can put principle above expediency because they will never have to come up for re-appointment.

Election by lot would be far cheaper than voting. The mechanics of election would be much less costly, and less open to fraud, than the collection and counting of votes. There would be no spending by candidates to get elected, and interest groups hoping to influence policy-making could do so only by talking to the general public about the issues.

Congressional campaign spending would disappear—without the government's having to address the matter directly or infringe upon the First Amendment. There would simply be no congressional campaigns. Indeed, there would be no particular reason to retain the practice of sweeping elections for many seats at once. Congressional seats could be re-allocated at, say, the rate of one per day.

The politics of sound bites, scandal-mongering, and negative campaign ads would instantly and completely cease. The expenditure of resources on revealing or covering up elected officials' past sexual indiscretions—which have absolutely no relevance to anyone's administrative competence or to the wisdom of his political program—would also largely end.

Denied the opportunity to spend money in order to affect the outcome of elections, pressure groups would allocate more money to their two remaining avenues of influence: working directly upon public opinion (so that those elected would be more likely to favor the positions the groups advocate), and lobbying incumbent congressmen. But such lobbying, though still possible, would be less effective because of the lack of a cohesive permanent caste of politicians. So pressure groups would be induced to "lobby" the whole adult population, stimulating wide debate and political education. In a very real sense, power would be returned to the people.

Some of those elected would not wish to serve in Congress. But this reality would make no more difference than the fact that many citizens today choose not to exercise their right to vote. The number of those elected by the lottery could be adjusted to take into account the fact that some would choose not to accept their own election.

Tried and Tested

Could election by lot work in practice? Well, it has worked in many places over many centuries.

Everyone knows that the democracy which was to be a shining beacon for later generations was developed in Athens. But an ancient Athenian would be surprised and suspicious at the notion of a "democracy" which confined itself to voting for representatives, without a major role for election by lot. And our Athenian would be dumbfounded by a "democracy" which lacked the principle of rotation: the iron rule of any true democracy that no one be permitted to hold the same political office twice.

As Athens became more democratic, it relied increasingly heavily on election by lot. At first the lottery was conducted by drawing white and black beans from a container, but by the fourth century B.C., a special randomizing machine, the *cleroterion*, was manufactured. Specimens have been recovered by archeologists.

In the Athenian democracy, most major political decisions were made by the *ekklesia*, the mass meeting of all citizens who cared to attend. But there were still many powerful public officials. All magistrates were chosen by lot, including the nine *archons* (usually translated as "chief magistrates," though this understates their political authority). All other public officials were also chosen by lot, except generals and some financial officials, who were elected by majority vote. The *boule*, or council of five hundred, was elected by lot, and its chairmanship rotated by lot. It met daily and actively supervised the performance of all public officials. Executive functions were broken down into small tasks, each entrusted to a board of ten members chosen by lot and serving for one year. Voting for representatives had some place in Athens, but it was looked at warily, as an inherently antidemocratic device that tended to oligarchy.

The lot was also widely used for political decisions in Rome, but here it had no democratic purpose. For example, which of Rome's two consuls could decide a matter was often determined by lot. With the capture of power by Julius Caesar, democracy in practice disappeared from the Western world for a while, although those writers who thought and wrote about it continued to associate it with election by lot.

Election by lot was employed in Venice and Florence during the Renaissance, and for a time in one Swiss canton. It prevailed in towns of the Basque region until it was stamped out by the Spanish crown.

It was only about 250 years ago that the prevailing concept of democracy lost its association with election by lot and became largely confined to majority voting. Montesquieu, in his *Spirit of the Laws* (1748) was the last major writer to take it for granted that, as he put it, "suffrage by lot is natural to democracy." Rather abruptly, election by lot disappeared from mainstream theoretical discussion. This may have happened in part because the English House of Commons, which had begun to serve as a model of representative institutions, evolved as an instrument of countervailing power. It was not seen as an organ of democracy, nor even as a governing body, but rather as a check upon the real government, the King and Lords. Positions in the monarchy and aristocracy, of course, are fixed by a different kind of lottery.

Voices for Democracy

Throughout the nineteenth century, election by lot continued to attract supporters, ranging from obscure pamphleteers like the author of *Election by Lot the Only Remedy for Political Corruption* to George Bernard Shaw. G.K. Chesterton toyed with the idea in *The Napoleon of Notting Hill*.

In recent decades a steadily growing number of academic political theorists have come to favor election by lot. Benjamin Barber's *Strong Democracy: Participatory Politics for a New Age* (Berkeley: University of California Press, 1984) is a typical product of Sixties "participatory" sentiment, of little interest except in that it recommends the "re-introduction of election by lot on a limited basis," mainly for local governing assemblies.

John Burnheim's *Is Democracy Possible? The Alternative to Electoral Politics* (Berkeley: University of California Press, 1985) takes a tougher line: "to have democracy we must abandon elections, and in most cases referendums, and revert to the ancient principle of choosing by lot those who are to hold various public offices."

A different kind of work is *A Citizen Legislature* by Ernest Callenbach and Michael Phillips (Berkeley: Banyan Tree/Clear Glass, 1985). Brief but economical, this book is entirely devoted to arguing for election by lot. The authors propose a House of Representatives chosen by lot, co-existing with other institutions chosen by majority vote in the present manner. The authors' approach is scrupulously practical; they recommend beginning the experiment with state legislatures. Though they make no secret of their leftist views, Callenbach and Phillips realistically note some of the policy issues where the House would be markedly more conservative than it is under the majority-vote system.

All these writers have been surpassed, at least in grandiosity of vision, by Barbara Goodwin, a leading British political philosopher, in her truly remarkable *Justice by Lottery* (Chicago: University of Chicago Press, 1992).

Professor Goodwin argues for what she calls the "Total Social Lottery," in which most aspects of life, including occupation, income, and the right to bear children, are allocated by lot. She does allow a few modifications, in such matters as the choice of a surgeon to operate on the anatomy of Barbara Goodwin.

Professor Goodwin's utopia is the *reduction ad absurdum* of the socialist view that the whole of life is political. Most notably, her conception of industrial efficiency is pitifully inadequate. When we consider, for example, that serious estimates of the cost to the US economy of the effective prohibition of IQ tests run as high as $145 billion, we can easily see that the immensely more devastating effects of randomly allocating people to jobs would threaten the very physical survival of the majority of the population. All equivocation about people being able to "learn to do a job" is fruitless: a substantially free labor market ceaselessly removes people who can "do jobs" from those jobs, replacing them with people who can do those jobs a shade better. We all benefit from the enormous efficiency of this system.

The Representative Sample

A standard objection to sortition is that not all the representatives elected by lottery would be capable or competent. But it's far from clear that they would, on average, be any less capable or competent—at governing rather than at running for office—than the political performers who entertain us today. Congress is already a home for comparative mediocrities. Many towering political personalities of today would be entirely undistinguished if employed in the middle management of industry, which is about a lofty a station as their talents might be expected to elevate them to.

It's true that *some* of the congressmen elected by lot would be unusually incapable, but they would be outweighed by their more nearly average colleagues. And exceptionally capable people would probably be at least as numerous as they are now. Leaders would emerge within the Senate and the House. Ordinary members, as now, would have the intellectually undemanding chore of voting for or against pieces of legislation prepared, as now, by professional staff. Voting in Congress requires opinions, not expertise.

Some may object that the people would not be choosing their own representatives. But this notion of representation evolved in small English communities, with obvious leaders of high traditional status, and with most people unable to vote, so that only a handful of people were actively involved in choosing each representative.

Given universal suffrage and the expansion of population, electoral districts have become so large at the state and federal levels that this old notion no longer makes any sense. Nowadays the voter gets to choose between two big packages, each containing many items he probably finds distasteful. Most voters now feel, deeply and instinctively, that their congressman does not represent *them* in any way whatsoever. This is not a passing mood, nor is it a failure of civic responsibility; it is the sober recognition of an indisputable and irreversible fact.

In actuality, election by lot would give ordinary people a greater sense of representation, even though congressmen would no longer have been theoretically delegated by them. Members of Congress would mostly be ordinary women and men, not individuals who had chosen the unsavory profession of politician. To the folks back home, electoral lottery winners would often appear to be true representatives, in the way that major celebrities are often so regarded by the communities from which they sprang. Most people in Dixon, Illinois, for example, viewed Ronald Reagan as representative of themselves and followed his political ascent with pride, long before they ever had a chance to vote for him.

A related worry is that members of Congress would no longer be accountable to the voters—the implication being that they could do anything they liked. But congressmen are accountable now only in the sense that they may wish to run again and may lose next time if they do something unpopular. Under sortition, all top office holders would have exactly as much accountability as any political office-holder does now in his final term, including every US president in his second term. Election by lot would in this respect be no different from the strictest term limits.

But winning an electoral lottery and becoming a member of Congress would undoubtedly be a stroke of luck for most winners: they would hope to capitalize on it for the rest of their lives, in the enhanced value of their experience and opinions. So they would still have some career motivation to please the public, as well as the natural desire to be highly thought of.

The recent growth of academic interest in sortition has been almost purely leftist in inspiration. There are at least three reasons for this. First, most academics are leftists. Second, in this century a concern with popular "participation" has been mainly a preoccupation of socialists. They sense there is something dreadfully wrong in the relations of government and governed, but rather than reduce the scope of government, they respond by trying to involve the subjects more actively in politics. Third, anything that offers to break up an ossified ruling group naturally appeals most to those who feel themselves unfairly excluded from political influence. Leftists felt this way very sharply in the Fifties and Sixties whereas conservatives came to do so in the Seventies. When the leftist participatory democrats of the 1960s began to reflect and to write books about their reflections, some of them gave birth to the modern intellectual movement in favor of election by lot.

Whatever its causes, the fact that the revival of sortition has occurred on the Left explains why it has made no contact with the term-limits movement, strongly linked to the Right. However, if the popular disaffection with majority-vote democracy continues to grow, as I expect it will, it is more than likely that this disaffection will join forces with the fledgling intellectual movement for sortition. Election by lot would then be revived as a serious contender in public discussion.

Sortition is particularly suited to the modern world of political entities with enormous populations and with the technical means to select randomly from large databases. And it is increasingly congenial to the contemporary worldview, shaped by the indeterminacies of quantum mechanics and chaos theory.

It is now widely believed that, while government is a necessary evil, rule by representatives chosen by majority vote is its least evil form. But election by lot may well be a decided improvement on majority-vote elections, and as long as people feel that they need some form of government, sortition is surely worth a try.

In any event, it probably will be given many a try in the coming century. We may as well begin to ponder that which we are going to confront in practice.

National Review, September 11th, 1995

4

YES, GAMBLING IS PRODUCTIVE AND RATIONAL (1997)

The War on Gambling is about to take its place alongside the War on Drugs as a crusade for decency which no ambitious politician may question. The present movement to legalize gambling, which got under way in the 1960s, is still making some gains, but has become increasingly unpopular. The momentum of legalization has been slowed, and will soon be reversed. Although some gambling is now legal in all but two states (Hawaii and Utah), gambling prohibitionists are confidently predicting absolute nationwide prohibition by early next century, and it's by no means self-evident that they are wrong.

Government policy on gambling has gone through successive cycles of liberalization, backlash, and renewed prohibition. In the US, we're currently experiencing the third nationwide backlash—the first was in the middle of the nineteenth century, the second during the 1940s.

The ease with which public opinion can be mobilized against gambling reflects a deep-rooted suspicion. Most people enjoy gambling in moderation, and will gamble occasionally if they can. Yet these same people often oppose further liberalization of the gambling laws. Gambling is one of those things which are obviously harmless when you or I do them, but fraught with menace if millions of other people can do them too.

Why is gambling, enjoyed by the vast majority of people, denounced day in and day out, with hardly any voices to be heard in its defense? The reigning ideology tells us all that gambling is evil, for several reasons. Gambling is selfish; it is addictive; it provides "false hope"; it is a dangerous competitor to some forms of religion because it too offers the prospect of a greatly improved future life at rather long odds.

Yet possibly the single most influential reason for holding gambling to be evil is the belief that it is unproductive and therefore wasteful. Today's hostility to gambling has much in common with the old opposition to "usury" (charging interest on loans) and the current fear of "deindustrialization" (replacement of manufacturing by service jobs). Money-lending, hamburger-flipping, and playing the lottery have all been maligned as essentially sterile pursuits whose expansion bodes ill for the health of the nation.

Simply Sterile Transfers?

Is gambling unproductive? We need to distinguish between the more or less remote *effects* of gambling and its *intrinsic nature*. It is sometimes claimed that gambling encourages people to dream impossible dreams about the future instead of working hard, or that gambling encourages crime at the expense of honest industry. Aside from these alleged effects of gambling, however, it is commonly believed that gambling is intrinsically unproductive—that in gambling, unlike farming or auto manufacture, nothing is produced.

Claims about the injurious *effects* of gambling don't seem to be factually correct. Freedom to gamble encourages hard work on the part of gamblers, especially those with low incomes, just as, broadly speaking, any enhanced opportunity to spend one's earnings as one pleases increases the incentive effect of a given wage. And gambling by itself does not attract crime: it's the illegality of some or all gambling which forces gambling to become a criminal activity.[1]

Is gambling, then, *intrinsically* unproductive? One very popular view was promulgated by Paul Samuelson in his once-canonical textbook: gambling "involves simply sterile transfers of money or goods between individuals, creating no new money or goods."[2] A footnote informs the reader

1   For some of the evidence for these statements, see the summary in Reuven Brenner, with Gabrielle A. Brenner, *Gambling and Speculation: A Theory, a History, and a Future of Some Human Decisions* (Cambridge: Cambridge University Press, 1990), pp. 37–42. The current anti-gambling campaign has begotten a spate of bogus scholarly "studies" purporting to show that gambling has deleterious consequences for the culture and economy. This literature consists largely of the same writers quoting each other's guesses about the evil effects of gambling, and passing these off as data. When one tracks down the ultimate sources in these works, one finds that they are often anecdotal impressions, for example: the opinions of people like Gamblers Anonymous activists. The methodology of this literature precludes the turning up of any findings other than those assumed at the outset. No studies with any semblance of rigor have yet confirmed the horrific fantasies of the anti-gambling ideologues.

2   Paul A. Samuelson, *Economics: An Introductory Analysis.* Seventh edition (New York: McGraw-Hill, 1967), p. 409.

that "in all professional gambling arrangements, the participants lose out on balance. The leakage comes from the fact that the odds are always rigged in favor of the 'house', so that even an 'honest' house will win in the long run." Notice the nasty quotes around "honest," and the use of the word "rigged" to represent the fact that these sneaky casino operators do not provide their services as a charity, but require to be recompensed for their efforts, just like college professors or writers of textbooks.

The Cannibals Are Coming

Before we look at the claim that gambling involves nothing but sterile transfers of money or goods, let's first consider a related charge leveled by anti-gambling propagandists. One of their leaders, Robert Goodman, contends that gambling, when it is permitted after a period of prohibition, displaces or, as he picturesquely terms it, "cannibalizes" other activities.[3]

Goodman continually reiterates this charge, and doesn't seem to notice that it applies equally to any activity which consumes scarce resources—therefore any activity whatsoever. If pizza restaurants were first prohibited and then legalized, the newly legal restaurants would attract some dollars away from other businesses. Buildings, kitchen equipment, tables, delivery vehicles, and employees would be bid away from other kinds of restaurants, and perhaps some resources would be bid away from non-restaurant activities, to cater to the consumers' newly liberated demand for pizzas. One might then observe that pizza provision grows only by hurting other occupations—that pizzerias "cannibalize" other trades.

If, after being prohibited, a casino is permitted to open, this may well cause people to spend in the casino some money they would formerly have spent in a restaurant. Perhaps that restaurant has to close because of reduced business. Precisely the same would apply in reverse: if casinos were legal, but restaurants prohibited, and then restaurants were legalized, the

---

3   *The Luck Business: The Devastating Consequences and Broken Promises of America's Gambling Explosion* (New York: The Free Press, 1995), passim. The term "cannibalization" seems to have arisen in business corporations, to denote new products which might take business away from a company's existing lines. Its application to gambling is unhappy; the word seems to have been picked up as a vacuous but ominous-sounding instrument of abuse.

newly legal restaurants would attract consumers' dollars away from casinos, and some casinos might have to close. Anti-restaurant fanatics could then proclaim that restaurateurs were nothing more than dastardly cannibals, gobbling up legitimate businesses such as casinos.

When a heretofore prohibited but widely desired activity is legalized, the expansion of this activity will necessarily curtail other activities, unless total output increases. This does not mean that the change is unimportant. The fact that people pursue the newly legal activity demonstrates that there is an unsatisfied appetite for that activity. The people who desire to take part in the prohibited activity, and are now free to do so, experience an improvement in their situation, in their own judgment. Their real incomes automatically rise, even though this increase is not captured in national income statistics.

There are two important qualifications to what I have just stated. First, the legalization of a formerly prohibited industry reduces the demand for other industries below what it would otherwise have been, not necessarily below what it has actually been. If total output rises—if there is economic growth—casinos may attract business from restaurants, and yet restaurants may keep the same business as before, or even expand. Second, prohibition of gambling does not succeed in stopping gambling. While prohibition reduces the total amount of gambling, some gambling goes on illicitly. A major part of the expansion of legal gambling following legalization takes away business from formerly illegal gambling rather than from non-gambling activities.

The assertion that gambling subtracts consumer dollars from other industries is precisely as true of gambling as of manufacturing refrigerators, providing health care, or running a church. Why then do anti-gambling zealots make such a fuss about cannibalization? There are two reasons.

First, in recent years politicians who favor legalization of gambling have scored points by appealing to local advantage. They have claimed that the local economy (city, county, state, or Indian reservation) would get a shot in the arm from an increased inflow of visitors. In this case, much of the money spent on local gambling is not withdrawn from some other local industry; it is withdrawn from industries outside the locality. There is a net gain to business in the locality, at the expense of reduced business elsewhere.

But this only works if gambling continues to be considerably more restricted outside the locality than it is within it. Las Vegas is now established as an exciting vacation center which would easily survive the complete legalization of all gambling in the US, but in its formative years Las Vegas would never have taken off if gambling had not been virtually illegal across nearly all of the country. The more gambling is legalized generally, the less any locality can attract visitors by legalization.

There has recently been so much legalization in various parts of the US that any locality which newly legalizes gambling cannot thereby attract many visitors.[4] The bulk of the new gambling business unleashed by a local legalization now comes from people who live nearby.[5] This has led to disappointment at the results of recent legalizations, disappointment which rabid anti-gambling demagogues like Goodman can cynically exploit.

The fundamental argument for legalizing gambling is not that it will bring in business from elsewhere, but rather that people are entitled to do whatever they please with their own lives as long as they don't invade other people's rights. More generally, it's good for people to be free to do what they want to do, so long as this does not impose on anyone else. The other reason why the "cannibalization" argument is so often made is that many people start with the prejudice that gambling is a waste. If gambling is unproductive, and if the growth of gambling subtracts from some productive activity, then this must, it seems, be bad. But if it is bad for gambling to cannibalize restaurants, yet okay for bookstores to cannibalize drycleaners or for churches to cannibalize bowling alleys, then cannibalization is not what is really being objected to. We come back to the inherent legitimacy of gambling, and the dominant view of that is mightily influenced by the popular theory that gambling is necessarily unproductive.

---

4   Gambling is still severely regulated everywhere, so a state or city which simultaneously repealed all restrictions on private gambling would at once become a shining beacon of affluence. But the restrictive climate of opinion makes such a bold move politically unfeasible.

5   As the anti-gambling enthusiasts succeed in repealing local legalizations, the process will go into reverse. Those localities which are slow to re-impose prohibition will begin to see big gains from visitors. The anti-gambling crusaders are keenly aware of this, hence their strategy of going for a "national gambling policy," in which the federal government takes over the states' and cities' traditional role of regulating gambling.

Production Means Satisfaction of Wants

What does it mean to say that some activity is unproductive? This question was picked over quite thoroughly by economists in the eighteenth and nineteenth centuries. One early view was that only agriculture was productive. Manufacturing (then a small part of total employment) was looked upon as unproductive, since it was obviously supported by agriculture—the manufacturers had to eat.

Another idea was that only products which could be turned into gold and silver were truly productive. Later these two theories lost any serious following,[6] but two others remained popular for a while: that anything which did not result in a new physical object was unproductive, and that what we would now call "service" jobs were unproductive. (These two views are not the same, and do not necessarily mesh together well, for a provider of services, such as an architect, may assist in the creation of a new physical object, such as a house.)

Adam Smith contended in 1776 that the labor of domestic servants, government officials, the military, "churchmen, lawyers, physicians, men of letters of all kinds; players, buffoons, musicians, opera-singers, opera-dancers, &c." were unproductive.[7] This contention, and the sloppy argument of which it forms a part, provoked much debate over the next century.

The attempt, by Smith and others, to designate some occupations as unproductive did not lead to convincing conclusions. Those who based productiveness on the making of a physical object were compelled to conclude, for instance, that the performance at a musical concert would be unproductive, whereas printing the tickets and programs for that same concert would be productive.

After the end of the nineteenth century, leading economists no longer paid much attention to the classification of activities as productive or

6   The first is now almost precisely reversed in the minds of many followers of Ross Perot and Patrick Buchanan: only the building of gadgets, preferably of metal, is considered truly productive. "Hamburger flipping"—providing meals for people—has become the very paradigm of unproductiveness.

7   *An Inquiry into the Nature and Causes of the Wealth of Nations*, ed. Edwin Cannan (Chicago: University of Chicago Press, 1976), p. 352.

unproductive. The new theory of value based on marginal utility shone a flood of light on the question, and clearly exposed many of the old arguments as fallacious.

The conclusion of the new approach was that "production" means satisfaction of wants. It is productive to make a physical object only insofar as that object enables someone to satisfy a desire. In satisfying desires, the physical object (such as a shirt) yields services. All production is ultimately production of services desired by consumers. The musician giving a live performance is being directly productive in the only way in which it is intelligible to be productive: he is satisfying the wants of consumers, in this case of listeners. The producer of a shirt is being productive more indirectly, by making an object which will yield a stream of future want-satisfactions to its wearer. If for some reason the shirt cannot yield these want-satisfactions, whether because everyone undergoes a conversion to an anti-shirt religion or because the shirt falls apart before it can be worn, then the labor of producing it has turned out to be unproductive, despite the fact that a physical object was made.

One way of describing want-satisfaction is to talk about "utility." An activity is productive if it yields utility. According to the modern view, which is no longer controversial among economic theorists, domestic servants, entertainers, priests, and physicians are indeed productive, because they produce services their customers want; they enable those customers to get additional utility.

The same applies to activities in which people may engage either individually or collaboratively. It is productive for a musician to give a recital, assuming that the audience likes it, but it is also productive for a group of friends to get together and perform music for their own enjoyment, or for an individual to perform alone for his own satisfaction.

"Productive" is not a value-judgment. If gambling turned out to be productive, that would not show that we would have to approve of it, but it would show that if we disapproved of it, we would have to do so on grounds other than its unproductiveness.

Does gambling satisfy the wants of its participants? Do gamblers enjoy gambling? If they do, then gambling is productive, in much the same way that sports, religious services, or psychotherapy are productive.

Gambling as Recreation

The outstanding theorist of gambling, Reuven Brenner, points out that it comes in two types.[8] There is gambling—call it "recreational"—which takes up a lot of the gambler's time, and gambling which does not. Many people derive considerable enjoyment from recreational gambling. Recreational gamblers do not gamble primarily to gain financially, but to enjoy themselves by playing a game. The possibility of monetary gain or loss adds spice to the game.

Many forms of recreational gambling involve some skill, and these games are therefore not sharply different from games like golf or chess, where there is some luck and people pay to play competitively, the winners receiving substantial prizes. In poker, the amount of luck per hand may be high, but this evens out with many hands, so that the element of skill will tend to predominate in the course of a few hours' play.[9] A serious chess game may easily take five or six hours; it is doubtful whether the outcome of five hours' poker is any less governed by skill. Recreational gambling is no less productive than tenpin bowling, ballroom dancing, or barbershop singing—all group pastimes which people pursue because they enjoy them.

8   Brenner, pp. 20–21. Brenner's is the best book ever written on gambling. Although I agree with nearly all of Brenner's criticisms of orthodox opinion on gambling, I reject the lynchpin of his own theory: that non-recreational gambling occurs only because people crave an increase specifically in their relative income, independent of their desire for an absolute increase in income.

9   Where there is recreational gambling with some skill involved, a resourceful player may win in the long run. There is no reason why the "house" or the "bookie" would necessarily object to some players making consistent gains. The majority of recreational gamblers, whose interest in winning is less predominant, or whose skill is unremarkable, ultimately pay for the winnings of the prize-winners and the gains of the "house." This majority may still be "ahead" in non-pecuniary terms, in the enjoyment they derive from playing. In utility terms, which is all that matters, everybody may be a net winner. An interesting case is that of blackjack, where there is a sure-fire method of winning consistently. Although the existence of this method is very widely known, most blackjack players don't bother to learn it (which takes a few weeks of intensive study), so casinos go on offering a game which they are bound to lose in the long run to any customers who apply the method. See the discussion of this in Willem Albert Wagenaar, *Paradoxes of Gambling Behavior* (Hove: Erlbaum, 1988), an interesting book which, however, like so many, never for a moment questions the reigning dogma that gamblers' motivations must involve irrationality.

Samuelson's mistake—a surprising blunder coming from an economist—lies in counting only the monetary transactions. Of course gambling does not create new physical goods; it directly yields utility to the players.

Are Lotteries Productive?

Many people will readily agree that if a concert, a baseball match, or an evening's conversation are considered productive, a poker game might also be judged productive.[10] But there is another kind of gambling: playing the lottery. Surely this can't be primarily an enjoyable way to pass the time. It seems to be done in hope of financial gain, but what if that hope is a product of delusion?

An activity may be anticipated to be productive, but found not to be productive after the fact. Drilling for oil may be unproductive if no oil is found. Technical terms sometimes used for such a distinction are *ex ante* (looking forward before the outcome) and *ex post* (looking backward after the outcome). The anti-gambling ideologue may say: Granted that gambling is productive *ex ante*, it is most often unproductive *ex post*.

Normally we would expect a person to learn from his mistakes, to give up futile endeavors and turn his attention to more successful avenues. Therefore, the mere fact that someone persists with some activity strongly suggests that this activity is productive for that person. It is claimed, however, that the gambler is unable to learn from experience. He is like a driller for oil who keeps coming up dry, but repeatedly pours money into an endless series of unsuccessful drills. Because of a flaw in his thinking, he is unable to learn from experience, despite the fact that he doesn't get what he pays for. Is playing the lottery inescapably irrational? If it is, then lottery playing may perhaps be considered unproductive *ex post*.[11]

10 Some writers castigate gambling because there is no "value added." This displays a misunderstanding. Gambling itself occupies the final stage of production: it's a consumer activity, like watching TV or jogging. Manufacturing TV sets, jogging shoes, casinos, lottery tickets, or roulette wheels "adds value." Incidentally, gamblers watch less TV than non-gamblers, though they read more, go to the opera and museums more often, and are more sociable (Brenner, p. 38).

11 Alternatively, the proponent of the irrationality of the lottery might agree that playing is productive both ex ante and ex post, but insist that the ex post judgment is necessarily based on error. The refutation of this position is along similar lines.

Anti-gambling dogmatists usually hold a distinctive interpretation of the motivation for gambling. They maintain that gambling occurs because individuals seek monetary gain, that this desire for monetary gain must be disappointed in most cases, and that therefore the persistence of gambling is irrational—either stupid or involuntary. It is often contended (or just assumed) that a rational person would never gamble. Gambling, on this interpretation, occurs only because gamblers fail to understand elementary probability theory, or, understanding it, cannot bring themselves to act upon it. The cliché that lotteries are "a voluntary tax on the stupid" echoes Sir William Petty (1623–1687), who argued for state management of lotteries on the grounds that the state already had the care of lunatics and idiots.

Gambling prohibitionists are always falling over themselves to "explain" (in the Lardnerian sense) that "gamblers must lose in the long run," that "the odds are stacked against the gambler," that "gamblers as a whole can only lose," and so forth. They pronounce these marvelous insights as though they were gems of wisdom which gamblers must have overlooked. And perhaps a tiny minority of gamblers have indeed missed these earth-shaking commonplaces—after all, people have been known to make silly mistakes in all departments of life, from music to marriage, so there's no reason why gambling should be immune. But I can't see any evidence that the general run of gamblers behave irrationally, or that they would stop gambling if they took a course in probability theory.[12]

Is Gambling Unproductive Ex Post?

On the most straightforward level the lottery player gets precisely what he pays for: an equal chance with other players of netting a very large sum of money, of becoming rich. The anti-gambling ideologue, however, will press the point: objectively, the lottery player gets exactly what he pays for, but

---

12 "Rationality" is a term with a range of senses. I don't use the term here in a sense so weak that any deliberate action, however foolish, would count as rational, nor in a sense so strong that any intellectual mistake would suffice for irrationality. My use of the term here covers any demonstrable mistake which, once understood, would necessarily cause the individual to stop gambling. Gambling is like piloting airplanes: the individuals involved may not always compute everything to perfection, but the very pursuit of the activity in question is not, I am claiming, typically dependent on error.

he is unable to evaluate it correctly, so he never gets what he believes he pays for. He does not appreciate how slim are his chances of becoming rich. His intuitive notion of his chance of winning is unrealistically high because of a peculiar mental defect.[13]

How does the anti-gambling preacher know that the lottery player over-rates his chances? Why don't we suppose that, on average, the player rates his chances exactly correctly?[14] Anti-gambling zealots reply that he then would never play the lottery! This argument is fatally circular and therefore worthless. Although antigambling zealots often insinuate that rational people would not gamble, there exists no serious argument for any such assumption.

The claim that the gambler overestimates his chances is usually asserted as a blind dogma, with no evidence offered. However, some anti-gambling propagandists mention, as though it were significant, the fact that the whole class of lottery players must lose on balance. In technical terms, playing the lottery is not a "fair" bet; the "expected value" of a lottery ticket is below the price of the ticket.[15]

The expenses of organizing a lottery have to be covered out of sales of tickets.[16] Therefore, the amount returned in prizes is lower than the amount paid for tickets. A technically "fair" lottery would be one in which the total prize money were equal to the total money paid for tickets. In such a lottery,

13 The case of a lottery is unusual, because we can't simply ask the individual what he thinks of the outcome after it has appeared. The fact that the player has not won does not prove that he was wrong to play (any more than the fact that a person wins proves that he was right to play): the player knew all along, of course, that he very probably would not win.

14 In view of recent evidence that smokers generally *over*estimate the health risks of smoking, we may suspect that lottery players underestimate their chances of winning. The smug, mindless propaganda of anti-smoking bigotry and anti-gambling bigotry, spraying over us day after day from all the major media, with no thought of "equal time" for dissidents, may well be reducing aggregate social utility by causing some people at the margins to misguidedly give up smoking or gambling. The clout of the tobacco industry or the gambling industry, which these bigots routinely revile, is as gossamer compared with the clout of the belligerent prohibitionist lobby.

15 "Fair bet" and "expected value" are technical terms. They have little to do with the vernacular sense of these words. An "unfair" bet may be entirely fair, or vice versa, while an "expected value" is not what anybody expects.

16 Under free competition, the return to investors in all industries, including gambling, will be roughly the same, on average, as the rate of interest.

what is called the "expected value" of a ticket would be the same as the ticket price. It is an error to suppose that this offers a criterion of rationality: that it must be irrational to play the lottery when the expected value is below the ticket price. That any such supposition is faulty can be seen upon a moment's reflection.[17]

The proportion of total ticket revenues returned in prizes from lotteries is commonly around 60 percent, though it is sometimes more than 70 percent, and with some of the new state lotteries is little more than 50 percent.[18] If lotteries were purely private and open to competition, this figure would immediately rise to well over 90 percent[19] (except where particular lotteries were openly allied with charitable donation), but it could never reach 100 percent without the lottery's making a loss. Just suppose, however, that a lottery were subsidized, so that 105 percent of the prize money were returned in prizes. Would it then become rational always to buy lottery tickets, and irrational to fail to do so? If so, how many tickets? How much of one's income would it be obligatory, if one were rational, to allocate to lottery tickets? Suppose now that the lottery were hugely subsidized, so that, say, five times the ticket revenues were returned in prizes (but most entrants would still win nothing), what then? At what point, as we increased the subsidy to the lottery, would it become incumbent upon any rational person to buy a ticket?

There is no such point—though there would empirically be a point where the majority of people, or the majority of people with math degrees, would judge that one would have to be a lunatic not to buy at least one ticket. This kind of thing is a matter of personal preference, a matter of one's personality and worldview. It is "subjective" in the sense that there is no single demonstrably correct answer for any rational agent. Such

---

17   Consider whether you would rather have a dollar or a one-in-50,000 chance of $50,000. The one thing you will not say is that you can see no difference between these options, that you are indifferent between them. But once a difference in the valuation of these two situations is acknowledged, it automatically follows that it may be rational to give up one in exchange for the other.

18   Anti-gambling preachers frequently include in the "costs" of gambling all of the money spent by gamblers, without subtracting the distributed winnings, which at a stroke multiplies the supposed costs several-fold. This is not willful deceit, just the normal intellectual laziness of these anti-gambling tub-thumpers.

19   About 95 percent of the money wagered in Las Vegas casinos is returned as winnings. An appreciable chunk of the remaining five percent goes in taxes.

judgments can be influenced by miscalculations or other mistakes, but if all mistakes were eliminated, there would remain a diversity of preferences. Given these preferences, one's behavior is also affected by objective circumstances like one's income.

A lottery player will usually prefer a lottery which returns 90 percent of the ticket revenues to one which returns only 80 percent. Therefore, some will be induced to play at 90 percent who would not play at 80 percent. But someone who plays the lottery buys a chance of being in for a big win, and there is no justification for the assumption that the individual's valuation of this chance, the amount of utility he derives from being aware of it, has to coincide with the "expected value" of a lottery ticket (the prize money multiplied by the chance of winning). There are many cases where it clearly ought not to do so (for example, if the price of a ticket is one's entire income for the next few weeks, so that one will die of starvation unless one wins the prize, it would not be sensible to enter with a one-in-a-million chance of winning, even if the prize were so heavily subsidized that the expected value of a ticket were a thousand times the ticket price).

A rational person doesn't have to value a one-in-a-million chance of getting a million dollars at precisely one dollar. You may value such a chance at one cent or at five dollars—either way (though this may tell us something about your personality) there's nothing wrong with you. If someone you loved desperately could be saved from a painful and potentially fatal disease only by getting a million dollars, and the only possible way to get a million dollars were to play the lottery, wouldn't you play? Of course you would: it would be contemptible not to do so. The principle is not altered if the person you love so much is yourself, and the disease is not being rich.

However, assume for a moment that the "expected value" theory of rational gambling were correct. Suppose that you paid a dollar for a ticket giving you one chance in a million of winning $700,000, with $300,000 of ticket sales going to run the lottery and payoff the state. The expected value of your one-dollar ticket would be 70 cents. Only 30 cents would have to be explained by non-pecuniary elements (a sense of participation, giving something to a good cause, and so forth, or, if we want to indulge in flights of fancy, by "irrational compulsion" or "enhanced daydreaming"). It would follow that at least 70 cents out of each and every dollar spent on lottery tickets would indisputably be rationally allocated. Is this better or worse than the dollars spent on furniture or books? Casual discussion of the rationality of buying a ticket often tacitly assumes that "expected value" is the rule, but then proceeds as though the entire sum spent on tickets would be shown to be irrationally spent, when in fact (on the erroneous assumption that expected value should fix the buyer's valuation of a ticket) only something less than half of the ticket price would then, arguably, be spent irrationally.

The fact that a lottery is not technically "fair" follows automatically from the fact that the costs of running the lottery have to be covered out of ticket sales, and is otherwise a complete red herring from which no conclusions about the rationality of the players may legitimately be drawn. It's a feature of any system for re-allocating existing endowments, such as a subscription to the March of Dimes: organizing a subscription costs something, so the total paid to beneficiaries must be less than the total contributed. This is ineluctable, and in no way sinister.

A lottery is very much like a charitable subscription, and may partake of some of its motivation. Begin with the benevolent idea that you would like someone on a low income to become rich, add the random selection of that person, and you have a lottery which might take place even under pure altruism. (The player would have to make himself eligible for a prize in order not to deny the other participants their share of altruistic utility; restricting the prizes to those who have entered would be justified by the consideration that some minimal level of goodwill, some spark of human decency, would be necessary to qualify. The fact that winners stop playing would be explained by the fact that they can now afford superior ways of being helpful to others.) The altruistic theory of the lottery would explain why players who never win rarely show any resentment against winners, but rather evince sympathetic delight.

A lottery is simply a way in which a lot of people each put in a small sum, and then a few of those people picked at random get large sums. Nothing in the world could possibly be more harmless or more innocent than this.

Is Insurance Irrational?

Insurance is a negative lottery. In buying insurance, we pay a small sum now to guard against the low probability of losing a large sum in the future, just as, with a lottery, we pay a small sum now to engineer a low probability of winning a large sum in the future. Insurance is always an unfair bet—much less fair than a competitively run lottery, because the costs of running an insurance company greatly exceed the costs of administering a lottery.

Do the ideologues who berate gamblers for their irrational shortsightedness also berate those who, for example, insure the contents of their houses against fire? Quite the contrary! This willingness to pay for insurance more (sometimes vastly more) than its "expected value" is lauded to the skies as the epitome of responsible behavior. Failure to take this unfair bet is commonly considered thoroughly foolish and even irrational. In the debate over Hillary Clinton's healthcare plan, it was generally considered a self-evident scandal that an appreciable number of young, fit, comparatively high-income people chose not to buy health insurance, such a scandal that it warranted their being compelled to buy it—forced to make this extremely "unfair" bet.[20]

What goes for insurance goes also for precautionary outlays of a non-pecuniary kind, like wearing a car seat belt or getting a polio shot. In a typical recent diatribe against gambling, totally bereft of any serious thought and seething with the malignant compulsion to control other people's lives, one Robyn Gearey blasts the New York state lottery because, *inter alia*, the odds of winning a big prize are less than the odds of being struck by lightning.[21]

First, the minor point of whether this is factually correct. The only way to defend this claim would be to suppose that Gearey was comparing, say, one's chance of being struck by lightning in a whole year with one's chances of making a big win by the purchase of one ticket. This would be deceptive in light of Gearey's evident reliance on the stereotype of someone

---

20 Some theorists have considered it puzzling that many people both insure themselves against risks and play the lottery. Various solutions have been offered to this supposed paradox. But there is no paradox. It is consistent for a person to pay a small amount to greatly reduce the already small likelihood of a big drop in income and simultaneously to pay a small amount to greatly increase the very small likelihood of a big rise in income. (It is sometimes claimed that the position I take here implies that the rich would not "gamble," and that it is therefore refuted by the fact that the rich do "gamble." But the rich do not play the lottery, a fact of which socialist opponents of the lottery as a devilish capitalist exploitation device remind us ad nauseam. The rich gamble recreationally; that's a different matter.)

21 "The Numbers Game," *The New Republic*, May 19th, 1997.

who plays the lottery habitually and heavily. A quick exercise with a pocket calculator will give us some rough idea of the comparison. One estimate of a US resident's chance of being struck by lightning in one year is 606,944 to 1 against (Heron House, *The Odds on Virtually Everything* [New York: Putnam's, 1980], p. 181). This means a probability of 1 in 606,945, or .000001648. Suppose a lottery in which a ticket costs $1, each ticket is entered for one draw, exactly half the ticket money is distributed in prizes, and each prize is $250,000. The probability of one ticket's winning is then 1 in 500,000, decidedly better than being struck by lightning. Suppose instead that every prize is $500,000; it follows that the chance of winning must be 1 in a million. Now you have to buy two tickets to make the probability of your winning a prize better than the probability of being struck by lightning. If every prize is $5 million, you need to buy 17 tickets, and if every prize is $10 million, you need to buy 33 tickets to improve upon your chance of being struck by lightning. Of course, the picture is complicated by a range of different prizes, and by other factors, but it's clear that anyone who buys several tickets a month for a year has much better prospects than someone who hopes to collect the insurance on being struck by lightning.

The more important aspect of Gearey's argument is that Gearey evidently believes that being struck by lightning is a negligibly unlikely event which shouldn't influence a rational person's plans, yet my guess is that Gearey does not inveigh with comparable enthusiasm against the installation of lightning rods.

The main thrust of Gearey's piece is that the New York State Lottery is described misleadingly by its promoters, which is doubtless true—it is, after all, an arm of the government. Yet her very article is filled with misrepresentations, beginning with the line at the top of the first page: "The Lottery: Ticket to Poverty." One only has to substitute some other item of working-class expenditure ("Video Rentals: Ticket to Poverty") to see the utter mendacity of this phrase. Gearey says people play because they believe the state's lies that playing the lottery might really lift them from poverty or drudgery" (p. 19). It's a fact well known to Gearey that the lottery not only might really lift players from poverty or drudgery but regularly does so. Gearey is so emotionally disturbed by her obsessional hatred of ordinary people spending their money as they choose to spend it that she does not balk even at the most patently ridiculous falsehoods.

Lottery Players Are Rational

Some months ago, a thousand-pound man was in the news. He had lain on his bed for years; his main physical exercise was calling the local deli to send round a few dozen sandwiches at a time. The medics had to knock down a wall to get him out of his house and carry him to the hospital.

It would not be sensible, in a discussion of whether to let individuals decide for themselves what to eat, to keep bringing up the case of this thousand-pound monster. Similarly, it would not be appropriate, in a discussion of whether to permit people to attend a church of their own choosing, to endlessly pontificate about the Heaven's Gate suicides.

Yet just such irrelevance is the normal practice with anti-gambling bigots, who compulsively prattle on and on about problem gamblers, people who gamble away their life savings and desert their families for the gaming tables. Such cases are a tiny proportion of gamblers, and most of the people who behave like this would behave just as badly if gambling did not exist. Typically, and overwhelmingly, gamblers practice strict self-discipline and moderation.[22] If they are on low incomes and play the lottery regularly, they often spend less than the price of a six-pack per week. Any freedom of any sort affords the opportunity for foolish behavior by a foolish minority, and that exceptional behavior can never justify clamping iron shackles on the overwhelming majority of people who are sensible and self-disciplined.

The allegation that gamblers are irrational can be tested.[23] We can look at their behavior for signs of irrationality. In all respects which I have seen reported, the vast majority of lottery players behave as if they were rational. They prefer games where the odds are better. (Everyone understands that, to maintain a viable state lottery, private lotteries have to be outlawed.) They bet only a small amount per week. When they win a big prize and become rich, they husband their winnings prudently.[24]

---

22 Brenner, pp. 37–42.

23 Abt and her colleagues summarize the research findings as follows: "Observations in a wide variety of times and places have shown that gamblers are realistically aware of their chances of winning and conduct their wagering with deliberation and disciplined concentration." Vicki Abt, et al., The Business of Risk: Commercial Gambling in Mainstream America (Lawrence: University of Kansas Press, 1985), p. 11.

24 Brenner, pp. 42–44.

People play the lottery more if they have few other options with lottery-like qualities: the stock market, venture capitalism, an exciting career, a songwriting avocation.[25] Young, talented people with few commitments have many such options, and will respond rationally by playing the lottery rarely. A fifty-five-year-old janitor with ten kids and no equity has hardly any options, and will respond rationally by playing the lottery more frequently. This is just what we observe; it fully corroborates the rationality of playing the lottery. Lottery tickets are the janitor's cattle futures. To blame him for playing the lottery is like reproaching him for not having the good taste to drive a Ferrari.

Lottery players seem to understand the odds quite well (unlike the anti-gambling lobbyists, who demonstrate their innumeracy every time they open their mouths); the players certainly do understand with perfect clarity that it is far more likely than not that if they play every week of their lives they will never win a big prize. They still think it is worth playing, and it's just ignorance to imagine that this judgment of theirs must rest upon a miscalculation.

Lottery players hold that it's better to have played and lost than never to have played at all. Who's to say that they're wrong?

Liberty, September 1997

---

25 The government has effectively eliminated high-risk, high-return opportunities for low-income people, such as the old "bucket shops," which enabled people to speculate on price fluctuations with only a few dollars' outlay.

5
THE MYSTERY OF FASCISM (2001)

You're the top!
You're the Great Houdini!
You're the top! You are Mussolini![1]

Soon after he arrived in Switzerland in 1902, eighteen years old and looking for work, Benito Mussolini was starving and penniless. All he had in his pockets was a cheap nickel medallion of Karl Marx.

Following a spell of vagrancy, Mussolini found a job as a bricklayer and union organizer in the city of Lausanne. Quickly achieving fame as an agitator among the Italian migratory laborers, he was referred to by a local Italian-language newspaper as "the great *duce* [leader] of the Italian socialists." He read voraciously, learned several foreign languages,[2] and sat in on Pareto's lectures at the university.

The great *duce*'s fame was so far purely parochial. Upon his return to Italy, young Benito was an undistinguished member of the Socialist Party. He began to edit his own little paper, *La Lotta di Classe* (The Class Struggle), ferociously anti-capitalist, anti-militarist, and anti-Catholic. He took seriously Marx's dictum that the working class has no country, and vigorously opposed the Italian military intervention in Libya. Jailed several times for involvement in strikes and anti-war protests, he became something of a leftist hero. Before turning thirty, Mussolini was elected to the National Executive Committee of the Socialist Party, and made editor of its daily paper, *Avanti!* The paper's circulation and Mussolini's personal popularity grew by leaps and bounds.

---

1   Original words from the 1934 song by Cole Porter. They were amended later.
2   At the Munich conference in 1938, Mussolini was the only person present who could follow all the discussions in the four languages employed.

Mussolini's election to the Executive was part of the capture of control of the Socialist Party by the hard-line Marxist left, with the expulsion from the party of those deputies (members of parliament) considered too conciliatory to the bourgeoisie. The shift in Socialist Party control was greeted with delight by Lenin and other revolutionaries throughout the world.

From 1912 to 1914, Mussolini was the Che Guevara of his day, a living saint of leftism. Handsome, courageous, charismatic, an erudite Marxist, a riveting speaker and writer, a dedicated class warrior to the core, he was the peerless *duce* of the Italian Left. He looked like the head of any future Italian socialist government, elected or revolutionary.

In 1913, while still editor of *Avanti!*, he began to publish and edit his own journal, *Utopia*, a forum for controversial discussion among leftwing socialists. Like many such socialist journals founded in hope, it aimed to create a highly educated cadre of revolutionaries, purged of dogmatic illusions, ready to seize the moment. Two of those who collaborated with Mussolini on *Utopia* would go on to help found the Italian Communist Party and one to help found the German Communist Party.[3] Others, with Mussolini, would found the Fascist movement.

The First World War began in August 1914 without Italian involvement. Should Italy join Britain and France against Germany and Austria, or stay out of the war?[4] All the top leaders and intellectuals of the Socialist Party, Mussolini among them, were opposed to Italian participation.

In October and November 1914, Mussolini switched to a pro-war position. He resigned as editor of *Avanti!*, joined with pro-war leftists outside the Socialist Party, and launched a new pro-war socialist paper, *Il Popolo d'Italia* (People of Italy).[5] To the Socialist Party leadership, this was a great betrayal, a sellout to the whoremasters of the bourgeoisie, and Mussolini was expelled from the party. It was as scandalous as though, fifty years later, Guevara had announced that he was off to Vietnam, to help defend the South against North Vietnamese aggression.

Italy entered the war in May 1915, and Mussolini enlisted. In 1917 he was seriously wounded and hospitalized, emerging from the war the most

3   Amadeo Bordiga, Angelo Tasca, and Karl Liebknecht.
4   Although Italy was a member of the Triple Alliance with Germany and Austria, support for the Central Powers in Italy was negligible.
5   It remained Mussolini's paper through the Fascist period. At first it was described as a "Socialist Daily." Later this was changed to "The Daily of Fighters and Producers."

popular of the pro-war socialists, a leader without a movement. Post-war Italy was hagridden by civil strife and political violence. Sensing a revolutionary situation in the wake of Russia's Bolshevik coup, the left organized strikes, factory occupations, riots, and political killings. Socialists often beat up and sometimes killed soldiers returning home, just because they had fought in the war. Assaulting political opponents and wrecking their property became an everyday occurrence.

Mussolini and a group of adherents launched the Fascist movement[6] in 1919. The initiators were mostly men of the left: revolutionary syndicalists and former Marxists.[7] They took with them some non-socialist nationalists and futurists, and recruited heavily among soldiers returning from the war, so that the bulk of rank-and-file Fascists had no leftwing background. The Fascists adopted the black shirts[8] of the anarchists and *Giovinezza* (Youth), the song of the frontline soldiers.

Apart from its ardent nationalism and pro-war foreign policy, the Fascist program was a mixture of radical left, moderate left, democratic, and liberal measures, and for more than a year the new movement was not notably more violent than other socialist groupings.[9] Among its first slate of candidates was a young orchestra conductor of quite liberal views, Arturo Toscanini. However, Fascists came into conflict with Socialist Party members and in 1920 formed a militia, the *squadre* (squads). Including many patriotic veterans, the squads were more efficient at arson and terror tactics than the violently disposed but bumbling Marxists, and often had the tacit support of the police and army. By 1921 Fascists had the upper hand in physical combat with their rivals of the Left.

---

6   It was first called the *Fasci Italiani di Combattimento* (Italian Combat Leagues), changing its name in 1921 to the National Fascist Party. *Fasci* is plural of *fascio*, a union or league. The word had been in common use for various local and ad hoc radical groups, mainly of the left.

7   Of the seven who attended the preparatory meeting two days before the launch, five were former Marxists or syndicalists. Zeev Sternhell, Mario Sznajder, and Maia Asheri, *The Birth of Fascist Ideology* (Princeton: Princeton University Press, 1994), p. 222. At the launch itself, the majority had a nationalist background.

8   Garibaldi's followers had worn red shirts. Corradini's nationalists, absorbed into the Fascist Party in 1923, wore blue shirts.

9   Stanley G. Payne, *A History of Fascism, 1914–1945* (Madison: University of Wisconsin Press, 1995), p. 95.

The democratic and liberal elements in Fascist preaching rapidly diminished and in 1922 Mussolini declared that "The world is turning to the right." The Socialists, who controlled the unions, called a general strike. Marching into some of the major cities, blackshirt squads quickly and forcibly suppressed the strike, and most Italians heaved a sigh of relief. This gave the blackshirts the idea of marching on Rome to seize power. As they publicly gathered for the great march, the government decided to avert possible civil war by bringing Mussolini into office; the King "begged" Mussolini to become Prime Minister, with emergency powers. Instead of a desperate uprising, the March on Rome was the triumphant celebration of a legal transfer of authority.

The youngest prime minister in Italian history, Mussolini was an adroit and indefatigable fixer, a formidable wheeler and dealer in a constitutional monarchy which did not become an outright and permanent dictatorship until December 1925, and even then retained elements of unstable pluralism requiring fancy footwork. He became world-renowned as a political miracle worker. Mussolini made the trains run on time, closed down the Mafia, drained the Pontine marshes, and solved the tricky Roman Question, finally settling the political status of the Pope.

Mussolini was showered with accolades from sundry quarters. Winston Churchill called him "the greatest living legislator." Cole Porter gave him a terrific plug in a hit song. Sigmund Freud sent him an autographed copy of one of his books, inscribed to "the Hero of Culture."[10] The more taciturn Stalin supplied Mussolini with the plans of the May Day parades in Red Square, to help him polish up his Fascist pageants.

The rest of *il Duce*'s career is now more familiar. He conquered Ethiopia, made a Pact of Steel with Germany, introduced anti-Jewish measures in 1938,[11] came into the war as Hitler's very junior partner, tried to strike out on his own by invading the Balkans, had to be bailed out by

---

10   Ernest Jones, *Life and Work of Sigmund Freud* (New York: Basic Books, 1957), vol. 3, p. 180.

11   Prior to 1938 the Fascist Party had substantial Jewish membership and support. There is no agreement among scholars on Mussolini's motives for introducing anti-Jewish legislation. For one well-argued view, see Gregor, *Contemporary Radical Ideologies: Totalitarian Thought in the Twentieth Century* (New York: Random House, 1968), pp. 149–159.

Hitler, was driven back by the Allies, and then deposed by the Fascist Great Council, rescued from imprisonment by SS troops in one of the most brilliant commando operations of the war, installed as head of a new "Italian Social Republic," and killed by Communist partisans in April 1945.

Given what most people today think they know about Fascism, this bare recital of facts[12] is a mystery story. How can a movement which epitomizes the extreme right be so strongly rooted in the extreme left? What was going on in the minds of dedicated socialist militants to turn them into equally dedicated Fascist militants?

What They Told Us about Fascism

In the 1930s, the perception of "fascism"[13] in the English-speaking world morphed from an exotic, even chic, Italian novelty[14] into an all-purpose symbol of evil. Under the influence of leftist writers, a view of fascism was disseminated which has remained dominant among intellectuals until today. It goes as follows:

Fascism is capitalism with the mask off. It's a tool of Big Business, which rules through democracy until it feels mortally threatened, then unleashes fascism. Mussolini and Hitler were put into power by Big Business, because Big Business was challenged by the revolutionary working class.[15] We

---

12   Among numerous sources on the life of Mussolini, see Richard Collier, *Duce! A Biography of Benito Mussolini* (New York: Viking, 1971); Denis Mack Smith, *Mussolini: A Biography* (New York: Knopf, 1982); Jasper Ridley, Mussolini: A Biography (New York: St. Martin's Press, 1998). All such works are out of their depth when they touch on Fascist ideas. For a superb account of all the fascist and other non-Communist dictatorial movements of the time, see Payne, *History*. On Mussolini's ideas, see A. James Gregor, *Young Mussolini and the Intellectual Origins of Fascism* (Berkeley: University of California Press, 1979); Sternhell, Sznajder, and Asheri, *Birth*, Chapter 5.

13   It's now usual to capitalize 'Fascism' when it refers to the Italian movement, and not when the word refers to a broader cultural phenomenon including other political movements in other countries.

14   Chicago has an avenue named after the brutal blackshirt leader and famous aviator, Italo Balbo, following his spectacular 1933 visit to the city. Chicago's Columbus Monument bears the words "This monument has seen the glory of the wings of Italy led by Italo Balbo." See Claudio G. Segre, *Italo Balbo: A Fascist Life* (Berkeley: University of California Press, 1987).

15   The evolution of this incredible theory is mercilessly documented in Gregor, *The Faces of Janus: Marxism and Fascism in the Twentieth Century* (New Haven: Yale University

naturally have to explain, then, how fascism can be a mass movement, and one that is neither led nor organized by Big Business. The explanation is that Fascism does it by fiendishly clever use of ritual and symbol. Fascism as an intellectual doctrine is empty of serious content, or alternatively, its content is an incoherent hodgepodge. Fascism's appeal is a matter of emotions rather than ideas. It relies on hymn-singing, flag-waving, and other mummery, which are nothing more than irrational devices employed by the Fascist leaders who have been paid by Big Business to manipulate the masses.

As Marxists used to say, fascism "appeals to the basest instincts," implying that leftists were at a disadvantage because they could appeal only to noble instincts like envy of the rich. Since it is irrational, fascism is sadistic, nationalist, and racist by nature. Leftist regimes are also invariably sadistic, nationalist, and racist, but that's because of regrettable mistakes or pressure of difficult circumstances. Leftists want what's best but keep meeting unexpected setbacks, whereas fascists have chosen to commit evil.

More broadly, fascism may be defined as any totalitarian regime which does not aim at the nationalization of industry but preserves at least nominal private property. The term can even be extended to any dictatorship that has become unfashionable among intellectuals.[16] When the Soviet Union and People's China had a falling out in the 1960s, they each promptly discovered that the other fraternal socialist country was not merely capitalist but "fascist." At the most vulgar level, "fascist" is a handy swearword for such hated figures as Rush Limbaugh or John Ashcroft who, whatever their faults, are as remote from historical Fascism as anyone in public life today.

The consequence of seventy years of indoctrination with a particular leftist view of fascism is that Fascism is now a puzzle. We know how leftists in the 1920s and 1930s thought because we knew people in college whose thinking was almost identical, and because we have read such writers as Sartre, Hemingway, and Orwell. But what were Fascists thinking?

Press, 2000), chs. 2–5. For a good brief survey of interpretations of Fascism, see Payne, *History*, ch. 12. For a detailed examination, see Gregor, *Interpretations of Fascism* (New Brunswick: Transaction, 1997).

16 Confronted with egregious high-handedness by authority, working-class Americans call it "Communism." Middle-class Americans, educated enough to understand that it's uncouth to say anything against Communism, call it "fascism."

Some Who Became Fascists

Robert Michels was a German Marxist disillusioned with the Social Democrats. He became a revolutionary syndicalist. In 1911 he wrote *Political Parties*, a brilliant analytic work,[17] demonstrating the impossibility of "participatory democracy," a phrase that was not to be coined for half a century, but which accurately captures the early Marxist vision of socialist administration.[18] Later he became an Italian (changing "Robert" to "Roberto") and one of the leading Fascist theoreticians.

Hendrik de Man was the leading Belgian socialist of his day and recognized as one of the two or three most outstanding socialist intellects in Europe. Many in the 1930s believed him to be the most important socialist theoretician since Marx. He is the most prominent of the numerous Western European Marxists who wrestled their way from Marxism to Fascism or National Socialism in the interwar years. In more than a dozen thoughtful books from *The Remaking of a Mind* (1919), via *The Socialist Idea* (1933), to *Après Coup* (1941) de Man left a detailed account of the theoretical odyssey which led him, by 1940, to acclaim the Nazi subjugation of Europe as "a deliverance." His journey began, as such journeys so often did, with the conviction that Marxism needed to be revised along "idealist" and psychological lines.[19]

Two avant-garde artistic movements which contributed to the Fascist worldview were Futurism and Vorticism. Futurism was the brainchild of Filippo Marinetti, who eventually lost his life in the service of Mussolini's regime. You can get some idea of the Futurist pictorial style from the credits

17   *Political Parties: A Sociological Study of the Oligarchical Tendencies of Modern Democracy* (New York: Macmillan, 1962).

18   Richard N. Hunt, *The Political Ideas of Marx and Engels* (Pittsburgh: University of Pittsburgh Press, 1974), vol. I, p. xiii, and vols. I and II, passim.

19   On Hendrik de Man, also known as Henri De Man, see Sternhell, *Neither Right Nor Left: Fascist Ideology in France* (Berkeley: University of California Press, 1986). Mussolini exchanged letters with de Man in which both tacitly recognized that de Man was following Mussolini's intellectual trajectory of ten to fifteen years earlier. Sternhell, Snajder, and Asheri, *Birth*, p. 246. To this day there are disciples of de Man who treat his acceptance of the Third Reich as something like a seizure rather than as the culmination of his earlier thought, just as there are a few leftist admirers of Sorel who refuse to admit Sorel's pre-fascism.

for the *Poirot* TV series. Its style of poetry was a defining influence on Mayakovski. Futurist arts activities were permitted for some years in the Soviet Union. Futurism held that modern machines were more beautiful than classical sculptures. It lauded the aesthetic value of speed, intensity, modern machinery, and modern war.

Vorticism was a somewhat milder variant of Futurism, associated with Ezra Pound and the painter and novelist Wyndham Lewis, an American and a Canadian who transplanted to London. Pound became a Fascist, moved to Italy, and was later found mentally ill and incarcerated by the occupying Americans. The symptoms of his illness were his Fascist beliefs. He was later released, and chose to move back to Italy in 1958, an unrepentant Fascist.

In 1939 the avowed fascist Wyndham Lewis retracted his earlier praise for Hitler, but never renounced his basically fascist political worldview. Lewis was, like George Bernard Shaw, one of those intellectuals of the 1930s who admired Fascism and Communism about equally, praising them both while insisting on their similarity.

Fascism must have been a set of ideas which inspired educated individuals who thought of themselves as extremely up-to-date. But what were those ideas?

Five Facts about Fascism

Over the last thirty years, scholarship has gradually begun to bring us a more accurate appreciation of what Fascism was.[20] The picture that emerges from ongoing research into the origins of Fascism is not yet entirely clear, but it's clear enough to show that the truth cannot be reconciled with the conventional view. We can highlight some of the unsettling conclusions in five facts:

Fascism was a doctrine well elaborated years before it was named. The core of the Fascist movement launched officially in the Piazza San Sepolcro on

---

20   The most illuminating single work is Sternhell, Sznajder, and Asheri, *Birth*. Other important accounts are: Gregor, *Young Mussolini*; Gregor, *Faces of Janus*; Sternhell, *Neither Right Nor Left*; Payne, *History*. A useful collection of old and new readings is Roger Griffin, ed., *International Fascism: Theories, Causes, and the New Consensus* (London: Arnold, 1998). Important works in Italian include those of Renzo de Felice and Emilio Gentile.

23rd March 1919 was an intellectual and organizational tradition called "national syndicalism."

As an intellectual edifice, Fascism was mostly in place by about 1910. Historically, the taproot of Fascism lies in the 1890s in the "Crisis of Marxism" and in the interaction of nineteenth-century revolutionary socialism with *fin-de-siècle* anti-rationalism and anti-liberalism.

Fascism changed dramatically between 1919 and 1922, and again changed dramatically after 1922. This is what we expect of any ideological movement which comes close to power and then attains it. Bolshevism (renamed Communism in 1920) also changed dramatically, several times over.

Many of the older treatments of Fascism are misleading because they cobble together Fascist pronouncements, almost entirely from after 1922, reflecting the pressures on a broad and flexible political movement solidifying its rule by compromises, and suppose that by this method they can isolate the character and motivation of Fascist ideology. It is as if we were to reconstruct the ideas of Bolshevism by collecting the pronouncements of the Soviet government in 1943, which would lead us to conclude that Marxism owed a lot to Ivan the Terrible and Peter the Great.

Fascism was a movement with its roots primarily in the left. Its leaders and initiators were secular-minded, highly progressive intellectuals, hardheaded haters of existing society and especially of its most bourgeois aspects.

There were also non-leftist currents which fed into Fascism; the most prominent was the nationalism of Enrico Corradini. This anti-liberal, anti-democratic movement was preoccupied with building Italy's strength by accelerated industrialization. Though it was considered right wing at the time, Corradini called himself a socialist, and similar movements in the Third World would later be warmly supported by the left.

Fascism was intellectually sophisticated. Fascist theory was more subtle and more carefully thought out than Communist doctrine. As with Communism, there was a distinction between the theory itself and the "line" designed for a broad public. Fascists drew upon such thinkers as Henri Bergson, William James, Gabriel Tarde, Ludwig Gumplowicz, Vilfredo Pareto, Gustave Le Bon, Georges Sorel, Robert Michels, Gaetano Mosca, Giuseppe Prezzolini, Filippo Marinetti, A.O. Olivetti, Sergio Panunzio, and Giovanni Gentile.

Here we should note a difference between Marxism and Fascism. The leader of a Marxist political movement is always considered by his followers to be a master of theory and a theoretical innovator on the scale of Copernicus. Fascists were less prone to any such delusion. Mussolini was more widely read than Lenin and a better writer, but Fascist intellectuals did not consider him a major contributor to the body of Fascist theory, more a leader of genius who could distill theory into action.

Fascists were radical modernizers. By temperament they were neither conservative nor reactionary. Fascists despised the status quo and were not attracted by a return to bygone conditions. Even in power, despite all its adaptations to the requirements of the immediate situation, and despite its incorporation of more conservative social elements, Fascism remained a conscious force for modernization.[21]

Two Revisions of Marxism

Fascism began as a revision of Marxism by Marxists, a revision which developed in successive stages, so that these Marxists gradually stopped thinking of themselves as Marxists, and eventually stopped thinking of themselves as socialists. They never stopped thinking of themselves as antiliberal revolutionaries.

The crisis of Marxism occurred in the 1890s. Marxist intellectuals could claim to speak for mass socialist movements across continental Europe, yet it became clear in those years that Marxism had survived into a world which Marx had believed could not possibly exist. The workers were becoming richer, the working class was fragmented into sections with different interests, technological advance was accelerating rather than meeting a roadblock, the "rate of profit" was not falling, the number of wealthy investors ("magnates of capital") was not falling but increasing, industrial concentration was not increasing,[22] and in all countries the workers were putting their country above their class.

In high theory, too, the hollowness of Marxism was being exposed. The

---

21 The Fascist government imposed measures which were intended to promote modernization. They were not necessary and their effectiveness was mixed. Italian output grew rapidly, but so it had in earlier years.

22 Many would not yet have acknowledged that there was no falling rate of profit and no concentrating trend in industry, but all had to agree that these were proceeding far more slowly than earlier Marxists had expected.

long-awaited publication of Volume III of Marx's *Capital* in 1894 revealed that Marx simply had no serious solution to the "great contradiction" between Volumes I–II and the real behavior of prices. Böhm-Bawerk's devastating critiques of Marxian economics (1884 and 1896) were widely read and discussed.

The crisis of Marxism gave birth to the Revisionism of Eduard Bernstein, which concluded, in effect, that the goal of revolution should be given up, in favor of piecemeal reforms within capitalism.[23] This held no allure for men of the hard left who rejected existing society, deeming it too loathsome to be reformed. Revisionists also began to attack the fundamental Marxist doctrine of historical materialism, the theory that a society's organization of production decides the character of all other social phenomena, including ideas.

At the beginning of the twentieth century, leftists who wanted to be as far left as they could possibly be became syndicalists, preaching the general strike as the way to demonstrate the workers' power and overthrow the bourgeois order. Syndicalist activity erupted across the world, even in Britain and the United States. Promotion of the general strike was a way of defying capitalism and at the same time defying those socialists who wanted to use electoral methods to negotiate reforms of the system.

Syndicalists began as uncompromising Marxists, but like Revisionists, they acknowledged that key tenets of Marxism had been refuted by the development of modern society. Most syndicalists came to accept much of Bernstein's argument against traditional Marxism, but remained committed to the total rejection, rather than democratic reform, of existing society. They therefore called themselves "revolutionary revisionists." They favored the "idealist revision of Marx," meaning that they believed in a more independent role for ideas in social evolution than that allowed by Marxist theory.

Practical Anti-Rationalism

In setting out to revise Marxism, syndicalists were most strongly motivated by the desire to be effective revolutionaries, not to tilt at windmills but to

---

23 Before the 1890s, there was no more impeccable a Marxist than Bernstein. He had been a friend of Marx and Engels, who maintained a confidence in his ideological soundness that they placed in very few individuals. His 1899 book, known in English as *Evolutionary Socialism* (New York: Schocken, 1961), is put together from controversial articles he began publishing in 1896.

achieve a realistic understanding of the way the world works. In criticizing and re-evaluating their own Marxist beliefs, however, they naturally drew upon the intellectual fashions of the day, upon ideas that were in the air during this period known as the *fin-de-siècle*. The most important cluster of such ideas is "anti-rationalism."

Many forms of anti-rationalism proliferated throughout the nineteenth century. The kind of anti-rationalism which most influenced pre-fascists was not primarily the view that something other than reason should be employed to decide factual questions (epistemological anti-rationalism). It was rather the view that, as a matter of sober recognition of reality, humans are not solely or even chiefly motivated by rational calculation but more by intuitive "myths" (practical anti-rationalism). Therefore, if you want to understand and influence people's behavior, you had, better acknowledge that they are not primarily self-interested, rational calculators; they are gripped and moved by myths.[24]

Paris was the fashion center of the intellectual world, dictating the rise and fall of ideological. hemlines. Here, anti-rationalism was associated with the philosophy of Henri Bergson, William James's pragmatism from across the Atlantic, and the social-psychological arguments of Gustave Le Bon. Such ideas were seen as valuing action more highly than cogitation and as demonstrating that modern society (including the established socialist movement) was too rationalistic and too materialistic. Bergson and James were also read, however, as contending that humans did not work with an objectively existing reality, but created reality by imposing their own will upon the world, a claim that was also gleaned (rightly or wrongly) from Hegel, Schopenhauer, and Nietzsche. French intellectuals turned against Descartes, the rationalist, and rehabilitated Pascal, the defender of faith. In the same spirit, Italian intellectuals rediscovered Vico.

Practical anti-rationalism entered pre-Fascism through Georges Sorel[25]

---

24 The impact of anti-rationalism on socialism not only helped to form Fascism, but also had a broad influence on the Left. Like Fascism, the thinking of leftist writers such as Aldous Huxley and George Orwell arises from the impact on nineteenth-century socialism of the fin-de-siècle offensive against rationalism, materialism, individualism, and romanticism.

25 The strong influence of Sorel on the formation of Fascism has now been heavily documented. See, for example, Sternhell, Sznajder, and Asheri, *Birth*. In earlier years, some writers used to minimize this influence or deny Sorel's close affinity with Fascism.

and his theory of the "myth." This influential socialist writer began as an orthodox Marxist. An extreme leftist, he naturally became a syndicalist, and soon the best-known syndicalist theoretician. Sorel then moved to defending Marx's theory of the class struggle in a new way, no longer as a scientific theory, but instead as a "myth", an understanding of. the world and the future which moves men to action. When he began to abandon Marxism, both because of its theoretical failures and because of its excessive "materialism," he looked for an alternative myth. Experience of current and recent events showed that workers had little interest in the class struggle but were prone to patriotic sentiment. By degrees, Sorel shifted his position, until at the end of his life he became nationalistic and antisemitic.[26] He died in 1922, hopeful about Lenin and more cautiously hopeful about Mussolini.

A general trend throughout revolutionary socialism from 1890 to 1914 was that the most revolutionary elements laid an increasing stress upon leadership, and downplayed the autonomous role of the toiling masses. This elitism was a natural outcome of the revolutionaries' ardent wish to have revolution and the stubborn disinclination of the working class to become revolutionary.[27] Workers were instinctive reformists: They wanted a fair shake within capitalism and nothing more. Since the workers did not look as if they would ever desire a revolution, the small group of conscious revolutionaries would have to play a more decisive role than Marx had imagined. That was the conclusion of Lenin in 1902.[28] It was the conclusion of Sorel. And it was the conclusion of the syndicalist Giuseppe Prezzolini whose works in the century's first decade Mussolini reviewed admiringly.[29]

The leadership theme was reinforced by the theoretical writings of Mosca, Pareto, and Michels, especially Pareto's theory of the Circulation of Elites. All these arguments emphasized the vital role of active minorities

26 Sorel's was the old-fashioned kind of antisemitism, which always made room for some good Jews. Among these Sorel counted Henri Bergson. Sternhell, *Birth*, p. 86.

27 It was also inferred from experience. It could be observed that if the one or two strongest personalities behind a strike were somehow neutralized, the strike would collapse.

28 In *What Is to Be Done?*, Lenin maintained that the working class, left to itself, could develop only "trade union consciousness." To make the working class revolutionary required the intervention of "professional revolutionaries."

29 See Gregor, *Young Mussolini*, ch. 4.

and the futility of expecting that the masses would ever, left to themselves, accomplish anything. Further corroboration came from Le Bon's sensational bestseller of 1895—it would remain perpetually in print in a dozen languages—*The Psychology of Crowds*, which analyzed the "irrational" behavior of humans in groups and drew attention to the group's proclivity to place itself in the hands of a strong leader, who could control the group as long as he appealed to certain primitive or basic beliefs.[30]

The initiators of Fascism saw anti-rationalism as high-tech. It went with their fast cars and airplanes. Fascist anti-rationalism, like psychoanalysis, conceives of itself as a practical science which can channel elemental human drives in a useful direction.

A Marxist Heresy?

Some people have reacted to Fascism by saying that it's just the same as socialism. In part, this arises from the fact that "fascism" is a word used loosely to denote all the non-Communist dictatorships of the 1920s and 1930s, and by extension to refer to the most powerful and horrible of these governments, that of German National Socialism.

The Nazis never claimed to be Fascists, but they did continually claim to be socialists, whereas Fascism, after 1921, repudiated socialism by name. Although Fascism had some influence on the National Socialist German Workers' Party, other influences were greater, notably Communism and German nationalism.

A. James Gregor has argued that Fascism is a Marxist heresy,[31] a claim that has to be handled with care. Marxism is a doctrine whose main tenets

---

30 *The Crowd* (New Brunswick: Transaction, 1995). The early nineteenth century had seen a fascination with hypnosis (then called Mesmerism). The late nineteenth century witnessed an extrapolation of the model of hypnosis onto wider human phenomena. Le Bon argued that in groups individuals become hypnotized and lose responsibility for their actions. Scholars, other than French ones, now believe that Le Bon was a dishonest self-promoter who successfully exaggerated his own originality, and that his claims about crowd behavior are mostly wrong. His influence was tremendous. Freud was steeped in Le Bon. The discussion of propaganda in Hitler's *Mein Kampf*, which strikes most readers as more entertaining than the rest of the book, echoes Le Bon.

31 Gregor, *Young Mussolini*. This was precisely the view of many Communists in the early years of the Comintern. Payne, *History*, p. 126.

can be listed precisely: class struggle, historical materialism, surplus-value, nationalization of the means of production, and so forth. Nearly all of those tenets were explicitly repudiated by the founders of Fascism, and these repudiations of Marxism largely define Fascism. Yet however paradoxical it may seem, there is a close ideological relationship between Marxism and Fascism. We may compare this with the relationship between, say, Christianity and Unitarianism. Unitarianism repudiates all the distinctive tenets of Christianity, yet is still clearly an offshoot of Christianity, preserving an affinity with its parental stem.

In power, the actual institutions of Fascism and Communism tended to converge. In practice, the Fascist and National Socialist regimes increasingly tended to conform to what Mises calls "the German pattern of Socialism."[32] Intellectually, Fascists differed from Communists in that they had to a large extent thought out what they would do, and they then proceeded to do it, whereas Communists were like hypnotic subjects, doing one thing and rationalizing it in terms of a completely different and altogether impossible thing.

Fascists preached the accelerated development of a backward country. Communists continued to employ the Marxist rhetoric of world socialist revolution in the most advanced countries, but this was all a ritual incantation to consecrate their attempt to accelerate the development of a backward country. Fascists deliberately turned to nationalism as a potent myth. Communists defended Russian nationalism and imperialism while protesting that their sacred motherland was an internationalist workers' state. Fascists proclaimed the end of democracy. Communists abolished democracy and called their dictatorship democracy. Fascists argued that equality was impossible and hierarchy ineluctable. Communists imposed a new hierarchy, shot anyone who advocated actual equality, but never ceased to babble on about the equalitarian future they were "building." Fascists did with their eyes open what Communists did with their eyes shut. This is the truth concealed in the conventional formula that Communists were well-intentioned and Fascists evil-intentioned.

32 Ludwig von Mises, *Omnipotent Government: The Rise of the Total State and Total War* (New Rochelle: Arlington House, 1969 [1944]), pp. 55–58.

Disappointed Revolutionaries

Though they respected "the irrational" as a reality, the initiators of Fascism were not themselves swayed by willfully irrational considerations. They were not superstitious.[33] Mussolini in 1929, when he met with Cardinal Gasparri at the Lateran Palace, was no more a believing Catholic than the violently anti-Catholic polemicist of his pre-war years,[34] but he had learned that in his chosen career as a radical modernizing politician, it was a waste of time to bang his head against the brick wall of institutionalized faith.

Leftists often imagine that Fascists were afraid of a revolutionary working class. Nothing could be more comically mistaken. Most of the early Fascist leaders had spent years trying to get the workers to become revolutionary. As late as June 1914, Mussolini took part enthusiastically, at risk of his own life and limb, in the violent and confrontational "red week." The initiators of Fascism were mostly seasoned anti-capitalist militants who had time and again given the working class the benefit of the doubt. The working class, by not becoming revolutionary, had let these revolutionaries down.

In the late 1920s, people like Winston Churchill and Ludwig von Mises saw Fascism as a natural and salutary response to Communist violence.[35] They already overlooked the fact that Fascism represented an independent cultural phenomenon which predated the Bolshevik coup. It became widely

33 "If by mysticism one intends the recognition of truth without the employment of reason, I would be the first to declare myself opposed to every mysticism." Mussolini, quoted in Gregor, *Contemporary Radical Ideologies*, p. 331.

34 Mussolini was openly an atheist prior to 1922, when his conversion was staged for transparently political reasons. In addition to his many articles and speeches criticizing religion, Mussolini wrote a pamphlet, *Man and Divinity*, attacking the Church from a materialist standpoint and also wrote a strongly anti-Catholic book on Jan Hus, the fifteenth-century Czech victim of Catholic persecution. Until it became politically inexpedient, Mussolini gave a speech every year on the anniversary of the murder by the Church of the freethinker Giordano Bruno in 1600. In office, Mussolini worked with the Church, generally gave it what it wanted, and was rewarded with its enthusiastic endorsement.

35 On Churchill's fulsome praise of Fascism throughout the late 1920s and early 1930s, see Ridley, *Mussolini*, pp. 187–88, 230, 281. For Mises's more guarded praise in 1927, see Mises, *The Free and Prosperous Commonwealth* (Irvington-on-Hudson: Foundation for Economic Education, 1962), pp. 47–51.

accepted that the future lay with either Communism or Fascism, and many people chose what they considered the lesser evil. Evelyn Waugh remarked that he would choose Fascism over Marxism if he had to, but he did not think he had to.

It's easy to see that the rise of Communism stimulated the rise of Fascism. But since the existence of the Soviet regime was what chiefly made Communism attractive, and since Fascism was an independent tradition of revolutionary thinking, there would doubtless have been a powerful Fascist movement even in the absence of a Bolshevik regime. At any rate, after 1922, the same kind of influence worked both ways: Many people became Communists because they considered that the most effective way to combat the dreaded Fascism. Two rival gangs of murderous politicos, bent on establishing their own unchecked power, each drummed up support by pointing to the horrors that the other gang would unleash. Whatever the shortcomings. of any such appeal, the horrors themselves were all too real.[36]

From Liberism to the Corporate State

In Fascism's early days it encompassed an element of what was called "liberism," the view that capitalism and the free market ought to be left intact, that it was sheer folly for the state to involve itself in "production."

Marx had left a strange legacy: the conviction that resolute pursuit of the class struggle would automatically take the working class in the direction of communism. Since practical experience offers no corroboration for this surmise, Marxists have had to choose between pursuing the class struggle (making trouble for capitalism and hoping that something will turn up) and trying to seize power to introduce communism (which patently has nothing to do with strikes for higher wages or with such political reforms as factory safety legislation). As a result, Marxists came to worship "struggle" for its own sake. And since Marxists were frequently embarrassed to talk about problems a communist society might face, dismissing any such discussion as "utopian," it became easy for them to argue that we should

---

36 The Fascist government was appallingly oppressive compared with the democratic regime which preceded it, but distinctly less oppressive than Communism or National Socialism. Payne, *History*, pp. 121–23.

focus only on the next step in the struggle, and not be distracted by speculation about the remote future.

Traditional Marxists had believed that much government interference, such as protective tariffs, should be opposed, as it would slow down the development of the productive forces (technology) and thereby delay the revolution. For this reason, a Marxist should favor free trade.[37] Confronted by a growing volume of legislative reforms, some revolutionaries saw these as shrewd concessions by the bourgeoisie to take the edge off class antagonism and thus stabilize their rule. The fact that such legislative measures were supported by democratic socialists, who had been co-opted into the established order, provided an additional motive for revolutionaries to take the other side.

All these influences might persuade a Marxist that capitalism should be left intact for the foreseeable future. In Italy, a further motive was that Marxists expected the revolution to break out in the industrially advanced countries. No Marxist thought that socialism had anything to offer a backward economy like Italy, unless the revolution occurred first in Britain, America, Germany, and France. As the prospect of any such revolution became less credible, the issue of Italian industrial development was all that remained, and that was obviously a task for capitalism.

After 1919, the Fascists developed a theory of the state; until then this was the one element in Fascist political theory which had not been elaborated. Its elaboration, in an extended public debate, gave rise to the "totalitarian" view of the state,[38] notoriously expounded in Mussolini's formula, "Everything in the state, nothing against the state, nothing outside the state." Unlike the later National Socialists of Germany, the Fascists remained averse to outright nationalization of industry. But, after a few years

---

37   Karl Marx, *Speech on the Question of Free Trade*. Karl Marx, Frederick Engels, *Collected Works* (New York: International, 1976), vol. 6, pp. 450–465.

38   The word "totalitarian" (*totalitario*) was first used against Fascism by a liberal opponent, Giovanni Amendola. It was then taken up proudly by Fascists to characterize their own form of state. Later the term was widely employed to refer to the common features of the Fascist, Soviet, and Nazi dictatorships or to denote an ideal type of unlimited government. In this sense, the word was in common use among Anglophone intellectuals by 1935, and in the popular media by 1941. Ironically, Fascist Italy was in practice much less "totalitarian" than the Soviet Union or the Third Reich, though the regime was methodically moving toward totalitarianism.

of comparative nonintervention, and some liberalization, the Fascist regime moved towards a highly interventionist policy, and Fascist pronouncements increasingly harped on the "corporate state." All traces of liberism were lost, save only for the insistence that actual nationalization be avoided. Before 1930, Mussolini stated that capitalism had centuries of useful work to do (a formulation that would occur only to a former Marxist); after 1930, because of the world depression, he spoke as if capitalism was finished and the corporate state was to replace it rather than providing its framework.

As the dictatorship matured, Fascist rhetoric increasingly voiced explicit hostility to the individual ego. Fascism had always been strongly communitarian but now this aspect became more conspicuous. Fascist anti-individualism is summed up in the assertion that the death of a human being is like the body's loss of a cell. Among the increasingly histrionic blackshirt meetings from 1920 to 1922 were the funeral services. When the name of a comrade recently killed by the Socialists was called out, the whole crowd would roar: "Presente!"

Man is not an atom, man is essentially social. These woolly clichés were as much Fascist as they were socialist. Anti-individualism was especially prominent in the writings of official philosopher Giovanni Gentile, who gave Fascist social theory its finished form in the final years of the regime.[39]

The Failure of Fascism

Fascist ideology had two goals by which Fascism's performance may reasonably be judged: the creation of a heroically moral human being, in a heroically moral social order, and the accelerated development of industry, especially in backward economies like Italy.

The fascist moral ideal, upheld by writers from Sorel to Gentile, is something like an inversion of the caricature of a Benthamite liberal. The fascist ideal man is not cautious but brave, not calculating but resolute, not sentimental but ruthless, not preoccupied with personal advantage but fighting for ideals, not seeking comfort but experiencing life intensely. The early Fascists did not know how they would install the social order which

---

39 On Gentile's ideas see Gregor, *Phoenix: Fascism in Our Time* (New Brunswick: Transaction, 1999), chs. 5–6.

would create this "new man," but they were convinced that they had to destroy the bourgeois liberal order which had created his opposite.

Even as late as 1922 it was not clear to Fascists that Fascism, the "third way" between liberalism and socialism, would set up a bureaucratic police state, but given the circumstances and fundamental Fascist ideas, nothing else was feasible. Fascism introduced a form of state which was claustrophobic in its oppressiveness. The result was a population of decidedly unheroic mediocrities, sly conformists scared of their own shadows, worlds removed from the kind of dynamic human character the Fascists had hoped would inherit the Earth.

As for Fascism's economic performance, a purely empirical test of results is inconclusive. In its first few years, the Mussolini government's economic measures were probably more liberalizing than restrictive. The subsequent turn to intrusive corporatism was swiftly followed by the world slump and then the war. But we do know from numerous other examples that if it is left to run its course, corporatist interventionism will cripple any economy.[40] Furthermore, economic losses inflicted by the war can be laid at Fascism's door, as Mussolini could easily have kept Italy neutral. Fascism both gave unchecked power to a single individual to commit such a blunder as to take Italy to war in 1940 and made this more likely by extolling the benefits of war.

In the panoramic sweep of history, Fascism, like Communism, like all forms of socialism, and like today's greenism and anti-globalism, is the logical result of specific intellectual errors about human progress. Fascism was an attempt to pluck the material fruits of liberal economics while abolishing liberal culture.[41] The attempt was entirely quixotic: There is no such thing as economic development without free-market capitalism and there is no such thing as free-market capitalism without the recognition of individual rights. The revulsion against liberalism was the outcome of misconceptions, and the futile attempt to supplant liberalism was the application of further

40   The most outstanding American scholar of Fascism is A. James Gregor. A shortcoming of Gregor's analysis is his tendency to assume that Fascist economic policy could work, that it is possible for a Fascist government to stimulate industrial growth. Any such view has to somehow come to terms with the fact that Italian economic growth was robust before World War I.

41   "Liberal" means classical liberal or libertarian.

misconceptions. By losing the war, Fascism and National Socialism spared themselves the terminal sclerosis which beset Communism.

"The Man Who Is Seeking"

When Mussolini switched from anti-war to pro-war in November 1914, the other Socialist Party leaders immediately claimed that he had been bought off by the bourgeoisie, and this allegation has since been repeated by many leftists.

But any notion that Mussolini sold out is more far-fetched than the theory that Lenin seized power because he was paid by the German government to take Russia out of the war. As the paramount figure of the Italian left, Mussolini had it made. He was taking a career gamble at very long odds by provoking his own expulsion from the Socialist Party, in addition to risking his life as a front-line soldier.[42]

Like Lenin, Mussolini was a capable revolutionary who took care of finances. Once he had decided to come out as pro-war, he foresaw that he would lose his income from the Socialist Party. He approached wealthy Italian patriots to get support for *Il Popolo d'Italia*, but much of the money that came to Mussolini originated covertly from Allied governments who wanted to bring Italy into the war. Similarly, Lenin's Bolsheviks took aid from wealthy backers and from the German government.[43] In both cases, we see a determined group of revolutionaries using their wits to raise money in pursuit of their goals.

Jasper Ridley argues that Mussolini switched because he always "wanted to be on the winning side," and dare not "swim against the tide of public opinion."[44] This explanation is feeble. Mussolini had spent all his life in an antagonistic position to the majority of Italians, and with the founding of a new party in 1919 he would again deliberately set himself at

---

42   Ignazio Silone held that Mussolini unscrupulously aimed only at power for himself. *The School for Dictators* (New York: Harper, 1939). While this is less preposterous than the theory that he sold out for financial gain, it too cannot be squared with the facts of Mussolini's life.

43   Angelica Balabanoff, socialist activist and Mussolini's mistress intermittently from 1904 on, was in Lenin's entourage, shipped with him into Russia in the famous German "sealed train."

44   Ridley, *Mussolini*, p. 67.

odds with the majority. Since individuals are usually more influenced by the pressure of their "reference group" than by the opinions of the whole population, we might wonder why Mussolini did not swim with the tide of the Socialist Party leadership and the majority of the party membership, instead of swimming with the tide of those socialists inside and outside the party who had become pro-war.

Although his personality may have influenced the timing, or even the actual decision, the pressure for Mussolini to change his position came from a long-term evolution in his intellectual convictions. From his earliest years as a Marxist revolutionary, Mussolini had been sympathetic to syndicalism, and then an actual syndicalist. Unlike other syndicalists, he remained in the Socialist Party, and as he rose within it, he continued to keep his ears open to those syndicalists who had left it. On many issues, his thinking followed theirs, more cautiously, and often five or ten years behind them.

From 1902 to 1914, Italian revolutionary syndicalism underwent a rapid evolution. Always opposed to parliamentary democracy, Italian syndicalists, under Sorel's influence, became more committed to extra-constitutional violence and the necessity for the revolutionary vanguard to ignite a conflagration. As early as 1908, Mussolini the syndicalist Marxist had come to agree with these elitist notions and began to employ the term *gerarchia* (hierarchy), which would remain a favorite word of his into the Fascist period.

Many syndicalists lost faith in the revolutionary potential of the working class. Seeking an alternative revolutionary recipe, the most "advanced" of these syndicalists began to ally themselves with the nationalists and to favor war. Mussolini's early reaction to this trend was the disgust we might expect from any self-respecting leftist.[45] But given their premises, the syndicalists' conclusions were persuasive.

The logic underlying their shifting position was that there was unfortunately going to be no working-class revolution, either in the advanced countries, or in less developed countries like Italy. Italy was on its own, and Italy's problem was low industrial output.[46] Italy was an exploited

---

45 Sternhell, Sznajder, and Asheri, *Birth*, p. 202.
46 It may seem odd that there was such anxiety about Italian development when the Italian economy was growing quite lustily: Precisely the same paradox arises with recent leftist attitudes to "poverty in the Third World."

proletarian nation, while the richer countries were bloated bourgeois nations. The nation was the myth which could unite the productive classes behind a drive to expand output. These ideas foreshadowed the Third World propaganda of the 1950s and 1960s, in which aspiring elites in economically backward countries represented their own less than scrupulously humane rule as "progressive" because it would accelerate Third World development. From Nkrumah to Castro, Third World dictators would walk in Mussolini's footsteps.[47] Fascism was a full dress rehearsal for post-war Third Worldism.

Many syndicalists also became "productionists," urging that the workers ought not to strike, but to take over the factories and keep them running without the bosses. While productionism as a tactic of industrial action did not lead anywhere, the productionist idea implied that all who helped to expand output, even a productive segment of the bourgeoisie, should be supported rather than opposed.

From about 1912, those who closely observed Mussolini noted changes in his rhetoric. He began to employ the words "people" and "nation" in preference to "proletariat." (Subsequently such patriotic language would become acceptable among Marxists, but then it was still unusual and somewhat suspect.) Mussolini was gradually becoming convinced, a few years later than the most advanced leaders of the extreme left, that Marxist class analysis was useless, that the proletariat would never become revolutionary, and that the nation had to be the vehicle of development. An elementary implication of this position is that leftist-initiated strikes and violent confrontations are not merely irrelevant pranks but actual hindrances to progress.

When Mussolini founded *Utopia*, it was to provide. a forum at which his party comrades could exchange ideas with his friends the revolutionary syndicalists outside the party. He signed his articles at this time "The Man Who Is Seeking." The collapse of the Second International on the outbreak of war, and the lining up of the mass socialist parties of Germany, France, and Austria behind their respective national governments, confirmed once again that the syndicalists had been right: Proletarian internationalism was

---

47   On the striking similarities between Fascism and African Socialism, see Gregor, *Contemporary Radical Ideologies*, Chapter 7.

not a living force. The future, he concluded, lay with productionist national syndicalism, which with some tweaking would become Fascism.

Mussolini believed that Fascism was an international movement. He expected that both decadent bourgeois democracy and dogmatic Marxism-Leninism would everywhere give way to Fascism, that the twentieth century would be a century of Fascism. Like his leftist contemporaries, he underestimated the resilience of both democracy and free-market liberalism.

But in substance Mussolini's prediction was fulfilled: Most of the world's people in the second half of the twentieth century were ruled by governments which were closer in practice to Fascism than they were either to liberalism or to Marxism-Leninism.

The twentieth century was indeed the Fascist century.

Liberty, November 2001

6
An Unexpected Discovery (2002)

On Friday evening, March 1st 2002, wanting to check a couple of points about Henri Bergson, I did a google search on him. I then had the thought: Why not do a google search on myself and find out what's out there? So I typed in the words David Ramsay Steele and got hundreds of results, many of which were about me and many of which were not.

The way these searches seem to work is that they look for any place where all the words entered occur close enough together. So, for instance, any document containing the names Bill Ramsay, Joe Steele, and David Jones in close proximity would have turned up on my search.

Very soon I noticed a result: "David Christopher 'Kit' Steele b. 1944 Edinburgh." Now, I was born in Edinburgh, Scotland, on 23rd June 1944, and I was christened David Christopher Ramsay Steele, but I have no recollection of being called "Kit," though Kit is a diminutive of Christopher (as in Kit Carson). I have never liked the name Christopher and stopped using it quite early. My first, slightly annoyed reaction was: There is another writer named Steele who was born in Edinburgh in 1944!

I therefore clicked on this search result, to find out who this upstart punk might be, and within a fifth of a second realized that I am Kit Steele. How is this possible? Here I have to fill in a bit of background.

A Murky Origin

As far back as I can remember, I disliked the woman I knew as my mother, and at some point began to suspect she was not my real mother. I didn't get on very well with my father either. One day at school, when I was eight, I found that all the other children in the class had brought copies of their birth certificates. I had been told nothing of this, but my father showed up later in the day and personally handed my birth certificate over to the teacher.

At the age of about ten, I went through some of my parents' documents which I wasn't strictly supposed to be looking at, and came across a letter implying that my "mother" was not my real mother, and possibly that I had an older brother somewhere. I accepted this thereafter but mentioned it to no one.

I grew up an only child in Birmingham, England. I clearly recall living in London before moving to Birmingham. My picture of my early life was that I had been born in Edinburgh, moved to London at the age of one or two, then to Birmingham at the age of four.

From an early age I loved the mother I could not remember, and dreamed of finding her again. I do not look much like my father, and I assumed I would look like my mother. I believed she would be very much like me in personal character, that if we ever met we would understand each other instantly, and that she would have been a remarkable beauty. I came to believe, and I do believe to this day, that while she was, of course, a normal human being who would therefore have made a lot of mistakes in her life, she must have had an excellent reason for anything she decided to do, and that she owed me nothing. But I did always miss her, and I do miss her now.

When I was eleven, my father became a born-again Christian, and this changed the family lifestyle for the worse. My father and stepmother became less happy (though committed, of course, to the public protestation that they were a lot more happy), and my life became more acutely miserable. I soon became a skeptic with regard to theistic religion, a position I have maintained ever since.

I left school at seventeen and went to work as a local newspaper reporter. I left home shortly afterwards, and then had little to do with my father and stepmother, though I did visit them occasionally, on amicable terms, and I ceased to dislike either of them, which is comparatively easy with persons one rarely meets. I became a great admirer of Bertrand Russell and an active member of CND (the Campaign for Nuclear Disarmament). Then I joined the SPGB (Socialist Party of Great Britain), a small Marxist group founded in 1904. After some years I went to the University of Hull and got a degree in sociology. I then (beginning in 1970) went through a profound crisis of ideology, which led me from Marxism to libertarianism. The story of that crisis and the ensuing transformation can be found in my book *From Marx to Mises* (1992), which doesn't seem anything like an autobiography, but really is.

I communicated rarely with my father and stepmother, though I did see them occasionally, and I visited my stepmother in hospital when she was seriously ill with cancer. After her death, I visited my father in (I think it must have been) early 1973, when I was twenty-eight, and he broached to me for the first time what I already half knew, with a few added details: that my late "mother" was not my real mother, and that I had an older brother somewhere, name of Bruce.

I asked my father about the possibility of tracing my mother and brother, and he said that my mother had been involved with a Pole, with a difficult-to-remember surname. He couldn't recall this Polish name and he had no idea what had become of my mother or my brother. I got the impression, though he may not have said this explicitly, that my mother had run off with her Polish boyfriend, taking her older son with her, and leaving behind her younger son, who was presumably more trouble. I inferred, for some reason, that this had happened when I was a few weeks old. My father told me that I had been raised for quite a while by his parents, in the attic flat above Charlotte Chapel, a big Baptist church in West Rose Street, Edinburgh, where they were the caretakers.

At this time and subsequently, I leaped to the conclusion that if I were going to find my mother and brother, it would be a matter of locating "Marjorie (difficult Polish name)" and her son "Bruce (difficult Polish name)." I decided this would be a time-consuming task, with very little likelihood of success, and that therefore it wasn't worth pursuing. I also subscribed to an ideological outlook which told me that blood is no thicker than water and that ancestry says little about who you are.

In recent years I have more often toyed with the idea of at least taking what I assumed would have to be the first step: having a search done at Somerset House in London, which holds records of all British births, marriages, and deaths, for anything they might have on Elsie Marjorie Allkins after her marriage to my father, or for anything on Bruce Ramsay Steele after his birth around 1942. But I never did get round to it. In addition to the other reasons there was the increasing possibility that she might already be dead.

In 1980 I got married and emigrated to the United States. In 1989 I divorced and remarried, and have since had four children: the second, Allan, was named after my father. The fourth, Duncan Bruce, was given the name "Bruce" after my absent brother. It hardly needs to be said that my views on kinship have undergone some subtle and not-so-subtle changes over the years.

And then on March 1, 2002, I stumbled on the fact that I am Kit and someone was looking for me.

Better Late than None

Google took me to genealogy.com, the place on the Web you go to find out about your family history and your lost relatives. I had never heard of it before. The post had been placed there by my brother's daughter, Jennifer Ramsay, who mentioned that she lived in Canada. I replied immediately, identifying myself. But then I realized that she had posted the message in November 2001, and she might well have given up looking at genealogy.com. It didn't occur to me at the time that I could have found her email address from genealogy.com, or at least what her email address had been back in November, and sent a message more directly.

I went home and told my wife, Lisa, the news. Later that night, she was messing around on the computer and when I asked her what she was doing, she said, "Never you mind. Go to bed." Next morning Lisa told me she had looked at a number of Jennifer Ramsays in Canada (Ramsay is a common Canadian name), and located the likely one: a researcher into salmon lice at the University of Prince Edward Island. Prince Edward Island is a province north of Nova Scotia. This Jennifer Ramsay seemed to be possibly the daughter of one William Bruce Ramsay, a professor of veterinary science at Nova Scotia Agricultural College. We were able to look at a picture of him on a faculty directory, and he did bear some resemblance to my father. Lisa downloaded the white pages for various towns in Nova Scotia. There were a number of William Ramsays and Bruce Ramsays. The most likely candidate was an entry for Bruce and Susan Ramsay in Truro.

Lisa also discovered that my mother, Marjorie Ramsay, had published a book of poetry, and Lisa even found some fragments of her poems on the Web. To judge from these, her poems are not very good. Her titles seem to be better than the poems themselves. The collection, published when she was approaching fifty is called *Half a Centennial Is Better than None,* and one of the poems is called "An Immigrant Remembers the Sea." If I'd been around, I could have told her it's a good idea to strive for that kind of economy in every line of a poem, but I suspect she would have gone her own way regardless.

I called the number for Bruce and Susan. A woman answered and told me they were in Cuba on vacation (the Canadian government, unlike the US government, permits its subjects to visit Cuba). After a few of my questions about Bruce, the woman became increasingly suspicious. I said: "I'm his brother." She was stunned and then overjoyed. She confirmed what I had deduced from Jennifer's post, that my mother had died—but only about two years ago.

The woman, who turned out to be Jennifer's younger sister, Robin, said: "I've got two surprises for them when they get back. I'm going to Japan, and his brother has called." In actuality she was holding out on her newfound uncle: She had three surprises for her parents. The third was: I've totaled the car and narrowly escaped with my life.

On March 3rd, I heard my brother's voice for the first time in fifty-five years. I also spoke with Susan and Jennifer. I was told of Christine, my first cousin in London, who is almost exactly the same age as I, and who played together with me when we were babies, when I was called "Kit," of course! I was able to talk to Christine, a big fan of my mother's, next day. It turned out that Christine, Jennifer, and Christine's sister and mother, had actually gone to some pains to find me in the UK, without success.

Susan and Robin scanned some family pictures and emailed them to me: For the first time since 1945, I saw what my mum looked like. She was lovely beyond my imagining, and facially she looked as much like me as a beautiful woman could. She was, by all accounts, opinionated, argumentative, articulate, and occasionally dogmatic in manner, though sometimes likely to change her opinions alarmingly. She was known as "Bobbo" and possessed a special kind of charisma - my cousin still speaks quite naturally of herself as "following Bobbo's banner."

Bobbo's Story

Bobbo was born during a Zeppelin raid on London in 1918, or so she later claimed—Bruce says there don't appear to have been any Zeppelin raids that late. Bobbo joined the British Union of Fascists, Sir Oswald Mosley's blackshirts, at the age of eighteen, and rose rapidly to become, by some accounts, "Mosley's right-hand woman." As well as being Mosley's secretary, she was the BUF's chief female public speaker, and was regularly to be heard in Hyde Park.

Bobbo met Jock Steele (my father, Allan Ramsay Steele) through "the movement." Soon after they began living together, they were burned out of their London flat by the Communists. At the beginning of the war in 1939, the leading blackshirts were jailed without trial—presumably on the theory that they might assist and collaborate with a German invasion. Bobbo was sent to Holloway (the women's prison in England) along with Lady Diana Mosley (one of the Mitford sisters) and was let out after two years. It seems likely that when Bobbo got out of the clink, doubtless some time between the commencement of Operation Barbarossa and the attack on Pearl Harbor, her joyful reunion with Jock produced my brother Bruce. A couple of years later, their mutual affections were evidently still intact, and they produced me.

For some reason, Jock and Bobbo later agreed to separate, and to split the kids between them. It may seem odd that she would take the older of the two, but for a woman who had to work, a child she could put into nursery school would have been less of a problem. So she didn't exactly run off with a man, and the separation happened when I was well over a year old. My later reconstruction of my early childhood was mistaken in some respects: I went to London later than I thought, and spent less time there before moving to Birmingham.

All witnesses seem to agree now that Bobbo was not involved with a man at the time of the separation. However, I believe that, just as no scientific theory is abandoned until a more attractive candidate theory comes along, so no romantic relationship is abandoned until a more attractive candidate partner comes along. Only a few days ago I learned that Jock and Bobbo and my stepmother and her first husband were two couples who knew each other well over a long period. So an alternative hypothesis naturally presents itself.

I used to think I might be the legendary Pole's natural son. For one thing, I have a very wide and short skull, a shape rare among the Anglo-Saxons and quite different from my father's, but common in Central and

Eastern Europe. I can never get glasses that are wide enough. But, as I now know, my mother had the wide skull too. Only DNA would settle it, but all the evidence I have suggests that I am indeed the offspring of Jock as well as of Bobbo. My mother took the child who looked like my father; my father took the child who looked like my mother. This kind of difference in the appearance of offspring is so striking that I find it remarkable that the true mechanism of inheritance was not discovered until 1865, and then was overlooked until 1900 because no one read Mendel's paper with any serious attention.

A few years after separating from Jock and me (and getting a divorce) my mother married a Czech Jew named Hajek, who legally adopted Bruce. Some years after that, the three moved to Canada. From then on my mother was generally known as Marje. Later, by some accounts, Hajek became increasingly violent, and my mother took Bruce and did a moonlight flit. Hajek disappears from the story, and is no doubt deceased. Marjorie and Bruce had changed "Ramsay Steele" to "Ramsay Hajek," then they dropped the Hajek and became just Ramsay, so my mother had four surnames in succession. and my brother has had three. The most likely hypothesis to account for my father's story of a "Pole" is that he heard about Hajek and got his Eastern European nationalities mixed up. My father confirms that this is possible, and that the 'Pole' he was thinking of was indeed Jewish.

My mother. and brother moved several times within Canada. My mother's obituary says, "She lived in five provinces and worked at a variety of occupations from furniture salesman to antique store owner and hotel maid to medical librarian." In her final residence, Truro, Nova Scotia, "she was active in such organizations as the Multicultural Society and Toastmasters."

I am now continually finding out new things about my mum, and there is a lot to learn. In Canada, she passionately advocated various leftist causes. Marje Ramsay invariably drew attention to herself by her vociferous promotion of her radical opinions and her British accent. She was an anti-war demonstrator who declared that she had "always been a hippie at heart." While a hospital employee in British Columbia she blew the whistle on some newsworthy scandal. She had received little schooling early in life and regretted her lack of academic knowledge; she took courses in social anthropology at the University of Winnipeg. She favored nuclear disarmament and later came to see the "First World" as the Earth's greatest threat. She admired Canadian environmental lobbyist David Suzuki. In the 1990s she was an environmental activist who pestered fellow-residents in her apartment building to consume less and recycle more. Even in her final days suffering severe complications of Parkinson's Disease, she initiated some kind of protest which became the occasion for a nursing home review. My brother Bruce, who turns out to be an excellent writer, is sending me his life story and my mother's in installments.

Into the Age of Lifestreams

This unexpected discovery has affected me in a number of ways and I will just mention a few of them.

I have become an Internet sap. When I heard people say "It changes everything; it's a miracle," I used to adopt a somewhat snooty and untrendier-than-thou posture. But now I have run out of superlatives. Yes, it's a miracle—but why confine oneself to understatements? It doesn't just change everything: it *changes everything!*

(A technical note: I know now that if you do a google search and enclose the words you enter in quotation marks, you will get only results which include those words in that order: this will exclude a lot of mainly irrelevant material. It was lucky that I did not know this on 1st March, however, for then I certainly would have missed the post looking for "Kit.")

In speaking to various people in recent weeks, I have been struck by the frequency of such incidents. Seeking long-lost relatives or friends seems to be a rapidly growing pastime—it must already be comparable, in the sheer number of people participating, to psychotherapy, church attendance, social work, or weight-loss programs. There is also a very widespread fascination in tracing back family trees without looking for any specific individual. The genealogical interest is exploding as the Internet makes it so much simpler and cheaper.

Another side to this is that there are quite a number of people who find such contacts unwelcome. A friend of mine was called, in her twenties, by her biological father, who had moved out of her life when she was an infant. She loves her adoptive father and was distinctly displeased that her biological father should presume that she wanted to be reminded of his existence. Biological relatedness does not give you the right to intrude into another person' life.

Finally, I'm impressed by the fact that some projects, which seem almost foredoomed, if analyzed methodically, turn out to be child's play. I now realize that I had all the information I needed to look for my mother, with very little expenditure of time or money and with a high likelihood of success. I knew her maiden name was Allkins. I knew enough to figure out (though I didn't) that she must have had family in London. I assumed that because Allkins is a very ordinary-sounding English name, it must be fairly common, but actually it turns out to be a northern English name and quite rare in London. I could have simply called every Allkins in the London phone directories, and would quite likely, within a few minutes, have contacted someone who knew her. The world is filled with opportunities, all just crying out to be missed.

Liberty, July 2002

7
TAKING THE JFK ASSASSINATION
CONSPIRACY SERIOUSLY (2003)

Thousands of books have been published on the Kennedy assassination, and about ninety-nine percent of them argue for a Conspiracy. The House Select Committee on Assassinations (1978) concluded there had been a Conspiracy. The successful movie *JFK* (1991) laid out an imaginative Conspiracy scenario as history. Not surprisingly, most people now believe there was a Conspiracy.

A vast amount of evidence has been marshalled in support of the Conspiracy theory, and I admit I cannot refute all of it. Yet I maintain that Kennedy was killed by the Lone Nut Lee Oswald,[1] roughly as determined by the Warren Commission report in 1964, by Jim Moore in his book *Conspiracy of One* (1990), and by Gerald Posner in *Case Closed* (1993).[2] I have become steadily more convinced of this over recent years, and here I want to explain why, despite all the arguments of the Conspiracy theorists, many of them unanswerable, the Lone Nut theory is the better theory.[3]

John Kennedy was fatally shot in Dallas at 12:30 P.M. on November 22nd 1963. Many concluded, especially following the shooting of

---

1   The Mel Gibson character in the movie *Conspiracy Theory* (1997) wonders why assassins always have three names. The answer seems to be that police and other bureaucratic reports tend to rehabilitate disused middle names. In life, Lee Harvey Oswald was commonly known as Lee Oswald.

2   *The Warren Commission Report: Report of the President's Commission on the Assassination of President John F. Kennedy* (St. Martin's Press, undated [1964]); Jim Moore, *Conspiracy of One: The Definitive Book on the Kennedy Assassination* (Summit, 1990); Gerald Posner, *Case Closed: Lee Harvey Oswald and the Assassination of JFK* (Random House, 1993; revised edition Anchor Books, 1994).

3   Predisposed to distrust the government, I tended to assume until 1992 that there had been a Conspiracy. I was wakened from my dogmatic slumber by Sheldon Richman's review of *JFK* (*Liberty*, March 1992) and then started to look into the subject.

Oswald by Jack Ruby two days later, that there had been a Conspiracy, but after publication of *The Warren Commission Report* (1964) the Lone Nut theory became widely accepted. This acceptance began to be seriously eroded by 1966, which saw the publication of the best-selling *Rush to Judgment*.[4] As the Vietnam war got worse and the Watergate scandal came to the boil, majority opinion swung heavily back to the Conspiracy theory.

The Conspiracy Theory Transformed

At times popular support for the Conspiracy theory has exceeded eighty-five percent. Today the Conspiracy theory is not as popular as it was twenty years ago, but still far more popular than it was thirty-nine years ago, immediately following publication of *The Warren Commission Report*. Meanwhile the factual arguments for a Conspiracy have been utterly transformed.

In the early years, Conspiracy theorists appealed to the publicly recognized evidence. They contended that if all this evidence were made available and properly interpreted, it would prove a Conspiracy. Some details of this evidence may have been tampered with, but most of it was assumed to be rock solid. Now, Conspiracy theorists generally maintain that the evidence itself was almost entirely fabricated by the Conspirators.

The two biggest examples of this radical change of approach are the autopsy pictures and the Zapruder film. Early Conspiracy theorists demanded the release of the autopsy photographs and x-rays, withheld from the public by request of the Kennedy family, but when these pictures were released in the 1970s they corroborated the Lone Nut theory. Conspiracy theorists then concluded that either the pictures or the wounds themselves, or both, must have been falsified.

---

4   Mark Lane, *Rush to Judgment* (Holt, Rinehart, and Winston). Other Conspiracy-theory works published in 1966 include Edward Jay Epstein, *Inquest: The Warren Commission and the Establishment of Truth* (Bantam) and Richard H. Popkin, *The Second Oswald* (Avon). Popkin is the outstanding historian of philosophical thought, author of *The History of Skepticism from Erasmus to Spinoza* and *The High Road to Pyrrhonism*. My theory is that *The Second Oswald* was really written by a second Popkin, who however was devious enough to make sure the royalties were mailed to the first Popkin.

The Zapruder film, a twenty-six-second movie of the assassination made by a spectator, Abraham Zapruder, used to be regarded on all sides as a record of fact. Aspects of this film were frequently employed to advance a Conspiracy theory. Now it is accepted by almost everyone that the Zapruder film, taken at face value, corroborates the Lone Nut theory. Most Conspiracy theorists therefore claim the film to be either altered in detail or a complete fabrication.

Most Conspiracy theory books since the 1970s have simultaneously relied upon the Zapruder film and alleged it has been tampered with.[5] In successive books, the trend has been to gradually rely less on the film as evidence and give more weight to tampering, culminating in recent allegations that Zapruder never made the Zapruder film but was paid by the Conspiracy to pretend that he had made it.[6]

The Body Snatchers

David Lifton's enormously successful 1988 book, *Best Evidence*, showed the way to rescue the Conspiracy theory from the evidence. Lifton maintains that Kennedy's body was stolen on the plane between Parkland Hospital, Dallas, and Andrews Air Force Base, Maryland, and elaborate alterations made in the corpse's wounds (in less than a couple of hours) so that the autopsy would be looking at reconstructed and therefore faked wounds.[7] Since the official coffin was now empty, there had to be a further elaborately planned conjuring trick, to get the body into Bethesda Naval Hospital for the autopsy. The body was then altered again for the autopsy photographs. This second alteration involved, not additional cutting or tissue damage,

---

5   Among numerous examples see Groden and Livingstone, *High Treason: The, Assassination of President John F. Kennedy and the New Evidence of Conspiracy* (Berkley, 1990 [1989]), pp. 117–18; Jim Marrs, *Crossfire: The Plot that Killed Kennedy* (Carroll and Graf, 1989), pp. 64–69, 86; Noel Twyman, *Bloody Treason: On Solving History's Greatest Murder Mystery, the Assassination of John F. Kennedy* (Laurel, 1997), pp. 117–166.

6   James H. Fetzer, ed., *Murder in Dealey Plaza: What We Know Now that We Didn't Know Then about the Death of JFK* (Catfeet Press, 2000); Fetzer, ed., *The Great Zapruder Film Hoax: Deceit and Deception in the Death of JFK* (Catfeet Press, 2003). A few Conspiracy theorists, notably Josiah Thompson, still insist on the reliability of the Zapruder film.

7   David S. Lifton, *Best Evidence: Disguise and Deception in the Assassination of President Kennedy* (Carroll and Graf, 1988), pp. 582–83 and passim.

but extensive rebuilding and remodeling, to replace large areas of skull which had been missing before.[8]

Lifton realized that if this were true, the Zapruder film must have been seriously falsified.[9] The Conspirators must have doctored the film to repair and conceal the enormous damage to the back of the head and add the eruption at the top right side of the head. Since the ballistics evidence is compatible only with a scenario of two hits from behind and none from anywhere else, the Conspirators must also have replaced the actual bullet fragments with planted fragments prior to analysis.[10] This might be a more challenging task than Lifton appears to recognize: the bullet which was designated by the Conspirators as the one which would appear to have hit both Kennedy and Connally would have to have been fired, and minuscule flakes extruded from it on impact would have had to be recovered and each separately planted somehow in Kennedy's body. Lifton's theory also requires that Kennedy's jacket, shirt, and necktie be faked to produce a false entry wound at the back and exit wound at the front.

High Treason by Groden and Livingstone appeared the following year and also became a best-seller. The authors scornfully dismiss Lifton's account for various reasons, including the impossibility of performing the surgery in the limited time and testimony that Kennedy's casket was always under observation.[11] Instead they propose that the body of someone else was substituted for Kennedy's just before the autopsy. The Conspirators faked the head and neck x-rays "by shooting a body in the manner in which they wished to have it appear that the President was killed." The Conspirators faked the autopsy photographs at a different time, and "No one among the conspirators realized the photographs were incompatible with the forged x-rays."[12]

Witnesses Against Oswald

I have said that I cannot answer many of the arguments for a Conspiracy. I am referring here to highly technical arguments involving medicine,

---

8   Lifton, pp. 560, 655–664, and compare the "Autopsy Photo 4," following page 682, with the right-hand drawing on page 310.

9   Lifton, pp. 555n–57n.

10   Lifton, p. 559.

11   Robert J. Groden and Harrison Edward Livingstone, *High Treason*, pp. 39–41.

12   Groden and Livingstone, p. 83.

ballistics, and photography.[13] Of course these physical arguments deserve to be addressed and answered by technical experts, and I am confident that in due course they will be.

Why am I so confident? Because of other arguments which trump the anomalies in the physical evidence. But before I get to those, it's worth pointing out that not all of the publicly recognized evidence can easily be dismissed as fraudulent, and much of this evidence favors the Lone Nut theory.

The Lone Nut theory requires that three and only three shots were fired from the sixth-floor window of the Book Depository. If there were more than three shots, or if any shots came from some other location, then the Lone Nut theory is refuted: there must have been a multi-shooter Conspiracy or at least a coincidence of two separate assassination attempts, with a Conspiracy to cover up one of these.[14]

The evidence for precisely three shots from that location, and the evidence for Oswald's involvement, is quite powerful.[15] Though the many witnesses differed in the number of shots they thought they had heard and where they thought these shots had come from, the biggest number of witnesses who had decided views on the matter favored three shots, and a plurality also favored the direction of the Depository.[16]

13   Examples of the arguments I have in mind are David Mantik's use of optical densitometry to analyze the autopsy x-rays, in James H. Fetzer, ed., *Assassination Science: Experts Speak Out on the Death of JFK* (Catfeet Press, 1998), pp. 121–139, and John P. Costella's discussion of the anomalies in the Zapruder film (Fetzer, *Great Zapruder Film Hoax*, pp. 164–221). I don't know enough about medical x-rays or film editing to answer these arguments, but for the reasons given in the text, I do not have to do this in order to decide that the Lone Nut theory is rationally preferable to the Conspiracy theory.

14   The single exception is the theory of Howard Donahue as presented by Bonar Menninger. In his well-argued book, *Mortal Error: The Shot that Killed JFK* (St. Martin's, 1992), Menninger contends that Oswald was the only one who intended to kill Kennedy, and that an accidental discharge of a Secret Service agent's gun also hit Kennedy. The only Conspiracy, then, was to cover up this embarrassing accident. Menninger's book contains a knowledgeable and lucid discussion of the firearms aspect of the assassination. (I believe the totality of the evidence now excludes the Donahue-Menninger theory.)

15   There is a difference between the views of most of the public and those of the active Conspiracy theorists. The former believe Oswald was part of the Conspiracy, that he "must've had help," while the latter maintain that Oswald was innocent.

16   Ninety-eight percent of the hundreds of ear-witnesses thought that the shots they had heard had come from just one location. While witnesses unused to gunfire might easily

The ceiling of the fifth story and floorboards on the sixth story were in disrepair, with actual gaps between the two floors. Three men working on the fifth floor, immediately underneath the sniper's nest, heard three very loud explosions directly above them, followed by the sound of the bolt action, and one of the three heard the cartridge cases landing on the floor. Several witnesses in the street saw the rifle sticking out of the sixth floor window, one actually saw it fire, and another saw the shooter's face and gave a description to the police, which may have led to the police picking Oswald up. Others saw a face like Oswald's in the window before the shooting, without seeing anything at the time of the shooting. Testimony as to shots from other locations tends to be a lot less definite, or to have become more sharply defined only years after the event.[17]

Conspiracy theorists have a difficult time with the eyewitnesses, notably Howard Brennan, who immediately following the shooting gave the shooter's description to the police. A few hours later Brennan failed to positively identify Oswald in a line-up, though he did say that Oswald most closely resembled the shooter. Brennan subsequently stated that he had really been in no doubt that the Oswald he saw in the line-up was the shooter but that he had been in fear for his life and the lives of his family from the presumed organized assassins, and annoyed with the authorities for allowing his own identity, as apparently the only witness to have seen the assassin, to become public knowledge. Therefore he had pretended to be unable to make a definite identification.

Stewart Galanor, in his beautifully succinct and predominantly fair statement of the case for Conspiracy, implies that the notion Brennan had refrained from making a positive identification when he could have done so originated from a Secret Service agent, who fed this suggestion to Brennan.[18] But let's get this in perspective. By Brennan's own account, a police

---

get the direction of shots wrong, it seems unlikely that they would think that shots from different directions all came from the same place.

17   After the shots rang out, some people started running. To a hardened cynic like me, one of the amusing aspects of Conspiracy speculations is the notion that these people would be running *toward* the sniper's perceived location, with the intention of "catching" him.

18   Stewart Galanor, *Cover-Up* (Kestrel, 1998), p. 91. Galanor says that Brennan "was unable" to identify Oswald, which is misleading.

officer suggested to Brennan at the line-up who the suspect was. In any case, Brennan had just seen the arrested Oswald on TV.[19] For both these reasons, any identification at the line-up would have been of small value. We do have Brennan's recollection that when he saw Oswald on TV he knew they had the right man. All this is precisely the kind of messy, unsatisfactory outcome you don't expect from a superbly orchestrated Conspiracy.

The fact remains that Brennan did report what he claimed to have seen to the police immediately after the shooting, giving a description of the sixth-floor shooter that led directly to a police radio bulletin incorporating that description, and thus perhaps to Oswald's apprehension.[20] If Brennan had just been making it up, what are the odds that someone conforming to the description, and arrested in Oak Cliff, over two miles from Dealey Plaza, would turn out to have been a Depository employee who frequently worked alone on the sixth floor? Alternatively, if Brennan were in the pay of the Conspiracy, then surely his eyewitness evidence could have been made airtight.

There is considerable additional evidence implicating Oswald, beginning with the simple fact that he, alone of all Depository employees, left the building within a few minutes of the assassination. He took a taxi to his rented room in Oak Cliff, changed his clothes, and picked up his revolver. Conspiracy theorists usually feel compelled to deny that Oswald then shot a police officer who approached him on the street, though a dozen eyewitnesses positively identified Oswald for this shooting.[21] And, to mention a circumstance no one disputes, what was Oswald doing, with a recently-fired revolver, sitting in a movie theater he had just run into without buying a ticket?

19   Howard L. Brennan and J. Edward Cherryholmes, *Eyewitness to History: The Kennedy Assassination as Seen by Howard Brennan* (Texian Press, 1969), p. 22.

20   Dale K. Myers, *With Malice: Lee Harvey Oswald and the Murder of Officer J.D. Tippit* (Oak Cliff Press, 1998), pp. 63–65, doubts that the description was what made Tippit approach Oswald. Twyman, *Bloody Treason*, p. 19, says "No one knows how the description was obtained," an untruth.

21   On Tippit's murder, see Myers, *With Malice*. Highly selective accounts of Tippit's killing by Conspiracy theorists such as Twyman should be compared with Myers's detailed and sober study.

What we have learned of Oswald's life, outlook, and behavior fits the Lone Nut theory. Norman Mailer, an early proponent of the Conspiracy theory, more recently wrote a "novelized" life of Oswald which purports to avoid taking any position on whether he was the assassin, sticking to those facts about Oswald which can be verified by biographical research. Whether intentionally or inadvertently, Mailer's account leaves an overwhelming impression of Oswald's guilt.[22]

Oswald's failed assassination attempt on General Edwin Walker, the photographs of him with a rifle, a pistol, and a leftist paper taken by his wife Marina, and his unprecedented behavior the morning of the assassination, leaving his savings and wedding ring behind, were all corroborated by Marina. As soon as she heard that the assassination shots had come from the Depository where Oswald worked, she thought her husband had probably done it, and she accepted this for years, later becoming an adherent of David Lifton's conspiracy theory. After her conversion to the Conspiracy theory, Marina stated she had been afraid of deportation to Russia, and eager to tell her interrogators what she thought they wanted to hear. She did not however claim that they had given her an elaborate structure of lies to memorize and repeat back to them.[23] Marina's story fluctuated in details; she was a quirky and unpredictable witness. But there is all the difference in the world, for instance, between telling varying stories about Oswald's rifle and making up the very existence of a rifle if she had not known he possessed one.[24]

A Colossal Conspiracy

In the early years, Conspiracy theorists used to argue that the Conspiracy need not have been on a vast scale. They maintained that it could possibly

22 Norman Mailer, *Oswald's Tale: An American Mystery* (Random House, 1995).
23 Over the years Marina—remarried, older, wiser, in no fear of deportation, and aware that our culture favors the Conspiracy theorists—has many times been questioned about whether she was pressured into saying anything that wasn't true to the Warren Commission. She has always firmly denied this, despite her latterly acquired belief that Oswald was innocent of the killings.
24 For a fresh look at this often-told story, see Thomas Mallon, *Mrs. Paine's Garage and the Murder of John F. Kennedy* (Pantheon, 2002).

have involved as few as a dozen people. This claim has gradually been abandoned. Years of close attention to all the details of the assassination have made it clear that if Oswald alone did not kill Kennedy then the majority of the physical and other evidence must have been systematically doctored or replaced, by advanced techniques not available to ordinary people, over a period of decades. This requires an immense and permanent Conspiracy.

Some Conspiracy theorists now hold that ever since the assassination there has been continual surveillance of conversations in Dealey Plaza, and continuous movement of such objects as lamp posts in order to confuse researchers.[25] Conspiracy theorists usually assume that the Conspiracy is still at work, and many believe that November 22nd 1963 was a coup d'état which installed what is now the real government of the United States, though why this inscrutable despotism should don the masks of Nixon, Carter, Reagan, and Clinton is one of its many unfathomable secrets.

Conspiracy theorists reasonably point out that not all participants in the Conspiracy would have to be aware of its real purpose. For example, some lower-level people working for the Conspiracy might have been told that Kennedy had been killed by a Communist plot, and that this had to be covered up to avoid a thermonuclear war. But then you would expect that as inquiries into the assassination progressed and became public, and as the Soviet Union staggered to its ignominious collapse, some individuals would realize they had been deceived, and would go public with any relevant information they might possess.[26] The rewards available for Conspiracy advocates greatly dwarf those of Lone Nut theorists. Fame and riches would accrue to anyone who produced a halfway plausible story about his personal involvement in the Conspiracy. Because of the transformation of the Conspiracy theory, the idea that the Mafia was a leading player in the Conspiracy has now gone out of fashion.[27] If almost all the physical and

---

25 Fetzer, *Great Zapruder Film Hoax*, pp. 223–234.
26 Many have confessed to being part of the Conspiracy, of course, just as many have confessed to being abducted by aliens, but none has produced names, dates, places, and other plausible touches.
27 Among many works promoting this theory, see G. Robert Blakey and Richard Billings, *The Plot to Kill the President* (Times Books, 1981); John H. Davis, *Mafia Kingfish: Carlos Marcello and the Assassination of John F. Kennedy* (McGraw-Hill, 1988); Seth Kantor, *Who Was Jack Ruby?* (Everest House, 1978); David Scheim, *Contract on America: The Mafia Murders of John and Robert Kennedy* (Shapolsky, 1988).

photographic evidence is a fabrication, this is obviously something way beyond the Mafia's capacities, though Conspiracy theorists usually still accord the Mafia a subordinate role.

My reproach to the Conspiracy theorists is that they don't take the Conspiracy seriously. They rarely make any sustained attempt to look at things from the Conspirators' point of view, and imagine how the Conspirators would rationally have executed their plan. Once we do this, we find that the hypothetical Conspiracy makes little sense.[28]

Typically, Conspiracy theorists chalk up any anomalies in the Lone Nut theory as plusses for the Conspiracy theory, but they are not interested in anomalies in the Conspiracy theory. The strategy of Conspiracy theorists is similar to that of defense attorneys in high-profile murder trials. Any discrepancies in the prosecution's case are given maximum emphasis, while the defense theory of what happened is not subject to the same scrutiny. The defense theory flows like wax into the cracks in the prosecution theory, and no one demands that it possess any inherent coherence comparable to that expected of a prosecution theory. In the Anglo-Saxon legal tradition, such a bias is to some extent justified, to protect the rights of the accused by the doctrine of "beyond reasonable doubt." But in historical enquiry, any such bias has no place. The only issue is which theory is best, and any theory can be evaluated only by comparing it with its strongest competitor. Both theories ought then to be given the same critical scrutiny.

Two related arguments convince me of the truth of the Lone Nut theory: 1. There was no sufficient motive for a Conspiracy to kill Kennedy, and 2. Assuming that there were such a Conspiracy, it makes no sense to conduct the assassination in the way that the Conspirators must have done.

Why kill Kennedy at all, and why do it by such a risky and gratuitously complicated method?

Where's the Motive?

Kennedy was not a wild radical and was not a serious threat to any major interest. His policies did not mark a sharp break from those of Eisenhower.

---

28 The closest approach to such an attempt is Twyman, *Bloody Treason* (currently the most impressive statement of the Conspiracy theory), pp. 25–64.

He tried to invade Cuba, bungled it, and then denied it. He went to Berlin and proclaimed: "I'm a jam donut," an eccentric remark, but not dangerous.[29] In the Cuban Missile Crisis he took the middle course favored by the majority of his cabinet,[30] which paid off in a kind of public victory. He talked of desegregation but shrank from doing much about it.

The usual claim is that Kennedy wanted to stop the US intervention in Vietnam but the evidence points the other way.[31] Aside from that factual question, people who make such a claim look at history as though the historical actors had the benefit of later hindsight. Proponents of the Vietnam war did not aim for long-drawn-out slaughter, with eventual humiliating withdrawal. If what ultimately happened in Vietnam could have been foreseen, some proponents of the war would have opposed it, while others would have argued for a radically different manner of waging it. Vietnam

29   In German, if you want to describe your profession or your citizenship, you do not use the article. "I am a Berliner" would be "Ich bin Berliner." Upon hearing someone assert "Ich bin ein Berliner," the assumption would be that the speaker was, claiming to be an object called a "Berliner," which happens to be a jam donut. Kennedy's posthumous admirers frequently dispute this serious charge of Quaylism, but they are wrong. It's clear from the context that Kennedy's speechwriter meant the sentence to be taken as "I am a citizen of Berlin," and to render this as "Ich bin ein Berliner" is most assuredly a comical error.

30   This account was widely accepted when I wrote this piece. It's now more commonly believed that Kennedy played a strong role in resisting calls for an immediate attack on Cuba.

31   There are still a few historians who oppose this conclusion, and the issue has some nuances we cannot explore here. Kennedy rapidly built up the number of "military advisers" in Vietnam from a few hundred to 16,000, then shortly before his assassination, he hesitantly agreed to the withdrawal of 1,000 of these, based on the mistaken premise that the South Vietnamese government (which had just been replaced in a Kennedy-instigated coup) was successfully subduing the insurgents. The general view, shared by Kennedy, Johnson, and nearly everyone else in ruling circles, was that it would be desirable to pull US troops out of Vietnam provided that the South Vietnamese regime could crush the Vietcong rebels. Some maintain that, faced with the new situation encountered by Johnson, which posed the no-longer-avoidable choice of either hugely increasing American military commitment or acquiescing in the loss of South Vietnam to the Communists, Kennedy would have made the latter choice whereas we know that Johnson did make the former. But the Conspirators could not have known either of these decisions (the actual or the counterfactual) in advance. We do know that Johnson's advisors who favored escalation of the war when that situation arose (including McNamara, Rusk, and McGeorge Bundy) were without exception former Kennedy men.

became highly divisive in American politics later; it was not highly divisive in 1963, and nobody knew that it would become so, any more than people today suppose that Liberia will be the dominant American political issue in 2008.

When Kennedy was killed, the presidential election was less than a year away, and it was entirely possible he would not be re-elected. What was so urgent about immediately getting rid of Kennedy, who might lose the election in 1964? Why not wait and see? And if some policy of Kennedy's really were felt to be so appalling, why wouldn't an immensely powerful Conspiracy instead blackmail this eminently blackmailable politician—or, rather than blackmail him, simply terminate his political career by making some of his private life public? Twyman argues (*Bloody Treason*, p. 34) that exposure could not be used because this "would have brought down both Lyndon Johnson and J. Edgar Hoover along with the Kennedys." So, if the public had been made aware of Kennedy's sexual activities in the White House, the Kennedys would have retaliated by publicizing, for example, Hoover's homosexuality and ties to organized crime, but the Kennedys would not retaliate in this way if Jack were murdered? And Hoover's control of files and agents sufficient to falsify almost all the evidence in the assassination case would not have enabled him to eliminate evidence of his active homosexuality (evidence which has still not turned up, this being a matter of surmise) and suitably doctor the records of his contacts with organized crime?

Twyman's implicit counter to this line of reasoning is to lay all the emphasis on the supposition that with Kennedy's re-election, Hoover and Johnson would be out of office and therefore impotent. But does this really work? A re-elected Kennedy asks for Hoover's resignation and Hoover (with all his loyal people in the upper echelons of the FBI, beginning with his presumed lover Assistant Director Clyde Tolson) responds that if he does not keep his job, items x, y, and z will be fed to the press. At that point Kennedy holds no cards, and withdraws the request for resignation. The Kennedy White House could never take on the FBI in a blackmailing contest. Furthermore, as Twyman fully acknowledges, Hoover and Johnson are not enough: other powerful interests have to be in the Conspiracy.

Judging by what actually occurred following the assassination, the likely political motive for a Conspiracy would have been to ensure that civil rights and racial integration were rammed through by the more resolute Johnson. But this motive is not popular with Conspiracy theorists, and it is, of course, preposterous. Why would high-level intelligence operatives favor acceleration of these policies so strongly that they would be willing to kill the president?

There did not exist a sufficiently powerful motive for the killing of Kennedy. There are always people who want the president out of the way, and Lyndon Johnson is the natural suspect, especially as the Kennedys might have succeeded in replacing him as vice president. But mere personal ambition or animus cannot account for a Conspiracy on so huge a scale. If Johnson were behind the hypothetical Conspiracy, he would need the collaboration of highly-placed intelligence chiefs, and no one has suggested a credible motive for such people to want Kennedy replaced with Johnson, and to want this so desperately they would kill the president.

Mark Lane has proposed that Kennedy planned to dismantle the Central Intelligence Agency, and that therefore the CIA had him killed.[32] The direct evidence that this was Kennedy's intention is flimsy,[33] and Kennedy took no steps to accomplish it, which presumably explains why those who advance this theory believe that he was planning to do it only after the 1964 election.[34] Again, the CIA would merely have had to make public one percent of what was known by insiders about Kennedy's private life to render him instantly un-re-electable.

---

32   Lane, *Plausible Denial: Was the CIA Involved in the Assassination of JFK?* (Thunder's Mouth Press, 1991), especially pp. 91–114.

33   It largely consists of the uncorroborated reminiscences of the fanciful L. Fletcher Prouty, former Pentagon liaison officer to the CIA and the real-life model for the Donald Sutherland character in *JFK*.

34   For an excellent refutation of Kennedy as a Vietnam dove, Kennedy as anti-CIA, and similar legends, see Noam Chomsky, *Rethinking Camelot: JFK, the Vietnam War, and U.S. Political Culture* (South End Press, 1993). Chomsky points out, pp. 144–45, that Johnson was more down on the CIA than Kennedy, and Nixon more so than Johnson. Note, however, that the anti-Conspiracy argument from motive does not have to show what Kennedy would have done, but something much weaker: that the Conspirators could not have been confident in advance that Kennedy would concede defeat in Vietnam while Johnson would not, that Kennedy would abolish the CIA while Johnson would not, and so forth.

An Over-Complex Plot

Let's now assume that a sufficient motive existed and that a Conspiracy to kill Kennedy was indeed planned. Why, on those assumptions, would the Conspirators choose to conduct the assassination in the manner in which it was supposedly conducted?

If we assume that all the evidence which seems to point to Oswald (the ballistics evidence, the eye-witness evidence, the autopsy records, the palm-prints and fingerprints, Oswald's purchase of the rifle, the Zapruder film, Oswald's unusual behavior the day of the assasination) is faked, that Oswald was entirely innocent,[35] we can develop a scenario which explains the apparent evidence against Oswald as the work of the Conspirators. We can always do this with any crime, provided we postulate a Conspiracy sufficiently powerful. All difficulties can be dissolved by asserting that the available evidence has been falsified, even if the means to do so would border on the supernatural.

But if we begin differently, assume that there was a powerful and far-sighted Conspiracy to kill Kennedy, and then ask how the Conspirators would set about their task, we encounter serious problems in explaining why they would decide to handle things the way they are supposed to have done. Take Lifton's theory that Kennedy's body was stolen and the wounds altered, so that front-entry wounds were made to look like rear-entry wounds. (Some such theory is essential for a Conspiracy, because the autopsy pictures are incompatible with anything other than two shots hitting Kennedy from the rear.) Lifton volunteers that the alteration of the dead man's wounds could only have been planned well ahead of time. Surgical teams had to be standing by ready to alter the wounds. The body had to be stolen and then switched back, and despite the fact that, according to Lifton, it arrived at Bethesda with different wrappings and in a different coffin, all the people most directly involved had to be made to swear that the body, its wrappings, and its casket were exactly the same when they arrived at Bethesda as whe

---

35   When arrested, Oswald claimed to be "a patsy." Whatever his motive for saying this, it should be considered along with uncontroversially false statements he made at the same time: for example that he had not used an assumed name when renting a room in Oak Cliff.

they had left Parkland. This prodigy of prestidigitation, worthy of an army of Houdinis, must have been planned with extraordinary precision, and with innumerable alternative plans to take account of the various uncontrollable twists and turns that events might take.

Yet it could not avoid being risky. And it was all required for one reason and one reason only: to make front-entry wounds look like rear-entry wounds. But why would intelligent conspirators take this tack at all? They must have planned the operation so that they would be compelled to accomplish the extraordinary feat of snitching the cadaver and altering the wounds, not to mention falsifying all the film, photographic, and ballistics evidence, when they could far more easily have planned it so that this problem just didn't arise.

If you're writing a murder mystery, it's good to construct a deceptive *mise en scène* which baffles the reader, but you have to guard against the narrative weakness of having the murderer do things just to make the story more engrossing. What the murderer does has to be credible given the murderer's aims and beliefs, and it's a badly constructed mystery story in which the murderer betrays the altruistic aim of helping the author by executing an ingenious plot purely for its entertainment value.

Making Things Difficult

Why did the Conspirators decide to shoot the president from a different direction than the one posited in the official public account? The Conspirators would not want to mislead us about the direction of the shots, except as this furthered their Conspiracy, but to read the Conspiracy theorists you might think that misleading us about the direction of the shots was an evil end in itself. If the Conspirators did mislead us about the direction of the shots, this must have been because they freely chose to plan the assassination in such a way that they would have to mislead us about the direction of the shots, and there is no credible reason for them to make this choice, as they could have much more easily arranged to allow the shots to appear to come from the direction they did in fact come from.[36]

---

36 Twyman claims that in order to persuade the real assassins that they would be able to escape alive, it was necessary for the shots of the decoy or patsy to come from some-

Similarly, Conspiracy theorists assume that there were numerous shooters in Dealey Plaza. To intelligent Conspirators possessed of vast resources, this would have appeared as a stupidly redundant complication. One well-aimed shot is all it takes, or two or three indifferently aimed ones. Fictional assassinations inspired by the Conspiracy theory, such as *The Parallax View* (1974), generally involve just one shot, revealing the film-maker's intuitive grasp of what makes for a believable assassination Conspiracy.

The method of reconstructing what would be likely to happen given the Conspiracy theorists' assumptions can be applied to minor details as well as to the broad framework of the assassination. We then see that flaws in the evidence which supposedly point to a Conspiracy would never have been permitted to appear if there really had been a Conspiracy. For example, Conspiracy theorists have always made much of the fact that pathologist Dr. James Humes copied out his original autopsy notes and then burned them. Humes says that the notes were covered with Kennedy's blood. Anxious to avoid sensational exploitation, he made a copy and destroyed the original. If Humes were lying about the copy being true to the original, because the original contained material pointing to a Conspiracy, why would Humes admit the copy was not the original? Why let on that the original had been burned?

The biologist J.B.S. Haldane was asked what he had learned from a lifetime's study of the natural world about the mind and character of its Creator. He gave the unexpected reply: "An inordinate fondness for beetles." If we ask ourselves what we can discern about the motives and aptitudes of the Conspirators from studying their handiwork, the answer must be: an all-consuming passion for doing everything in the most difficult and costly way imaginable.

---

where else. But a little thought will show that this is not the case. After all, Oswald left the Depository and got well away, despite Twyman's belief that the Conspirators planned to have him bumped off at that point. If Oswald had kept away from his known haunts, and acquired a suit, a hat, and $50, this rank amateur would probably have made it as far as Mexico. How much easier it would have been to secure the escape of the assassins if there had been a faked gunfight, leading to the patsy's immediate death and therefore the speedy public acceptance that the sniper was no longer at large. The obvious disguise for the real assassins would have been as police or Secret Service, and getting them away would have been fairly straightforward.

Picture the first planning meeting of the Conspirators. "So that's carried then, nem. con. We'll kill the president. Please come to order; we have a lot of business to get through. Thank you. Next item, gentlemen, how do we do it? Anyone got any ideas? Chair recognizes the gentleman from Langley."

Well, we could kill him, as the motorcade comes through Dealey Plaza. This would be real neat[37] because we would do it in full view of hundreds of people. Just for the hell of it, we could place several shooters in positions where they might be easily spotted, and put our non-shooting patsy in a terrific concealed position where he could hardly miss. Then we could have our patsy run around all over the place, trusting to luck that he would not do anything which would give him an alibi, have him shoot a policeman and then have him picked up, and shot later by a loony strip club owner. Meanwhile, we would be stealing the body of the president, having a crack team of surgeons alter the wounds so that the shots would seem to have come from the patsy's location. We would also make sure we got our hands on the hundreds of still photographs and the several movies of this event, and substitute fakes which we would have prudently concocted in advance, and we would remove all the real bullets and substitute fake ones. . . . How am I doing?

Surely this guy's career as a Conspirator would be over at that point. I have heard some dumb suggestions in meetings, but this one fairly bristles with absurdities. If you're going to shoot the president in public and frame an innocent patsy, you obviously have the patsy killed right away, in fact probably before the assassination, though the story would be that he was killed in an exchange of fire immediately afterwards. The public would readily have accepted that it was necessary to shoot the sniper. The mere fact that Oswald was free to move around at will at the time of the assassination goes against the hypothesis that he was a preselected fall guy. The actual shooting of the president would of course be done from the patsy's real

37   This is around 1962, remember.

location (or at least what could be represented as such), and if for some unknown reason you wanted the real assassins to be somewhere else, you wouldn't put them in an exposed public place like the Grassy Knoll, where anyone might stumble upon them.

A well-conducted Conspiracy would not merely plan for what actually happened, since this would be uncertain before the event. The Conspiracy would plan for what conceivably might happen. For example, if there had been a sniper on the Grassy Knoll, he might so easily have been caught unambiguously on film, and the filmer might have published the film before it could be intercepted by the FBI or Secret Service.[38] This is just one of many possible accidents which could not be ruled out. Their possibility would occur to any prudent Conspirator and this would guarantee that he would never be so careless as to put a shooter on the Knoll.

The Conspiracy must have included highly placed people in intelligence and law enforcement. These would naturally tend to come up with a scenario where intelligence and law enforcement personnel would look at least competent. Confusion, sloppiness, and lack of direction on the parts of the FBI, the Secret Service, and even the police would tend to be eliminated at the planning stage. But all these are rife in the actual playing out of the events in Dallas forty years ago.[39]

38 Conspiracy theorists claim that shooters can be discerned in photographs of the foliage at the top of the Knoll. See for instance the photographs in Fetzer, *Great Zapruder Film Hoax*, pp. 50–53.

39 One of the more general conclusions arising from my rejection of the Assassination Conspiracy is that any high-level Conspiracy to create an enormous web of falsehood about specific, concrete occurrences is by no means child's play. When the US invaded Iraq this year, Bush asserted that Iraq possessed newly developed weapons of mass destruction ready for immediate delivery against other countries. This was a calculated lie, but the administration probably supposed that these imaginary WMD would be forgotten after a brief and successful war, as the nonexistent Kosovo "mass graves" were forgotten after Nato's occupation of Kosovo, and as Bush's other big lie, that Saddam Hussein had something to do with 9/11, was in fact forgotten. When the issue wouldn't go away after the American occupation of Iraq, the question arises why the administration didn't simply plant some of its own WMD in Iraq. The answer is that this would be difficult and risky: it could not be done without quite a number of people knowing that the object was public deception, and this operation might later be exposed. This doesn't, of course, imply that such a massive operation of deception could never happen or never has happened, merely that it would be difficult and risky, and less likely under a liberal-democratic than under a totalitarian political system.

Why a Public Shooting?

If we accept the premise that a public shooting might be the Conspirators' chosen method, many of the details are incomprehensible. But why would the Conspirators opt for a public shooting? In the movie *Godfather III* (1990), Pope John Paul I is assassinated. I don't know whether he really was or not, but the depicted method of the assassination is highly plausible. Something was slipped into his morning coffee and the public never learned that the death was other than natural. Surely this is the kind of thing we expect from a formidable, intelligently conducted Conspiracy.

One assassin acting alone is a Lone Nut. Two or three assassins acting together is a weak Conspiracy. Even a much larger number can still be judged weak if the Conspiracy has little or no access to people in political administration, police, or intelligence. A public shooting is the preferred method of a Lone Nut or a weak Conspiracy. This method might therefore be selected by a powerful Conspiracy which wished to represent the killing as done by a Lone Nut or a weak Conspiracy.

Twyman conjectures that the Conspirators wanted to lay the blame for the assassination on Cuban Communists,[40] but there are two difficulties with that hypothesis. Granted that the Conspirators would like to incriminate Castro in some way, it doesn't follow that they would make the assassination thousands of times more costly by tying it to this incrimination exercise. And if they were setting up Oswald as a Cuban agent, why is there no prima facie evidence of this Oswald role? The paper trail indicates that Oswald was pro-Castro and at one point wanted to move to Cuba, but was rebuffed by the Cuban authorities. The Oswald-Cuba relationship was entirely one-sided. The Conspirators oddly failed to plant any evidence showing Oswald's links with the Cuban government, or for that matter his involvement in any type of Conspiracy. In an elementary oversight, the Conspirators did not even ensure that Oswald came into any money; he was always close to broke.

Kennedy had fleeting sexual encounters with hundreds of partners and longer-term sexual relationships with a dozen more. It would have been a simple matter to supply him with an attractive and willing woman in the

---

40   *Bloody Treason*, pp. 57, 832.

pay of the Conspiracy.[41] He took drugs for his complicated and dangerous medical conditions, as well as for recreational purposes. There are poisons which mimic the effects of natural diseases, and which would not be detected unless foul play were suspected and a deliberate search for traces of those specific poisons were made. If Kennedy had really been murdered by an immensely powerful Conspiracy, he would have passed away serenely in his sleep from seemingly natural causes, and we would never have heard of Lee Oswald or Jack Ruby, let alone Clay Shaw and David Ferrie.

EDITOR'S NOTE: The above article purports to be the work of the Lone Nut David Ramsay Steele (notice the three names). Some allege there is evidence of a Second Writer, who wrote parts of the article from a diametrically opposite direction. The article was then intercepted while on its way to *Liberty* by email, and surgically modified by skillful insertion of the opposing arguments. Skeptics retort that Steele's troubled history of confused and contradictory reasoning is notorious. We take no position on the matter, but we do feel obliged to point out that on the day this article was submitted, one of our editors had a bad cold. The odds against this being pure coincidence have been estimated at 800 trillion to one. If you look closely at a photograph of Steele, you will eventually begin to notice a striking resemblance to the foliage at the top of the Grassy Knoll. Evidently there is much more here than meets the eye, and the case is still wide open.

Liberty, November 2003

---

41 Kennedy's henchmen would not permit the Secret Service even to quickly check the purses of the new prostitutes who were supplied to Kennedy daily. Seymour M. Hersh, *The Dark Side of Camelot* (Little, Brown, 1997), p. 229. But even without such lax security, getting a female assassin into close personal contact with Kennedy would have been many times less costly than arranging for a shooter on the Grassy Knoll. An incidental benefit of the former method is that if assassination were ever suspected, the White House staff would have had a powerful self-interested motive to cover up the circumstances of the killing, to protect themselves from public disgrace.

8
THE SACRED ELEMENT (2003)

Listen children, this story is more than just true. It's true many times over, for the very same sequence of events has happened thousands of times on different worlds.

Once upon a time there was a well-positioned planet endowed with much carbon. And sure enough, on this planet there developed a marvelous array of living organisms. Out of these myriads of species, there emerged, by a succession of lucky accidents, one intelligent animal, with the capacity for building civilization and the indefinite development of knowledge. So far, so good.

As these intelligent animals exulted in their technological and artistic achievements, they little suspected that a terrible, malign force was pitilessly draining away the life's blood from their world. They were living in a shadowy and attenuated time, the darkness of death closing in on the biosphere, the light of life sputtering feebly amid the encircling gloom.

Of course you all know the explanation. For millions of years of evolution, countless living organisms had been dying every day, and some of these dead organisms became trapped deep in the planet's crust, their precious carbon locked out of circulation. Since biomass is fixed by the quantity of available carbon, the continual removal of carbon spells shrinkage and degeneration.

Left to itself, life automatically eliminates the conditions for its own existence, though thankfully it does so quite slowly. Occasional volcanic eruptions do liberate some carbon, but this is a mere trifle compared with the enormous losses inflicted by the formation of peat, coal, and petroleum deposits. Forests are the number one menace to life, for any tree will eventually die, and who can say what will then become of its priceless carbon?

A momentary reprieve came along when some of the intelligent animals began to dig for coal and drill for oil and gas. They thought only of the profits to be earned by providing their fellow species-members with cheaper fuel, but unbeknownst to themselves, they were benefitting their own population and their biosphere in an entirely different way. By liberating the imprisoned carbon, they helped—though this was no part of their intention—to counteract the insidious shriveling of the biomass.

But these intelligent animals soon abandoned fossil fuels—while the vast bulk of the lost carbon still lay entombed beneath the planet's surface. Nuclear, solar, and other forms of energy completely superseded oil and coal, when only a minute proportion of the carboniferous deposits had been reclaimed for the benefit of life. The March of Death recommenced!

Eventually, however, a few of these intelligent animals—on our world we know them as the Six Prophets—began to preach the revolutionary new idea, though to us it is common sense, that carbon must be disinterred from the geological graveyard if life is to fulfill its potential. The holy cult of carbon redemption was born: the saints pledged themselves to donate a sixth of their income to extract coal and oil, solemnly oxidizing these organic minerals in magnificent public rituals and also in millions of humble household shrines.

New coal mines and oil wells were created, far more than in the days of fossil fuels, with the single intention of resurrecting these substances and reclaiming their carbon to sustain the living world. It was soon realized that it was often easier to pump oxygen down below and burn the deposits where they lay, but millions of tons and barrels were brought to the surface so that the devout could personally witness their reclamation. The liberation of carbon became the biggest of charities, and later (when every individual had become immensely wealthy by primitive standards), the sole charity, the last surviving philanthropic "good cause."

In our world, this all happened a long time ago. The observable benefits have been spectacular, even over just the last six thousand years. Our climate is more lovely and more temperate. The sky is bluer and the rain finer. The air is filled with the bright plumage of wondrous new birds. Vegetation springs up everywhere with an eager rapidity that would have astonished our ancestors, the dazzling effulgence of its emerald verdure far outshining the drab coloration of earlier times.

The redemption of carbon has already created a worldly paradise, yet the great work has barely begun. Our machines have sniffed out every ounce of coal, oil, and diamonds for thousands of meters below the surface, they continue to go deeper—and there are vast reserves of limestone, chalk, and marble down there, just waiting to be converted.

We award our most distinguished medals and our most prestigious prizes to those members of our species who redeem lost carbon and restore it to the living world, thereby triumphing over death. And that's why we're going out today, children, for six hours, to watch the ceremonial burning. For today, the Sixth of June, is Carbon Redemption Day, or Life Day, the most glorious holiday in our calendar. The redemption of carbon is a voluntary act, a noble deed of unsullied virtue. No pastime is more strictly righteous. "All religion is folly save only the sacrament of carbon redeemed and life amplified" (Third Prophet, 46:656).

Children, you are now six years old, and you may look back on this day as the most momentous of your lives. The torch of life now passes to you. No one can make you dedicate your life to burning fossilized mineral compounds. Only you can decide, of your own free will, to undertake that heroic commitment for the benefit of future life on this planet and its many far-flung colonies.

I know that you are good children and that all six of you will do your bit to save the planet. Please don't let me down. Now let's go and have fun watching all that wonderful smoke. A happy Life Day to one and all!

Liberty, March 2003

9

LIFE, LIBERTY, AND THE TREADMILL (2005)

Gregg Easterbrook, *The Progress Paradox: How Life Gets Better While People Feel Worse*. New York: Random House, 2003.

Barry Schwartz, *The Paradox of Choice: Why More Is Less*. New York: Harper-Collins, 2004.

Raymond Angelo Belliotti, *Happiness Is Overrated*. Lanham: Rowman and Littlefield, 2004.

I can remember the day I learned to ride a bike. I must have been about eight. In those days, at least in that part of England, there were no such things as training wheels and the smallest bicycles had twenty-four-inch wheels. I just kept pushing, wobbling, and gliding along, and suddenly, I could do it!

The sun came out from behind a cloud and the entire world shone with warm and radiant delight. Every day for the next few weeks, I spent hours just cycling up and down or round and round in circles. Could there be anything to beat this?

Six months later I was still pleased I could ride a bike, and I still got some direct fulfillment out of this activity, but I would not have dreamed of riding around just for the sheer pleasure of it—not for more than a couple of minutes, anyhow. Cycling had become about ninety-eight percent instrumental, a way to get from one place to another, and only about two percent intrinsically gratifying.

This well-known phenomenon, called "adaptation," is key to the thinking of psychologists who maintain that our level of happiness is a "set point" to which we always tend to return, largely irrespective of our circumstances. Typically, we look forward to some consummation, and when we achieve it, we're pleased. From that moment on, the glow of gratification dims like dying embers. It's essential to being human that the joy resulting from the attainment of any goal starts to fade as soon as it begins.

Most people believe that if their real income were to be suddenly doubled, they would feel a lot happier. And so they would, for the first week or two. After that, the happiness would have perceptibly diminished, and six months or a year later, they would be only slightly happier than before their financial improvement.

And it works in reverse. People who go blind or deaf, lose their limbs, or become paralyzed are usually acutely miserable for a month or two, after which the gloom begins to evaporate. A year later, they are approximately as happy as they were before they were afflicted. Research indicates that people with extreme physical disabilities are, on average, slightly happier than the general population.

We were made by millions of years of natural selection of genes. From a gene's point of view, the happiness of the organism which temporarily houses the gene is not an end in itself. The gene 'wants' its host organism to reproduce, which entails surviving for at least a while, the longer the better if repeated reproduction is possible.

It's advantageous for pleasure to be associated with successful action, and pleasure often tends to promote happiness. But pleasure too intense and too prolonged might be detrimental. If we now have something we have wanted, and we know we can keep it, what would be the point of perpetual euphoria? It could distract us from the immediate tasks of survival and reproduction. Continual misery would be pointlessly distracting too. It's entirely authentic, as well as poignant, that the slave-labor-camp inmate protagonist at the end of the harrowing *One Day in the Life of Ivan Denisovich*, reflects that, all in all, this has been a pretty good day.

Is Progress Pointless?

All this is straightforward, and not even controversial, but it does raise an interesting issue with political implications. Liberals, and especially that subspecies of liberals known as libertarians, tend to accept as a premiss that *it's good for people to be able to get what they want.* If asked why, we are apt to say, with the framers of the United States Constitution, that only then can people pursue happiness. This can easily lead to the reasoning: *it's good for people to be able to get what they want, because if they get what they want, they will be happier than if they don't.*

But what if having more of what we want does not ultimately add to our happiness? What if the pursuit of happiness is a "hedonic treadmill," as some psychologists have contended? In recent years a lot of research has gone into finding out how happy people actually are and what makes them happy or unhappy. Some of the conclusions of this research suggest that increasing real incomes—increasing ability to get what we want—does not make us very much happier, once we have passed a certain minimum level of comfort. What, then, is the point of further industrial and technological progress?

This question has been raised in a number of recent writings, most influentially in Lane's book, *The Loss of Happiness in Market Democracies*.[1] Easterbrook's work is a more popular treatment of the same issues. Both Lane and Easterbrook start from the finding that Americans in the 1990s were no more happy, and perhaps even a bit less happy, than they were in the 1950s, although real incomes had way more than doubled in that period. Lane refers to the "paradox of apparently growing unhappiness in the midst of increasing plenty" (Lane, p. 4), a theme echoed in Easterbrook's more popular work. Contrast this with the 1930s complaint of 'poverty in the midst of plenty'. It's hard to uncover real old-fashioned poverty in twenty-first-century America, but it's easy to find any amount of dissatisfaction.

Ascertaining how happy people are is mainly a question of asking them, and it may be doubted whether this is always perfectly reliable. However, the results of numerous questionnaires, painstakingly designed and scrupulously interpreted, exhibit a consistency, a stability, and a clear pattern which suggest that people's happiness self-ratings are generally quite accurate.[2] Various attempts have been made to check the results (for instance by comparing individuals' self-ratings with the ratings of those individuals by people who know them) and they look quite solid. I'm convinced that

1   Robert E. Lane, *The Loss of Happiness in Market Democracies* (New Haven: Yale University Press, 2000).

2   Ed Diener and Eunkook M. Suh, eds., *Culture and Subjective Well-Being* (Cambridge, Massachusetts: MIT Press, 2000), pp. 5–7.

the data emerging from these studies do indeed measure happiness (or SWB, subjective well-being, as it's known in the trade).

If these studies of SWB are at all accurate, then there has been little, if any, gain in happiness in advanced industrial countries of the West over the past half-century. In the United States, people are no happier than they were in the 1950s. To be more precise, the percentage reporting themselves as just "happy" is close to identical in the 1990s and the 1950s, while the percentage in the "very happy" category has fallen slightly, and the percentage classified as "depressed" has increased.

The Specter of Futility

Easterbrook starts out with impressive boldness and clarity. He makes two assertions: 1. that in almost every measurable respect, life for nearly everyone in the western world has been getting better at a spectacular rate, and 2. that people's happiness or satisfaction with their lives has stayed about the same or slightly diminished. Both of these claims are well documented by an accumulation of interesting and often surprising facts, which Easterbrook presents skillfully and entertainingly.

Easterbrook poses his "paradox" boldly, but as his book continues, the thrust of the argument falters. Just over halfway through the book, Easterbrook switches to throwing out a number of conjectures about influences which might account for the loss of happiness, along with his policy solutions. He voices the usual leftist gripes about consumer capitalism, though the relation of these to the findings of SWB research may be tenuous. He is furious at greedy CEOs, and favors raising the minimum wage, imposing universal health insurance, and increasing foreign aid. These chapters are still well-written and they contain nuggets of fascinating information, but they do not resolve or even seriously confront the ominous "paradox" he has laid out at the beginning.

Easterbrook, like Lane, makes the most of the startling juxtaposition of declining happiness and increasing affluence, and doesn't want to spoil a good story by drawing too much attention to considerations which might blur the stark drama of this incongruous outcome. Neither author gives the reader even an outline of the basic facts from which a few items have been plucked for close attention.

Lane actually volunteers that he does not place any reliance on the declining SWB trend, and wouldn't be surprised to see it reversed.[3] This admission contrasts strangely with the strident rhetoric of *decline* and *loss* in Lane's book. Granted, the fact that the amount of happiness has been roughly the same and has not increased, while incomes have made spectacular gains, is notable enough to be well worth discussing. But if we take *The Loss of Happiness in Market Democracies* and substitute some word like 'conservation' or 'stability' for 'loss', it would not have the requisite quality of 'Man bites dog'. The same applies to Easterbrook's subtitle, *How Life Gets Better While People Feel Worse*. "How Life Gets Better While People Feel about the Same" would be more defensible, and still quite intriguing, though less of a shock.

Most People Are Happy!

By far the biggest and most imposing fact to emerge from the empirical studies of SWB is that a substantial majority of people in advanced capitalist cultures are happy.[4] In Easterbrook's and Lane's books, and a number of other writings, there is so much emphasis on the disquieting fact that the amount of happiness has not increased, and may even have slightly declined, that one is apt to lose sight of the mundane fact that *over eighty percent of people in advanced industrial countries rate themselves as more happy than unhappy*.[5]

This is worth italicizing because it is so frequently denied. Down the centuries, innumerable sages have opined that most people were not happy.

---

3   "My argument does not depend on the evidence of growing unhappiness in the postwar period (which may be a mere blip in a long-term curve)" (Lane, p. 5). The rhetoric of "growing unhappiness and depression" is heavy throughout his book, but if his argument really does not depend on this, it must depend on the mere fact that there is some remaining unhappiness in "market democracies," even though this is less than in any other kind of social order.

4   A good source for recent findings in this area is Diener and Suh, which I draw upon freely here. Useful background for some of the psychological and methodological issues is Daniel Kahneman, Ed Diener, and Norbert Schwartz, eds., *Well-Being: The Foundations of Hedonic Psychology* (New York: Russell Sage Foundation, 1999).

5   Eighty-five percent of people in the U.S. are above the neutral mid-point between unhappiness and happiness (Ed Diener and C. Diener, "Most People Are Happy," *Psychological Science* 7 [1996]), and the corresponding number for several European countries is higher.

In his 1930 classic, *The Conquest of Happiness*, Bertrand Russell asserted that very few people were happy, a fact he inferred from the expressions on the faces of people in the street.[6] From all that we know now, it seems inescapable that the majority of the readers of that book were happier than its author, at least in the 1930s. (In his nineties, convinced that the world was overwhelmingly likely to be destroyed in a thermonuclear conflagration, Russell became extremely happy, illustrating both adaptation to a set point regardless of perceived circumstances and the common pattern of individuals growing steadily more serene with age.)

Thomas Szasz has famously defined happiness as "An imaginary condition, formerly attributed by the living to the dead, now usually attributed by adults to children and by children to adults."[7] Most readers take this as an amusing overstatement of a truism. There prevails a strong tradition for intellectuals to believe that ordinary people are incapable of happiness, or at least of 'true' happiness, as well as being wretched and not even truly alive.[8]

Facts about Happiness

Another downplayed fact is that *people in rich countries are, on average, much happier than people in poor countries.*[9]

Surely it is in the light of these huge general findings—that the great majority of people are happy and that people in developed countries are happier than people in less developed countries—that we ought to look at the extremely interesting possibility that aggregate happiness in the United States may have declined slightly.

Here are some other assorted facts to emerge from the SWB research.

Older people have higher SWB than younger people,[10] a fact all the more significant because it is an aggregate outcome which presumably has

6   Bertrand Russell, *The Conquest of Happiness* (New York: Liveright, 1930), p. 13.

7   *The Untamed Tongue* (Chicago: Open Court, 1990), p. 139, though this *bon mot* had appeared in print earlier.

8   See John Carey, *The Intellectuals and the Masses: Pride and Prejudice among the Literary Intelligentsia, 1880–1939* (Chicago: Academy Chicago, 2002).

9   Diener and Oishi, in Diener and Suh, pp. 198–201.

10   According to some studies, older people are slightly less "happy" but more "satisfied with life." SWB usually averages different entities like this. I skip over these distinctions here.

to include gains in SWB more than enough to compensate for some cases of acute misery caused by terminal disease. Men are almost exactly as happy as women, though women experience more extremes of happiness and misery (one of the exceptional cases where women go to extremes more than men do). American blacks are just about as happy as American whites.

Consistently cohabiting married people of either sex are happier than the divorced, the separated, or the never-married. Analysis of the data suggests that the causality runs in both directions: being married makes you more happy and being happy makes you get and stay married. Churchgoers are slightly happier than non-churchgoers. Ethnic diversity within a country is not associated with higher or lower happiness.

The happiest populations in the world are the people in Scandinavia, Netherlands, and Switzerland, though the United States and most other wealthy countries are not very far behind. From all that we know, it seems a reasonable surmise that the present populations of Scandinavia, Netherlands, and Switzerland are very close to being, and may actually be, the happiest sizeable populations that have ever existed in human history, and not very distant from the maximum aggregate happiness attainable in any large population, absent some future biological or other revolutionary breakthrough.

Both within and between countries, high-income people are happier than low-income people, though the advantage becomes very slight above a quite modest level of income. Although "more money" is definitely associated with high SWB, individuals preoccupied with money-making tend to be less happy than those who seek fulfillment in other ways. Gregarious, extraverted types are happier than loners.

There are wide variations in SWB among different populations, independent of income. Some very poor tribal cultures, such as the Maasai of East Africa, are not far below the affluent world in SWB, while within that affluent world there are very sizeable differences between countries. The populations of Japan, Italy, and France are distinctly less happy than their level of income would predict. People in the Irish Republic have been consistently happier than people in Germany, which until recently had twice Ireland's real income per head. (Rapid growth in Ireland and slow growth in Germany have been closing the gap in incomes.) Adjusting for income, Hispanic people are the happiest broad segment of world population, while Asians are the least happy.

Within countries, very low-income people are on average decidedly less happy than people of modest income or above, but high-income people are not tremendously happier than middling-income people. The very rich are indeed happier than the average for the population, but only by a small margin.

A common prejudice among intellectuals is that people generally want higher incomes primarily because this will improve their status relative to other people. While many writers are so convinced of this theory that they often assert it in blithe disregard of the facts, the SWB research does not afford the theory much comfort. For instance, poor people in rich countries are decidedly happier than poor people in poor countries. In fact, living in a rich or poor country has a stronger effect on your SWB than being rich or poor yourself. "Inequality" does not reduce happiness (Diener and Oishi, in Diener and Suh, pp. 205–07).[11] Detailed studies show that, for example, people of moderate income are equally happy whether they live in predominantly poor or predominantly affluent areas.

A view compatible with the data is that if you're poor, more income will enable you to become appreciably happier, but once a quite modest level of income has been achieved, further increases will bring very little greater happiness. (Money does buy happiness, but for most people in advanced industrial cultures, it takes a lot of money to buy a tiny increment of happiness.) This general result could be explained in a number of different ways. For instance, it could be that all the components of real income begin to plateau, as regards conduciveness to happiness, once a modest income level has been reached. Or it could be that one or two key components of income do all the heavy lifting with respect to happiness, and once consumption of these goods has reached a certain point, any further income increments go to goods which don't add to long-run happiness. As with so many puzzles in this area, empirical work may soon provide a definitive answer.

Liberty Promotes Happiness

It used to be thought that people in "individualist" cultures are happier than people in "collectivist" cultures, but one major study has failed to

---

11   The data actually show that there is more happiness with greater inequality. Diener and Oishi decide to abstain from any causal inference on this point.

confirm this and it is now in doubt, though most SWB theorists still seem to hold to it. Individualism and collectivism in this context do not relate to the system of industrial ownership or administration. They are terms employed by sociologists and social psychologists to distinguish cultures which value individual self-realization from those which lay more emphasis on group solidarity. Thus, Japan and South Korea are classed as collectivist cultures.

At any rate, people in individualist countries, contrary to the folklore of intellectuals, don't appear to be any less happy than people in collectivist countries (though it could reasonably be contended that people in collectivist cultures would be more inhibited about highlighting their own feelings, and would therefore tend to have a downward bias in rating their own happiness).

Freedom generates happiness. Veenhoven classified three kinds of freedom: economic, political, and private. He found that all are correlated with happiness, but economic freedom much more so than political or private freedom. Veenhoven candidly remarks: "This is a pleasant surprise for the right-wing free market lobby but a disappointment for liberals like me" (Veenhoven, in Diener and Suh, p. 276).

Economic freedom does not merely contribute to happiness by raising incomes; controlling for income, economic freedom still clearly promotes SWB, a fact which seems to puzzle Veenhoven. I see nothing puzzling here. To most people economic freedom is the very substance of their lives as creative, purposive beings. Compared to the option of living and working where you please, at whatever occupation you wish, doing what you choose to do without permission from anyone on high, the liberty to vote in elections or to pass out leaflets on the street is, for the great majority of folks, rather a minor consideration, especially in poor countries.

As Veenhoven suggests, the strong positive association between freedom, especially "economic" freedom, and happiness will very likely turn out to be even stronger, because his results are heavily affected by the temporary situation in post-Communist countries, which possess some freshly-won freedoms but are currently undergoing a historically brief, acutely painful industrial transition.

Veenhoven's results refute the familiar conservative contention that freedom reduces human well-being by atomizing individuals, by inducing anomie, by imposing a crushing burden of responsibilities, by removing the security of fixed status, or by offering a vertiginous variety of choices. The findings also refute the related view that people cannot benefit from freedom until they have been sufficiently prepared. Rich or poor, ready or not, people feel better if they are more free. They do not suffer by being cut loose from traditional folkways or from the kindly direction of their betters, or if they do, they somehow find more than adequate consolations for these losses.

Some popular legends have become casualties of the SWB research. The "midlife crisis" is a myth: on average, emotional crises get steadily fewer and less severe as people grow older, and there is no blip at midlife. Neither is there any such thing as an "empty nest syndrome": middle-aged people whose children have moved out are in fact happier than those whose children stick around.

Happiness and Economic Growth

The fact that joy of attainment always fades suggests that happiness may be pursued by keeping a succession of new attainments coming, just as the fact that every note sounded on a piano declines in volume very rapidly from its inception does not prevent a piano piece maintaining a high, or even an increasing, level of volume. This would mean that at any time some attainments were close to their maximum in terms of contributing to subjective well-being.

That line of thought might suggest that the rate of growth of income may be more relevant than the current amount of income. Some such notion may have influenced the great proponent of economic growth, Adam Smith, who evidently held that higher incomes do not make people happier, but that fast-growing incomes do. Before reading any of the recent research I would have bet on this Smithian view, but the facts now appear to be exactly contrary: there is a high correlation between absolute level of real income and happiness, and no significant correlation between rate of economic growth and happiness (Diener and Oishi, in Diener and Suh, p. 203).

All the same, I still feel that something like this ought to be true. Perhaps, for instance, people in countries with positive GDP growth are happier than those in countries with zero growth, who are in turn happier than those experiencing negative growth. Few countries have experienced zero or negative growth over the last few decades and SWB research has not made a special effort to focus on these places, so there is presumably insufficient data to test this. But thanks to the valiant efforts of helpful souls like Hugo Chavez, we will not run out of examples of countries with falling incomes, and perhaps this theory can be tested before long.

In Defense of Progress

What are the implications of SWB research for those who favor progress, and in particular for libertarians? I believe that the liberal, progressive, and libertarian commitment to advancing technology and indefinitely expanding material prosperity can be defended against the new attack based on the SWB findings.

My defense is in two parts. First, I claim that these findings, properly understood, are less disturbing for advocates of progress than the popularizers of SWB research have reported. Second, I point out that happiness, though important, isn't everything, and I maintain that modern, high-income, capitalist cultures score higher on most of the other salient values than do traditional or pre-industrial cultures.

We should separate two theses: 1. that for comparatively high-income people the level of happiness has remained approximately the same while real incomes have expanded enormously, and 2. that there has been a slight, long-term decline in happiness in the more affluent countries. While the first of these now seems to be strongly indicated by the data, the second looks dubious.

Most of the evidence for the decline in happiness over the past half-century comes from the rising incidence of "depression". This invites the obvious response that what fifty years ago was called being down in the mouth is now called "depression," "depressive disorder," "unipolar depression," or, forsooth, "clinical depression." Easterbrook dismisses such objections as follows (p. 165):

> though the rising rate of Western depression may relate to some
> extent to better diagnosis and the loss of taboo associated with

> this topic . . . a tenfold increase in two generations is far too
> great to be an artifact of improved diagnosis alone.

This is the reader's first introduction to the statistic of a "tenfold increase" in depression (no source is cited for the factor of ten). Easterbrook later discloses (p. 181) that "tenfold" is the upper limit of a range of controversial estimates, the lower limit being twofold (or, as he puts it, "on the order of two- or threefold"). Twofold still sounds like a lot, but the likelihood that an increase is due to "better diagnosis" (meaning greater readiness to apply the label "depressed") has little to do with the size of the increase as a multiple of the starting point and much to do with the size of the increase as a proportion of the total population. This, of course, is small.

It's often claimed that twenty-five percent of Americans undergo an experience of depression at least once in their lives, and that six or seven percent have experienced depression at least once in the past year. These numbers can't easily be compared with the statistics for SWB, which tend to focus on how people are feeling at one point in time or how they feel on average over a period of time. We typically don't ask people whether they have been blissfully happy at least once in their lives or at any time during the past year. And someone who currently feels fine but at one time felt sad and fell into the clutches of the mental health profession may now be classified as depressed and "managing" his depression.

Where such small shifts in numbers are at issue, it's remarkable that so little attention is paid to two great demographic trends: aging of the population and immigration. How many of those labelled "depressed" are over eighty? Both average overall life satisfaction and the small percentage of "depressed" increase with age.

Millions of people from the less developed countries have come to the United States recently, and have prodigiously amplified both their real incomes and their SWB. Still, they are genetically and culturally products of countries with much lower levels of SWB than the United States (all the data point to a major genetic component in the determination of SWB). These folks might well be immensely happier than they would have been in Guatemala or Cambodia, and still embody a decline in United States SWB. Improvement could thus possibly masquerade as deterioration.

Another element usually undiscussed in this connection is the enormous growth in the ingestion of mood-modifying substances like Prozac. At first blush, we might suppose that this collective swilling of antidepressants and tranquilizers must be counteracting a powerful tendency for misery to increase. I am more inclined to the view that these drugs, on average and in the long run, do not increase happiness, or more precisely, that substituting these newfangled concoctions for the tried and trusted intake of good old alcohol, good old tobacco, good old cocaine, and good old opiates does not increase happiness. The bigoted "Just Say No" zealots of our day strive to replace drugs which give people enjoyment with drugs which deaden people's sensibilities, and regrettably they have had some success.

I discount the suggestion that there's an inherent tendency for happiness to decline in industrially advanced countries. But I think it has to be admitted that the level of happiness in these countries is either roughly stationary or climbing very, very slowly. This does raise the question of whether further increases in incomes can be defended as additions to human wellbeing.

It won't be a practical issue for at least another couple of centuries. There are still hundreds of millions of people in the world who are desperately poor, and whose SWB will be greatly augmented by raising their incomes. It's not a feasible option to increase the incomes of the poor while holding the incomes of the well-off at a constant level: hold down the rich and you ineluctably hold down the poor. It's not possible to have economic growth in the less developed countries while halting it in the more developed.

Since modern, affluent, high-tech lifestyles are demonstrably highly conducive to human happiness, to oppose further gains in material prosperity from free trade and globalization is objectively to favor the perpetuation of wretched misery for hundreds of millions of poor people. Extrapolating from the SWB data, the conversion of the entire Third World to first-world standards will generate an enormous gain in happiness.

At a more general level, it's fallacious to conclude that because increases in already high incomes yield only very slight benefits for SWB, therefore only those very slight gains would be lost if we froze incomes at some arbitrarily high level (supposing this were feasible). Humans are plan-pursuing entities who achieve fulfillment from striving to improve their condition. What happiness they have now is an attribute of this broad purposive framework. If this framework were to be destroyed, there could be a major reduction in happiness. That this might be so is corroborated by Veenhoven's demonstration that economic freedom confers happiness independently of its income-raising role.

On this argument, then, the very existence of free-market capitalism would in itself add substantially to long-term happiness, and it's just an inseparable concomitant that free-market capitalism indefinitely increases median real income, which does not add very much to long-term happiness for the already well off. In short, even if *having* more of what we want does not add greatly to our happiness, *being able to pursue* more of what we want may still add greatly to our happiness.

What certainly has to be acknowledged is that it is false to suppose that every increase in GDP represents an actual gain in the joyfulness of daily experience, or that in some future high-income world every quotidian moment will be lived in a perpetual state of bliss. But I do not know of anyone who has ever held this view.[12] Probably those who came closest to it were Marxists around 1890.

Happiness Isn't Everything

The second part of my defense is to point out that happiness, though important, isn't everything. As many have insisted, happiness is not the *summum bonum* (all-important good). Other values are vital in setting our requirements for a good social order.

Easterbrook repeatedly states that it is "far better" to have high incomes even if these are not matched by high SWB. He even says that it's better to have high rates of depression than to have a world so poor that people are so caught up with survival they have no time to become depressed (Easterbrook, p. 165). I agree, and I applaud him for saying it, but he does not make explicit the values which may legitimately compete with happiness.

If you could convince me that a return to a world of recurring plagues and famines, children without shoes, their ribs poking out because of

---

12 "Utility" in economic theory is not happiness. It is an abstract concept defined as want-satisfaction. This is not unconnected with happiness but shouldn't be identified with it.

malnutrition, most of them dead before the age of ten, and the average woman requiring to give birth about nine times to maintain a stable population, would somehow leave people no less happy than today, I would still feel that you had not made a case for returning to that pre-industrial world. Dignity, charity, intelligence, and exploration of new opportunities are values which, though of course most often conducive to happiness, are in principle independent of happiness and may occasionally clash with it. The realization of these values is far more in evidence in today's Europe and America than in medieval Europe, medieval Islam, or the Third World.

Although happiness is extremely valuable, it is not the only thing of value, nor can it measure the value of every other thing. The arguments here are as familiar as they are sound. A cheap and infallibly happiness-inducing drug, added to the water supply, would not make us lose all interest in justice or human betterment. Most people would not choose to undergo a kind of brain damage which would make them simultaneously a lot happier and a lot more stupid. "Ignorance is bliss" can be uttered with many shades of emotional tone, but never admiringly. As Nozick's argument from the "experience machine" brings out,[13] most people do not want a happy life in a state of comprehensive delusion. A survey has found that less than one percent of people would choose to be plugged in to an experience machine.

Possibly neither "La Belle Dame Sans Merci" nor "The Bucket Rider" could have been written by a happy person—at any rate they weren't—yet the creative lives of John Keats and Franz Kafka are enviably worthy. It can even plausibly be argued that a certain modicum of suffering is essential to the best possible life, though I would add that one can get too much of a good thing, and I have it on the best authority that my suffering quota has been filled.

Happiness: The Final Frontier

How much further can we go in raising SWB in affluent modern cultures? My view is that people do have a set point which is most often on the happy side of neutral, but which varies individually, and which is largely but not

13   Robert Nozick, *Anarchy, State, and Utopia* (New York: Basic Books, 1974), pp. 42–43.

entirely genetic. Once certain sources of acute misery are removed, which they generally are by industrial development, the set point rules. Thus, although I see abundant opportunities for augmenting happiness, I don't see the scope for anything which could again repeat the staggering achievement of free-market capitalism in raising SWB to its present high levels.

Modern society is a marketplace for lifestyles, religions, psychotherapies, and interpersonal arrangements. There's a continual process of discovery by trial and error, which may lead over a long period of time to an approach to the optimum in these areas, yielding some gains in happiness.

In the area of religion, I see much hope in replacing the Abrahamic creeds (which, in one of their recent manifestations, can make millions of people think it inspiring to watch a movie of a man being tortured to death for a couple of hours) with a new synthesis of Buddhism and other religions of enlightenment.[14] The Abrahamic religions, aside from being composed mainly of untruths about nonexistent entities, are not well-suited to a culture of real abundance, security, and glorious opportunities.

In psychotherapy, which I expect to eventually become one with religion, all psychodynamic doctrines, derived from Freud, which seek to terrify people by imagining a world of inscrutable unconscious forces, are rapidly being replaced by an effective cognitive-behavioral approach of the sort pioneered by Albert Ellis, which effectively teaches people how to reduce their sources of unhappiness.

It's unclear whether the general tone of the culture or the reigning ideology can have much effect on people's happiness, but if it can, there is certainly room for improvement here. To take one simple example, the modernist movement in the arts, and its various offshoots and successors, have driven a wedge between music, fiction, drama, and pictorial representation as readily appreciated by the mass of the population and as sanctified by the approval of intellectual elites. This wedge was not always there, and will not always be there. It's largely a matter of intellectual fashion. But as long as the wedge is there, opportunities to develop great works of art with a popular audience tend to be closed off, and a potential avenue to the enrichment of the lives of the majority of people is not explored.

---

14   See the remarks by Andrew Rawlinson in his *The Book of Enlightened Masters: Western Teachers in Eastern Traditions* (Chicago: Open Court, 1997), pp. 33–36.

Ultimately, drugs may be helpful for some, not because of the questionable notion that "depression" is an "illness," which can be "treated" by "medication," but rather because of the fact well known to Fitzgerald's Khayam and to countless others down the ages, that taking drugs can make you feel better. If you belong to the one, or five, or ten percent of the population genetically most prone to melancholy, maybe some drug or other will help you to be happier.

Surfeit of Options

Barry Schwartz is an avowed enemy of the free market (one of his earlier books is subtitled *How Market Freedom Erodes the Best Things in Life*). But most of *The Paradox of Choice* is advice about making the best decisions within a free market. To the extent that people take his advice and find that it works, his anti-market complaints lose some of their force.

He thinks that we are overwhelmed by too many choices. But he accepts that how many choices confront us is itself a result of our choices. It's easy, for example, to adapt our shopping habits so that the number of purchase decisions is greatly reduced. It would even be feasible to join a club, like a book or record club but concerned with all kinds of consumer goods, so that we had to make almost no further choices at all—we would simply accept the groceries and other provisions selected for us each week by the club. Perhaps this is why some people join cults with apparently absurd dietary and other restrictions, because in this way they reduce the need to consider too many options.

Schwartz begins the book with an anecdote about his visit to The Gap in search of a pair of jeans. The salesperson asked:

> Do you want them slim fit, easy fit, relaxed fit, baggy, or extra baggy? . . . Do you want them stonewashed, acid-washed, or distressed? Do you want them button-fly or zipper-fly? Do you want them faded or regular?

I didn't expect the Spanish Inquisition! What a burden to drop onto the shoulders of a mere college professor! Buying the jeans, he says, became "a daylong project." The jeans he ended up with "turned out just fine." But, reports Schwartz, "it was a complex decision in which I was forced to invest time, energy, and no small amount of self-doubt, anxiety, and dread." Forced? He could have just left and gone to Penney's.

People can choose to make fewer choices. Schwartz gestures a few times in the direction of the brainwashed zombie theory, the victim of consumer capitalism who cannot choose to make fewer choices because he's addicted to consuming. But it wouldn't do to elaborate that theory, as it would undercut eighty percent of Schwartz's book, which gives you advice on how to choose to make fewer choices.

Much of this advice is quite sound. There's plenty of experimental evidence that most people typically make wrong-headed decisions. For instance, they erroneously count sunk costs. Schwartz gives many of these examples, some of which have no bearing on overabundance of choices. There's certainly scope for educating people in fallacies of practical decision-making, but this aspect would be more helpful if detached from his preaching about the baleful influence of too many choices.

Another anecdote refers (pp. 18–20) to a study in which either twenty-four or six varieties of jam were displayed. Thirty percent of people who visited the display of six varieties bought jam, while only three percent bought jam from the display of twenty-four. Problems of this kind tend to solve themselves: sellers of jam have an incentive to set up the smaller display. Managers of stores as a matter of course do limit the number of varieties of all goods they offer for sale.

Schwartz is perturbed (p. 9) that his local supermarket carries 285 varieties of cookies, but evidently if all 285 keep taking up shelf space, all 285 are selling. Anyone upset by the spectacle of 285 types of cookie can go to a corner or specialty store where the range is far more limited. Costco or Sam's Club attracts people prepared to buy in bigger quantities at bargain prices, from a more limited range. What many people do, of course (p. 19), is to settle on a cookie they like, and then always look for just that one, tuning out the other 284. Those on the Atkins diet tune out all 285. Taking this further, you can request the supermarket to send you the same list of groceries every week, and give no more thought to choices. Some busy yuppies use services like Peapod in this way.

Schwartz's advice is to adopt a "satisficing" rather than a "maximizing" strategy. Settle for what's good enough without looking for the very best.

Most people do this anyway, instinctively adjusting their searches among goods to take account of the opportunity cost of their own time (satisficing is only a special case of maximizing). Some others, mainly women, seem to derive intense gratification from the actual activity of researching what's available. Who, aside from the Taliban, would want to deny them this indulgence?

Even supposing that some people find the multiplicity of options irksome, the benefit they derive from having that many options may more than compensate them for the irksomeness. Therefore, it's possible for people to dislike the situation of having so many choices and still be net gainers from the availability of those choices, a possibility Schwartz never mentions. He thus confounds some specific loss from more choices with net loss from more choices, and wrongly supposes that by making a case for the prevalence of the former, he makes a case for the prevalence of the latter.

For those stressed-out shoppers who really do find choosing oppressive, much of Schwartz's advice may prove helpful, and the free market will then work even better. Thank you, Barry Schwartz.

Happiness in Its Place

Raymond Belliotti evidently started out to write a work with the challenging title, *Happiness Is Overrated*, and when he was well into it, suddenly realized that his crucial argument is misconceived. Instead of scrapping that book or turning it into a different kind of book, he went ahead and published the thing.

The problem becomes clear when we ask: Just who has overrated happiness? It turns out that there are two broad ways of defining "happiness," the way it is defined in ordinary English, as subjective contentment or good feeling, an enduring pleasant state of mind, and the way it is defined by some philosophers, as encompassing much more than that, perhaps a *merited*, or *worthy*, or *virtuous* pleasant mental state.

As Belliotti must have realized late in his composition of the book (see Belliotti, p. 93), those philosophers who have defined the word "happiness" in the normal vernacular manner have generally stated that happiness is not the *summum bonum*, but that other values are independently important, and may trump happiness. And those philosophers who have proclaimed happiness as the *summum bonum* have generally proposed an expanded definition of the word "happiness."

Consequently, Belliotti cannot name anyone around today who really overrates happiness, in the sense he specifies. A possible historical exception is Bentham, but on this point Bentham has no following. Belliotti's own views, while often correct, are equally often much more commonplace than he supposes them to be. In an effort to come up with a real "target" for his "thesis," he finally identifies "those who formally define happiness as a relatively enduring, positive state of mind and who take happiness to be (at least) a great good" (p. 94). This is indeed a popular position—I adhere to it myself—but I cannot find any arguments in Belliotti's book directed against it. The most he seems able to claim is that happiness is "not always a personal good," which presumably means that there are some situations where happiness is not a relevant value.

While he does not advance happiness as the *summum bonum*, Belliotti does recommend an expanded definition of "happiness." His attempt to argue for an expanded definition is bedeviled by the problem that he apparently does not understand that the meanings of words are conventional, and therefore writes as though there is a correct meaning of "happiness," independent of actual usage or of usefulness in argument. So he sets out on a wild goose chase to discover the true meaning of happiness or what happiness really is. He maintains, for example, that defining 'happiness' in the normal way ignores or slights values other than subjective contentment. This is like saying that we had better define a car's "maximum speed" to include its comfortable seats or fuel economy, and if we don't, we are ignoring or slighting these other desirable attributes.

Belliotti provides a readable survey of philosophers' views on happiness and finding meaning in life, but sheds little new light on these topics.

Liberty, February 2005

10

Is God Coming or Going? (2010)

No one predicted it. No one expected it. It was completely unprecedented in American history. It began in 2004.

What happened was an explosion of public discussion about atheism. The most obvious sign was a boom in sales of books about atheism. The huge sales of Harris, Dawkins, and Hitchens were only the tip of the iceberg. Dozens of other books on atheism, for and against, have been published, many selling far more than would have been expected a few years earlier. What's the explanation for this astonishing upsurge of interest in atheism?

Has God Returned?

According to some Christian critics of the New Atheists, the spate of successful atheist books is a response by atheist intellectuals to the disconcerting fact that religion, instead of dying away as expected, has made a comeback. According to Marvin Olasky, a well-known Evangelical Christian writer, atheists are "cornered and desperate" because of the shocking revival of religion in the US. Similar claims have been by Dinesh d'Souza, and by John Micklethwait and Adrian Wooldridge, co-authors of *God Is Back* (2009), who refer to the New Atheism as "secular fury."

There must be something wrong with this theory. First, it presupposes that the New Atheist boom has been engineered by its authors. But books by atheists attacking Christianity have been appearing by the truckload every year for the past hundred years, without any significant sales or impact until 2004. Authors and publishers wish they knew of a trick for ensuring that a book will become a bestseller, but they don't. What we have to explain is not why these books were produced, but why they have been bought and read by so many people.

In America, the great majority of the readers of these books cannot be atheists. All surveys of American religion indicate that more than ninety percent of the US population say they believe in God, while those who call themselves 'atheists' comprise about two percent. Even if we suppose that atheists read more books than other people, basic arithmetic compels us to acknowledge that the book buyers responsible for the success of Harris, Dawkins, and Hitchens in America must consist overwhelmingly of people who believe in God. Second, the theory presupposes that there has in fact been a recent revival of religion in the US. If this is interpreted to mean that religion plays a more important role in the lives of typical Americans than it did fifty years ago, this is a false claim—though it's frequently voiced, and many people believe it.

Let's see how this story of a comeback for American religion, like other resurrection stories, came to be believed despite its demonstrable falsity.

Secularization Challenged

Until the 1960s, social scientists and journalists almost unanimously accepted the *secularization thesis*—broadly, that life under modern capitalism tends to erode the importance of religion (which for our purposes here means monotheistic religion, chiefly Christianity). Adherents of this thesis did not claim that there would be a growth of atheism; simply that religion would have less and less importance in people's lives.

Beginning in the 1960s and becoming more audible in the 1970s, a minority of social scientists and popular writers began to challenge the secularization thesis. Observers of American religion noted the curious fact that the churches known as 'Mainline Protestant' were dwindling as a proportion of the total population, while the 'Evangelical' churches were growing. Evangelicalism has an 'old-time' Biblical literalist perspective, whereas Mainline Protestantism appears to have accommodated itself to the scientific worldview, accepting evolution, for instance, and also accepting that the Bible is not infallible in its historical claims. So the growth of Evangelicalism and the decline of Mainline Protestantism look like the *opposite* of secularization. It has indeed been hailed as an example of *de*secularization.

In 1972, Dean Kelley published an influential book, *Why Conservative Churches Are Growing*. He later pointed out that a more accurate title would have been *Why Strict Churches Are Strong.* Kelley argued that religion loses appeal if it becomes lax and accommodates to the secular world. Evangelical churches were growing at the expense of Mainline churches because they made fewer concessions to the secular world and more demands on their members.

This message was taken up the sociologist Rodney Stark, who argued in *The Churching of America* and numerous other writings that religious commitment has been growing in America since the early nineteenth century. As Stark sees it, when churches accommodate themselves to the non-religious world at the behest of well-educated and comfortably-off ministers, they lose members. New, enthusiastic, and more demanding sects then spring up and attract worshippers away from the more complacent liberal congregations. While some secularization is always going on, it is always being made up for by energetic new sects. In Stark's view, desecularization has outweighed secularization over the past two hundred years in America.

Since 1939, the Gallup organization had been asking a random sample of Americans 'Have you been to church in the last week?' In 1939 the affirmative response was forty-one percent. In the 1970s and 1980s, affirmative responses still hovered around forty-one percent! This too didn't look like secularization.

Other developments seemed to give credibility to the view that religion was on a roll. For instance, there was the activity of the Religious Right (later called the New Christian Right), associated with Jerry Falwell's Moral Majority and then with Ralph Reed's Christian Coalition.

The desecularization theory has attracted many active proponents, and is regularly repeated in a stream of popular books and articles. The writers usually agree that Christianity is in its death throes in Europe, but so much the worse for Europe! The desecularizers insist that what goes for Europe does not go for America—America is different. In America, as in the Third World, religion is alive and well, even expanding its influence.

A recent example of this type of writing is *God Is Back.* Yet if we look at the evidence its authors offer, we find it consists of a breathless recitation of disconnected factoids. Those from the industrialized world are seriously misrepresented, while those from the Third World are beside the point. There is no dispute that the sheer amount of religious activity going on in the world is growing, simply because religion is stronger in the poorer half of the world, where population growth is still rapid. (The richer half of the world would show declining populations if it were not for immigration from the poorer half.)

To gauge the global trend, what we need is not a rag-bag of anecdotes, but a systematic survey of religious commitment compared with economic development. The best thing we have along these lines is the study by Pippa Norris and Ronald Inglehart reported in their book *Sacred and Secular* (2004). They looked at seventy-four countries, classified as agrarian (poorest), industrial (richer), and post-industrial (richest). They found that religious belief and commitment is dramatically higher in agrarian than in industrial societies, and is higher in industrial than in post-industrial societies. So the facts indicate that secularization is a worldwide industrial and post-industrial reality. What we want to know next is whether the United States of America is an exception to this. Contrary to what is frequently asserted, we'll see that it is not.

Secularization Vindicated

Do the growth of Evangelicalism and the emergence of a Christian Right in the second half of the twentieth century indicate a comeback for American Christianity? If we put these developments in context, we have to say No.

In the 1990s, sociologists took a harder look at the Gallup responses about church attendance. Different ways of asking the question elicited a much lower rate of reported church-going; and comparisons with the direct observation of people attending church showed that the responses to the Gallup question exaggerate actual attendance by up to one hundred percent. We now know that US church attendance has actually been falling steadily, and averages around twenty percent—higher in the South and Midwest, lower in the rest of the country. US church attendance is about four times that of the UK, yet still, church-going is distinctly a minority activity in today's America.

Most of the churches we now call Mainline (Methodist, Presbyterian, Congregationalist, and so on) used to be Evangelical. Methodism was the original Evangelical church—the first denomination in the English-speaking world to lay great emphasis on a 'born again' conversion experience. As a form of Evangelicalism, Methodism spread like prairie fire at the end of the eighteenth and beginning of the nineteenth century. But in the course of the nineteenth century, Methodism evolved into a Mainline denomination.

Evangelicalism was at its peak in America before the Civil War. Whereas Evangelicalism, if generously defined, now accounts for over a quarter of the US population, in 1860 it accounted for more than eighty percent! The proportional growth of Evangelicalism compared to the Mainline after World War II was not due to conversion of adults from Mainline churches, but was primarily due to the fact that people in Mainline churches became less fertile: they had fewer babies, and started to have them later in life, while Evangelicals tended to stick to a more old-fashioned reproductive pattern, women generally beginning to have babies by their early twenties.

Indications are that the higher fertility of Evangelicals was merely a lag in the adjustment of Evangelicals to the newer, less fertile pattern, associated with the fact that Evangelicals are concentrated in the (until quite recently) least economically advanced parts of the country. The story that large numbers of adults left Mainline churches to join Evangelical churches is an unfounded legend. It's just not true that adult Americans have turned away from liberal Protestantism to conservative Protestantism because they found the latter more appealing.

America is a big country, and religious participation statistics are misinterpreted if regional differences are ignored. It would be like taking similar statistics for the whole of Europe, thus lumping Slovakia in with Sweden. Many parts of the US, like Washington State or New Hampshire, are just as irreligious as the more irreligious parts of Europe. If we break down the US geographically, we see the same configuration as the worldwide pattern found by Norris and Inglehart: the more advanced, urbanized, and educated areas are consistently more secular in outlook than the less developed areas. But since many parts of the formerly backward South have achieved spectacularly rapid economic growth in the past half-century, this connection becomes even clearer if we match up present-day religious patterns with economic development fifty years earlier.

Until the 1950s, the South was a Third World country within the US—desperately poor and overwhelmingly rural. Economically, it was like a colony, comparable to Algeria or the Philippines. And virtually all well-known evangelistic preachers since World War II have been Southerners. As the South rapidly industrialized, there was an export of Southern culture to the rest of the US. This process has been called 'the country-and-westernization of America' (and indeed the story of country music closely coincides with that of Evangelicalism). Now most of the South is affluent, we can witness the reciprocal 'Americanization of Dixie': the South is now experiencing steady decline of Evangelical affiliation, alongside the comparative growth of Mainline churches. This is comparable to what happened in the North after the Civil War. American exceptionalism turns out to be 'recently-undeveloped-and-backward-rural-American' exceptionalism—and therefore no exceptionalism at all.

The new prominence of Evangelicals in rightwing politics in the 1970s did not occur because there were more Evangelicals around, or because Evangelicals had become more active, but because Evangelicals were breaking with a strong tradition of non-involvement in politics. As a young minister, the Reverend Jerry Falwell was opposed to men of the cloth becoming politically active: he was talked into changing his mind by entrepreneurial lobbyists.

There is one under-publicized fact which puts the whole secularization/desecularization issue into perspective. The category of religious affiliation which has shown the greatest change over recent decades in America is those with *no* affiliation. The category of people who disavow any religious label has shown steady growth over many years, and is now sixteen percent of the entire adult population, and twenty-five percent of the population aged 18–29. Of course, they're mostly not atheists: they're just uninterested in belonging to a church.

Thus the growth of Evangelical Protestantism at the expense of Mainline Protestantism occurs within a shrinking proportion of the population. But there's worse news for those who would like to see God return. Evangelicalism is being diluted from within. Estimates of Evangelicals as constituting over a quarter of the population rely on self-identification in polls. Many in this group are the grown children of Evangelical parents, and less connected to the church than their parents: they are religiously inactive, and most of them are ignorant of the beliefs which define Evangelicals. Their lifestyles are not much different from the general population; for example, their divorce rate is somewhat higher. The Barna Group, a research organization run by Evangelicals, but widely respected for its scrupulously objective methods, estimates the proportion of genuine Evangelicals among the US population at seven percent.

Roman Catholics have remained a steady proportion for a long time, at about a quarter of the US population; but this statistic hides a steep decline, only compensated for by heavy Catholic immigration, as native Catholics defect to Protestantism or become unaffiliated. Regular attendance at mass among self-identified Catholics has plummeted even more dramatically, and it has become almost impossible to recruit new priests from the US or from any other affluent industrial country.

Apart from American churches classified as 'historically black', which have exhibited no net growth, that leaves small Christian groups like the Mormons and Jehovah's Witnesses (Jehovah's Witnesses are less than one percent of the US population, Mormons less than two percent), and the non-Christian religions (Hinduism, Islam, Judaism, Buddhism), which together amount to less than four percent. Both Mormons and Jehovah's Witnesses have grown very rapidly, Mormons primarily by having babies rather than by making adult converts. Jehovah's Witnesses make a lot of converts, but also face a very high rate of defection in each new generation. A look at Mormonism also discloses the emergence of a 'liberal' wing within the Mormon Church. This maintains, for example, that *The Book of Mormon* need not be relied upon as accurate history, but should be valued only for its spiritual message.

Though both Mormons and Jehovah's Witnesses will certainly become larger proportions of the US population, and will therefore exert a more noticeable impact on public awareness, there is no indication that these denominations can ever make up in absolute numbers for the steady fall in church attendance. And as these two churches grow, we can expect their members' fertility to decline, and the proportion of their offspring who lapse into purely nominal attachment to increase.

So, is God back? The truthful answer from within the US is that God never left, but lately has been looking distinctly unwell, and is now a pale shadow of His former self.

Explaining the Explosion

If the New Atheist explosion in America can't be explained as a reaction to a Christian resurgence, what does account for it? I have a two-part answer: the polarization of American political culture, and the impact of 9/11 on left-leaning American intellectuals.

Polarization in American attitudes has been widely documented. On many religious, social, and political issues, support for extreme positions has grown, while support for intermediate positions has waned. For example, there's been growth in the number of young people who think abortion is murder; yet also in the number who think abortion should be freely available. We see a growth of those who reject evolution because it contradicts the Bible, yet also a growth of those who think the Bible is just a collection of ancient writings deserving of no authority. The polarization is documented and analyzed in Robert Wuthnow's fine book *After the Baby Boomers* (2007).

We've already seen this polarization as the simultaneous growth of the religiously unaffiliated and the Evangelical churches. It manifests itself in elections as the red state–blue state opposition. (Confusingly for non-Americans, 'red' means rightwing and 'blue' means leftwing.) The polarization is due to two influences working in opposite directions. More children grow up in red-state households because these households have higher fertility. However, exposure to life in big cities, higher education, and other features of advanced industrial culture, tends to influence people toward a more secular or progressive outlook.

Polarization also means that atheists see a growth of fundamentalist religion, which alarms them, while conservative Protestants see a growth of militant secular humanism, which alarms *them*. However, they're both right, because the extremes are growing and the center is shrinking. And so we see that the theory of a religious comeback, while generally false, contains a nugget of truth. There has indeed been a growth of 'extreme' and enthusiastic religiosity, which has alarmed the more secular-minded people, even though, viewing US society as a whole, commitment to religion has shown net decline. Bold and explicit atheism is generally a response to bold and explicit religiosity.

Most Americans today are secular-minded nominal theists. They say they believe in God, but they have no time for church. They are not alarmed by atheism, and they often hold the same blue-state social and political attitudes as the tiny minority of atheists. They think of atheists as intelligent people with interesting ideas, whereas they think of Evangelicals as a bunch of kooks who might become dangerous. And so they take readily to books like *The God Delusion*.

The second stage of my explanation for the New Atheist Explosion in America centers on 9/11. American intellectuals needed a story which would put 9/11 in context and confirm their assumptions. What they came up with was the view that the Muslims who perpetrate terrorist attacks and the New Christian Right are *the same enemy* (fringe elements of Evangelicalism have perpetrated terrorist attacks on abortion clinics). This is the dominant theme in *The End of Faith* by Sam Harris, and it looms large in *The God Delusion*, and in *God Is Not Great* by Christopher Hitchens. The New Atheist story, marketable to the American intelligentsia as a whole, is that extreme religion commits atrocities, and even moderate religion may be dangerous because it provides cover for extreme religion.

Is this story defensible? I don't think it is. But that's another argument.

Philosophy Now, April–May 2010

11
SAFE DEX (2011)

Arthur Mitchell, the misnamed Trinity Killer, surmises for one fleeting moment that Dexter aspires to be a vigilante ("The Getaway," *Dexter*, Season Four). Our Dex, however doesn't want to be a vigilante, though the net result is that he acts just like one.

Well, maybe not *just* like a vigilante: occasionally saving killers from being picked up by the police so that he can have the satisfaction of slaughtering them himself isn't VSOP (vigilante standard operating procedure). But even this Dexter quirk has its helpful side: it does save the taxpayer all that expensive crap about appeals, psychiatric evaluations, and maybe in some cases, life sentences for the killers (which come with a life sentence for the taxpayers who have to feed, clothe, accommodate, and entertain them).

Dexter the Just Man

One hundred and four years before Season One of *Dexter*, when the word "vigilante" was still confined to westerns and was fairly obscure even there, and the term "serial killer" had not even been coined, Edgar Wallace published *The Four Just Men*. It instantly became, and remained for the next fifty years, a super-hyper-mega-bestseller, and was followed up by several sequels, both novels and collections of stories, including *The Three Just Men* (there had really only been three all along). The Just Men are rich, well-connected (one is a European prince), ruthless, cosmopolitan individuals with secret lives and a secret plan. They ingeniously conspire to assassinate evil-doers who have somehow escaped the law. In the main story of the first book, however, their target is not an especially wicked person, merely somewhat misguided, in their opinion, about current politics. The Just Men publicly announce that they will kill the British Foreign Secretary (equivalent to Secretary of State) if a certain piece of legislation goes through the British Parliament. It does and they do.

Good job, killers! Sometimes even non-evil persons may have to be eliminated, in the interest of the greater struggle against evil.

The Four Just Men is not a whodunnit but a howwilltheydoit: how can the Just Men manage to kill the illustrious cabinet minister at a precise pre-announced time, under the eyes of the entire Metropolitan Police Force and the secret service? The Just Men always keep their word to the very letter, so it's understood that if they don't succeed in killing the minister at exactly that time, they will have to abandon the attempt to kill him altogether. If we want to understand why our cuddly monster Dex is a true hero of our time, we can begin by asking why nothing like *The Four Just Men* could possibly be a major hit in the early twenty-first century.

Both the Just Men and Dexter kill bad guys. Both the Just Men and Dexter have secret lives, respectable public faces contrasting with their clandestine callings. Both the Just Men and Dexter are dedicated, disciplined, charming, *muy sympatico*. Both the Just Men and Dexter are, if you want to get technical about it, murderers, serial killers, dangerous criminals who, if caught, would be executed. Both the Just Men and Dexter are strongly identified with by readers or viewers, who want them to keep on getting away with their killing.

As far as I know, there were no protests or complaints about the morality of the Just Men. I've come across several disdainful references to Wallace in writings of the 1920s, 1930s, and 1940s. Snobbish literary people dismissed Wallace, along with Agatha Christie, Edgar Rice Burroughs, and sometimes even the Sherlock Holmes canon, as vulgar and escapist. They considered this stuff to be trash, though many of the literary intellectuals who took this line still thoroughly enjoyed reading that kind of slickly executed trash. But I have not encountered anyone from that period saying that there is something unhealthy about encouraging millions of readers to identify sympathetically with people who cold-bloodedly break the law in myriad ways, and commit numerous murders for which, if caught, they would be executed. And this was at a time when hardly anyone doubted that such people should be executed.

Rooting for a Killer

When we turn to *Dexter* and our own time, things are different. *Dexter* is continually being denounced by people whose denunciations are well publicized. The Parents Television Council (PTC), which claims membership of over a million, has called for action against advertisers who support *Dexter*, and has repeatedly agitated for confining the show to cable and keeping it off the broadcast channels. Although explicitly concerned about sex, violence, and profanity in TV shows which might be watched by children, the PTC is well aware that *Dexter* does not have a higher level of sex, violence, and profanity than some other shows, but still singles *Dexter* out as the worst offender because (as their President, Timothy F. Winter, puts it) "the series compels viewers to empathize with a serial killer, to root for him to prevail, to hope he doesn't get discovered."

There must be more to it than that, though. To pick just one obvious example, since 1844, readers of *The Count of Monte Cristo* have been "compelled" by Dumas's story-telling magic to empathize with Edmond Dantès, root for him to prevail, hope he doesn't get discovered. And Dantès, the Count of Monte Cristo, like the Just Men, is literally a serial killer. What's going on here?

No doubt part of the answer lies in the fact that TV is easily accessible in a way that books aren't. But there seems to be something else. As a first stab at the answer, Edmond Dantès has a personal motive: revenge for a terrible wrong. And the Just Men had a moral purpose—though we don't know that the PTC wouldn't object to the Just Men if they were popular today. But Dexter Morgan is addicted to the thrill of slaughtering humans for its own sweet sake. He's not just a serial killer, he's a psychotic serial killer, addicted to ritual killing—or so we're told.

What's the attitude of Wallace (and presumably many of his readers) to the operations of the Just Men? It's an attitude which no thriller writer or TV scriptwriter could get away with today. The killings of the Just Men are depicted as a rational plan, and are tacitly commended, at least to the extent that the reader is expected to identify with the Just Men and hope that they keep getting away with it. Each killing is one more happy ending. The Just Men are smooth operators, fully in control. Most of their victims (with the notable exception of the Foreign Secretary in the first story) are evil characters who thoroughly deserve their fate.

In conversation, the Just Men good-humoredly compare their own notoriety with that of Jack the Ripper, then as now the most famous of all serial killers. (The Ripper is more legend than fact. The press, with the connivance of the police, conspired to pad his resume by crediting him with murders committed by several different unconnected people.)

Our Killers, Right or Wrong

What about the rightness or wrongness of what the Just Men are doing? Wallace's attitude, as storyteller, seems to be: 'There are big ethical issues here, and they add to the excitement, but we don't want to get sidetracked into debating them.' The authorial voice betrays no defensiveness, even though we're continually reminded that the Just Men have to outwit official law enforcement as well as the bad guys. The Just Men never falter in their belief that what they're doing is absolutely right. The writer seems to be saying to his readers: 'I have a story to tell, and part of the charm of my story is that you and I can imagine what it's like for scoundrels to be brought to justice. There are powerful, influential, or very slippery people who commit a lot of evil acts but are outside the reach of the law, but wouldn't it be wonderful if ruthless, glamorous persons, with efficiency and panache, could give these disgusting villains their comeuppance?'

Could something like *The Four Just Men* be made today, say as a TV series, and be successful? Can you imagine a show something like *Criminal Minds*, in which the heroic team is a self-appointed group of private crime-fighters, who illegally execute bad guys? To make the parallel close, suppose that the pilot episode shows our heroes assassinating the Secretary of State because she supports a piece of over-intrusive homeland security legislation—and imagine that this episode is wildly popular, with no one voicing a qualm about its propriety.

This is extremely unlikely, for two related reasons. First, any such series would provoke a storm of controversy about the choice of targets for assassination, as well as the general immorality of endorsing murder. Second, and more importantly, today's writers would be quite incapable of presenting the Just Men as entirely rational. They would be unable to stop themselves from finding the origin of the Just Men's plans in their troubled childhoods. The ideology of childhood trauma is now so very powerful. But if the writers took care to present the team of killers as victims of their demons or their 'issues', this would tend to defuse the former kind of objection. We see here how currently dominant ideology automatically pushes any acceptable vigilantism in the direction of *Dexter*.

What became of Edgar Wallace? He persuaded his employers at the *Daily Mail* (a major UK national newspaper) to serialize *The Four Just Men*, with a generous prize to readers who could guess the ending (just how the Foreign Secretary was killed). Although the book sold millions, boosted the circulation of the *Mail*, and made Wallace famous, Wallace was careless with the wording of the prize offer, so that everyone, without limit, who guessed the ending was entitled to the prize. Wallace's book sold millions but the prize competition drove Wallace himself into bankruptcy.

After that, he wrote many successful stories, including a series about "the Ringer," a glamorous revenge killer. He earned a lot of money, but always spent far more than he earned, gripped by the superstition that if he failed to spend lavishly, his run of success as a writer would come to an end. His final project was the script for *King Kong*. In 1932 he went to Hollywood to work on that movie, but quickly fell ill and died.

Wallace's Just Men are the crystallization of a common theme in popular fiction: the hero will sometimes break the law in a good cause. Sherlock Holmes, aside from such trivialities as burglarizing houses in search of evidence, sometimes lets killers go free. Unlike the irreproachable Just Men, Holmes also displays another common trait of the storybook hero: he has his Dark Passenger. His major motivation is the fascination of solving problems and if he has no criminological problems to occupy him, he injects himself with cocaine and plays inchoate dissonant chords on the violin.

The Retribution of Raffles

While Conan Doyle's Holmes mostly upheld the law, Conan Doyle's brother-in-law, E.W. Hornung, created A.J. Raffles, a proper gentleman and "the greatest slow bowler of his generation." Raffles has a public face and mingles with the rich and fashionable, but also leads a secret criminal life. He is a jewel thief constrained by an idiosyncratic code of honor. When Raffles's confidant, accomplice, and narrator, Bunny Manders suggests that being a well-known cricketer would be a hindrance to a life of burglary, Raffles responds:

> My dear Bunny, that's exactly where you make a mistake. To follow crime with reasonable impunity you simply must have a

parallel ostensible career—the more public the better. . . . it's my profound conviction that Jack the Ripper was a really eminent public man, whose speeches were very likely reported alongside his atrocities. ("Gentlemen and Players")

I suppose that in this day and age we do have to mention that Bunny is a member of the male sex, and to explain that to be most revered as a cricketer in those days, you had to be a gentleman, and therefore someone who was not paid to play. In *Mr Justice Raffles*, the great jewel thief steals no diamonds, but utilizes all his skills to bring retribution on an evil man and restitution to some of his victims. The retribution does not extend to the arch-villain's death, but, presumably sensing that anything less than death would leave the reader's sense of justice unsated, the bad guy is slain by someone else. *Mr Justice Raffles* is now the least anthologized and least reprinted of the Raffles stories, presumably because of its rather numerous unpleasant comments about the villain's ethnicity.

Enter the Bulldog

Eighteen years after the Just Men made their appearance, along came Bulldog Drummond, in stories penned by the writer who wrote under the name 'Sapper'. Drummond was the James Bond of his day, and later became Ian Fleming's major inspiration for Bond, just as Drummond's arch-villain Carl Peterson was the inspiration for Ernst Stavro Blofeld (if you're rusty on your Bond movies, he's the guy with the long-haired white cat). Drummond in 1920 is a former British army officer who finds life dull after World War I, but then stumbles on a secret conspiracy aiming at the total ruination and humiliation of Britain. Drummond briefly considers informing the police of Peterson's foul plot and criminal deeds, but decides that he, Drummond, would be just as liable to prosecution as Peterson.

The first four Drummond novels describe Drummond's epic battle to thwart Peterson's vile schemes. Drummond has a secret life like that of the Scarlet Pimpernel. He and his friends, all rich young men who seem to have nothing more on their minds than getting sozzled in the posh London clubs, have secret lives as ferocious fighters against evil. In *The Black Gang*, Drummond and his associates, all dressed in black, terrorize the evil-doers and run rings round the police. A vast malign conspiracy is afoot. Jews and Communists (the latter indifferently described as Bolsheviks or anarchists) figure prominently in the conspiracy, but these individuals, though degenerate and malevolent enough, are simple-minded dupes of the mastermind Carl Peterson, a German who can pass for English or American, and whose goals, aside from the obvious enormous piles of money and despotic power, include the destruction of the British Empire.

Apart from administering executions, floggings, and other punishments, the Black Gang is responsible for the disappearance of many leftist agitators and the reader wonders what has become of them. Perhaps they have been chopped into pieces and . . . well, there were no plastic bags in those days, and no cordless circular saws. On the other hand, manual labor was cheap and forensics was pretty basic. However, near the end of the book, the disappeared ones turn up, in a rehabilitation camp run by the Black Gang. Here the former subversives are made to work hard under the fist of a drill-sergeant, thus teaching them (a touch of irony here, old chap) what socialism is really all about.

In the climactic scene of *The Black Gang*, Drummond and the Gang have captured Peterson and his leading cronies. Peterson, a wizard with disguises, is in the persona of a sweet American clergyman.

> [Drummond] swung round on the cowering clergyman and gripped him once again by the throat, shaking him as a terrier shakes a rat. . . . And still the motionless black figures round the wall gave no sign, . . . They knew their leader, and though they knew not what had happened to cause his dreadful rage they trusted him utterly and implicitly. Whether it was lawful or not was beside the point: it was just or Hugh Drummond would not have done it. And so they watched and waited, while Drummond, his face blazing, forced the clergyman to his knees, . . . It was Phyllis who opened her eyes suddenly, and, half-dazed still with the horror of the last few minutes, gazed round the room. She saw . . . the Black Gang silent and motionless like avenging judges round the walls. And then she saw her husband bending Carl Peterson's neck farther and farther back, till at any moment it seemed as if it must crack. For a second she

THE MYSTERY OF FASCISM

stared at Hugh's face, and saw on it a look which she had never seen before—a look so terrible, that she gave a sharp, convulsive cry. "Let him go, Hugh: let him go. Don't do it." Her voice pierced his brain, though for a moment it made no impression on the muscles of his arms. A slightly bewildered look came into his eyes: he felt as a dog must feel who is called off his lawful prey by his master.

So Drummond relents, and so (women never think about the trouble they cause by their sentimental interventions) we have another two novels in which Drummond battles the arch-fiend Peterson before finally seeing him off.

What was it that dear little Phyllis saw in hubby's eyes, and what was it doing there? We're repeatedly reminded that Drummond had nothing but wholesome fun in the Great War, cruising through No-Man's Land in search of Germans whom he could savagely throttle. Presumably he had that look in his eyes then. And what's the big deal, since Carl Peterson is more of a threat and more of a monster than Kaiser Willy? The incident may show feminine frailty, or it may show that even in the struggle against absolute evil, the decent Britisher is restrained by civilized inhibitions unknown to the filthy Hun. On the droll side, it seems to show that the immensely muscular Drummond takes a suspiciously long time to break someone's neck. But what it most clearly shows is that Drummond, like Dexter, has his Dark Passenger. There's a monster within, and somehow, it's for the good if that monster is sometimes let loose.

Enter the Saint

At school in England, the young boy who would later be Leslie Charteris thought carefully about his optimal future career, a career that would suit his personality and make him rich, and eventually he hit on the answer: he would become a professional burglar. The record is silent on whether he actually tried out this profession, but he was a supremely practical person and we can draw our own conclusions. And then Charteris discovered that the writing which came easily to him was saleable. He gave up burglary for writing, and systematically developed a hero, Simon Templar, a fearsome vigilante who kills bad people ("the godless," as he refers to them, though this is his only symptom of piety), and who continually has to outwit Inspector Teal of Scotland Yard.

Teal, not knowing the whole story about Templar, considers him a dangerous criminal, and to be strictly accurate, Teal happens to be technically correct. Templar's true purpose is proclaimed early on:

> We Saints are normally souls of peace and goodwill. But we don't like crooks, bloodsuckers, traders in vice and damnation. We're going to beat you up and do you down, skin you, smash you, and scare you off the face of Europe. We are not bothered by the letter of the law, we act exactly as we please, we inflict what punishment we think suitable, and no one is going to escape us. (*Enter the Saint*)

As a typical example, in "The Death Penalty," the Saint runs into Abdul Osman, a drug dealer and white slaver whom he's already met some years before. On that earlier occasion, the Saint had contented himself with branding both of Osman's cheeks with a nasty Arabic word. Now the story ends with Osman's death, though at whose hands remains a mystery until the very end. The Saint has no qualms about forging evidence and presenting a fabricated story to the inquest on Osman, and laying the blame for Osman's killing on another drug dealer and white slaver, who ends up being hanged for a crime he didn't commit. Thus, the Saint hoodwinks the official machinery of law enforcement into killing a man because the Saint believes he deserves it. The Saint's moniker is quite consciously ironic.

In popular fiction before World War II, "white slavery" is a code term for prostitution. Prostitutes and pimps make appearances in these stories, but these words are generally considered too indelicate. By the 1940s, for instance in *The Saint in Miami* (1944), the word 'pimp', at least, has become permissible. Both Drummond and the Saint speak in a kind of chummy public-school argot (the Saint's owing something to Bertie Wooster) which a later generation might consider somewhat campy. But the concept of camp lay in the future, and if you could've explained what it meant to the Bulldog or the Saint, you'd earn yourself at least a sock in the jaw.

The Saint is flamboyant, abrasive, and often inconsiderate of bystanders.

These were the days of the great sports cars with magical names, the Hispano-Suiza and the Lagonda. The greatest of all these cars was the Hirondel, as driven by Simon Templar, terrorizing other drivers as well as pedestrians in his ruthless, high-velocity pursuit of his own brand of justice.

> Some who saw the passage of the Saint that night will remember it to the end of their lives; for the Hirondel, as though recognizing the hand of a master at its wheel, became almost a living thing. King of the Road its makers called it, but that night the Hirondel was more than a king: it was the incarnation and apotheosis of all cars. For the Saint drove with the devil at his shoulder, and the Hirondel took its mood from his. If this had been a superstitious age, those who saw it would have crossed themselves and sworn that it was no car at all they saw that night but a snarling silver fiend that roared through London on the wings of an unearthly wind. (*The Saint Closes the Case*, also sometimes titled *The Last Hero*)

Now that's a car. And that's what we call writing. Those who have hoped to acquire a genuine old Hirondel have been disappointed, for this make of car lived entirely in the imagination of Leslie Charteris and his millions of readers. What such passages illustrate is that we always (at least, since Lord Byron) like our heroes to have an anti-social streak. They have their Dark Passengers. If they're too utterly sane, like R. Austin Freeman's Dr. Thorndyke, they lack an essential ingredient and come across as bloodless cyphers.

Charteris often described the Saint as a "buccaneer," but in later stories the Saint is co-opted by the authorities. In *Angels of Doom* (1931), he seems to be working with his old enemy, Inspector Teal of Scotland Yard, then seems to have double-crossed Teal and become an outlaw vigilante, then turns out to have been working for the Secret Service (thus outranking Teal) all along. But it wouldn't do for him to become entirely respectable and above board. Part of the mystique of the Saint is that he's a criminal, so this image is continually toyed with in subsequent stories.

The Saint never had much success on the big screen, but a fairly close imitation, The Falcon, had a good run in the 1940s (Charteris sued the

RKO studio for plagiarism and made contemptuous fun of the Falcon in *The Saint Steps In*). Charteris lived in the United States, but was unable to obtain permanent residency because of the Chinese Exclusion law (which kept out people with fifty percent or more Chinese ancestry). Charteris had a Chinese father and an English mother; his real name was Leslie Bowyer-Yin.

Eventually a special Act of Congress was passed, just to enable Charteris to stay in the US. But after marrying his fourth wife, the Hollywood starlet Audrey Long, he moved back to England, and lived there till his death in 1993. Charteris wrote over a hundred lucrative books, mostly about the Saint. His last few Saint stories were mainly written by other people; he just looked them over and made a few changes before attaching his name. The writers chosen were highly competent, and the books remained excellent, but the Saint's popular appeal was waning.

Decline of the Vigilante Novel

At first glance, if we look at what happened after World War II, we may get the impression that systematic private enforcement of justice went into eclipse. Even as the word 'vigilante' became popular, the vigilante novel almost disappeared. Simon Templar was now working for the government, at least some of the time. Bulldog Drummond's fan following dwindled and his niche was filled by James Bond, a civil servant 'licensed to kill' by a government department.

Mickey Spillane's Mike Hammer and the hero of the *Death Wish* movies, played by Charles Bronson, were exceptions, but in spirit they did not go very far beyond revenge. Revenge is a form of justice and has its own rules just as onerous as any other form, but revenge is personal retribution and does not extend to punishing offenders with whom the punisher has no personal connection. Still, some revengers may graduate to vigilantism.

In the late twentieth century, private enforcement of justice is more usually presented as a fearsome threat. Harry Callahan, hero of *Dirty Harry* is sometimes idiotically called a vigilante. *Magnum Force* (1973), the second Dirty Harry movie, shows a group of cops who bump off evil-doers in their spare time. These vigilante cops are not presented at all sympathetically, and the law-abiding Callahan is compelled to waste them in order to uphold the law.

In *The Star Chamber* movie (1983), a group of judges assassinate killers who have managed to escape official justice by legal technicalities. The true plot begins when they realize they have made a mistake and their hired executioner is already on his way to kill the designated target. One of the judges, played by Michael Douglas, decides to intervene personally to protect the target. At the end of the movie, Douglas is delivering up the other vigilante judges to the official police force. The movie's point of view is one of bland confidence that the Star Chamber, the unofficial conclave of judges, is dangerous and indefensible. It does not explore the irony in the fact that the Star Chamber has made one rare mistake and that in all its other operations it is rectifying mistakes by the official system. Nor does it confront what should be done on those occasions when the official system makes the same mistake as the Star Chamber had made: punishing the innocent. Should a judge with a conscience then intervene physically to thwart the implementation of official justice?

Despite appearances, vigilantism had not died. It had merely moved from the bookstores to the newsstands. Comic-book superheroes took over most of the illegal enforcement of justice. These new heroes have superhuman powers, not just figuratively, like the Saint's amazing agility, quick-wittedness and extraordinary reflexes, but literally. The most outstanding of the superheroes not to have superhuman abilities is Batman, who—like the Just Men, Bulldog Drummond, and the Saint before him—is independently wealthy.

The eviction of vigilantes from popular novels and their relegation to the disreputable underworld of comics does seem to reflect an increased hostility to vigilantism, connected with the growth of state worship in the twentieth century, the age of totalitarianism.

Dexter, Hero of Our Time

In the early twenty-first century, the ideology of childhood trauma reached its peak in popular culture, even while psychological research had largely undermined it as scientifically acceptable. Look at the difference between the first movie made of *Willy Wonka and the Chocolate Factory* (1971) and the remake, *Charlie and the Chocolate Factory* (2005). The first movie, following the Roald Dahl story, presents Willy Wonka as a somewhat inscrutable, interestingly dangerous, quirky, but fundamentally benign person, a formidable godlike figure. The remake depicts Wonka as a dude with serious issues, a man who worships chocolate because his father, a dentist, did something terrible to him all those years ago, as well as forbidding him to eat chocolate.

The director of the remake, Tim Burton, repeatedly voiced his opinion that Wonka just has to be seen as "screwed up" and that therefore some explanation of his mental disorder is required. The explanation, of course, has to be childhood trauma—what else? Another example is the 1997 movie, *The Saint*, with Val Kilmer, which borrows a few plot devices from Charteris but is basically about an entirely different character. The Saint of this movie has not dedicated his life to punishing bad guys, and instead of being self-assured and confident in his righteous mission, he is driven by—a childhood trauma.

The Kilmer Saint is a professional thief who has become very wealthy and plans to retire after one more job. He is clever and resourceful, but helplessly possessed by an irrational compulsion, flowing from his childhood mistreatment by priests. Childhood trauma plays the same role in modern popular culture as used to be played, in traditional folk tales, by love potions. Like a love potion, a childhood trauma compels the hero to behave in an irresponsible way, takes possession of him, and leaves him no choice. These magical effects of childhood trauma are as mythical as those of the love potion, but they seem to be passionately believed in by most of today's writers.

The storyline of Dexter is popular because it's safe—ideologically safe. A story about someone who bumps off people for carefully calculated reasons, in pursuit of a strict code of justice, would make too many people too uncomfortable. Today's ruling ideology (at least among the intellectual class from whom scriptwriters are chiefly recruited) holds that motiveless, irrational killing is tasty, especially if it can be linked with childhood trauma, while calculated killing in a worthy cause, by a hero without hang-ups, is almost unthinkable, and if thinkable at all, painfully embarrassing. Every age is as straitlaced as every other, but the specific taboos change.

Dexter adroitly accommodates itself to the reigning ideology. It gives us the glamour of the Secret Life and of the anti-social 'bad boy', the narrative appeal of the supernormal hero who fights his way out of adversity and triumphs, the satisfaction of seeing the most cunning and elusive evil-doers getting their just deserts. Instead of inviting criticism or derision by having the hero take a strong moral line against the villains he executes, any questions about the rightness of the hero's cause are defined away: the hero is not responsible for his actions.

To make the hero a puppet of his bloodlust seems, on the surface, outrageous, provocative, audacious. But really it's the very safest way to go. This is not to denigrate the artistic quality of *Dexter*, which is superb. Nor is it to criticize *Dexter* on ideological grounds. We should be no more troubled by the childhood-trauma ideology of *Dexter* than by the antisemitism of A.J. Raffles and Bulldog Drummond, the ultra-politically-correct feminism of Stieg Larsson, or Jack London's amalgam of Marxism and Social Darwinism.

Outside the context of the story, these belief systems may be criticized and rejected, while within a work of fiction or drama, they can be accepted as features of the landscape. It was inevitable that the indestructible popular hunger for stories of unofficial justice would meet the rampant ideology of my-childhood-makes-me-do-it. It was not inevitable that the artistic result would be as intelligent, as witty, as well-plotted, and as brilliantly produced and acted as *Dexter*.

Dexter and Philosophy: Mind over Spatter, 2011

12

THE BIGOTRY OF THE NEW ATHEISM (2014)

If there's anything new about the New Atheism which erupted in 2004, it's the strident proclamation that belief in God is a powerful force for evil. All kinds of atrocities are laid at the door of "religion," equated with belief in God.

The central message of the New Atheism is that 9/11 and similar outrages have occurred because their perpetrators believed in God. This is explicitly stated and reiterated many times by Sam Harris, but the same tune has been hummed and whistled in several keys by Richard Dawkins and the late Christopher Hitchens.

If you believe in God, then you have been infected and (twenty-eight days or years later) this belief is going to prompt you to kill yourself and your fellow-humans. So the New Atheists tell us. I view this as a fairytale, just as far-fetched as anything in the Bible or the Quran.

Atheists Do It Better (Mass Murder, That Is)

There's an obvious problem with the New Atheist claim that theistic religion is peculiarly conducive to atrocities. The last hundred years have seen the rise to power of secular, in some cases overtly atheistic, ideological movements, and these movements have been responsible for the killing, torture, enslavement, and terrorizing of many millions of people.

By any measure, the evil deeds done by these secular regimes within a few decades have vastly outweighed the evil deeds done by Christianity and Islam combined, throughout their entire history—not by a factor of just two or three, but by a factor of hundreds, if not thousands. Institutions claiming to embody Christianity or Islam have murdered thousands. Institutions claiming to embody Marxism, National Socialism, or other types of socialism, have murdered tens of millions.

Since this factual point is so conspicuous, the New Atheists have naturally attempted to account for it. Their most common response is that whereas theists (like Torquemada) committed atrocities because they believed in God, atheists (like Stalin or Mao) did not commit *their* atrocities because they disbelieved in God. This strikes me as a very strange claim.

Even if this strange claim were true, it would not address the difficult point. The New Atheists maintain that "religious," meaning theistic, ideologies generate atrocities. History shows that non-theistic or secular ideologies have generated atrocities on a vastly greater scale than theistic ideologies. Now, even if the religious atrocities were committed because the perpetrators believed in God while the secular atrocities were not committed because the perpetrators disbelieved in God, this does nothing to get around the stark fact that ideologies without belief in God have motivated more and bigger atrocities than ideologies incorporating belief in God, and that therefore it looks dubious to single out belief in God as an especially virulent intellectual source of atrocities.

However, the strange claim, if we can make any sense of it at all, can only be false. Belief in God is an integral part of Christianity and disbelief in God is an integral part of Marxism. Torquemada committed his atrocities because of a belief system which included belief in God. Stalin and Mao committed their immensely more ambitious atrocities because of a belief system which included disbelief in God. I can't imagine how you extract from these facts the conclusion that theists committed their atrocities "because" they believed in God while atheists did not commit *their* atrocities "because" they disbelieved in God.

Another argument offered by the New Atheists is to cite ways in which the churches were complicit in the crimes against humanity committed by Fascist and National Socialist regimes. The New Atheists don't seem equally concerned about the complicity of atheist intellectuals in the greater crimes against humanity committed by Communist regimes.

But, in any case, what do such examples really show? Fascism and National Socialism were not Christian movements. The distinctive elements in their ideologies and policies were not derived from what the churches were teaching. When the Fascists and the Nazis were new, small parties with little following, they did not seek, nor did they get, the slightest bit of support from the churches. Until 1933, for instance, Catholics were forbidden by the German bishops to join the Nazi Party.

By the time Fascism and National Socialism became contenders for power, and then achieved power, many people compromised with them, including most of the churches. So did other groups, for example, the majority of scientists, scholars, and journalists in the affected countries. Both totalitarian movements, Fascism in Italy and National Socialism in Germany, gained electoral support at the expense of specifically Christian political parties, which were closed down when the Fascist and National Socialist parties came to power.

It's also true that some Christians, motivated at least in part by their Christianity, resisted these regimes and paid for it. The truly heroic Claus von Stauffenberg, leader of Operation Valkyrie, the plot to assassinate Hitler, was a devout Catholic.

As well as the Soviet repression of theists, both Christian and Muslim, and such well-known instances as the mass killings directed by the atheist Khmer Rouge in Cambodia, it's worth mentioning a couple of other, lesser-known cases where specifically atheist persons or groups were responsible for horrible acts of violence.

In 1924, the Mexican government ramped up its already severe restrictions on the activities of the Catholic Church. Hundreds of priests and other Catholics were imprisoned or executed because they refused to comply with new regulations (requiring, for example, that priests not criticize government officials and not wear clerical garb outside a church). The brutal repression of Catholics led to the "Cristero war" between Catholic rebels and the government, followed by further government assaults on Catholics. The government hunted down and killed priests, just because they would not give up being priests. Graham Greene wrote about this in a documentary work, *The Lawless Roads* (1939), and then in a novel, *The Power and the Glory* (1940). The former president and de facto ruler of Mexico at this time, Plutarco Elias Calles, was a highly enthusiastic atheist.

The traditional anticlericalism, often atheism, of Mexico's ruling elite stems mainly from Positivism, the atheist belief system promulgated by Auguste Comte, a form of pre-Marxist socialism which took root among the Mexican intelligentsia in the nineteenth century. Vicente Fox Quesada, elected in 2000, was the first Mexican president for ninety years who could openly admit to being a believing Catholic, and even today, a few remnants of the old restrictions remain, for example ministers of religion are banned from holding political office in Mexico.

In another example, the Spanish anarchists, atheistic followers of Mikhail Bakunin ("If God existed, it would be necessary to abolish him"), had come to control some regions of rural Spain by the 1930s. They committed numerous outrages against Catholics, not just the desecration of churches, but also occasionally the killing and mutilation of priests and nuns. These atheist-inspired attacks alarmed many Spaniards, and stimulated support for rightwing enemies of the Republic, helping prepare the way for extraordinary brutality by both sides in the Spanish Civil War. Numerous leftist supporters of the Spanish Republic, like George Orwell, were fully aware of these anti-Catholic crimes and never uttered one word of criticism. Yes, it's true that these atrocities were "exaggerated by the Right for their own purposes." But the Right had something to exaggerate.

Atheist Terrorism

Harris's explanation for the current spate of suicide terrorism is that the terrorists believe they will be rewarded as martyrs in Heaven. The religious zeal of fundamentalist Muslims is the explanation for suicide attacks. This entertaining story has been continually reiterated by journalists, but it will not withstand scrutiny.

Harris, and following him Dawkins, have asked, rhetorically, whether we can imagine any atheist group conducting suicide terrorism. In actuality, a rather high proportion of suicide terrorists have been atheists. In the years up to 2009, the pre-eminent perpetrator of suicide bombings in the world was the group known as the Tamil Tigers, in Sri Lanka. They were of Hindu background but led by atheists. Opinions differ on whether the Tamil Tigers could accurately be described as "Marxist-Leninist," but it's not disputed that they were belligerently anti-religion.

Another atheist group responsible for suicide terrorism was the Kurdistan Workers' Party (PKK), a Kurdish nationalist and Marxist-Leninist group active in Turkey. These suicide bombers were atheists and their victims were mostly Muslims. Around 1999 the PKK leadership abandoned its Marxism-Leninism and its practice of suicide bombings, and later changed its name.

Suicide terrorism is primarily political in its aims and rationale. Suicide bombers have political objectives which provide the reason for their actions. Suicide terrorism is the recourse of members of ethnic populations who find themselves completely outmatched by vastly stronger military might. It's their way of hitting back at the occupying troops, whom they are too feeble to confront directly. It is particularly effective if the occupying power is a democracy. Robert Pape's study of the backgrounds of Muslim suicide terrorists (*Dying to Win: The Strategic Logic of Suicide Terrorism*, 2005) shows that many of them are not especially religious.

If suicide bombers knew of a way to kill an equal number of the enemy without also killing themselves, they would act upon it. The reason that suicide bombing has become much more frequent since 1983 is that it works. The Israeli government, for example, while usually unmoved by peaceful overtures or by (comparatively ineffective) non-suicide attacks, has made concessions to the Palestinians following suicide bombings. Reagan pulled US troops out of Lebanon because of suicide attacks, intended precisely to get US troops pulled out of Lebanon. Pape, who made a thorough study of all cases of suicide terrorism (up to 2003), calculated that about fifty percent of suicide attacks had some demonstrable success in achieving their political objectives—an amazingly high success rate for terrorism, or indeed for any form of political operation by small groups not in control of a government.

This is not to say that suicide terrorism has any moral justification. It is merely to say that it works extremely well. Suicide terrorism is far more effective than any of the alternatives open to militant political groups acting, as they see it, on behalf of comparatively powerless ethnic communities under foreign military occupation. It's a highly rational, expertly calibrated activity which delivers the political goods.

Some readers will no doubt protest that some of the Muslim suicide bombers really do believe they will enjoy the attentions of seventy-two virgins in paradise. (Some Muslims have told me this is a mistranslation and it should read "seventy-two raisins," which confirms my view that Islam isn't much fun.) It wouldn't astound me to learn that one or two members of IRA-Sinn Fein did believe they would have a friendly chat with St. Peter at the Pearly Gates before being issued with harps. But Al-Qaeda, like the IRA, is an organization all of whose activities are strictly determined by its assessment of how these activities will serve its political objectives. Being prepared to give up one's life for a great cause is a commonplace of all national cultures, and always positively valued when done for the side we favor.

It's understandable that someone who picks up his knowledge of Christianity and Islam from the TV news would be innocent of the above facts. (In the wake of 9/11, an operation carried out by Saudis, I kept hearing about seventy-two virgins, but not once did I hear a single murmur on the major TV networks about US troops stationed in Saudi Arabia. These troops were pulled out eighteen months after 9/11, rendering that operation a brilliant success.) Still, anyone of a curious disposition might pause to wonder why, if belief in God explains 9/11, the first fifteen centuries of Islam passed by without a single suicide bombing or anything comparable, whereas suicide bombings (usually assassinations of public figures) were well-known in nineteenth-century Europe. We see this awareness reflected in such stories as *The Secret Agent* by Conrad and 'The Stolen Bacillus' by Wells. Again, we can generally assume that the "anarchists" who committed suicide bombings in nineteenth-century Europe were atheists.

What Makes Religion Dangerous?

Confronted by the fact that atheists have been implicated in both state repression and terrorism to an extent hugely disproportionate to their numbers, the New Atheists offer the rejoinder that these dictators and terrorists, though they may not believe in God, still think in ways that are unreasonable. In one formulation of this rejoinder, Harris says that "although these tyrants [Stalin and Mao] paid lip service to rationality, communism was little more than a political religion" (*End of Faith*, p. 79).

The first thing to note about this is that in making such a move, the New Atheists casually abandon what had been their central claim—and continues to be their central claim, because they don't acknowledge that they have abandoned it, but go right back to repeating it. They keep drumming into their readers that religion must be defined as belief in God (or occasionally, the supernatural), and that specifically belief in God is the pathological meme which causes terrorism and mass murder.

If 'religion' is to be used to characterize all belief systems which have ever led to terrorism and mass murder, then in shifting from religion-defined-as-theism to religion-which-may-just-as-well-be-atheistic, the New Atheists have tacitly accepted that their original claim is false.

The second thing to note is that while Harris will not apply the term 'religion' to his own beliefs, he does not give us a litmus test to distinguish 'religion' from non-religious beliefs. But a favorite rhetorical trope of his is to assert that people he disagrees with accept things without evidence, and so I think we can assume that Harris defines 'religion' as accepting things without evidence, or, as he sometimes says, without justification.

However, virtually all spokespersons for Christianity, Islam, Communism, or even National Socialism, would hasten to insist that they do not, repeat not, accept anything without evidence. They would go on to assert that Harris ignores the relevant evidence for their doctrines. Harris would naturally reply that he's not very impressed with their evidence, and interprets it differently. On this point I agree with Harris (as I have unpacked at length in my *Atheism Explained: From Folly to Philosophy*).

But the crucial thing to remember here is that anyone who takes up any point of view on any subject whatsoever will always claim that the evidence supports this point of view and that the evidence goes against people who espouse a different point of view. So what Harris is saying is that he is right and the theists are wrong. But we are all right about some things and wrong about others, and, while we ought to strive to increase the ratio of our true beliefs to our false beliefs, this in itself says nothing about which false beliefs have the effect of increasing the predisposition to kill people.

And so we find that, in practice, what Harris is saying amounts to the claim that 'religion' means belief systems he disagrees with, and people who think precisely the way he does would never commit atrocities. Any Marxist around the year 1900 would have said exactly the same thing.

Why Atheists Have More Blood on Their Hands

While I point out that atheists have perpetrated more and bigger atrocities than theists, I do not attribute this to an inherently greater tendency on the part of atheists to commit atrocities. If the historical facts were the other way around, with theists having committed more and bigger atrocities than atheists, I would then be pointing out that it is a logical error to conclude that theism is inherently more inclined than atheism to perpetrate atrocities.

As I see it, there's no direct causal link between atheism and atrocities or between theism and atrocities. Neither theism nor atheism is significantly conducive or unconducive to atrocities (or to happiness or health, as I argued in *Atheism Explained*). But I do have a historical theory explaining why atrocities by atheists in the twentieth century vastly exceeded the far smaller-scale atrocities perpetrated by Christians and Muslims in all centuries up to and including the twentieth.

Enthusiastic ideologies or belief systems, especially when they are able to capture a monopoly of governmental authority, are liable to give rise to atrocities. It doesn't make any difference to the body count whether such a belief system encompasses theism or atheism. The rise of secular belief systems such as Positivism, Marxism, Fascism, and National Socialism coincided historically with the greatly enhanced technology for committing atrocities. If Torquemada had possessed the administrative and personnel resources of Stalin, he might have more nearly approached Stalin as a superstar of mass murder.

Modern capitalism produces improved techniques and it also produces secularization. But secularization does not mean the disappearance of belief systems with fanatical adherents. Spiritual religions are replaced by purportedly scientific religions, from Mesmerism to Global Warming. Socialism has come and gone, and has now been replaced by Environmentalism. When Environmentalism passes away, it will be replaced by some new enthusiastic belief system, perhaps one associated with Mental Health or the need for contact with space aliens.

In the "third world," the poorer half of the world, which is now the stronghold of both Christianity and Islam, there remains some danger of atrocities perpetrated in the name of Christianity or Islam, but in the advanced industrial countries, most of the danger of future holocausts arises from secular-minded and pseudoscientific belief systems.

The New Illiberalism

Do we have anything to fear from the New Atheists themselves? Some of the things they say aren't very reassuring.

Harris informs us that "belief is not a private matter." (p. 44). The phrase "a private matter" has a specific meaning in the history of liberal thought. It means an area which is none of the business of the authorities, an area where whatever you may choose to do will not cause you to fall into the hands of the police. Hence the chilling quality, to any liberal, of the phrase, "Thought Police."

Maybe this was just a slip by Harris? Not a bit of it. "Some propositions are so dangerous," he explains, "that it may even be ethical to kill people for believing them" (pp. 52–53). The whole thrust of his book conveys the message that belief in God is the most dangerous of the dangerous ideas for which it is ethically permissible to kill people who have done absolutely nothing wrong. Harris reasons that since thoughts give rise to actions, it's okay to coerce people on account of their dangerous thoughts alone. The rhetorical tone of *The End of Faith* suggests that Christian fundamentalists have the moral standing of insect pests.

Just imagine the fuss the New Atheists would be making if Jerry Falwell or Pat Robertson had so much as hinted that it might be ethically permissible to kill people simply for believing there is no God. But the late Reverend Falwell said: "We [meaning traditional-minded Americans] honor the unbeliever." You can't imagine Harris saying anything this nice about Christians.

Commenting on the fact that most Muslims living in the West are tolerant of the non-Muslim beliefs of their neighbors, Harris points out that Muslims in the West are in a small minority, so their seeming tolerance may be just a sham (p. 115).

Quite possibly. And if the New Atheists today, when atheists constitute about two percent of the US population, can cheerfully entertain the ethically permissible liquidation of some unspecified segment of the dangerous eighty-plus percent who believe in God, what should we expect from the New Atheists when atheists have increased their following to forty, fifty, or sixty percent of the population?

The London Libertarian blog, April 12th 2014

13
THE FALLACY OF SHEER BULK (2014)

I've been having a lot of fun reading the works of the big-government anar-chist David Graeber. Superficially he embodies everything I most loathe, yet actually I like his writing. One reason is that he's completely unpreten-tious. He lays out what he believes with perfect clarity and no mystifying tricks. This is very unusual for someone on today's extreme left, especially when that someone is a professor of social science with a considerable aca-demic reputation. So, if for some reason you've been swallowing some toxic swill like Deleuze and Guattari, to cleanse the palate, try a swig of Graeber.

One thing that makes Graeber somewhat unlike most of today's left and very much like the left of the 1930s is his powerful conviction that cap-italism cannot possibly last much longer. He suggests different reasons for this belief on different occasions, but here I just want to look at a single sentence:

> There is good reason to believe that, in a generation or so, cap-italism will no longer exist: for the simple reason that (as many have pointed out) it's impossible to maintain an engine of per-petual growth forever on a finite planet. (page 31 in *Revolutions in Reverse: Essays on Politics, Violence, Art, and Imagination*, not dated but probably 2011)

Here I'm not going to look at the intended meaning of this sentence in the context of Graeber's overall political outlook (I'll do that sometime) but I'm just going to comment on its figurative and rhetorical aspect as a typical cliché of today's left.

Walking in Chicago's Loop a couple of weeks ago, I was stopped by a pleasant young woman who asked me to sign something for Greenpeace. I said, apologetically, that she was wasting her time on me because I am opposed to Greenpeace. She donned a maternal frown of concern and asked why, and I responded: "Because I'm evil" (though with the twinkling smile of a rough diamond, and if I'd had a mustache I would have tweaked it roguishly; the English accent always counts for something too; in England my voice betrays me as a prole, but over here the natives can't tell me from Hugh Grant).

So, I had to explain about how we need economic growth to industrialize the poorer half of the world so that millions of third-world babies can be rescued from heartrending deaths and how Greenpeace is among the enemies of economic growth and therefore of human happiness. And I threw in a few of my best lines, like the way wind farms mangle and rip apart the poor little bodies of millions of innocent birds and bats, and I can't understand how anyone can defend such a horrible practice. (Nor could she, for a few seconds.) I was heavily bundled up against Chicago's global warming (10 below zero Fahrenheit), and she probably couldn't see that I was nearly four times her age. So this was working, trust me, it really was.

Then she asked, no doubt rhetorically, whether we could go on indefinitely expanding aggregate real incomes, whether we could do this, as she put it, infinitely. I was trapped by my damnable candor, and in all honesty I had to say: "Yes indefinitely, yes infinitely." So now I was the escapee from the psych ward and that was that. Another lamb lost to the wilderness.

Back to Graeber's sentence. If we look at this sentence, we see that it relies on the metaphor of physical quantities. *Perpetual growth forever* (strictly redundant, but I think the redundancy works well as a bit of prose) *on a finite planet.* We immediately think of something physically expanding forever within a fixed perimeter. Obviously, this is impossible, at least in Euclid's world, and Euclid has to be good enough for this, I think.

The metaphor hides a simple mistake. Economic growth—growth of incomes—need not be growth of physical mass. For example, my iPhone is much smaller than an old-fashioned telephone, and even smaller than a telephone-plus-camera-plus-music-player-plus-computer. It is less massive yet more valuable.

A Ferrari 458 Italia sports car weighs 3,274 lbs. A Ford F-150 pickup truck weighs 4,013 lbs. So the mass of the Ford is more than a fifth greater than the mass of the Ferrari. But the Ferrari will cost you around $250,000 while you can pick up the pickup for around $25,000. The Ferrari currently has ten times the value of the more massive Ford.

Since something smaller can have more value than something bigger, economic growth does not always mean accumulating more and more physical stuff. Growth may sometimes coincide with reducing the amount of physical stuff. A CD is less massive than a vinyl LP, and any number of downloadable tracks account for no mass at all in the hands of the listener. Yet the progression from LP to CD to online song is an example of economic growth. As people move from books made of paper to e-books, there is a reduction in the assembly, storage, and transportation of physical stuff. Yet this is an example of economic growth.

It's not a novel phenomenon. Observers of the early factory system noted that, compared with domestic production, it uses less of certain kinds of equipment and supplies. Take a hundred weavers out of their homes and put them side by side in a factory, and they don't need as much backup equipment or stocks of yarn or even auxiliary labor as they all did in aggregate when they were working separately. This isn't the whole story, of course, but it's one reason why the factories could be more economical than the scattered domestic system. In this case, economic growth means getting the same output with less equipment.

Economic growth is not accumulation of more and more physical stuff. It primarily consists of the re-arrangement of physical stuff in new ways. Matter-energy can't be created or destroyed, but only re-arranged. Human activity can convert matter into energy, but the amount of matter lost in this way is minute. What producers are doing under capitalism is not to add bulk but to re-arrange the existing bulk in ways more suited to human gratification. And if we're worried about sheer bulk, several tons of cosmic dust land on the Earth every day (or even every hour, as most of the relevant scientists say), so the sheer bulk of the planet is always growing, do what we will. (Unless, of course, the incoming dust is compensated by gas and dust *leaving* the Earth. I've never seen anyone look at this, but probably someone has.)

At times, a reduction in the amount of physical stuff being used in production can be a form of economic growth. And it seems reasonable that these times would get more frequent once a lot of basic infrastructure has been built.

Economic growth also means more free time, more leisure. People have far more free time than they did a hundred years ago. People choose to take some of the gains of economic growth in shorter working hours and some in more stuff (where 'more stuff' means more valuable stuff, stuff affording greater satisfaction of wants). The proportions are determined by people themselves, not by something else such as 'the system'. In my judgment, income statistics would be more accurate if they included the amounts of free time, but in practice this doesn't matter much, as people always choose to take most of the gains of economic growth in goods other than leisure, rather than sharply reducing their working hours. We just have to bear in mind that the gain in human well-being from economic growth measured by national income statistics is usually understated: we have to add something for the bonus of shorter working hours.

Is it possible to maintain perpetual growth forever on a finite planet? Well, it can't go on forever, because as the sun very slowly gets hotter, in 3.75 billion years from now, the oceans will boil away and we'll be dead or gone. Even before that, since our galaxy, the Milky Way, is colliding with another galaxy, Andromeda, death by cosmic accident seems likely, not to mention more ordinary catastrophes like an asteroid hit, which can easily happen at any time (Our only hope there would be SDI; thank you, Ronald Reagan). And the next glaciation presents a problem, though per capita growth might go on, close to the equator, if we can reduce population by 96 percent.

But with those qualifications, yes, it's perfectly possible to maintain perpetual growth forever on a finite planet. Just as there will always be new songs to be sung, new stories to be told, new discoveries, new achievements, new debates, new adventures, new worlds of imagination and experience, so there will always be new ways to re-arrange the material structure of capital to make it ever more adaptable to human gratification and therefore human happiness. And that is all that we mean by economic growth. Capitalism could last forever and economic growth could go on, somewhere, until the heat death of the universe, with everyone getting richer indefinitely. There is no contradiction, and what "many have pointed out" is, as so very often, quite wrong.

Actually, I think that we'll probably evolve beyond capitalism within the free market economy. But that's a story for another day.

The London Libertarian blog, February 24th 2014

14

A MORAL DEFENSE OF MEAT-EATING (2014)

A moral case for vegetarianism has been made by some philosophers and has become popular among a small group of people not noted for their reticence. The most influential of these philosophers is Peter Singer. Singer's argument is that it's immoral to cause suffering, that the suffering of non-human animals has equal weight with the suffering of humans, that you can't eat meat without patronizing and encouraging the inflicting of suffering on animals, and that therefore it must be immoral to eat meat, except in cases of dire necessity.

I think this argument is mistaken, and I will now give you my chief counter-argument. My counter-argument contains a lemma—an intermediate conclusion that I can then use as a premiss for my final argument. To keep things short and simple, I'm not going to argue here for the lemma (though I am going to briefly explain the point of it), since I believe that most people, if they think about it even briefly will agree with it. I'm just going to state the lemma and then move on from there. (Although I say "my" counter-argument, I don't mean to imply that there's anything original about this. I've heard something similar to this before, though I have no idea who first came up with it. After all, it's pretty obvious.)

> LEMMA: We're not under any moral obligation to act so as to reduce the total amount of animal suffering below what it is in the wild, or below what it would be if humans didn't exist. In other words, if the immorality of eating meat is dependent on humans causing animals to suffer, then it can't be immoral to eat meat if the production of meat for human consumption does not increase the suffering of animals above what it would have been in the absence of any human intervention.

Explanation of the lemma: In the absence of human intervention, animals like deer and oxen would be eaten by non-human predators. When humans eat meat, they're competing with other meat-eating animals, such as lions and wolves. If the predators disappear, this may lead to overpopulation of the former prey animals and consequent unwelcome environmental effects such as deforestation followed by soil erosion.

The situation is not changed in principle if we move from hunting to the raising of livestock: the morally relevant issue is whether the cows or sheep we're raising would suffer more, or less, or the same, if they were in the wild and being eaten by lions or wolves.

The lemma allows the possibility that some ways of treating animals may be immoral, but the lemma rules out the presumptive immorality of all cases of treating animals in such a way that their situation is no worse than they would face in the wild. In the case of hunting, this is clear enough. Anyone who knows cats knows that they love to keep their prey alive and toy with it before finally killing it, and this causes more suffering than would be caused by a quick kill with an arrow or a bullet. So human hunting causes less suffering than hunting by at least some other predators.

Could it be argued that by hunting deer, humans are causing suffering to lions and wolves by taking away their prey? This doesn't look like a promising line of argument. Humans are hunters by nature, and it's not clear why we would feel obliged to let other species of hunters have prey that we could have. A lion whose potential prey is killed by a human is no worse off than a lion whose potential prey is killed by another lion, and in either case the total lion population adjusts to the availability of prey for lions, with marginal lions always dying or otherwise failing to reproduce because of competition.

As we move from hunting to raising livestock, no important new issues of principle arise. Do farm animals suffer more or less than animals in the wild? It's not clear that they suffer any more, and it seems likely that they suffer a lot less. The day-to-day life of a cow munching the grass and chewing the cud has less excitement than that of the wild ox, continually fearful of sudden attack by a predator, but I doubt that the cow would get a thrill from dangerous adventures the way some humans do. When death comes to the cow, it does not seem to cause any more suffering than death in the wild—and if we ever found out that it did, we could adjust our techniques of slaughter, without abandoning the practice of killing animals for food. My argument is not that all and any ways of raising and killing animals for food are morally acceptable, but merely that some feasible ways are morally acceptable, and therefore morality does not require vegetarianism.

Some people may feel that the life of an animal in the wild is in some way better than that of a farm animal, even though the farm animal experiences less actual pain and fear. Well, we observe, as real incomes rise, that there is a growing interest in both recreational hunting and in the demand for game animals, animals killed in the wild, in preference to farm-raised animals. The meat of game animals is leaner and tastes better. This trend is merely the tip of a broader movement towards free-range raising of animals. Suppliers of meat can charge more for meat that has been produced in a 'more natural' way, partly because of superior taste and partly because consumers feel better knowing that what they were eating was produced in a more natural way. As our incomes rise, we spontaneously move away from factory farming toward free-range farming, and then ultimately to preferring meat from animals that have been hunted in the wild.

If we accept the lemma, then the mere fact that some suffering occurs to animals when they're raised for meat production is not enough to show that this is immoral. Instead, we have to show that they necessarily suffer more than they (or corresponding animals, which might be a bit different in a hypothetical alternative world) would suffer, if the human population were much smaller and the populations of lions and wolves much bigger.

Although I'm not offering arguments for the lemma, I do want to look at three possible ways of rejecting it. Someone could maintain that our obligation is simply to stop suffering wherever we can. One way to stop the suffering that comes from animals being harvested as prey would be to wipe out those animals. Thus, we could kill all oxen (including beef cows). At the same time, we would wipe out all the predators, the animals that would have eaten the oxen. This would mean wiping out virtually all animal species, including insects, birds, and fish, for all these animals are either predators or likely prey. Some folks would feel sad that all these species had disappeared, but they could console themselves with the thought that being extinct means you never have to suffer, whereas being extant means you do have to suffer.

Consistently, we should extend this to humans: they should be killed off, and then no human would ever suffer again. (Just to keep an eye on things and make sure everyone follows the rules, I'll be the last one to go.) If allowing suffering is decisively immoral then every sentient living thing, including humans, should be made extinct, because this and only this guarantees no more suffering.

Another person might, however, approach the issue a bit differently. Instead of killing all animals, we could take over and manage the entire animal kingdom, transforming it into something very different from the way it has evolved, intervening with birth control drugs, factory-produced food, analgesics, and anesthetics. The former predators could be fed substitute foods made in factories from soybeans, or even directly from industrial chemicals. Since they would suffer somewhat from not being able to hunt, we would have to provide them with robotic imitation-prey, so that they could continue to experience the activity of hunting. Herbivores could be left to graze the wilderness, but fed fertility-reducing drugs to keep their populations stable. There would still be some suffering: accidents do happen, and every animal has to die, though we could try to limit this suffering by infiltrating the natural world with robots using analgesic and anesthetic dart guns, watching all the while for any impending pain or anxiety.

There are various aspects of this scenario which may not be very appealing. Be that as it may, it is not feasible right now, and won't be feasible without a huge investment over many decades, if not centuries (think about the difficulty in ensuring that every fish in the oceans is guaranteed never to be eaten). So, even assuming that this ambitious intervention is morally required, we're stuck for a while with the choice between a certain amount of suffering in the wild and a certain amount of suffering (probably the same or a bit less) down on the farm. And therefore, if we accept the lemma, we must reject the case for vegetarianism on grounds of the suffering caused by meat-eating.

Of course, most vegetarians will reject those two approaches and go for a third approach: simply have humans abstain from meat-eating. But what the lemma helps to bring out is that this option has an arbitrary quality. Turning humans into herbivores means excluding other herbivores from a large area of land, reducing the world's populations of non-human herbivores. So the third approach is a kind of partial and inconsistent version of the first approach. Either we have an obligation to reduce animal suffering every chance we get, or we don't have such an obligation. Eschewing the first two approaches means admitting that we have no such obligation.

We can kill animals for food without adding to the total net suffering in the animal kingdom, so killing animals for food is morally okay.

The London Libertarian blog, May 6th 2014

15
How I Could Have Made Hillary President (2018)

In his book *Win Bigly: Persuasion in a World Where Facts Don't Matter*, Scott Adams analyzes the formidable persuasion skills of Donald Trump and the comparatively feeble persuasion techniques of the Hillary Clinton campaign of 2016. The book is very funny, full of insights, and well worth reading. For those who haven't read it, what I'm going to talk about here is a tiny sliver of the richly entertaining material in the book, but it does illustrate Adams's approach.

Adams compares what he calls Trump's "linguistic kill shots" with the attempted kill shots of the Hillary campaign, and he compares Trump's slogan, "Make America Great Again" with the numerous easily forgettable slogans considered or actually employed by the Hillary campaign.

Here are the more powerful of Trump's linguistic kill shots:

• Low-energy Jeb

• Crooked Hillary

• Lyin' Ted

• Lil' Marco

• Pocahontas

Scott Adams analyzes these in detail to show exactly why they're so effective. They all appeal to the visual and they all plan for "confirmation bias." Probably the best of them is "Low-energy Jeb." The very day this nickname came out of Trump's mouth, Scott Adams blogged that Jeb was finished, as indeed he was, though no other commentator saw what had just happened. Recall that Jeb Bush had a war chest of many millions and spent far more than Trump. He was a natural for traditional Republican voters and for the fabled "Republican establishment," as yet another dynastic Bush but a more likeable personality than the preceding two Bushes.

Even after Trump had released his kill shot into what we can call the *rhetorosphere*, most seasoned pundits were still naming "Jeb!" as the most likely nominee. Yet, Trump had given Jeb Bush what Adams calls his "forever name," and it was henceforth to be altogether impossible for anyone to see Jeb or think about him without instantly thinking *low-energy*. His presidential ambition had been killed stone dead, not just for that electoral cycle but for all time, in about half a second, "in front of your eyes," by the Master Persuader, Donald Trump.

Adams offers similar analyses for the other nicknames. "Pocahontas" was the name given to Elizabeth Warren, one of the leading Democratic Party politicians and a likely future Democratic presidential candidate. Warren, a blue-eyed blonde, had claimed to be of Native American, specifically Cherokee, ancestry and had gotten an academic job at Harvard by impersonating a "minority." The Cherokee Nation, which has a database of everyone they have been able to find with Cherokee ancestry, has repeatedly protested against Warren's claim. Warren also once contributed a "Native American" recipe to a book of supposedly Native American recipes called . . . wait for it . . . *Pow Wow Chow*. It turns out that Warren is not Native American, the recipe was not Native American but French, and the recipe itself was plagiarized from another source.

A look at this book on Amazon shows that Warren is in even deeper trouble. The subtitle of *Pow Wow Chow* is *A Collection of Recipes from Families of the Five Civilized Tribes*, and the book is published by Five Civilized Tribes Museum. This blatantly insinuates that the Apache didn't routinely solve quadratics or use trig to calculate the circumference of the Earth, and this is indisputably the filthiest kind of racism.

I would be irresponsible if I didn't point out that this kill shot illustrates Donald Trump's disgraceful carelessness with facts. The Cherokee belong to the Iroquoian group, whereas the historical Pocahontas belonged to an Algonquian-speaking tribe. How low have we sunk when our president can tell such appalling lies?

Everyone could see that Trump's nicknames were effective, and so the Hillary campaign burned the midnight oil to discover an effective nickname for Trump himself. They tried three in succession:

- Donald Duck

- Dangerous Donald

- Drumpf

"Donald Duck" is obviously the sort of thing a committee would come up with. "Duck" tries to make the point that Trump was "ducking" various issues and various criticisms, including releasing his tax returns. But of course, associating Trump with a beloved if distinctly ridiculous cartoon character doesn't mesh well with the idea that Trump is a fearful Hitler-like menace.

"Dangerous Donald" doesn't really work, especially because a large portion of the electorate positively wanted someone "dangerous," someone who would go to Washington and break things.

"Drumpf" was claimed to have been the earlier name of Trump's ancestral family, changed to "Trump" around the year 1600. This story now appears to be just made up "fake history." The idea that having a non-Anglo-Saxon name in your family tree is a dirty little secret is not a winner.

As everyone knows, Trump's election slogan was "Make America Great Again." This is a brilliant slogan which can hardly be faulted. Adams lists its strong points (*Win Bigly*, pp. 155–56).

As against this, the Hillary campaign considered eighty-five slogans (yes, 85!, according to Scott Adams, p. 157, citing the *New York Times*) and eventually ended up with "Stronger Together." Here are the ones which were actually tried out:

- Love Trumps Hate

- I'm with Her

- I'm ready for Hillary

- Fighting for Us

- Breaking Down Barriers

- Stronger Together

These all have the flavor of mediocrity and ineffectiveness that comes out of committees, and especially committees of bigoted leftists. "Love Trumps Hate" literally begins with "Love Trump," and as Scott Adams points out, people's attentiveness declines steeply, so they often pay more attention to the beginning than to the end of a sentence.

"I'm with Her" and "I'm Ready for Hillary" both have a patronizing tone, as though you can prove yourself by being open to a female candidate, just because she's female; that kind of thing is off-putting to some voters. And as Bill Maher pointed out, "Ready for Hillary" evokes the resignation of being "ready" for that uncomfortable tetanus shot from that possibly sadistic nurse.

"Fighting for Us" makes you wonder who the "Us" really is. During World War II, George Orwell pointed out how a British working man might interpret the government poster that said: "*Your* Courage, *Your* Cheerfulness, *Your* Resolution, will bring *Us* Victory" (the first three sets of italics in the original, the fourth definitely not!).

"Breaking Down Barriers" has good rhythm but an uncertain appeal because most people feel strongly that they really want some barriers between them and some kinds of other people.

"Stronger Together" was the final throw, and it came just as voters could hardly ignore the fact that violence was coming from the left. Some of Hillary supporters were bullies, and bullies are always stronger together. The news was already out that the "violence at Trump's rallies" was deliberately engineered by paid agents of the DNC.

Scott Adams Doesn't Give His Alternatives!

Although Scott Adams does an excellent job of identifying the strengths of Trump's slogan and nicknames for opponents, and the weaknesses of Hillary's, he doesn't come up with his own, better proposals for Hillary.

This is a bit of a disappointment, and a surprise, as he emphasizes that it's all a matter of conscious technique, not instinct.

And so, I decided to cook up my own suggestions. Here goes!

My proposal for the nickname Hillary should have given Trump is:

● **The Don**

Here's how this works. Before Trump announced for president, he was often called "The Donald," a phrase which usually went along with either patronizing amusement or mild and grudging admiration. Use of "The Donald" died out, presumably because the US population was mobilizing into two great camps, one of which viewed Trump as a satanic monster, the other of which saw him as the nation's redeemer, and neither of these would perceive "The Donald" as entirely apt.

My plan would be for Hillary supporters to refer to him several times as "The Don," and just occasionally, for those who might be a bit slow on the uptake, "The Godfather" (or variations like "The Godfather of Greed"). Hillary would then take up "The Don," as an already established nickname for Trump.

Trump has many of the popular attributes of the Mafia boss: a commanding presence and a weakness for vulgar display (his golden toilets). All the points actually made against Trump's character by Clinton could have been given a slightly different coloration. Thus, when making the allegation (which the Hillary campaign did) that Trump had stiffed some of his subcontractors, this would be described as "making them an offer they couldn't refuse." You could throw in a reference to one of Trump's business dealings with someone who has since passed on, and add the jocular remark, "He now sleeps with the fishes." When complaining about the fact that Trump wouldn't release his tax returns, this could be framed as "the Trump Family [Family, get it?] has sworn the oath of *Omertà* never to reveal their sources of income."

But aren't mafiosi supposed to be Italian? Yes, but now they're often Russian too. Hillary's campaign promoted the story that Trump had "colluded with the Russians." This appears to have been a pure fabrication, simply made up (no one has ever faulted Hillary for being over-scrupulous or excessively candid) but it would have been so much more believable if associated with the Russian mafia.

It's a self-evident truth that every Russian has "ties to Vladimir Putin," and this can always be asserted of any Russian without fear of rebuttal. Similarly, it's a self-evident truism that every Russian businessman has "ties to the Russian mob." It would have been a simple matter to dig up every occasion when Trump did business with a Russian, call that Russian an "oligarch" (who could deny it?) and declare that this Russian oligarch had ties to organized crime (or deny that?). In this way, it would have become impossible for voters not to think of Trump's business activities as steeped in criminality.

Now, what about a campaign slogan for Hillary? This is quite difficult, because of the fact that Hillary had spent four of the previous eight years as Secretary of State within the Obama administration. She could not therefore put any emphasis on "change," and it would be hard to imply anything radically new. But anything that looked like a defense of the last eight years could only run the risk of implying that "the status quo is fine and we just want to keep things the way they are." This is a disadvantageous position to be in.

A slogan that goes negative and tries to focus on the evil of Trump is liable to boomerang—remember that meeting of Democrats, where a speaker referred to Hillary using the word "honest," and the entire room spontaneously erupted into laughter?

As Scott Adams hilariously points out (p. 159), a rather different kind of boomerang was a major feature of the campaign. One of Trump's problems, as a former reality TV host, was to get voters to take him seriously as a real president. Hillary continually urged voters to "imagine" Trump as president, and thus provided Trump with exactly what he needed. He needed people to imagine him as president, and Hillary did an excellent job of helping voters to do just that.

The Hillary campaign slogan has to have the following qualities:

- It mustn't directly mention the rival product.

- It mustn't be easily interpreted as merely a response to Trump's slogan or campaign.

- It can't, unfortunately, make a bold plea for change.

- It can't, unfortunately, make a bold claim for Hillary's trustworthiness or other personal virtues.

- It must have rhythm.

- It mustn't allow the interpretation that some special interest will be benefited.

- It must take the high ground.

So here's my proposal:

- A Win-Win for America

This slogan would occasionally follow the words "Hillary Rodham Clinton." (It's bad luck that "HRC" doesn't trip off the tongue like "LBJ" or even "JFK." There is no other memorable version comparable with "Doubleya". "HRC" might evoke "hardcore," but we probably don't want to go there.)

The slogan is positive and inclusively patriotic. It therefore crowds out the undesirable thought that Hillary appeals chiefly to welfare recipients, criminal aliens, and billionaire hedge-fund managers. "For America" takes the high ground and crowds out the thought that Hillary's election would be a win for Hillary, an undesirable thought because Hillary might be considered a loser, and also because we don't want voters thinking about any personal advantage Hillary might reap.

The term "Win-Win" has several functions. Literally it refers to a situation where we win, whichever of two alternate possibilities occurs. There would have to be a story about this, ready for those times when Hillary or her henchmen were directly asked about the meaning. But that's unimportant. We could even come up with a dozen different stories and get people arguing about which one was true. (Someone might suggest that it referred to the two Clintons in the White House again, and we might let that kick around for forty-eight hours before squashing it.) Really the term is simply a repetition of the positive word "win," and gives the slogan distinctiveness and rhythm.

It also has something which Scott Adams has talked about on a number of occasions: he has pointed out how President Trump utilizes the tried and tested marketing ploy of putting slightly "wrong" formulations into his tweets to enhance their effectiveness. A slightly doubtful formulation or a feeling that something is not quite conventionally correct helps a phrase to lodge in the memory. "Win-Win" therefore gains something from the fact that what it means is slightly obscure and off-key, while its emotional associations are entirely positive.

So there we are, Trump is *The Don* and Hillary's slogan is *A Win-Win for America*. This would have been enough to give her the electoral college, though it wouldn't have hurt to have also done a bit more campaigning in Michigan and Wisconsin.

Hillary threw tens of millions of dollars at various "consultants" who were out of their depth and out of touch with public feeling. As I've just proved, I could have gotten Hillary elected by a few commonsense marketing touches. Given my unpretentious proletarian origins and unimpressive net worth, I would have done it for, say, half a million dollars. That would have been a terrific deal for Hillary, and would have enabled me to pay off a good chunk of my debts.

But, I can already hear you saying, you'd be enabling this disgusting warmonger, purveyor of PC bigotry, and criminal sociopath to take power. Could you really live with yourself?

Yes, I have to admit, I would feel bad about that. So, make it a round million.

The London Libertarian blog, 22nd February 2018

16

SCOTT ADAMS AND THE PINOCCHIO FALLACY (2018)

Ever since 1999, many popular writers have been telling us that we're very probably all "living in a simulation." Scott Adams is one of these many. On his Periscopes and on his blog, Scott often returns to this theme. And in *Win Bigly*, he asserts it strongly (p. 35) and actually has an appendix where he tells us how he thinks we can prove it (pp. 267–270).

The idea that we might all be living in a simulation was given its biggest boost by the 1999 movie *The Matrix*. In *The Matrix*, the world we think is real is in fact a gigantic simulation: all the seemingly real facts about the world are not what they appear to be. The human beings who inhabit this world are real, but their bodies are actually being maintained in tanks, and their brains are being fed with information about a physical world which does not truly exist, or if you want to quibble, exists in a form very different from the way it appears. This world can be seen as an involuntary collective delusion, a delusion from which a few have managed to free themselves by "taking the red pill."

The Matrix has some puzzling features which have exercised the minds of fans ever since it appeared. It raises some questions which are not very well answered in the story. For instance, the movie definitely conveys the idea that the electronic "machines" or "Agents" who police the Matrix desperately need the humans, but why they need them is unclear and still controversial among *Matrix* fans. Why keep billions of humans in tanks, at enormous expense?

We're told that the humans are being exploited for the "energy" they provide and they are called "coppertops" (a reference to Duracell batteries). But in terms of literal energy output, measured in watts, this makes no sense. It would not be feasible to recover from the humans more than a minute fraction of the energy required to keep them alive and functioning in their tanks.

This, like many other questions, can be brushed aside with the defense that it's fiction and not everything has to be explained. There are things going on which we're not told about, and which the characters in the story don't know about. Morpheus doesn't explain everything, and the things he does tell Neo and the others, with a great show of certainty, could be his mistaken conclusions (as we eventually learn, at least in a few particulars, they are).

Since the readers of this chapter will all have an IQ above the fortieth percentile, you don't need me to tell you that the point of *The Matrix* is an allegory of the Marxist theory of exploitation and the Marxist theory of ideology. The theory that workers are exploited by capitalists for their "surplus-value" is just as wrongheaded and untenable as the theory that we're all in a computer simulation being exploited for our "energy," but here I'm going to take the *Matrix* story seriously and look at the notion that we're literally "in a simulation."

In *The Matrix*, the humans like Neo, Trinity, and Morpheus really are flesh-and-blood humans. It's just that, before they take the red pill, their bodies are actually inert in tanks, and the world they think they experience is only virtual, a computer simulation. So the human inhabitants of the Matrix do have bodies, and the story requires they must have bodies for the whole shebang to work.

But the "Agents" do seem to be purely electronic entities, able to manifest themselves as fake flesh and blood in the Matrix, but actually without any flesh and blood counterpart. There are also entities like "the Woman in the Red Dress," who are probably not conscious beings but merely programs inserted into the Matrix, or in this case into a training duplicate of the Matrix. We don't know how many of these entities there are in the actual Matrix.

The version of the "simulation" theory which has now become popular, and which is advocated by Scott Adams, dispenses with the bodies in tanks. It asks us to accept that we are all nothing but pieces of software, chunks of code. So, according to this theory, we're more like the Agents or like the Woman in the Red Dress than like Neo or Trinity. As Scott Adams recognizes, this means that in the simulation theory, we are not merely *in* a simulation (as in *The Matrix*), but we *are* simulations (p. 35).

But is it possible for software code to be conscious? Consider another question. Pinocchio is a boy made entirely of wood. Pinocchio gets the idea he would like to be "a real boy," not just a wooden boy. Could this story possibly be true? Of course not! And why not? Because to develop even a vague hankering to be a real boy entails being conscious. And a block of wood is not the sort of thing that could ever be conscious. A living body containing a nervous system is the sort of thing that could be conscious, and a block of wood is not very much like a living body containing a nervous system.

Why You Can't Be (in) a Simulation

The theory that "we're all (very probably) living in a simulation" was given another big boost by the philosopher Nick Bostrom. Numerous people outside philosophy have taken Bostrom's argument seriously, and it has spread like a prairie meme among people who write and talk about society, politics, and popular culture.

Bostrom is a serious philosopher and his argument, if you look at it closely, is much more tentative and qualified than the arguments of those, like Scott Adams, who have popularized this approach. I think that Bostrom is mistaken, but I'm not here directly refuting Bostrom, only some of his popularizers like Scott Adams.

The reason you can't be a simulation is because you have conscious experiences. For example, you have sometimes been sick to your stomach and you have sometimes felt euphoric. You have sometimes been sad and sometimes elated. You have sometimes felt itches and sometimes tickles. You have sometimes dreaded something and sometimes eagerly anticipated something. Of course, if you never have experienced anything like those things, you probably are a simulation. You don't know what you're missing, but then, you don't know anything.

Can these conscious experiences be simulated? Of course they can, but a simulation is never the real thing. A simulation of a weather system does not create real thunderstorms or real hurricanes. No one gets wet when a rainstorm is simulated. No trainee pilot has been burned to death in a flight simulator which simulated a crash. In exactly the same way, no one has a conscious experience when a conscious personality is simulated. A *simulation* is not a *replication*. A simulation of consciousness is not consciousness and does not create any consciousness. A simulation of a mind is totally mindless, just like sticks and stones and blocks of wood.

So, can conscious experience be *replicated*? Of course it can. We do this every time we produce a baby. Our babies have conscious experiences, just as we do, and as they grow up, their conscious experiences become even more like ours. We could, perhaps, one day grow brains outside animal bodies, human or non-human, and these brains could have conscious experiences.

It is possible to imagine humans one day designing and creating new kinds of conscious animals "from scratch," so to speak. But these would be real, bodily creatures (literal "creatures" in this case, since we would have created them). Nothing can be conscious without a body; nothing can be conscious except a body.

This isn't at all what the "simulation" proponents like Scott Adams have in mind. What they do have in mind is a situation somewhat like that in *The Matrix*, except that there would be no bodies in tanks. There would be no bodies at all. Instead, conscious thoughts would be generated within electronic computers.

This, I maintain, is quite clearly out of the question. It can never happen and therefore we can never "make progress" towards it. We can be as certain as we can be of anything at all that we are not simulations living in such a simulation world. The world we perceive is real, not fake, and our flesh and blood bodies are parts of this world.

The Simulated World

When popular writers like Scott Adams claim that we're probably living in a simulation, they make a number of assumptions. They take it for granted that the inhabitants of this fake world are just the same kinds of minds, and just the same particular individual personalities, as would inhabit the real world (supposing that the fake world were actually to be not fake but real).

Scott Adams betrays no doubt that the personality of Scott Adams is real, the personality of Donald Trump is real, the personality of Hillary Clinton is real, and the personality of all the minor member of the cast, such as David Ramsay Steele, are real. In this respect, the "simulated" world is just like the world of *The Matrix*: all of the personalities, or at least many of them, do exist, but each is experiencing a fake reality, artificially constructed.

These writers, including Scott, also assume that it's the same, identical fake reality for all the billions of us. Scott doesn't suppose that he's the only "simulated" mind, and that the rest of us are just props in his fake reality (like the Woman in the Red Dress). If he did allow this possibility, it might reduce his incentive to convince us that we're probably living in the fake reality—since he would be trying to convince what amount to little more than figments of his imagination that they are little more than figments of his imagination, and why bother? Especially as Scott keeps reminding us that he has "fuck-you money," is happier and healthier than he has ever been before, and is generally thoroughly chuffed about life.

Scott also doesn't generally doubt that the laws of nature, and the laws of mathematics, are pretty much the same in the fake reality as they would be in the fake reality if it were in fact not fake but real. All proponents of the fake reality theory, and most definitely Scott Adams, argue for the likelihood of the fake reality by appealing to laws of nature and logic (including mathematics) as we discover them in what we take to be reality, which is actually, according to their argument, likely to be fake reality. So they assume that the laws of nature and of logic are the same in the fake reality as they would be in the fake reality if it were not actually fake but real, and presumably also the same as they are in the real reality that underpins the fake reality (for we mustn't forget that for the theory of a fake reality to be true, there has to be a real reality which generates the fake reality).

Scott makes the interesting suggestion that some of the laws of the universe may have been concocted to put limits on what we can find out (because the architects of the simulation face cost constraints). So, we can't travel at above the speed of light, and therefore can't get beyond a certain distance in the universe (*Win Bigly*, p. 268). Scott apparently doesn't notice that if the fake universe we think we're living in includes ad hoc adjustments to physical laws, then the whole argument for thinking we're probably in a simulation is undermined.

What Is Consciousness?

Consciousnesss involves inner, subjective experience. Here are some examples of conscious states:

- feeling happy
- feeling miserable
- feeling pain
- feeling an itch
- feeling a tickle
- feeling apprehensive because there is an earthquake
- feeling apprehensive for no apparent reason
- believing something (feeling convinced that something is true)
- believing that the world we live in might be some kind of fake construction
- hoping that things will get better
- fearing that things will get worse
- feeling hungry or thirsty
- feeling that something is meaningful
- feeling that something is not just meaningful but very important

No one, at the present time, has the *slightest* idea how to design a computer or any other machine that experiences any of these states, *except* by reproducing or somehow reconstructing a living animal with a brain. And, related to that, no one has the *slightest* idea how to design a computer that can understand what it's doing or can attribute meaning to anything.

Now, you might raise the objection that these inner, subjective states are of no importance. If we can construct a simulation of interacting conscious minds, what does it matter that it's just a simulation, that there is actually no consciousness?

Well, suppose I were to tell you that I'm about to give you an injection. After that injection, your body will continue to behave, so far as anyone can observe, just like it does now. It will talk in coherent sentences and give the appearance of expressing emotions, but really it will be bereft of emotions or of any conscious feelings. Your inner subjective state will be that of someone in a deep coma—that is, you will not have any inner subjective state. You will never again have any *experiences*, even though your body will continue to behave normally.

Assuming you understand me and believe what I'm telling you, you will view the injection as lethal. I will be threatening you with murder.

From the moment of that injection, you'll be dead meat, even though your body will continue to operate normally. You will be legally alive but there will be no "you" any more.

So, *nothing is more important than consciousness*. Nothing could ever be more vital than consciousness, because without consciousness nothing can have any meaning. Paraphrasing the King James version of 1 Corinthians 13, we may say:

> Though I speak with the tongues of men and of angels, and have not *consciousness*, I am become as sounding brass or a tinkling cymbal.

That would indeed be precisely the death of being turned into a mindless robot.

However, the question of the vital importance of consciousness is, strictly speaking, a side-issue. More fundamental to the argument is the fact that you are conscious, and you know you are conscious, whether or not you or I judge this to be of any importance. So it doesn't matter *for the argument* whether it's important that you're conscious. All that matters is that your being conscious proves that you cannot be a simulation.

But now you might say, granted that no one has the slightest idea how to make a machine, other than an animal body, have conscious experiences, who's to say that some way of doing this might not be discovered, perhaps thousands of years from now? The quick answer is that we can't rule out this possibility, but that the making of an artificial consciousness will require the arrangement of matter and energy in a particular way, in effect the creation of a new kind of conscious body—even thought it might, conceivably, be a conscious body based on a different kind of chemistry—and that this arrangement of matter and energy can't possibly be simply lines of code, because simulation can never amount to replication.

Scott refers to "the simple fact that we will someday be able to create software simulations that believe they are real creatures" (p. 35). But this "simple fact" is a simple falsehood; the simple fact is that we will never be able to make software that believes anything at all. Believing, like understanding, is just one of those things that computers can't do (see Hubert Dreyfus, *What Computers Still Can't Do*).

How Some People Typically 'Argue'
for the Simulated World

When popular writers explain to us why they think we're probably living in a simulation, they all say more or less the same thing. First, they soften us up by suggesting that computers are "intelligent," and as they get better and better, they will become more and more "intelligent."

However, the word "intelligent" is ambiguous. Deep Blue, the program that won a chess game against Garry Kasparov, was intelligent in one sense but not in another. Deep Blue had no inkling of what it was doing. Deep Blue, just like a ten-dollar pocket calculator, had not the faintest notion of what was going on. It understood nothing. It was unable to see meaning in anything. It had no idea it was playing a game, and no notion of what playing a game means.

The use of the term "processing power" is then brought in to add to the ambiguity. The inattentive reader may pick up the idea that there is some general thing called "processing power" which can produce consciousness if there is enough of it. Computers do processing and so does the brain, right? But then, so does a sewage treatment plant and so does a soap factory, and we don't expect either of them to create consciousness, no matter how much processing they do.

We may be tempted to think like this: computation is somewhat analogous to thought, and thought is a conscious process, therefore computation is close enough to a kind of consciousness. But no amount of computation can produce consciousness. We do not know of any "processing power" that could ever produce thought.

We will then be told that we can assume "substrate-independence" meaning that consciousness doesn't depend on any particular type of physical system. Here two confusions are combined. First, the fact that we don't know enough to rule out the possibility that some other substrate might work is rephrased to suggest that we know that some other substrate might work.

Second, the issue of whether there might possibly be a different kind of substrate is confused with the issue of whether a particular system picked at random might be that different kind of substrate.

Sometimes confusion is piled upon confusion when it is suggested that the issue is between carbon-based systems (like us) and silicon-based systems (like computers). A computer could be built using carbon instead of silicon, and it would be equally incapable of consciousness or thought. Carbon has amazing properties unlike any other element, which is why chemistry is divided into two great kingdoms: organic (involving carbon) and inorganic (without carbon). To surmise that life above a certain level of complexity might just *have* to be carbon-based is not at all crazy.

But more crucially, let's suppose that one day we can discover, or create, a physical body based on silicon instead of carbon, and this body is conscious. This is conceivable—meaning only that we don't yet know enough to rule it out. Such a body would not be a computer, and the conceivability of such a body has no bearing on the fact that a computer can't be conscious.

(Here, to avoid unnecessary verbal complications, I'm skipping over the fact that according to the quaint argot of "artificial intelligence," *any* object, such as a screwdriver or a paperweight, or a brain, is *defined* as being "a digital computer." Here I'm following ordinary speech, where "a computer" is something like my laptop, whereas a screwdriver, a paperweight, or a human brain are not "computers.")

We can transfer the substrate 'argument' to the case of Pinocchio. Since we can't rule out the possibility that consciousness could have a different substrate, therefore (logical slip) we can't rule out the possibility that a block of wood could become conscious, and therefore (another logical slip) a block of wood could "in principle" be conscious. We seem to have proved that a block of wood could do the trick as well! But we know that can't be right, because we happen to know that the idea of a block of wood becoming conscious is totally silly. We have been handed something that looks a bit like an argument but is actually bogus through and through.

As far as we can tell, the cosmos is empty of consciousness except as this has arisen in animal brains. But this, of course, does not show that consciousness *couldn't* arise in a different physical system (or hasn't already). So, we may speculate, there could be consciousness arising from a different type of physical system, perhaps very different in some ways from the animal brains we know about.

In *Whipping Star* (spoiler alert), Frank Herbert supposes that stars are conscious and that they can intervene in the interactions of other conscious beings such as ourselves. We can't prove this isn't true, but I suspect that if civilization and science survive for a couple of hundred more years, we will establish the physical essentials of consciousness, and thus be able to prove that stars can't possibly be conscious.

We do not know of any consciousness except in animal bodies. At one time people attributed consciousness to natural forces, but we now know this to be false. At one time people believed they had observed ghosts or other disembodied consciousnesses (though in many versions the ghosts have bodies of sorts). But we have learned that ghosts, like the Martian canals, or like the Loch Ness Monster, or like the spontaneous generation of living organisms from dirt, though once frequently observed, simply cease to be observed when the observation procedures are tightened up.

Consciousness is a real physical property produced by a physical system. Consider any other property which can be produced by a physical system—say, stickiness (I mean literal stickiness, like the stickiness of Scotch tape). Can we write a computer program that would produce stickiness? No, never. Stickiness arises because of the specific structure of certain kinds of molecules. We can simulate stickiness in a computer program, that is, we can generate mathematical models of physical bodies which are sticky—they behave in the simulation as if they were sticky. But they are not really sticky. It's no use saying that if computing power can be increased billions-fold, we will one day be able to get stickiness out of software. This is forever an absurdity. We may, of course, find or create sticky physical substances that have not existed before, and no doubt there are ways to do this. But we have to step outside the software to do it. We are then no longer simulating; we are replicating.

As it is with stickiness, so it is with consciousness. We may, perhaps, be able to bring into being new types of physical systems, in some ways radically unlike the animals we're familiar with, which will be conscious. The argument that we don't know that today's animals are the only things which can be conscious points to the possibility of different types of physical systems which might be conscious; it doesn't point to the possibility that software might become conscious.

One More Thing

If we did create a new type of physical system which could be conscious, it doesn't follow that we would inflict upon these creatures a purposely false understanding of their place in the world.

We've seen that the arguments for software becoming conscious are more rhetorical than reasonable, and that the idea is, when all's said and done, more than a bit fanciful. But there is another point we can raise against it. That is the question of the motive for any advanced civilization to create such a "simulated" fake world. Just as fans of *The Matrix* have trouble with the motive, so the theorists of a simulated world have trouble with the motive.

To condemn millions of minds to living in a fake world is obviously immoral, especially if that fake world is full of terrible suffering (real suffering, actual agony, not simulated suffering, which would be no suffering at all) which could easily have been eliminated by writing the program differently. And if it were possible to create real minds within software, then such minds would have their own way of experiencing the world, their own emotions, objectives, and sensibilities, no doubt dramatically different from those of mammals like us. There would be a moral imperative to provide conditions conducive to the flourishing and fulfillment of such software creatures (or not to create them in the first place).

No one will ever be able to create conscious software. But just supposing they could, it would be morally wrong for them to do it in such a way that these new software-minds were trapped in a fake world of illusion, instead of being able to reach out and grasp reality, as we do.

Scott Adams and Philosophy: A Hole in the Fabric of Reality, 2018

Part II
More Scholarly than Popular

17

HAYEK'S THEORY OF
CULTURAL GROUP SELECTION (1987)

Hayek suggests that there are two ways in which we might think of society's having come to be what it is.[1] There is the "constructivist" way, social institutions having been designed for a known purpose, and an alternative, evolutionary way, analogous to Darwinian selection, "a process in which practices which had first been adopted for other reasons, or even purely accidentally, were preserved because they enabled the group in which they had arisen to prevail over others."[2] In this context, Hayek does not contemplate the possibility of any third way.

In this paper I establish what Hayek's evolutionary theory is, and argue (by reference to the preconditions of Darwinian natural selection) that it is scarcely tenable. I advance a third possible way in which social institutions might develop, and contend that this third way is the mode of social evolution envisaged by liberal social theorists such as Hume, Ferguson, and Carl Menger, mistakenly cited by Hayek as proponents of his own theory of cultural group selection. (I even toyed with the notion of entitling this paper "Hayek versus the Liberal Theory of Social Evolution.") In the course of these arguments, it will emerge that the refutation of Hayek's theory of cultural group selection knocks away the main support for Hayek's doctrine that reliance on human reason is hazardous in deciding matters of social policy. It will also emerge that Hayek's later thinking involves a curious convergence with the holistic and organicist theories he criticized so bitterly in his earlier writings.

---

1 F.A. Hayek, *Law, Legislation, and Liberty*, vol. 1, *Rules and Order* (London: Routledge, 1973), pp. 8–9.
2 Ibid.
3 F.A. Hayek, *Studies in Philosophy, Politics, and Economics* (London: Routledge, 1967), p. 111.

What Is Hayek's Theory of Cultural Group Selection?

There are at least three reasons why the peculiarities of Hayek's conception of social evolution have generally escaped notice and criticism:

1. Hayek's theory is singular, even bizarre, and readers tend to put their own commonsensical glosses on it.

2. Whilst Hayek frequently states his theory in unmistakable terms, he at least as often employs phrases that could describe either his theory or the liberal trial-and-error theory I shall recommend as more convincing. For example, the formulation "what proved conducive to more effective human effort survived"[3] is general enough to cover both theories.

3. Hayek undoubtedly takes for granted the liberal or trial-and-error scenario in some contexts (though he makes no mention of it in those contexts where it would be relevant to his treatment of cultural group selection).

However, such passages as the following leave little room for doubt about Hayek's commitment to an original and distinctive theory of social evolution:

In the process of cultural transmission, in which modes of conduct are passed on from generation to generation, a process of selection takes place, in which those modes of conduct prevail which lead to the formation of a more efficient order for the whole group, because such groups will prevail over others.[4]

In so far as such rules have prevailed because the group that adopted them was more successful, nobody need ever have

4 F.A. Hayek, *New Studies in Philosophy, Politics, Economics, and the History of Ideas* (London: Routledge, 1978), p. 9.

{226}

known why that group was successful and why in consequence its rules became generally adopted.[5]

[Cultural evolution is] a process of winnowing or sifting, directed by the differential advantages gained by groups from practices adopted for some unknown and perhaps purely accidental reasons.[6]

[Civilization] was made possible, at least as much if not more than by the growth of knowledge or intelligence, by some moral beliefs that asserted themselves, not by men increasingly understanding their advantages, but simply and solely by the selection of those groups which by adhering to them became able to build much better than they knew. . . . It had been mystical or supernatural beliefs that made groups stick to the traditions of certain practices long enough to give natural selection time to pick from the great variety of groups those with customs which most effectively assisted the growth of their numbers.[7]

Such passages have become increasingly common in Hayek's more recent writings, and they present a coherent and unambiguous theory, which I call natural selection of group cultural systems, or for short, cultural group selection. Among significant points, we should especially notice the following:

1. A selection process, analogous to Darwinian natural selection, is posited as operating in human society.
2. This process operates on groups, distinct populations of humans, each with its distinct culture.

5   F.A. Hayek, *Law, Legislation, and Liberty*, vol. 2, *The Mirage of Social Justice* (London: Routledge, 1976), p. 5.
6   F.A. Hayek, *Law, Legislation, and Liberty*, vol. 3, *The Political Order of a Free People* (London: Routledge, 1979), p. 155 (footnote number omitted).
7   F.A. Hayek, "The Rules of Morality Are Not the Conclusions of Our Reason," Plenary Lecture, Twelfth International Conference on the Unity of the Sciences, pp. 5, 7 (grammatical correction: "became" substituted for "becoming").

3. What are selected for or against are practices that benefit or hurt the "whole group," and not individuals or subgroups within the group.

4. What are selected for or against are entire group cultures, total group systems or aggregates of practices, and not particular practices.

5. There is no need for humans to possess any rational comprehension of this process, which occurs independently of anyone's intellectual understanding.

6. The process ensures that customs, morals, laws, and so forth, are useful to human group survival and expansion, even though the reason for their usefulness (or the fact that they are useful at all) is not understood by anyone.

7. We should therefore respect traditional ways even where we can see no good in them, and even where we find them abhorrent, because they serve a function for human society that we may not appreciate. (In fact, Hayek holds that we are bound to find them abhorrent, since he advances the theory, which we will not consider here, that the cultural traditions that have proved vital for the "Great Society" are in conflict with our genetically favored gut reactions, which evolved earlier and are inherently socialistic.)

Thus Hayek's repeated insistence on the importance of cultural group selection is part of his general case against what he regards as excessive reliance on reason.

Immediate Doubts and Puzzles

So much is clear, but there are obscure areas in Hayek's exposition of cultural group selection. The following three questions spring to mind at once:

1. *When did all this take place?* Did it happen in prehistoric times, and if so, does it happen today among primitive groups? Has it happened in recorded history, or is it even still supposed to be going on among industrialized societies?

2. *How do groups succeed or fail?* Do the successful groups exterminate or enslave the unsuccessful groups? Or do the successful groups merely

outbreed the unsuccessful groups, by a faster rate of population growth due to superior productive powers? Or is it rather that in some way "success" manifests itself as glamour, so that the successful groups are more widely imitated, and their efficient practices thus disseminated more readily than less efficient practices?

3. *How narrowly defined are the practices selected?* Are they so broad that all, or nearly all, existing societies exhibit these practices, or are they, for example, characteristically "Western" or even "Liberal"?

Each of these three mutually interrelated questions has the two characteristics that: 1. different answers are implied by Hayek on different occasions, and 2. whichever answer is given raises problems for his theory. In some places Hayek suggests that cultural group selection occurred in prehistory and was responsible for the transition from a primordial socialistic band to the "Great Society" of trade and division of labor.[8] Indeed, he seems to recognize that only in a vanished age no longer available for inspection could the conditions have obtained that would enable cultural group selection to take place, at least if it occurred by the physical disappearance of the unsuccessful groups. For the groups must be separate entities, not interdependent, and they must impose strict rules upon their members. The rules must be inflexible enough not to change to any appreciable extent, either by internal evolution or by random contacts with other groups. Hayek's recent emphasis on a sharp demarcation between membership and non-membership of the primordial bands, and on the intensely held supernatural beliefs hypothesized to have accompanied observance of group rules, may be an attempt to establish the (historically unknown) conditions that would make cultural group selection possible.[9] He also suggests that the evidence of social-anthropological field studies has no bearing on the transition from the primordial band to the Great Society, apparently an attempt to cover his theory against the observation that no group of people has been discovered with the characteristics of his hypothetical primordial band.[10]

---

8   Hayek, *Law*, vol. 3, p. 160.
9   Ibid.
10   "On this the study of still surviving primitive people can tell us little." Ibid., p. 156.

On the other hand, Hayek predicts, "Sometimes whole groups, and perhaps entire nations, will decline, because they chose the wrong values."[11] The context suggests that this will occur by a process similar to that which operated in the past to weed out unsuccessful values, and thus that cultural group selection is still operative. But apart from the consideration that the conditions for cultural group selection to be possible have not existed in historical times, immediate reflection on the well-known events of history prompts the conclusion that the process has not in fact occurred. For example, the English polity evolved over centuries, and not by the most generous application of any version of cultural group selection could any part of that evolution be convincingly explained. There were not thousands of separate Englands, with the "unsuccessful" ones being killed off or absorbed, for reasons of comparative efficiency that no one understood. There was a single continuous social grouping, which evolved in large part by intelligent individuals improvising on the basis of their theories about the world, by the unintended results of the clash of interest-groups and factions, by calculating statesmen responding to the military fortunes of various European leaders, and so forth.

To the second question, Hayek seems to allow all possibilities, with references to population growth,[12] conquest,[13] and imitation.[14] But each of these has its problems, not the least of which is that any one of them can be swamped by either or both of the others working in a contrary direction. It is difficult to accept that the most rapid population growth is always an infallible sign of "success." Civilization is based on cities, yet throughout much of history, population growth has been lower in the cities than the surrounding countryside, and in many cases the urban population's fertility was below replacement, so its maintenance relied upon immigration of rustics. This process continues today on an international scale, with the most technologically advanced societies facing the prospect of declining populations except for immigration from the (intuitively) "less successful"

---

11   Hayek, *New Studies*, p. 20.
12   Hayek, "Rules of Morality," p. 5.
13   Hayek, *Law*, vol. 3, p. 202, n. 39.
14   Ibid., pp. 159, 166. In particular, Hayek lays greatest emphasis on the successful society's greater ability to increase its size by recruiting new members voluntarily.

countries.[15] (In some cases, like the United States, this effect is being temporarily masked by the fact that some internal groups, only a few generations away from backward agrarian social conditions, have high enough fertility rates to keep the average for the native population above replacement.) As for conquest, Marx states somewhere that it is a "law" that societies founded on conquest adopt the culture of the conquered population. While no doubt a gross oversimplification, this is certainly far closer to truth than the reverse would be. The most prominent of several reasons is that conquerors take the conquered women, who play a major role in bringing up children. The grandchildren of the Scandinavian conquerors of Normandy spoke only Norman French. In some cases of conquest, even the women are exterminated, but this reduces the efficacy of conquest as a means of spreading the practices of the conquerors to a larger population. In some cases vigorous attempts are made to stamp out the native culture and replace it with the conquerors' culture, but this is rarely completely successful and is probably more common in recent centuries than earlier. (Another reason may be that society is big and complex, while conquest by a comparative handful may be easy, as in the repeated conquests of ancient Egypt.)

Furthermore, ability to conquer is not a very satisfying index of civilized "success." Historically, many comparatively civilized, productive peoples were conquered by rougher and less cultivated sorts. This raises the wider question of whether there is any necessary connection between "success" in the selective process and "success" in any sense we might wish to preserve and extend. We must resist the slovenly inclination to lump together all the things we like about civilization, assume that they are mutually conducive, and assume that whatever favors any one of them (or even, whatever favors some entirely different "success" trait) favors them all. That a culture has prospered by rapid population growth shows only that it permits, and probably favors, rapid population growth, or rather, that it did so under past conditions. That a culture prospered by military conquest shows only that it was good, or at least not hopelessly bad, at military conquest.

Selection by imitation of societies that are glamorous or awe-inspiring because of their success is the least convincing of all the alternatives,

15 See, for instance, Eugene Grebenik et al., Council of Europe, *Population Decline in Europe: Implications of a Declining or Stationary Population* (London: Arnold, 1978).

because it introduces the element of conscious, rational appraisal with which the entire argument is supposed to dispense. It is very rare—virtually unknown—for all of the culture of an alien people to be imitated, except by the occasional individual "convert." Usually the imitators are selective in what they imitate, and they select according to some theory of what makes the glamorous group so glamorous. Indeed, imitation often goes along with a certain amount of contempt for the people imitated, and precisely for that reason a desire to learn the tricks that have regrettably made them so successful; the adoption of some European behavior-patterns by Eastern peoples such as the Japanese illustrates this.

Further, Hayek emphasizes the whole pattern of practices in a group's culture, and if this whole pattern is not taken over, what will result by imitation will not (according to Hayek's argument) partake of the effectiveness of the whole pattern. It may well be less adaptive than what was abandoned; anecdotes abound of the kind in which a tribal chief buys an alarm clock though he cannot tell the time. An extreme example is the case of the Pacific cargo cults.[16] Like the Japanese, Koreans, and others, the cargo-cult members are rationally exercising discrimination in their choice of Western practices, but unlike those others, the cultists are operating according to a mistaken theory of the reasons for Western success.

Selection by imitation also has the difficulties that 1. stray, random influences of imitation may proceed in either direction, and 2. the imitating and imitated groups may be linked in some systematic way, the most probable and significant being that they each benefit from specialization and therefore from their differences. If we postulate that members of group A copy the practices of group B because group B impresses by its glamorous success, it follows that information about B is available to members of A. It is therefore highly likely that information about A is available to members of B. All this cosmopolitan cultural exchange seems difficult to reconcile with the granite inflexibility of rules within each group, which is required for natural selection to work. But in any case, we should be clear

16 Peter Worsley, *The Trumpet Shall Sound: A Study of 'Cargo' Cults in Melanesia* (London: MacGibbon and Kee, 1975); and Peter Lawrence, *Road Belong Cargo: A Study of the Cargo Movement in the Southern Madang District, New Guinea* (Manchester: Manchester University Press, 1964).

about what is envisaged: A member of group A must know something about group B; based upon his knowledge, he concludes that B is more successful than, or in some way superior to, A; he forms a theory that certain of the practices of B are responsible for the superiority; he rejects any theory that asserts that his own group is fated to remain inferior to group B, or that he ought to be loyal to A regardless of the remote consequences for group success; he then decides that the costs to him of adopting the new B practices are less than the benefits that thereby accrue to him; he next makes an analysis of the relevant group B practices, and manages to correctly copy them; he copies enough of them, and the right ones, to bring about the same benefits for his own group; and the condition must also be fulfilled that members of group B are not simultaneously copying practices from group A. Whatever we may think about all this, it can hardly be considered to form part of an argument that is going to result in the conclusion that rational appraisal should be limited in policy issues.

The elusiveness of the route by which one group supplants another appears in passages such as this, on the prehistoric transition to the "abstract" society:

> It is very likely that in the course of this development a wealthier urban and commercial population often imposed upon larger rural populations a law which was still contrary to the mores of the latter, just as after the conquest by a military band a military land-owning aristocracy imposed in feudal ages upon the urban population a law which had survived from a more primitive stage of economic evolution. This is also one form of the process by which the more powerfully structured society, which can attract individuals by the lures it has to offer in the form of spoils, may displace a more highly civilized one.[17]

Since Hayek has not discussed the displacement of more civilized by more powerfully structured societies, the final sentence is puzzling, perhaps pointing to future works in which Hayek will explicate his conception of social evolution. It is not clear whether he regards such "displacement" as

17   Hayek, *Law*, vol. 3, p. 202, n. 39.

an unfortunate occasional occurrence or thinks it valuable for a society to be "more powerfully structured." If the latter, it is a mystery why he should think that. The significance of the "spoils" is unclear, since in the two examples given it is the extension of the law to the subjugated, not any distribution of spoils, that is important. As to the two examples supplied, we may note that 1. a hypothetical process by which a more advanced culture subdues a more primitive culture is supported by a historical case where a more primitive culture subdues a more advanced one, and 2. the case of the towns under feudalism is one in which precisely what is supposed to happen in Hayek's scheme does not happen, viz., the towns retain their culture, alien to that of the feudal rulers. We may similarly suppose that the rural populations subdued by Babylonians, Incas, or their unknown prehistoric predecessors might retain their separate cultures (the story of the Jews' Babylonian captivity and return suggests as much) and that these might indeed survive long enough to modify the culture of the rulers.

On the question of how broadly or narrowly Hayek conceives the cultural practices selected, clues are scant. Although Hayek in one place seems to suggest that existing primitive peoples are unlike the primitives left behind by the advance to civilization in the past,[18] in another place he does imply that existing primitives, equally with those of the past, lack something vital that they would have to acquire before becoming civilized.[19] Private property, trade, contract, and a judicial system appear to be as prominent in most primitive societies as they are in industrialized ones, though naturally less elaborate.[20] Social-anthropological fieldwork has uncovered a great range of existing primitive societies, enough to scotch any fondly held prejudices about the necessary attributes of different "stages" of development, but nothing has turned up remotely like the Hayekian primordial band, untrammeled by customary rules, guided only by immediately perceived benefit. This seems to be equally as uninstantiated in the realm of the actual as are the promiscuity and primitive communism beloved of Morgan and Engels.

18   Ibid., p. 156.
19   Ibid., p. 160.
20   See, for example, C. Daryll Forde, *Habitat, Economy, and Society: A Geographical Introduction to Ethnology* (New York: Dalton, 1963); and Edward A. Hoebel, *The Law of Primitive Man: A Study in Comparative Legal Dynamics* (New York: Atheneum. 1968).

Hayek's conception of the necessary elements of the Great Society, which survive because they were selected out during a process that preceded the birth of the Great Society, defies criticism on account of its nebulousness. But however broadly or narrowly we conceive these elements, history must place a great strain on the theory. As far as is known, Sumer was the first great civilization. It seems to have been extraordinarily "liberal,"[21] at least immensely more liberal than many later civilizations, notably the "totalitarian" Assyrian, and perhaps more so than much of the world today. A very large proportion of the features of the Great Society, and especially those features which particularly appeal to Hayek, just seem to have appeared full-blown at the very dawn of history, to have died away, and then to have appeared full-blown elsewhere, essentially independently.

General Difficulties with Biological Parallels

There are difficulties with the notion that culture can evolve in a manner that parallels evolution of living organisms. In the biological case, natural selection depends upon a definite distinction between individual and population. The population adapts via its members' differential prospects for reproduction. Individuals reproduce by a process that preserves likeness, with some—usually comparatively slight—variations. An individual that survives to reproduce passes on an enormous collection of characteristics, mostly similar to those of its fellows that failed to reproduce or to reproduce so plentifully. In cultural group selection, where is the population and where the individual? One might regard each performance of a practice as an individual, the kind of practice as the population (for instance, one historical act of genuflection as an individual, genuflection as the population). But here the parallel fails because in Hayek's account there is no selection for particular practices, such as genuflection, but only for the entire set of practices carried by the group.[22] In nature this is true for the individual, which is selected for or against because of its entire makeup rather than a single characteristic. One trait might be conducive to reproductive performance

---

21   Samuel N. Kramer, *The Sumerians: Their History, Culture, and Character* (Chicago: University of Chicago Press, 1963).

22   Hayek, *Studies*, pp. 663–672.

in combination with other traits, but not with a different set. The individual is selected out of a pool of largely similar individuals; thus the effect is usually to select for one or a few differentiating characteristics according to their efficacy in combination with most of the others.

We are then tempted to try a different analogy: of the biological individual with the social group, the population with the set of all social groups with similar cultures. That does not work very well either. Rarely are there numerous social groups with highly similar cultures. Either groups are so closely linked (coming to each other's aid in war, for instance) that they must be regarded, from the point of view of natural selection, as one individual, or they differ very considerably in culture. In this respect, human groups are unlike small populations of organisms, upon which natural selection most effectively operates. We do not find batches of very similar cultures, differing in a few details, so that this replicated order can be honed toward adaptiveness by progressive selection of those details which work best as part of that order. It is as if we had a few thousand organisms, each potentially immortal occasionally splitting into two, occasionally fusing, each preserving some continuity but changing spontaneously in many details at all times. Anything like Darwinian selection is out of the question here.

Flies or rats can become resistant to poisons faster than can human populations, because flies and rats have shorter generations. In view of the acknowledged importance of the rapidity of cultural change, it seems relevant to ask for the length of a cultural generation, or rather (since potentially immortal organisms can breed rapidly), for the reproduction rate. Since for Hayek the reproducing entity is a group's whole system of cultural practices, such questions appear to have no sensible reply. The reproduction rate of a cultural system maintained by a group seems to be meaningless. Ordinarily, groups, and group cultural systems, do not reproduce at all in any sense that would fit. The founding of new Greek colonies in ancient times would be about as close as we could get, but even here the new colonies started to evolve apart once founded, and since they continually interacted with the other Greek communities, we could hardly regard each colony as a separate organism for selective purposes.

Hayek reminds us that human culture evolves much more rapidly than human biology.[23] But if cultural group selection is to be relied upon, human culture would evolve much more slowly than human biology. For the selection of groups is a slower process than the selection of individuals, and group selection according to culture cannot be expected to proceed any faster than group selection according to genes.

Evolution within the Group

Inasmuch as Hayek emphasizes the importance of the total system of a group's cultural practices, it is necessary to sharply distinguish internal changes in this system from those changes that result from selection among total systems. The latter kind of adaptive change is menaced by the former, not assisted by it. To take the biological parallel, if the genes of a living organism were to improvise their own changes, so that an individual organism at one point in its life were changed out of all recognition from the same individual at a different point (unpredictably, and not according to any programmed developmental scheme), this would not help out natural selection; rather it would prevent natural selection from making much progress.

Hayek often suggests that we should make changes in particular details of our customs, morals, and laws, in the light of our appreciation of the way in which these changes will enhance the working of the whole system. Nowhere does he seem to recognize that such a mode of conscious adaptation is incompatible with cultural group selection. Hayek appears to think that these two processes are almost the same, or complementary, when they are mutually incompatible. Hayek's account of the spontaneous evolution of law depicts judges applying old rules to new situations, and testing any doubtful rule by its consistency with the totality of inherited rules, which ought not to be open to question.[24] Hayek praises the Common Law tradition, in which precedents are regarded as embodying general principles, which are then applied to new situations as they arise. Sometimes, however, legislation must step in when some consequences of the direction taken by successive legal rulings "are seen to be clearly undesirable."[25] Neither the

23 Hayek, *Law*, vol. 3, pp. 154, 156; and Hayek, "Rules of Morality," p. 4.
24 Hayek, *Law*, vol. 1, pp. 85–88, 94–123.
25 Ibid., p. 88.

evolution by accumulation of precedents nor the legislative intervention can be squared with cultural group selection; in both cases the law is changed according to individuals' conscious awareness of what is desirable. In neither case is there any automatic selective check on the wisdom of the decisions, much less any check that operates by enabling some groups to prevail over others.

Hayek repeatedly insists that the merit of laws and other rules inherited from the past is that the process which selected them was independent of any human design, and that the adaptiveness of these rules rests in their total concatenation. But if the array of inherited rules is to be modified piecemeal by conscious decisions according to perceived desirability, then even the rules that remain unmodified lose (following Hayek's argument) any claim to respect, because they have become parts of a different system of rules. It is almost as though Hayek believed that cultural group selection selected general, abstract principles, and that conscious decisions which made the rules more conformable to those principles thereby aided the selection process. But the fact that the new decisions can be classified along with the old decisions does not mean that a selection process which favored the old decisions will favor the new decisions. What has not been selected is no more likely to be adaptive merely because it can be classified with what has been selected. We may suppose that along with the features selected, there are other adaptive features which could be classified together with them. But nothing entitles us to assume that that hypothetical classification can be known, or that it corresponds to the classification judges might make. In a reference to the evolution of systems of morals, Hayek contends that it is "only by recognizing the conflict between a given rule and the rest of our moral beliefs that we can justify our rejection of an established rule."[26] It is permissible, or at least, in Hayek's opinion the idea may be countenanced, to change one detail of the inherited system of moral rules, if this introduces greater consistency into the whole system of rules. But there is no reason to suppose that if the system of morals has been arrived at by a form of natural selection, intellectual consistency will be of any consequence. Perhaps the most adaptive system of moral rules is one riddled with absurdities and incongruities. The Stickleback does not bother its head try-

26   Hayek, *Law*, vol. 3. p. 167.

ing to render the quirky patterns of its nesting and territorial behavior into a harmonious series of propositions. Hayek also claims that a moral innovator must first purchase the esteem of his fellows by strict adherence to the established rules.[27] Elsewhere he proposes that the social group is governed by "dominant old individuals who are firmly set in their ways and not likely to change their habits, but whose position is such that if they do acquire new practices they are more likely to be imitated than to be expelled from the group."[28] Such remarks, endorsing the cautious traditionalism that Hayek recommends as a matter of settled policy, may be very valuable on other grounds, but they do not harmonize with cultural group selection, which if true would not indicate caution as a desirable policy. It might indicate either blind adherence to tradition and resistance to all change, or that we could have no sound basis for any sensible decisions at all.

In numerous discussions of Hayek's theory, I have been offered the failure and consequent disappearance of hippy communes and producers' co-operatives as examples of Hayekian selection. But these will not do, because they are parts of a wider society. Suppose that communes and co-operatives benefited the whole of society but that no one recognized this. It would not have helped them. It is entirely possible that a subgroup may act beneficially for the whole group and be selected against, or that it may act harmfully and be selected for. It might be thought that a subgroup's benefits for the group would result in prestige, imitators, and the wherewithal to support large families all being "awarded" to the subgroup. We are tempted to think this likely because we assume that someone recognizes the subgroup's benefits, but this would make the selection process dependent upon someone's intellectual grasp of the subgroup's importance. Alternatively, there might be some invisible-hand process by which rewards accrue to the beneficial subgroup regardless of anyone's conscious recognition of benefit, but this will happen only if institutions favor it. Frequently the activities of small minorities, such as Jews in medieval Europe or Asians in twentieth-century East Africa, are hugely beneficial to society as a whole, but this leads neither to disproportionate minority expansion nor to large-scale emulation of minority ways by the majority.

27   Ibid.
28   Hayek, *Studies*, p. 79.

Application of cultural group selection to modern history must fail because of the interdependence of all groups. Although Hayek predicts that "whole nations" will decline "because they chose the wrong values," it seems unlikely (given some of his other views) that he would grant that Soviet Russia was demonstrated to possess the right values by its successful expansion. It is a commonplace in liberal circles that the Soviet Union is able to progress, or perhaps even to maintain itself, only by drawing upon the technological achievements of the more market-oriented West. Hayek seems to share this view.[29] Hayek would probably insist, in the context of any past or future Soviet expansion, that the West and the Soviet Union are components of a complementary system. But that is not compatible with treating the Soviet Union or any modern nation as a separate culture susceptible to natural selection.

There are familiar ways in which nations may get on the wrong track and visibly decline, with the result that inappropriate practices are replaced. For example, they may adopt unwise economic policies and become materially impoverished, so that various individuals around the world—academics, journalists, and others—see the wrongness of those policies and broadcast their conclusions. Or the nations' governments may find that international lending agencies make their loans conditional on the adoption of new policies which increase the likelihood that the loans will be repaid. So it is not denied that nations may decline because they chose the wrong policies, and even the wrong "values." But this has nothing to do with cultural group selection.

There are, then, three major problems for a theory of cultural group selection in conditions where there are frequent contacts between "groups":

> 1. The groups may function interdependently, and therefore be better viewed as complementary sub-groups. 2. Where there is transmission of practices from one group to another by imitation, there can be no assumption that the transplanted practices will have the same significance in their new soil. 3. We cannot assume that the transmission of adaptive practices will be favored over maladaptive practices. (Members of rich and powerful social groups often imitate the customs of poorer and

29   F.A. Hayek, *The Constitution of Liberty* (London: Routledge, 1960), p. 47.

weaker peoples, as when Lowland Scots adopted a copy of the tribal "clan" system, plaids and all, of the Highland savages.)

Adaptiveness Cannot Be Inferred from Survival Alone

According to the views prevailing among evolutionary biologists,[30] natural selection operates only in conditions where there is a substantial number of similar entities with the capacity for self-replication at a potentially geometric rate.[31] The sole mechanism of selection is the arithmetic mean of the reproductive success of those entities endowed with a particular characteristic, compared with the arithmetic mean of the reproductive success of those entities endowed with an alternative characteristic. The forces making for selection must be high relative to the rates of change of the selected entities. Natural selection cannot look ahead and engineer developments because they will have beneficial consequences at the end of the selection process. Nor can it operate for the benefit of anybody or anything except via reproductive performance. These ideas are in stark contradiction to commonplace notions of evolution, which generally share a viewpoint that might appropriately be labeled "providentialism." Providentialists (who probably include most educated laypersons who have not made a special study of evolutionary biology) tend to assume that a. anything in nature of any benefit (for any organism) has been selected because of that benefit, or b. anything at all in nature must have been selected for in order to survive, and therefore must be of some benefit. Since almost anything that can be imagined will benefit some organism, these two formulations are in practice equivalent.

For example, many people probably suppose that senescence (deterioration through old age, leading to death) is prevalent in nature because it

---

30 What follows is heavily indebted to George C. Williams, *Adaptation and Natural Selection: A Critique of Some Current Evolutionary Thought* (Princeton: Princeton University Press, 1974).

31 At least, this is often stated. But David Hirshleifer pointed out to me that any potentially continuous increase will do; it does not have to be geometric. However, any increase becomes geometric if we assume that the average individual in each generation has the same reproductive capacity.

is somehow beneficial. They may suppose that it is nature's way of clearing the ground and making a fresh start, preventing overpopulation and making room for new generations, but this line of thinking has to he rejected as incompatible with natural selection. Any individual that had the potential for living longer than others in full reproductive vigor must gain a selective advantage, and no selective disadvantage, thereby. There is no reason why this advantage would stop accumulating with any given increase in longevity, short of potential immortality. Surprising as it may seem, death from "old age" has no "biological function" whatever. It may have benefits, but since there is no way that those benefits could be selected for by superior reproductive performance, the benefits do not account for its occurrence, and its occurrence does not show that there are any benefits. It is only when this has been comprehended that one is in a position to appreciate the ingenuity and elegance of Medawar's explanation of senescence.[32]

There is similarly no justification for supposing that occasional drownings of lemmings (which gave rise to tales of their "mass suicide"), the individual "suicide" of a moth flying into a flame, homosexuality (which occurs in all mammals), the pain suffered by a fatally wounded animal, sexual arousal in a female past her fecund stage of the life cycle, the fact that blood is red, the fact that you can sometimes hear your own heartbeat, the susceptibility of humans to backache and delusions, or millions of other persistent features of the natural world, have any adaptiveness. Influenced by the providentialist outlook, some sociologists and social-anthropologists adopted a "functionalist" approach to institutions, an approach which produces explanations that can never be refuted, since anything benefits someone.

Hallpike provides a salutary dismissal of functionalist theories of war.[33] In his critical comments on Hallpike's paper, Eibl-Eibesfeldt asserts that as wars have been going on since the dawn of humankind, they must serve some function.[34] He triumphantly follows this "refutation" with a list of

---

32   Peter B. Medawar, "An Unsolved Problem in Biology," in Medawar, *The Uniqueness of the Individual* (London: Methuen, 1957), pp. 44–70.

33   C.R. Hallpike, "Functionalist Interpretations of Primitive Warfare," *Man* 8, no. 3 (September 1973), pp. 451–470.

34   Irenäus Eibl-Eibesfeldt, *The Biology of Peace and War* (London: Thames and Hudson, 1979), p. 182.

ways in which war has contributed to humankind's development. One might as well argue that as human beings have always been falling from heights and breaking their necks, this must fulfill some function. And sure enough, these falls help to select those with stronger bones and the intelligence to calculate dangers accurately!

Although natural selection is a spontaneous process that hits upon devices a conscious designer might easily miss, it is subject to many of the same limitations as a designer. It must make use of the materials available, and in gaining one advantage, it may have to pay a price in associated disadvantages. An architect can decide to save space by putting in fewer supporting walls, or gain security by putting in more. The former choice leads to more collapses of buildings; the latter to less freedom of movement within. It would be a mistake to look for the purpose of roof collapses or constricted movement. (Hallpike satirizes the functionalist interpretation by suggesting that the function of dry rot is to ensure that houses are periodically overhauled and redecorated.[35])

Vestigial features (such as the rudimentary legs on the bodies of snakes) remind us that natural selection is imperfect and bound by the past. Any organism can be adapted only to its past environment; any recent environmental change throws open anew the whole question of adaptiveness.

An important prerequisite of natural selection is stability of replication. Occasional mutations can be coped with, but the rate of mutation has to be low in relation to the pressure of selection on different characteristics. It is no use expecting natural selection (or trying to practice artificial selection) if what you are selecting among changes too much, independently of the selection process. Selection works cumulatively only if what is selected in each generation is likely to remain largely unaltered for many successive generations.

Spiders keep down the number of flies, and this benefits humans, but that fact plays no part in explaining why spiders keep down flies. Economists will recognize this as a "free rider" problem: The spiders have no way of charging humans for their benefit, because the spiders have no way of selectively excluding humans. Many relationships in nature are of the free rider sort.

---

35   Hallpike, "Functionalist Interpretations," p. 451.

All these points can easily be applied to society. The survival of some persistent feature does not show adaptiveness, and no matter how beneficial that feature, this does not necessarily explain its persistence. Even if natural selection is responsible, adaptiveness applies only to the past. And "benefit" does not account for survival except as conduciveness to improved reproductive performance in competition with similar societies lacking the putatively beneficial feature. A benefit that accrues only via the modern international economy, united by the world market and division of labor, cannot account for the existence either of practices which gave rise to that social unification of the world or of practices which have been enabled to develop since. Just as there is no natural selection for the adaptiveness of the totality of living things on Earth, so there can be no natural selection accounting for the adaptiveness of a world social order. It is a paradox of Hayek's account that he seeks to explain the rise of the Great Society by the evolution of groups fitted to the Great Society, when it would be possible to realize the benefits of the Great Society only by obliterating the group's discrete and independent character, essential to the alleged evolutionary route.

Adaptiveness applies only to the environment within which selection occurred, and this must be true for any natural selection of culture. The environment of a human group seems to be very largely a matter of its relations with other groups, and the assumption of environmental constancy is questionable. But the necessity for stability of replication is even more dangerous to Hayek's theory. If Hayek relied upon the physical extermination of groups with maladaptive practices and the repopulation of their former habitats by colonists from the surviving groups, this would be a slower process than that of individual genetic selection. Even so, and even postulating groups with a monolithic intolerance and rigid orthodoxy of a degree never encountered historically, it defies belief that the formation of colonies would produce near-perfect copies of the mother society. Yet Hayek wants a process that works faster than individual biological selection and therefore has to rely upon the making of converts from those impressed by the evident success of groups with more adaptive practices. Sufficient stability of replication could scarcely be maintained under these conditions.

In nature, natural selection does not only introduce novelties, but at least equally importantly, it is necessary to maintain existing adaptations.

Selection must ensure that there is permanent pressure to eliminate random departures from existing structures. A convincing theory of social evolution would likewise have to show, not just that certain practices were favored, but that there remained a ceaseless tendency to revert to those practices.

Group Selection

In developing his theory of cultural group selection, Hayek was influenced by biological theories of "group selection."[36] Although such theories were given wide popular exposure, especially by Robert Ardrey,[37] they were always a controversial minority view among evolutionary biologists, and in recent years have increasingly been rejected on theoretical and empirical grounds. There is no doubt that group selection occurs, in the sense that a population can be wiped out and its habitat taken by a different population, but it is only under unusual conditions that this could effectively counteract selection of individuals, which may often work against group benefit. Part of the reason is simply that, as individual selection is bound to proceed much faster than selection of populations, any trait that benefited groups at the expense of individuals would normally dwindle within all groups faster than it could spread by expansion of favored groups.

It used to be claimed by some writers that animals would restrict their individual rates of reproduction in order to avoid overpopulation, and this example is cited by Hayek.[38] It was later shown that although higher population density leads to fewer offspring in many species, this maximizes the number of individual parent's offspring that can be successfully reared.

36 Hayek, *Studies*, p. 70, and *Law*, vol. 1, p. 18.
37 Robert Ardrey, *The Territorial Imperative* (London: Collins, 1967). Hayek was impressed by the later works of Ardrey; see, for example, Hayek, *Law*, vol. 3, p. 197, n. 7.
38 Hayek, *Studies*, p. 70, and *Law*, vol. 1, p. 164, n. 8. Although Darwin had no place for group selection counter to individual selection, group selection theories were frequently advanced by biologists and nonbiologists from at least as early as the 1920s, but no concerted criticisms or extended debate on the subject transpired until V.C. Wynne-Edwards, *Animal Dispersion in Relation to Social Behaviour* (Edinburgh: Oliver and Boyd, 1962), which evoked a considerable controversial literature. See George C. Williams, ed., *Group Selection* (Chicago: Aldine, 1971); and Robert N. Brandon and Richard M. Burian, eds., *Genes, Organisms, Populations: Controversies Over the Units of Selection* (Cambridge: MIT Press, 1984).

It is individually advantageous, and group selection is unnecessary for its explanation. Advantage to the group is fortuitous.[39] Thus Darwin's position that evolution proceeds by individual and not group selection has substantially been reasserted, though the issue is not entirely settled, and a few biologists still champion group selection.[40] Hayek clearly developed his theory of cultural group selection unaware of the trend of biological theory. In a discussion of various group patterns, including the "arrow formation of migrating wild geese, the defensive ring of buffaloes, or the manner in which lionesses drive the prey towards the male for the kill"[41] as well as the co-ordinated activities of ants, termites, and bees, Hayek quite correctly observes that such group patterns do not depend upon the individual organism's awareness of them but merely on the individual's following certain rules. He then goes on to apply this idea to human social patterns (in itself, not unwarranted), and adds, "Yet all the individuals of the species which exist will behave in that manner because groups of individuals which have thus behaved have displaced those which did not do so."[42]

This leap is unjustified. For instance, the behavior of a lioness in driving prey toward the male is likely to show a net benefit (to be reproductively profitable) for that individual lioness. Group benefit is incidental, and as an explanation, redundant. This discussion, written no later than mid-1966 and therefore quite early in the development of Hayek's cultural group selection theory, helps to uncover the assumptions underlying it and is significant in that it already shows Hayek posing the exclusive alternatives of design and group selection.[43] By 1979 Hayek had become aware of the trend

39 David Lack, *Ecological Adaptations for Breeding in Birds* (London: Methuen, 1968). Recent textbooks of evolutionary biology generally have less than two pages on "group selection," and that dismissive. Paul Ehrlich, Richard W. Holm, Dennis R. Parnell, *The Process of Evolution*, second edition (New York: McGraw-Hill, 1974), p. 119. And see the forceful statement in Egbert Giles Leigh, Jr., *Adaptation and Diversity: Natural History and the Mathematics of Evolution* (San Francisco: Freeman, Cooper, 1971), pp. 245–250.

40 For example, David Sloan Wilson, *The Natural Selection of Populations and Communities* (Menlo Park: Benjamin/Cummings, 1980.

41 Hayek, *Studies*, p. 69.

42 Ibid., p. 70.

43 Hayek here cites Alexander M. Carr-Saunders, *The Population Problem: A Study in Human Evolution* (Oxford: Clarendon, 1922), which contains an anticipation of the

in biological thinking, and asserted in a note to the third volume of *Law, Legislation, and Liberty*: "Although the conception of group selection may now not appear as important as it had been thought . . . there can be no doubt that it is of the greatest importance for cultural evolution."[44]

An Alternative View of Natural Selection of Culture

The rapidity of cultural transmission and innovation may mean that natural selection of culture should be separated from the notion of selection of human groups. Following this line of reasoning, we regard the individual practices or ideas as organisms, analogous to fleas or bacteria in their relation to the human groups that bear them. We ask what causes a particular sort of practice or idea (what Dawkins calls a "meme"[45]) to survive or die out, perhaps independently of the fortunes of the human hosts. Natural selection of human groups is an unlikely path for natural selection of memes, since culture is so contagious. Fashions and religions are often compared to epidemics. It would be unconvincing to propose that bacteria have evolved to benefit humans because the human groups infected by harmful bacteria must have died out. The unconvincingness arises only partly because bacteria can live outside human bodies; it is mainly due to the fact

main outlines of Wynne-Edwards's theory, with the emphasis on humans rather than other animals. The influence of other parts of this work upon Hayek is also highly evident, a fact of interest to students of Hayek's intellectual biography and the "LSE connection."

44 Hayek, *Law*, vol. 3, p. 202, n. 37. In the lecture "The Rules of Morality Are Not the Conclusions of Our Reason," Hayek asserts: "It is at the moment the predominant view among biologists that such group selection is at least not important in Darwinian evolution. I am not wholly convinced by this, but this is a matter for biologists to decide. All that matters to me is that, in the explanation of cultural evolution, group selection is of crucial and central importance" (p. 4). Hayek fails to address the fact that the considerations which led biologists to this conclusion apply a fortiori to cultural evolution, along with additional difficulties.

45 Richard Dawkins, *The Selfish Gene* (Oxford: Oxford University Press, 1976), p. 206. And see L.L. Cavalli-Sforza, "Similarities and Dissimilarities of Sociocultural and Biological Evolution," in F.R. Hodson, D.G. Kendall, and P. Tăutu, eds., *Mathematics in the Archeological and Historical Sciences* (Edinburgh: Edinburgh University Press, 1971), pp. 535–541.

that their rate of transmission is so rapid as to make the reproductive performance of their hosts a negligible consideration for their own reproductive performance. I suggest that cultural practices are the relevant self-replicating entities, and as with biological organisms, individual selection is overwhelming. (An important aspect of selection of individual practices is their compatibility with group-borne systems of cultural practices. That, of course, is quite different from selection that works upon the systems as wholes.) Hayek says that the success of groups is influenced by the sorts of cultural practices they maintain (True), with the result that those groups which happen to adopt beneficial practices will have a better chance of survival (True), and therefore the practices handed down from the past are likely to be useful to humans, even if they cannot understand why. Hayek would not say that the success of groups is influenced by the sorts of fleas, lice, and tapeworms they maintain (True), so that those groups which happen to adopt beneficial fleas, lice, and tapeworms will have a better chance of survival (True), and therefore the fleas, lice, and tapeworms handed down from the past are likely to be useful to humans, even if they cannot understand why. The latter conclusion is false. The former conclusion might be true, but like the latter, it does not follow.

The importance of this point can be illustrated by comparing a couple of imaginary histories. First, suppose that at a certain time a continent is inhabited by ten tribes, of equal population and level of civilization (by whatever standards may be supposed to be relevant). The continent is sealed off from outside cultural influences, and all cultural influences of one tribe on another are somehow prevented. We return to this continent a few thousand years later. We find that nine of the tribes have expanded enormously in population and have achieved dazzling successes in the arts and sciences. The tenth tribe has dwindled, and its people are as wretched and ignorant as can be imagined. Further, the culture of this tenth tribe has changed little, while the cultures of the nine tribes have undergone repeated transformations, so that the continuities are less easy to trace than are those between the Hittites and the inhabitants of Los Angeles. For our second historical scenario, suppose that everything is just like the first, except that 1. intertribe cultural influences are permitted, and 2. on our return visit we find that all of the ten tribes are profoundly affected by the culture of the tenth tribe. (For instance, they have all been converted to the tenth tribe's language and religion, and (mistakenly) identify themselves as descendants of the tenth tribe.) In the first case, we would not be tempted to conclude that the culture of the tenth tribe possessed, or was likely to possess, superior conduciveness to human survival and well-being. In the second case we might be so tempted, but this conclusion would be just as unwarranted as in the first case.

A theory of natural selection of memes is worth elaborating, but it is surely liable to be limited. In particular, we cannot help noticing that humans are inclined to discard those practices they come to believe to be harmful, and adopt those practices they find useful—a fact excluded alike from Hayek's theory and from the above.

Traditional Practices as Instruments

Hayek presents two alternatives: Either an institution was designed by a single mind and its operation conceived in advance, or it evolved by a group selection process entirely independent of human understanding. But there is a third possibility, which I suggest accounts for most of cultural evolution: that evolution proceeds by a process in which design and insight play an indispensable role, though the process as a whole is undesigned.

Consider the evolution of the bicycle (or of the piano, military strategy, the suit, the rifle, numbers, musical harmony). Here each model is produced consciously by a designer, guided by a traditional pattern the designer did not invent. The modifications are not random; they could be made only by conscious intelligence, though some might have been originated unreflectively or even by mistake. These modifications are not based on an exhaustive knowledge of the artifact; it is an error to suppose that because we have designed and built something we know much about it. Many proposed modifications are stillborn, others have their vogue and are then abandoned, whilst a few endure for a considerable period, perhaps becoming permanent features-like the bicycle chain or zero in mathematics. What determines the fate of an innovation is a "community judgement" (i.e., the judgments of numerous individuals) on whether the innovation works. People have common standards they can use to settle this question, at least provisionally.[46]

---

46 This does not commit me to pragmatism. Whether something "works" is a brief way of discussing whether it does what is required of it by certain common theoretical stan-

The evolution of the bicycle shares some qualities with Hayekian evolution. The course of the development is spontaneous, and it would obviously be unwise to try to direct it along a predetermined path. It may even be seen as a form of natural selection, since although conscious choice is vital, no single person's choices (or the choices suggested by a single formulated program) determine the evolutionary path. Indeed, it is just about conceivable that an innovation might be made and disseminated by an almost unconscious process, a slip of the pen at the drawing board, or a misreading of figures at the factory, followed by careless imitation. A modern bicycle could not have been devised "from scratch," without generations of experience of trial and error. Numerous promising-looking innovations that were unsuccessful and a few, perhaps inauspicious, departures that worked have cumulatively resulted in something that embodies, in a sense, more knowledge than any individual could possess.

On the other hand, we did not have to wait, in order for the bicycle to improve, for those civilizations which chose silly bicycle designs to be exterminated, outbred, or conquered by those with better bicycles, nor for the bicycle to make such a contribution to the efficiency of one group that this group became mysteriously yet evidently superior to other groups, so that members of the other groups applied to join the superior group, thereby incidentally and uncomprehendingly adopting its bicycle design. It would not matter if the more successful bicycles were made by patently unsuccessful, declining, and despised groups; insofar as the bikes worked, they would be copied. Every stage in the bicycle's evolution depended upon some people's being able to appreciate what was an improvement and what was not. Even the hypothetical case of the error at the factory leading to an almost wholly unconscious innovation depends upon conscious judgment in a negative way; this departure was preserved, whereas most would have been corrected, because it failed to obtrude upon anyone's attention as an inferior construction. People had to have some idea of what a bicycle was *for*. The evolution of the bicycle would not be explicable on the hypothesis

dards. One might have to decide whether a line of verse, a passage of counterpoint, the dénouement of a whodunnit, a scientific explanation, or a mathematical proof "worked." The expression helps to remind us that we may be able to decide that something works without understanding how it works—though in some cases we might have to understand in order to decide.

that they thought it was a sewing machine, still less on the hypothesis that they had no idea what it was.

The bicycle evolved by trial and error. This phrase is literally somewhat misleading, since in the notion it conveys, the preservation of success rather than recognition of error is the important thing. Deliberate trial is not essential. A cat learns how to get out of a box by pressing a lever. The cat could have fallen against the lever at a time when it had, so to speak, given up trying to get out of the box. What matters is that the cat will repeat the lucky motion in future, whenever it wants to get out. Trial and error does presuppose goal-seeking, and the capacity to preserve those practices that improve prospects for goal attainment. Intellectual insight will probably help. The application of the phrase "trial and error" to Darwinian selection is much looser and inclined to be misleading, since no goal-seeking is involved. One would be unlikely to say that sand and pebbles had come to line seashores because of trial and error. In Hayek's account of cultural group selection, there is strictly no trial and error.

I propose that social practices, or assemblages of practices, no matter how narrowly or abstractly conceived (a handshake, punishment for adultery, private property), evolve in much the same way as did the bicycle. They are vehicles, implements, or instruments that enable people to get what they want, and people cling to them or discard them according to whether they have been found to work. This hypothesis accounts for all of the facts accounted for by Hayek's natural selection theory, and there are numerous facts Hayek's theory does not explain, and indeed prohibits, that are easily explained analogously with the evolution of the bicycle. Most striking of these is the rapid pace of cultural evolution, far too fast for the weeding-out of whole societies.

The bicycle evolved in the way it did not only because of improvements in design, but also because of changing purposes (traveling to work, traveling as part of work, recreation, exercise, sport) and a changing environment (changes in roads and paths, other forms of transport, cyclists' incomes). Similarly, a traditional practice will respond to environmental changes, which will largely be changes in other practices. Practices have to be compatible with other practices, and it may help if they are complementary. A social practice may work at one time, and cease to work because of changes in other practices. Here we make contact with one of the well-worn themes of sociology, the interaction between different institutional spheres: the economy, family, state, religion, and so forth. We also encounter the theory associated with historical materialism: that changes in technical methods of production ("productive forces") will cause people to change their traditional ways of organizing themselves interpersonally in production ("relations of production"). In turn these changes will cause other kinds of practices to fail to work as satisfactorily as they did before. Adjustments will be made gradually where possible, but occasionally some cumulative changes will build up an increasing tension with respect to some traditional practices that cannot be adapted in the desired direction except by sudden, radical transformation.[47]

A practice may be regarded as valuable in itself, much in the way that a cyclist might develop an affection for a particular bicycle or model of bicycle. When we say that a practice is "valuable in itself," we mean that the production structure is less roundabout; utility is derived more directly, in the same way that eating provides utility more directly than does ploughing. And where practices enhance their utility by being similar or mutually interlocking, there are economies of standardization. Greetings, word usages, family obligations, or property rights derive some advantage for their practitioners from being standardized throughout society, in much the same way as electric power points, coins, or tape cassettes come to be standardized. Out of a range of possible practices, there are advantages in picking one option and sticking to it, quite apart from the comparable merits of the options. There is a built-in traditionalism, since the cost of switching to a new standard may be higher than the increased utility derived from an alternative practice, which would therefore be better only in an imaginary universe where we could start from scratch.

Cultural evolution depends upon humans being able to judge what is useful to them, and generally does not operate independently of utility; it cannot be ruled out that humans may improvise themselves into a corner, so that they have to take a fresh look at their overall situation, and sweep aside many customary ways in order to release constraints upon progress. There is no area of cultural life that proceeds without the need for conscious

---

47   Karl Marx, *A Contribution to the Critique of Political Economy* (Moscow: Progress, 1970), pp. 20–22.

commitment by individuals. No consciously maintained rule or practice would last long in any society unless large numbers of individuals saw good reason to persist with it. Few refrains are more common, throughout history and throughout the world, than that of elders bemoaning the fact that youngsters are deserting the old ways. And it's true—they always are. Hayek suggests that people follow rules without thought, and the rules endure. This is true in some cases, like unnoticed regularities in language (dubiously called "rules"). But in the sorts of cases with which Hayek is more concerned, like property, law, and morality, I suggest that typically people strive hard to maintain rules and are often doomed to fail.

An explanation of the origin of private property in terms of trial and error on the basis of perceived advantage goes back some centuries and has recently been restated by economists specializing in the study of property rights.[48] Recorded instances of the development of private property among peoples formerly adhering to common property[49] accord well with this theory and do not corroborate cultural group selection. I suggest that private property was never introduced or maintained because it "benefited society" or "helped groups to survive," but for reasons of evident practical utility noted by Aristotle, Cicero, Grotius, and Pufendorf. Private Property was maintained because, in the judgments of numerous individuals over the centuries, it worked. It led to the growth of a market whose extent and intricacy could never have been foreseen. Intelligent improvisation opened up possibilities for human welfare unsuspected by the improvisers.

Nonhuman Cultural Evolution

Hayek makes references[50] to the celebrated account of the macaque monkeys observed by Kawamura on Koshima Island, but this appears to bear

---

48 Furubotn and Pejovich, in a summary of this literature, assert that "changes in property rights are triggered by the interaction between the prevailing property rights structure and man's search for ways of achieving more utility." Eirik G. Furubm and Svetozar Pejovich, eds., *The Economics of Property Rights* (Cambridge: Ballinger, 1974), p. 9 (emphasis removed).

49 See Harold Demsetz, "Toward a Theory of Property Rights," in ibid., pp. 34–37. Originally in *American Economic Review* 57 (May 1967).

50 Hayek, *Studies*, p. 79, and *Law*, vol. 1, pp. 163–64, n. 7.

out the cumulative trial-and-error theory sketched above and to be difficult to reconcile with cultural group selection.

To lure monkeys to a place where they could be more easily observed, scientists scattered grain and sweet potatoes on the beach. One monkey invented the washing of sweet potatoes in the sea. This innovation was copied by other moneys, until it spread by imitation to most of the population. The same "genius" then invented the separation of sand from grains by throwing them on the water surface, and this too spread by imitation. Because of their new-found interest in the sea, the monkeys learned to swim and dive for seaweed, which in turn led them to travel to other islands.[51] A cultural revolution occurred without any group selection, and many thousands of times faster than would have been possible by group selection. The new practices persisted both with inventor and imitators because they enabled these individuals to be more effective at attaining their prior goals.

The practices were not preserved because they helped the group, though presumably they did that incidentally. Even if they had resulted in net harm to the group, they would still have spread among individuals and, given some stray interchange of individuals among groups, could have spread among all groups long before there was any appreciable differential effect upon groups. Irreconcilable with cultural group selection, the Koshima observations are also incompatible with Hayek's alternative hypothesis, that new practices become established only when the respected elders accept them. Among the Koshima macaques, new practices were always invented and most readily imitated by the young. The old either followed tardily or died off without benefit of the innovation.[52]

Earlier Liberal Writers on Social Evolution

Hayek frequently refers to earlier liberal writers in such a way that the reader might conclude that they too advocated cultural group selection in

51   A summary is provided in Edward O. Wilson, *Sociobiology: The New Synthesis* (Cambridge: Belknap, 1975), pp. 170–71, which cites M. Kawai, "Newly Acquired Pre-cultural Behavior of the Natural Troop of Japanese Monkeys an Koshima Islet," *Primates* 6, no. 1 (1965). See also S. Kawamura, "The Process of Sub-cultural Propagation among Japanese Macaques," in C.H. Southwick, ed., *Primate Social Behavior* (Princeton: Princeton University Press, 1963).

52   Hayek, *Studies*, p. 79.

some form.[53] This inevitably follows from dividing all accounts of the origin of social institutions into non-evolutionary and group-selectionist.

I will here briefly mention three of the thinkers most often cited by Hayek in this connection: Hume, Ferguson, and Carl Menger.

Hume presents the growth of social institutions as the outcome of individuals consciously pursuing their own interests.[54] Humans improvise their social order by developing what they find to hand. For example, the first social group was a natural extension of the family.[55] Because their "self-love" tends to lead to conflicts, individuals see the need for general rules that apply to everyone. Hume cautions: "I here only suppose those reflections to be form'd at once, which in fact arise insensibly and by degree"[56]— a different matter from saying that the conscious "reflections" do not arise at all, though even that could occur in an improvisatory, trial-and-error scenario.

Adam Ferguson sees Man as an ingenious contriver, and it is precisely from this inventive faculty that he sees social change flowing, though not in the direction anyone expects.[57]

Menger distinguishes between two sorts of social phenomena, those which are "the results of a common will directed toward their establishment (agreement, positive legislation, etc.)" and those which are "the unintended result of individual human effort (pursuing *individual interests*)."[58]

---

53 Hayek, *New Studies*, p. 9. Here Hayek propounds group selection and refers to his earlier essays, "The Results of Human Action but Not of Human Design" (*Studies*, pp. 96–105) "The Legal and Social Philosophy of David Hume" (ibid., pp. 106–121). But nowhere in these essays does Hayek clearly ascribe any form of group selection to the writers discussed (Mandeville, Savigny, Montesquieu, Ferguson, Josiah Tucker, Hume, Adam Smith), though he occasionally employs phrases that could be taken to describe either cultural group selection or individualistic trial-and-error. Between the *Studies* (1967) and the *New Studies* (1978), cultural group selection had moved to the center of Hayek's thinking.

54 David Hume, *The Philosophical Works*, ed. T.H. Green and T.H. Grose (Aalen: Scientia, 1964, reprint of London, 1886), vol. 2, pp. 258ff.

55 Ibid., pp. 259–260.

56 Ibid., p. 274.

57 Adam Ferguson, *An Essay on the History of Civil Society, 1767* (Edinburgh: Edinburgh University Press, 1966), pp. 6–7, 122.

58 Carl Menger, *Problems of Economics and Sociology* (Urbana: University of Illinois Press, 1963), p. 133. The same idea is repeated many times, e.g., on p. 158.

In Hume, Ferguson, and Menger, social evolution is an outcome of intelligent individual behavior, and there is no hint of cultural group selection, which would seem to offer a belated rationale for the organicist and historicist notions that both Carl Menger and Hayek have been at pains to repudiate.[59]

A Few Conclusions and Suggestions

Among considerations arising from the above discussion, I would urge that 1. It is a mistake to appeal to cultural group selection to provide a defense for policies that rational appraisal would on other grounds reject; 2. there is nothing that makes social orders optimal or efficient, except insofar as many seriously suboptimal or inefficient formations may he eliminated incidentally by rational policy-making or trial-and-error groping; 3. Hayek views society as a frail hothouse bloom that requires the most delicate care, whereas it is more in the liberal tradition (and more accurate) to regard civilization as a robust weed, virtually impossible to stamp out; and 4. cultural group selection, which became prominent in Hayek's writings in the late 1960s and has grown in prominence ever since, tends to go against some of his earlier (and sounder) arguments against methodological collectivism and historicism.

Journal of Libertarian Studies, Summer 1987

---

59   Ibid., passim, especially pp. 144–159; F.A. Hayek, *The Counter-Revolution of Science: Studies on the Abuse of Reason* (Indianapolis: Liberty, 1979), passim, especially pp. 93–152.

How We Got Here (1988)

The Principles of Social Evolution
by C.R. Hallpike
New York: Oxford University Press, 1987. 426pp., $59.00

Culture and the Evolutionary Process
by Robert Boyd and Peter J. Richerson
Chicago: University of Chicago Press, 1985. 339pp., $29.95

Functionalism is one of the reigning myths of our time. The paradigm of a functionalist is the social anthropologist who observes an exotic tribe with apparently crazy customs, and then comes home and explains how these customs are really superbly adapted to the welfare of the tribe. In a typical example, members of one community of hunters (the Montagnais of Labrador) determine the direction in which they will set off looking for game by holding an animal shoulder-blade over heat until it cracks. The pattern of cracks tells them the direction.

O.K. Moore (quoted by Hallpike, 116–17) interprets this as a randomizing technique, though Moore accepts that the hunters have no idea that this is what it is. Moore argues that any systematic pursuit of clues to the animals' whereabouts would give the animals the opportunity to learn how to anticipate the hunters' movements. The hunters' false theory that cracks in the bones can tell them where the game is located is actually an efficient way to maximize the long-term yield of game, by preventing the emergence of a locational pattern to which the animals could adapt.

Characteristically, no attempt is made by functionalists to test this theory, by actual comparison of the effectiveness of randomized versus non-randomized hunting. Nor is there any attempt to explain how it is that the great majority of hunting communities do *not* employ any such alleged

randomizing technique. Nor is there any attempt to explain how such a for-
tunate method could be guaranteed to be hit upon unconsciously. Nor is
any serious attention paid to an alternative interpretation: that the hunters
who use bone-cracking to find game are just making a mistake, acting upon
an erroneous theory, in much the same way that some people consult horo-
scopes and others adopt functionalist theories of culture.

The Poverty of Functionalism

Many anthropologists go to their fieldwork completely sold on the idea
that the culture they are about to study is made up of efficiently adjusted
components, like the parts of a watch, and that it is the anthropologist's job
to determine just what the 'functions' of the various parts are. As Mali-
nowski put it: "in every type of civilization, every custom, material object,
idea and belief fulfills some vital function, has some task to accomplish,
represents an indispensable part within a working whole" (quoted in
Hallpike, 95). Anthropologists are disinclined to find that they are studying
people who do many things for mistaken reasons, and that this explanation
is sufficient. Since almost any social arrangement that can be imagined will
have *some* benefits to *someone,* it is quite easy to dream up 'functions' for
anything. This all-purpose applicability and irrefutability is enhanced by
the ambiguity of the functionalist theory. For instance, is the 'function' to
maximize the welfare of the members of the community, or to perpetuate
existing social institutions?

The functionalist outlook spills over from anthropology into other
areas, and also infects the popular conception of biology, according to which
evolution has occurred so as to guarantee the welfare of large populations
of organisms. In some cases, this takes the form of species patriotism; it is
widely supposed that the function of reproduction is to ensure the survival
of the species, and that the function of mortality is to prevent overpopulation. In other cases, this form of biological functionalism (or providentialism) manifests itself as devotion to the welfare of all living things. Thus,
the function of Canadian wolves is to keep the caribou fit and healthy by
preventing overpopulation and weeding out the weaker individuals. The
function of earthworms is to aerate the soil and mix it thoroughly with de-
caying vegetation, so that agriculture is made easier. Given such elfin views

among the populace, it is hardly surprising that some people conclude that the function of the AIDS virus is to discourage rectal intercourse, or that the function of nuclear war is to cure the world's overpopulation crisis.

A good example of vulgar functionalism in popular attitudes to social institutions can be found in the popularized teaching of Christian theology, where it is explained that the old Jewish law, with its intricate regulation of diet and other matters, was functional for a primitive Middle-Eastern tribe. The dietary restrictions, it is somewhat obscurely hinted, were health measures, no longer necessary with modern sanitation and refrigeration. Thus both the old Law and the modern neglect of it are given a scientific validation. But it seems obvious that obeying the instructions of Leviticus will be deleterious and crippling for any society (except in the sense that individuals may derive satisfaction directly from following these instructions), and in this case there is no good reason to doubt that the obvious is correct. (Naturally, with regulations so numerous, a few of them will by chance have some beneficial results, and some of them may incorporate bits of primitive knowledge about the effects of various foodstuffs.)

Functionalism seems to be congenial almost right across the political spectrum. Among conservatives, functionalism harmonizes with the notion that society is an organic unity transcending individual reason. The Hayekian version of functionalism, even more brazenly fallacious than most, is eagerly embraced by many conservatives, and has introduced an irrationalist strain into the thinking of some libertarians. To rely upon science or reason to redesign traditional institutions is held to be dangerous "constructivist rationalism." Society has its reasons, which Reason knows not of. Among Marxists a sort of historicist functionalism tends to prevail, with things going on under capitalism because they are necessary to the survival of capitalism—but not because anyone knows this. Somehow, the sociological entity 'capitalism' instinctively looks after itself, a doomed and bad-tempered but highly purposeful beast. More fundamentally, certain functionalist assumptions seem to be inherent in the materialist conception of history. Perhaps the greatest tribute to functionalism, however, is the growing use of the term 'dysfunctional,' which means: 'having consequences I dislike'.

Of all anthropologists, the one who has done most to challenge the loose thinking of the functionalists is C.R. Hallpike, whose arguments are presented afresh in *The Principles of Social Evolution,* along with much new material, including an attempt to explain certain features of human culture which might at first blush seem to demand a functionalist explanation.

Hallpike's antifunctionalist case is, aside from a very few details which may need sharpening up, virtually watertight. He shows the implausibility of most of the "adaptationist" scenarios by which social institutions would be made functional (though I question some of his criticisms of this "adaptationism"; see below). He exposes the incoherence of the view (Durkheim, Radcliffe-Brown) that social systems have 'needs' (86ff). He refutes the theory that warfare among tribes is an adaptive device for adjusting population to resources (105–113).

One form of "adaptationism" is the view that the mode of subsistence, the way people get a living, determines or greatly influences the rest of the social organization. Hallpike tests this hypothesis by cross-cultural comparisons, and finds that, for most cultural traits, there is little or no consistent relationship. He classifies 113 societies by mode of subsistence (gathering, hunting, fishing, pastoralism, and three types of agriculture), codes each society for each of 14 features of its institutions, and then tests for correlation (150–165). The results go against the theory that a society's organization is heavily determined by its environment or mode of production. Hallpike concludes that primitive social organization is extremely open and underdetermined: that on the one hand any one of a great range of alternatives will work about equally well, and on the other, there are certain simple forms of organization which are likely to arise in any society, no matter what its method of subsistence.

Social scientists generally believe that primitive societies are tightly-adapted, efficiently-organized structures, and they have managed to sell this theory to a large portion of the public, but they do not normally extend this to their own society, which typically they see as jam-packed with dysfunctions, especially of the sort that require advice from social scientists in order to be cured. Somehow, the automatic forces ensuring functional efficiency are thought to have been destroyed by the juggernaut of capitalism. Hallpike instead advances the highly suggestive, and I think possibly correct, view that primitive societies can be organized in a great variety of possible ways—almost anything will do—while advanced societies are far more constrained. (The design of a paperweight is presumably less determined than that of a car, and arguably that of a car less than that of a spaceship. This principle suggests the possibility that there may be only *one* way to organize a *very* advanced society.) The functionalist illusion arises, in part, because anthropologists read the usefulness of institutions in their own society back into those of primitive societies.

One variant of functionalism is the view that the religious or magical theories held by individuals in a particular culture are actually 'about' the social relationships of that culture. Thus the anthropologist Fortes could make the preposterous statement that "The Tallensi have an ancestor cult . . . because their social structure demands it" (124). This sort of thing reminds me of the comical Jungian idea that the theories of the alchemists, admittedly inaccurate as representations of chemical substances, were actually extraordinarily accurate depictions of the human psyche.

A few years ago I saw a TV documentary about the Amish. The documentary gave absolutely no information about the ideas of the Amish, their religious reasons for rejecting much modern technology, for example, but obligingly translated these into sociologese and social-workerese, cant about tradition and social relationships, which the writer of the documentary knew to be what the Amish were really trying to tell us. Fortunately I was able to decode the Amish documentary correctly: it was really expressing something about the social structure of college sociology departments and TV networks.

Survival of the Mediocre?

Hallpike rightly insists that people's ideas are not determined by the social structure, and will themselves have effects on social institutions. But he seems to under-rate the importance of ideas in influencing social development, and the extent to which the evolution of ideas exhibits adaptiveness (122–138). This is connected with what Hallpike claims to be "one of the fundamental principles of social evolution," "the survival of the mediocre" (113). He provides some good examples of technological devices which survived for many centuries even though, with hindsight, they were dreadfully and obviously inefficient (114–16). However, the term "survival of the mediocre" suggests that the mediocre possesses some advantage over the more efficient, which is not borne out by Hallpike's argument. His principle might better be called 'survival of the optimal', with the proviso that what hasn't yet been tried cannot survive. (I don't mean optimality in the sense of 'optimal to an omniscient intelligence,' which is never achieved nor closely approximated, and is therefore a red herring.) What applies here to the making and use of tools, applies to other systems of ideas too.

Although I do not doubt that, as Hallpike says, many historical technologies were capable of great improvement with only a little insight, we have to be cautious about making such judgments. The fact that one technology succeeds another and seems an 'obvious improvement' does not show that it could advantageously have been made earlier, if only someone had thought of it. This is especially so if the new technology requires more investment. Hallpike gives the example of the Oldowan hand axe, which remained in use for well over a million years before being replaced by the Acheulian flint axe about half a million years ago. It is not self-evident that the Oldowan axe survived so long merely because no one thought of a better design. Perhaps game was so abundant that most of an animal could be discarded, and later became less abundant. While the flint axe could be used to do new things, such as cutting wood, it had higher production costs, requiring more work and expertise to manufacture. The flint axe, though sharper, was also more fragile, and required more frequent maintenance and replacement. Flint was probably scarcer than pebbles or cobblestones, and would have necessitated living near chalk beds, or being linked by trade with those who did. Perhaps there was eventually an increased demand for wood-cutting, or increased availability of time to spend making flint tools. (Stone Age axes were produced in large factories with specialized capital— tools just for making tools—and distributed hundreds of miles away by trade.) We should look at the 'obvious' explanation that no one had thought of an improvement earlier with the same skepticism we should show toward myths like little James Watt watching the kettle-lid. Furthermore, both the Oldowan and Acheulian axes underwent continuous, though very slow, improvement in design detail—a fact which does not harmonize well with "survival of the mediocre."

Cumulative Rational Selection

It appears from several passages, but especially his remarks on Durkheim (94), that Hallpike sees only three alternatives: 1. that people employ techniques and perpetuate institutions because they can perceive and understand the advantages of them; 2. the view implied by functionalism, that there is some mysterious process, in which intelligent insight plays no part, which guarantees that techniques and institutions are advantageous or even optimal; 3. that any advantage or benefit is due to pure chance. But there is a fourth possibility, which may be thought too obvious to need pointing out, but which Hallpike's argument often seems to leave out of account. I will here call it "cumulative rational selection" (I have elsewhere referred to it as "cumulative trial and error." See "Hayek's Theory of Cultural Group Selection," *Journal of Libertarian Studies* 8, no. 2).

If we find a tribe using optimally weighted and balanced, aerodynamically sophisticated feathered arrows with points and barbs made from some carefully processed substance admirably suited to this purpose and a shaft made from the best possible wood available, we do not conclude that some super-genius of a tribal engineer invented all this in one afternoon, or in a lifetime, nor that the arrow design appeared by a mysterious process in which conscious intelligence played no part, nor that this arrow design was adopted by pure chance. The arrow in question is the result of a process lasting millennia, in which innovations were made within a tradition of arrow-making. Some departures from tradition could be incorporated into the tradition and thus preserved. This process requires that people should, most of the time, copy the existing pattern without fully understanding it—a perfectly sensible thing to do, since they can see that this pattern (embodying the results of generations of past improvement) is more effective than anything they could have personally invented. But the process also requires that changes should occasionally be accepted and retained. For the process to be progressively advantageous, there must be some relationship between an innovation's benefits and the likelihood that it will become part of the tradition, and there is such a relationship: people can discern what works better. People who use arrows know what arrows are for, and they can tell a better arrow from a worse one. (In situations where they cannot—where benefits are hidden, or where individuals hold a mistaken theory which leads them to think that something works better than it really does—cumulative rational selection will not be progressively advantageous.)

Cumulative rational selection in the evolution of tools has some of the characteristics of Darwinian selection, and was in Darwin's mind at the time he wrote *The Origin of Species*. ("Almost every part of every organic being is so beautifully related to its complex conditions of life that it seems as improbable that any part should have been suddenly produced perfect, as that a complex machine should have been invented by man in a perfect state." Near beginning of Chapter II, page 58 in Mentor edition.) An artifact may have many advantageous features that no one in the community understands or knows about. The process of evolution of an artifact, such as an arrow, is consciously guided by no one. Picturesquely, and at some risk of being misunderstood, we may say that an artifact or technique contains the accumulated knowledge and wisdom of the ancestors. Yet at each stage the process depends upon rational evaluation of effectiveness. The whole process is a form of 'natural' selection, but each stage in the process (unlike genetic evolution) depends upon literal selection (except in the possible but certainly not predominant case where accidental, unnoticed changes are preserved merely because they fail to force themselves on the attention of the individuals concerned; here it should be noted that conscious attention is still important, in the form of a filter). Just as Darwinian theory requires that the adaptations of living things have come about by natural selection of genes—and thus rules out many possibilities which would have been useful, but could not arise because no natural-selection route was available—so cumulative rational selection cannot be used to account for the occurrence of practices where no plausible cumulative-rational-selection route exists. An arrow can be explained by this hypothesis, but not bone-cracking as a randomizing device, because no succession of intermediate steps, each perceived to be effective, could have led to that outcome.

I agree with Hallpike that generalizations can be made from technology to social institutions. In fact I think that all beliefs and institutions can be seen as instruments enabling people to get what they want. "Mediocrity" explains nothing, since it means no more than 'progress which, with benefit of hindsight, seems rather slow.' This may just be an anachronistic or ethnocentric judgment; where it is more than that, it calls for a historical explanation (Why didn't they discover improvements? Or if they did, why did the tradition resist modification?)

Cumulative rational selection applies to all aspects of culture—to religious and kinship beliefs, for example. Hallpike fully acknowledges that institutions prevail only because they "are perceived as useful by individual people" (214). He apparently views this as a transparent commonplace which cannot take us any further, and turns for help to "the structural properties of each society's institutions and their developmental potential," abstracting from people's motives. Structural properties are seen as the sole source of those important features of institutions which individuals do not understand. This overlooks the fact that institutions are continually subject to evaluation and modification, and that this process may produce adaptive features which no individual comprehends.

There are many reasons why cumulative rational selection, though it is a strong adaptive influence, cannot result in anything approaching the optimality implied by functionalism. People often make mistakes, employing an erroneous theory of what works. Different institutions tend to evolve piecemeal; hunting technology and marital relationships will be adapted and improved largely independently, with little thought to their compatibility, which is, as Hallpike rightly says, not much of a problem anyway, since a great range of marital systems are, as far as anyone can tell, all equally compatible with a given method of hunting. (Still, there will be some modification of institutions to render them more adjusted to others.) Changes in circumstances may make yesterday's practices ineffective. A community may by chance be 'trapped' in a set of practices which are not particularly fruitful in permitting new advantageous developments. And so forth. Recognition of cumulative rational selection permits a modest form of adaptationism which does not rest on mysterious or providentialist scenarios, and does not entail the extravagances of functionalism.

Cumulative rational selection requires that individuals hold a theory of what a technique or institution is for, and so are able to recognize whether something works well or badly. It ranges from groping, unreflective 'trial and error' to deliberate innovation after careful investigation, but it always presupposes 'rationality' in the broad sense that individuals employ means to attain their objectives, and are capable of choosing one means rather than another because they judge that their objectives will be better served by the former. Humans in all times and places are rational in this broad, general sense, and therefore cumulative rational selection is always a possibility. (As with Darwinian selection, prolonged stasis also requires an explanation: some process must be weeding out deleterious mutations, and that process in human culture is application by individuals of shared rational means-ends theories.)

Hallpike's Core Principles

Having dismissed all "adaptationist theories," Hallpike requires an alternative way of explaining how societies develop. A key element in his theory is the notion of "core principles," which he elucidates by a comparison of the histories of Chinese and Indo-European society.

Drawing heavily on the writings of Georges Dumézil, Hallpike argues that many significant features of modern European and European-derived societies can be understood as continuations of the institutions of the prehistoric Indo-Europeans. For example, Indo-European society, unlike Chinese society, has a high regard for war and warriors. Indo-Europeans saw society as composed of three essential segments: farmers, fighters, and priests, a conceptual division which is absent in other societies, and which has re-surfaced repeatedly among Indo-Europeans over the millennia.

The theory of "core principles" is like historical materialism or Weber's theory on the relationship of Protestantism and capitalism: it is easy to find striking confirmations, but difficult to test the theory, since just what would count as a refutation is elusive. And Hallpike gives his theory that great advantage which Marx and Weber gave theirs: a passage where the theory is so heavily qualified as to be all but taken back (370). Like all such ambitious theories some rather general statements can be drawn from it which are certainly true, and perhaps worth saying: that ideas or institutions may tenaciously survive numerous upheavals and social revolutions over thousands of years, a fact which itself tends to refute the functionalist notion that the parts of a social system are well-adapted to each other (or does it?).

The core principles are a mixed bunch, and it seems that they could be just a catalogue of those things which happen to have survived. If that is what they are, then it is, of course, no surprise that they have survived. Perhaps everything exerts some influence, and the influence exerted by those things which have survived a long time has been important just insofar as they have survived a long time. Hallpike does not explain how the core principles are determined, where they come from, or why they stay around. The Indo-Europeans were polytheistic, but they became converted to monotheism. Why? They were adherents of sacred kingship, but they became secular-minded republicans. Why? Are these core principles which were dropped or does their abandonment show that they were never core principles?

Hallpike suggests that the liberal political doctrine of separation of powers is rooted in the Indo-European tripartite view of society, the connection being "the idea that society is inherently composed of different functions, which *must not* be performed by the same people" (342). I said above that it is easy to find striking confirmations for these kinds of theories, but I should add that their devotees will always manage to sniff out confirmations that are far from easy to find, or even recognize once found. If this kind of breathtaking leap were performed by a sociobiologist or cultural-selectionist, how scathing Hallpike would be! The connection is remote and altogether dubious, and one can immediately call up a dozen equally plausible connections with other factors—one might say, for instance, that the separation of powers is rooted in Christianity, and I can imagine a pedantic epigone of Hallpike's arguing about whether 'Render unto Caesar' came from the Semitic or Indo-European strands in the New Testament.

Core principles apparently "are more resistant to change than others, and exercise a general regulatory influence" (288). But it is possible that something is resistant to change because it is inert and adapts itself with little resistance to whatever is happening, i.e. exercises no general regulatory influence. (Writing from left to right, or right to left, is extremely resistant to change, but conceivably it has very little influence on social development.) Suppose that I instance Russia as an exception to the tripartite view of society, since Russian farmers, many of them virtual slaves, have been treated so terribly and not granted any respect or recognition. Possible Hallpikian responses might be: 1. that the landowning aristocrats represented the food-producers in the tripartite scheme, or 2. that leading Russians often waxed sentimental about the sacred virtues of the peasants. Either of these would suggest that the tripartite view were inert and accommodating rather than regulatory. An alternative would be to admit that in many Indo-European cultures the tripartite scheme has been as absent as in many non-Indo-European cultures.

It is suspicious that the Indo-Europeans are compared with the Chinese, who have been ruled by a single state for so long. Since the Chinese have been dominated by a single state staffed by conformist scholars, and therefore a single broad tradition of ideas, some peculiarities of Chinese institutions may just represent the 'fixing' of elements that happen to have been associated with that one state. Similarly, we could take a single Indo-European society and quite easily define its core principles with emphasis on those that were distinctive, and do the same for the remaining Indo-European societies taken collectively. In this way we could plausibly contrast the core principles of Russian, or Iberian, society with those of Indo-European society. The only reason we cannot do this is because we happen to know that Russia and Iberia are Indo-European. We could equally well take 'Mediterranean society,' aggregating its Indo-European and Semitic elements, and probably find many common features, contrasting with those of either Northern Europe or sub-Saharan Africa. This sort of exercise is made much easier because, on Hallpike's own showing, many of the "Indo-European" core principles occur separately in some non-Indo-European societies, and do not manifest themselves in some Indo-European societies. My impression is that Japanese society sits more comfortably with his Indo-European than with his Chinese core principles.

Hallpike maintains that common linguistic origins between societies will be a comparatively good predictor of other forms of institutional similarity (370), implying that this substantiates the influence of core principles. But all this would show would be that some practices could survive a long time. It then automatically follows that there will be correlation of practices among those communities of common descent or subject to the same cultural influences in the past. This doesn't support the view that any of these practices regulate or dominate the others, or in any way form a "core." To take a trivial instance, there is an extremely strong correlation between those communities using an Indo-European word for 'one' and those communities using an Indo-European word for 'two', but this doesn't indicate that either word regulates the other, or that there is any necessary or intrinsic connection between the two.

The Market and the State

Hallpike gives considerable attention to the origins of the state, which he views as a test case for his contention that social evolution can be directional without being adaptationist. He concludes that the state could have arisen by various different routes. (I will not comment directly on his discussion of state-formation, which would require an extended and specialized analysis, but his observations will have to be taken seriously by all students of this problem.) In the course of his argument he advances the principles of "multiple properties" and "equifinality" (209–213).

Equifinality means that different routes may lead to the same destination (as with the invention of agriculture and the origin of the state). Multiple properties means that institutions have many properties, some of them unsuspected by individuals in the society. Hallpike appears to think that much more can be deduced from these two principles than seems to me to be possible. He states that "Because certain institutions . . . have multiple properties, there is a high probability that they will occur frequently" (211). This simply doesn't follow—the number of properties (even the number of *desirable* properties, which is not what Hallpike says) has no bearing on how frequently an institution will occur. And the principle of equifinality doesn't explain how similar institutions are arrived at by different routes: If there is a great number of alternative potential institutions which can be reached by a great number of alternative routes, the upshot should be a great number of actual institutions—not, as Hallpike implies, a smaller number than if each of these alternatives could be reached by only one route. On the other hand, a small number of alternative potential institutions would help to explain the independent emergence of similar institutions (120), but in that case equifinality is redundant. Having rejected all "the various selectionist and adaptationist theories of social evolution" (375), Hallpike turns to such principles as equifinality and multiple properties to account for the directional character of social evolution, but these principles are quite impotent to yield direction without being supplemented by some element of adaptationism.

Hallpike seems to misconstrue the role of the market in social evolution. He even seems to regard the market as an ancillary of the state (256). But the market predated the state by many thousands of years, and the market is of special interest because it is 'functional' in the sense of having a tendency, under certain restricted but not fantastic conditions, to reach optimal outcomes without anyone consciously aiming at them. As cumulative rational selection is able to crystallize the knowledge gained successively by many generations, so the market is able to crystallize the knowledge gained contemporaneously by many mutually distant communities.

Hallpike states that trade can arise only when there is a surplus (256), a statement one often encounters, but which doesn't become coherent, let alone true, by being affirmed. He quotes someone else quoting Karl Polanyi to the effect that ancient traders weren't like modern traders (257). What seems to be true is that the earliest empires regulated trade and gave monopolistic privileges to particular people, but there was no doubt an underground or black economy upon which the state regulation was erected, just as there is in present-day Italy or Burma. The market displays precisely the same laws wherever and whenever it occurs; for example, a good harvest means lower food prices.

An Inadequate Critique of Adaptationism

Hallpike's long second chapter opposing the application of quasi-Darwinian notions of "adaptiveness" to social evolution is the weakest, although I think that most of his broad conclusions here are correct. He tends to lump together all the differing adaptationist approaches, often making criticisms which apply only to some of these approaches. He should have classified different kinds of adaptationist arguments, then dealt with them separately. Thus, there is a big difference between arguing that social structures are genetically adaptive and arguing that they are adaptive in the sense of serving the subjective needs of individuals or the survival demands of institutions. Different considerations are relevant to adaptiveness for individuals, for genes, for little groups, and for big groups. There are major differences between arguing (as some sociobiologists do) that social practices serve genetic adaptiveness, arguing (as other sociobiologists, such as Daniel G. Freedman do) that practices serve some kind of "holistic" group adaptiveness, and arguing (as Cavalli-Sforza or Dawkins do) that practices are themselves subject to natural selection for their fitness at replicating themselves culturally. Hallpike emphasizes that among many primitive social groups there is little competition; but there could be fierce competition among forms of behavior without much competition among individuals or groups. He tends to misrepresent Richard Dawkins's position (in *The Selfish Gene*) by discussing Dawkins's argument in the context of the genetic adaptiveness of individual behavior in recent human society. Dawkins actually takes the view that human cultural evolution has become to a large extent autonomous, guided by memes rather than genes.

Aside from this, many of Hallpike's anti-adaptationist arguments just don't have much force. Arguing that cultural transmission is not analogous to genetic inheritance, he points out (44–46, 55–56) that human activity is structured, and that therefore individuals do not adopt practices or memes in isolation, but he doesn't identify specifically how this differs from the case of genes. An animal has a lifecycle, it has feeding and reproductive behavior, it is part of a population which is part of an ecological community, all highly structured. This doesn't mean that talking about one gene and its effects is of no explanatory value, and certainly not that it in any way contradicts the description of the animal's behavior. A way of building an arch fits into a complicated social structure, but this doesn't mean that it is of no explanatory value to talk about the transmission and natural selection of a particular way of building an arch, and certainly not that this in any way contradicts the whole theory of architecture in a given society, or the purposes for which humans erect buildings. The structure is itself dictated by genes/memes, and the environment of a gene/meme is mainly other genes/memes. The fact, for instance, that one kind of variation of a particular practice would 'make no sense' in a particular structured context, and therefore would hardly arise, is analogous to the fact that many genetic mutations are simply breakdowns to be eliminated.

In his contentions that structures are important, Hallpike is groping for a sound argument against complete reliance on natural selection of memes but he has not managed to frame it accurately, perhaps because he wants to do too much: to rule out all (natural-) "selectionist" theories completely. It may be promising to develop a reconciliation between structured institutions, especially those structured by purposes, and natural selection of culture. (Whether such a reconciliation would merely find a place for natural selection of culture in the spaces left by purposive action and conscious scrutiny, or whether purpose and consciousness could be brought within a general theory of natural selection of culture, I am not sure.) Just as we do not expect genetics to *supplant* descriptions of goal-seeking behavior in animals, but rather to shed light on them, so natural selection of culture may help to illuminate purposive action and structured institutions.

Hallpike claims that there is no evidence that memes exist, since there are no criteria for identifying them, "unlike genes, atoms, and molecules" (45). This is strange because: 1. for a long time genetics developed without any idea of what genes actually were; their existence was imputed in order to explain their effects, and their effects constituted the only empirical evidence for their existence (the same applied to atoms; as with genes, there were some people who argued that they were merely useful fictions); and 2. if it is impossible to identify a cultural unit, what is Hallpike doing all through this volume, where he talks about Oldowan axes, the East Cushitic *gada* system, or Indo-European sacred kingship?

Hallpike states that social evolution is quite unlike biological evolution because the latter requires that the organism be adapted to an environment "which *is not itself changed* by this adaptation," whereas in social evolution "we have a continuous process of *mutual adjustment*" (36, and see 208). But this sort of thing happens all the time in biology. For instance, an animal living in an arid environment becomes more efficient at extracting water from the environment, making it more arid. Or a beaver constructs dams, leading to a transformation of the landscape, with wider and deeper waterways. Again, Hallpike makes much of the fact that for natural selection, variation has to be blind (50—55), whereas in human society it may be the result of conscious action. Hallpike has a good point here against those cultural-selectionists who argue or imply that cultural variation has to be completely random, or that new discoveries are always accidental. But there is no need for variation to be entirely random for natural selection theory to have some explanatory value. When geneticists studying fruit-flies deliberately stimulate certain kinds of mutations by, for example, radiation, this does not mean that the usual corpus of neo-Darwinian theory has to be abandoned. Nor would this be the case if humans started to control their own evolution by genetic engineering or by deliberately stimulated mutations plus artificial selection. This would mean that an adequate account would have to include this conscious policy of control, but humans would still be subject to Darwinian selection for survival of the genetically fit. The two theories—natural selection and artificial selection—would have to be integrated to give an adequate account. This leads directly to another problem with Hallpike's discussion: he tends to assume that if he can show the great importance of processes which (he thinks) are quite different from and pre-empt natural selection, then natural selection is of no importance. But it is possible that human culture has evolved partly by quasi-Darwinian and partly by other mechanisms. These mechanisms may exist side by side, and may interact. This 'all or nothing' assumption is a mistake also often made by Hallpike's sociobiologist or cultural-selectionist opponents.

Natural Selection of Culture

The book by Boyd and Richerson (B&R) gives grounds for questioning Hallpike's sweeping dismissal of selectionist theories, though Hallpike's book also calls into question many of B&R's assumptions. Each of these books is a fine corrective to the other. B&R are concerned with natural selection of cultural traits. (In "natural selection" I include all processes where there is non-contrived differential survival of replicating entities, which may include hair styles or hymn-tunes. Unfortunately B&R employ the term in a more restricted and somewhat arbitrary sense.) They proceed by examining different scenarios of cultural selection, in the form of simple mathematical models. As far as I could tell, though, there is no mathematical mystification. The models are used to test the scenarios, and to generate sometimes unexpected results. Everything makes sense verbally. Not only is this work a systematic exposition of almost every simple mode of cultural transmission yet proposed; it fits them all together into a coherent typology, and it treats many positions in social theory from the culture-selection standpoint. The theories of 'human sociobiology' and those of the cultural symbolists are all brought within the range of different models; the circumstances in which they might hold are identified, and criticisms made of each.

Guided Variation

The book is really divided into two parts. Chapters 1–6 develop the cultural transmission processes B&R term "guided variation" and "direct bias." Chapters 7–9 explore the possibility of other kinds of cultural transmission. Guided variation and direct bias do seem to be very important, but the authors assume too readily that these processes are likely to work toward genetic adaptiveness. They therefore turn to the other processes in part to find possible explanations for genetically maladaptive cultural practices. I think they overlook the extent to which human cultural and intellectual evolution is cut loose from control by the genes. Therefore, their approach is unnecessarily elaborate; they strain to find sophisticated explanations for facts that can be explained more simply.

Following Rosenthal and Zimmerman, B&R explain guided variation as follows (80, 95–98). Suppose that an individual becomes a castaway in a strange, new, unknown environment. That individual could try to learn the best way to get along by individual trial and error, but if there were other people living in that environment, it might be less risky to observe them closely and copy their behavior. The new-born child is indeed a castaway in a strange, new, unknown environment, and the infant may benefit, therefore, from imitating his elders. This assumes that the elders are doing better than acting as an uninstructed newcomer would, and this seems plausible if we assume past trial-and-error learning. The picture is one of individuals copying the traditional practices of their society, and making some changes—which can then be copied by others, notably their offspring.

Is B&R's "guided variation" the same as what I have called "cumulative rational selection"? It seems so on its first introduction (9), where B&R mention the importance of "rational calculation" which, however, they distinguish from "trial and error." But thereafter, rational calculation is largely ignored, and trial and error comes to be interpreted as entirely non-rational. The reader gets the impression that, without being given a systematic examination of rationality in human affairs, he is being softened up, as B&R's argument develops, to accept the notion that humans are scarcely rational. The main rhetorical device to this end is the familiar one of appealing to an impossibly sophisticated model of rationality, in this case the Bayesian model (87–94).

In their discussion of guided variation, B&R tend to overlook—perhaps they even intend to deny—the fact that the process depends at each step upon rational evaluation. Their position is somewhat obscure; it could be that they are endeavoring to describe an abstract, unconscious process, which they accept will be heavily supplemented in practice by intelligent deliberation, creative thought, and deliberate testing. However, this is far from clear, and there are indications that they wish to resist this interpretation, which would greatly limit the applicability of their models.

I contend, against B&R, that guided variation or cumulative rational selection immediately establishes the possibility of cultural evolution in a genetically deleterious direction. An individual may prefer one practice over another because he judges that the preferred practice helps him better achieve his goals, yet it may not be conducive to the maximum spread of his genes. B&R seem to resist this conclusion, and make unnecessary difficulties for themselves, because of their presumption that guided variation must have genetically adaptive consequences or it would not have come to prevail.

Biased Transmission

Suppose that there are various alternative and mutually exclusive practices in a given generation of adults. The newcomer or infant has to copy one of several possible alternatives. If the child copies either one parent or the other, with a fifty-percent likelihood of each, the results for cultural transmission will be closely analogous to. genetic inheritance. Another possibility is "direct bias": the child imitates (not necessarily from its parents) the practice the child finds most attractive, perhaps by testing out each practice, perhaps not. "Indirect bias" arises when the child chooses whom to copy by some other criterion: choosing whose hunting practices to copy by looking at who brings back the most game, or who is the tallest, or who has the longest beard. An example of "frequency-dependent bias" would be always to copy the most common of the rival practices. Direct, indirect, and frequency-dependent bias can all be observed quite commonly in various cultures.

Purposive Behavior in Cultural Evolution

B&R play down the fact that all these transmission processes can operate by means of rational appraisal. Moreover, in many cases the imitator has to grasp abstractly what the practice is before he can imitate it. Imitation requires understanding the 'point' of what is imitated—not necessarily the 'real' point, but some kind of imputed point, at least. What is transmitted culturally is not merely a series of actions, but also the meaning or point of those actions, the intention behind them.

Consider the making and use of a bow and arrow. Does anyone suppose that this complex series of operations could have come about without the individuals concerned having some idea of what it was *for*? The technology is so complicated that some minute divergence from the appropriate procedure would render the entire, highly expensive process totally ineffective. On the other hand, quite substantial departures from tradition could be incorporated by a person who knew what he was doing. The more elaborate the series of actions, the more likely it is that some slight change, in the actions or in the environment, will cancel all or much of its effectiveness. But if the individual has an intellectual insight into the point of the actions, enabling him to tell whether they are working well or not, considerable variation is possible without disastrous results. It might be pointed out that very complex series of actions sometimes are transmitted genetically in some animals, but in that case individual variability through trial-and-error learning must generally be reduced to within very narrow limits. Once an organism has evolved some way along the path of a rigid genetically-programmed complex series of actions, the complexity of the pattern will itself intensify the pressure against any variation: the organism will increasingly become locked into rigid patterns of behavior which discourage the plasticity necessary for cultural transmission.

It would be futile to try to explain the evolution of bow-and-arrow technology without reference to the *intentions* of the hunters. As Hallpike has perceived, the fact that humans do things on purpose limits the scope for explaining the determination of culture purely by unconscious transmission processes; perhaps ultimately the main explanatory arena for some of the scenarios outlined by B&R will be found to be those cultural practices which no one considers of any importance, and especially, those cultural practices which are subliminal, which no one notices, like certain grammatical features of language of which the language-users are oblivious.

Some element of natural selection of culture will enter wherever the transmission of an idea is governed by a factor other than the ostensibly most important one. For instance, some things are easier to memorize than others (often for genetic reasons). This influence must often have prevailed at a cost; the 'Rule of Three' in early arithmetic and notions like the Kuhnian 'paradigm' among present-day intellectuals are concepts which manage to survive and reproduce themselves more because of their ability to stick in the mind than because of their ability to do the analytic job ostensibly required of them. On the other hand, it would be silly to omit the fact that one idea sometimes does displace another because it works better according to the overt intellectual standards applied. To expect to explain exhaustively all of human behavior by natural selection of culture is like assuming that Greta Garbo must have slept with thousands of directors.

Insofar as large complexes of practices are held together by some scheme or theory (which may, for instance, be a spirit-filled community cosmology), the elements of the scheme will have a rationale within the scheme, and will be resistant to spontaneous or 'natural' selective pressures. Part of what Hallpike is getting at in his criticisms of selectionism is that it would be curious, for instance, to theorize about selective pressures for the common practice of putting oil in the car. Any such influences on putting oil in the car, or failing to do so, must conform to an explanation which refers to the rational means-ends scheme. A society which left it to the unregulated forces of natural selection to have any significant part in determining whether oil gets put in the car could never develop the production and use of cars. The same tendency of a rational scheme to dominate explanation by natural selection of cultural practices holds equally well for those schemes which are mistaken, or whose evaluation is less straightforward. A society which had to leave it to natural selection of culture to decide whether baptism were conducted with water or with sand would never have developed Christianity.

Imitative behavior is a subsequent and more elaborate development of individual learning based on individual evaluation. Learning by imitation is founded on individual learning by trial and error—even though, from the viewpoint of an individual human, it may superficially appear that the reverse is true, since imitative learning is so important in human infancy. As imitative learning arises out of individual trial-and-error learning, and never eliminates it (even in infant imitation, individual trial and error is at work), individual learning is always liable to be directed by individual evaluation.

B&R seem to think that guided variation and direct bias would cause all cultural groups to respond in the same way in the same environment (157–160). If so, they are mistaken. Take guided variation. One individual improves an inherited practice; later his son copies it, then improves it a bit more, and so on. There are obviously different ways of improving something. A knife can be improved by being made more quickly, being sharper, sturdier, and so forth. An individual in one tribe may notice an improvement that no individual in another tribe happens to notice. Once some variations have appeared through chance, others will appear, not only through chance, but also because the cultural context helps to determine what constitutes an 'improvement.' Furthermore, we are dealing with 'improvements' as judged by the individual at the time, and he may be mistaken in his judgment, or he may apply standards different from those prevailing in another culture. We are dealing with successions of improvisations, and it should be clear that, from the same starting point, two chains of improvisation can turn out entirely differently. Guided variation alone could in principle lead to virtually indefinite divergence in cultural forms.

Human cultural transmission is never exact, because in order to imitate something effectively you have to possess some understanding of it. You have to form a theory of what the meaning or essence of the practice is. In acquiring that understanding, you make it your own. No matter how orthodox and conformist you may strive to be, you cannot avoid innovating, perhaps in very small ways. Commenting on the paradox implicit in the fact that many individuals can learn 'the same' language, J.N. Hattiangadi *(How Is Language Possible?)* points out that they do no such thing; they each learn a different language, which however has many points of similarity or overlap with the languages learned by the other individuals in the community. What Hattiangadi says about language applies to all cultural practices. Strictly speaking, there is no 'Nuer kinship system'; there are as many Nuer kinship systems as there are Nuer. The Nuer kinship system is an abstraction of some of the features common to the beliefs of all Nuer, or to most of them.

B&R seem to assume that rationality and conscious choice are inimical to stability of cultural transmission; but this is not always so. A person may abandon traditional ways because of rational reflection, yet rationality also helps to explain the stability which exists. If people lost any intellectual grasp of the point of making and using bows and arrows, and somehow kept on imitating these behaviors blindly, then accumulation of random variations would soon make these operations unrecognizable. Instead, an intellectual grasp of the point of bows and arrows is the core of continuity and cohesion in the practice of making and using these implements. The persistence of perceived meaning helps to stabilize human culture.

Are People Rational?

B&R survey the evidence from behavioral decision theory showing that "humans ordinarily make quite poor judgments" (168). This body of findings, they conclude, "paints a depressing picture of human decision-making abilities" (169). As they acknowledge, the decision-making procedures of ordinary people can be defended on various grounds; for example, it is sensible to employ a crude rule of thumb if it is right a lot of the time and cheap to apply. But this is not the main point. The question is whether rational choice is an important factor in human affairs, not whether it is commonly executed with virtuosic brilliance. The fact that people are *stupid* should not blind us to the fact that they are *rational*. It is a popular theory that people are very clever but highly irrational; I think this theory could only have been devised by people who are rational but not very bright.

The importance of rationality in culture helps to answer the question posed by B&R (130–31): Why is culture so rare in non-human animals? An animal with little insight into what it is doing can easily waste its time if conditions are not exactly as they were in the evolutionary past, as when a cat of my acquaintance scratches furiously at the tiled floor near her litter box. Protracted series of actions are highly vulnerable to slight departures from past conditions, but this can be compensated by the animal's having general goals to which it can adapt the details of the actions. If the animal knows what it is doing, it can pursue elaborate series of actions (as when a chimpanzee uses a stick to get a fruit out of reach) without being locked into them genetically, and the actions can be varied considerably and still be effective.

Once we acknowledge that people are rational, some of the distinctions made by B&R lose their precision and force. They make a sharp distinction between individual trial-and-error learning and cultural transmission, to such an extent that they counterpose "learning" to "culture," which is odd since culture is usually defined (in the social sciences) in terms of learned behavior. But learning by imitation is a certain kind of learning by trial and error. The child is not a passive receptacle for culture, but an active explorer, all the time trying to get satisfaction, trying out the available options to see what works. The difference between direct bias and guided variation is not very fundamental: in both cases, an individual evaluates two or more rival practices and chooses the one that she likes. Indirect bias is not so very different from direct bias: in either case a fallible judgment is made about whether a practice is worth adopting. B&R counterpose rational action to cultural transmission (40), but they make no attempt to argue that the transmission of culture is not made up of rational decisions on the parts of both teachers and imitators. As their own introduction to guided variation implies, a rational decision-maker who found himself suddenly stranded amid a strange culture would find it useful to learn its traditions. Since it generally pays the individual to imitate, and since there are demonstrable cases where individuals fail to imitate when it doesn't pay, rational decisions alone are sufficient to explain the existence of cultural transmission.

In turn, biased transmission and guided variation are together distinguished from "natural selection," defined by B&R as "all the things that happen to an individual because it performs a given behavior, and that, in turn, affect the probability that the individual will be available as a model for naive individuals" (175). Suppose an individual does something that results in his being consigned to a despised group of outcasts. This is 'not being available as a model' yet its effects are cases of biased transmission. The term 'guided variation' is itself somewhat misleading, since although each variation is chosen (literally selected), the cumulative process of many variations over many generations is not guided by anyone. Thus 'guided variation' is no more guided than 'biased transmission,' and both of them are forms of natural selection. B&R seem to want to emphasize the distinction between natural selection of cultural traits through reduced fertility and death of humans, and other kinds of natural selection of culture. But if we are going to take cultural transmission seriously, we must view the cultural practices as the relevant organisms or replicating entities, and the humans as aspects of their environment. To a meme, as to a flea, it may not be very important whether it kills a human; the meme's progeny may be able to jump to many other humans before being adversely affected. (In some cases, humans have been especially imitated after, and because of, their deaths.) Parasites may change the behavior of their hosts, but it is probably not very common for parasites to pursue their own interests by the indirect route of causing their hosts to reproduce faster. In some cases, memes may flourish by increasing the genetic reproductive performance of their human hosts. This is a special case, and only one part of the explanation of cultural change. Probably no one believes that the future of the United States belongs to the extraordinarily fertile Hutterites, though it is reasonable to suppose that the Hutterites will become a more important factor in American life.

Cultural Selection Is Not Genetically Adaptive

Guided variation and biased transmission will spread the variants favored by accumulated choices and by bias. In no way can this outcome be equated with genetic fitness. If people don't know what's good for them, or if they define 'good' in ways other than spreading their genes as widely as possible, then these forms of cultural transmission could favor behavior which was extremely maladaptive (though it is adaptive for *the memes*). The elaborate lengths B&R go to in order to develop models which favor genetic unfitness are therefore not as important for their argument as they imagine, interesting though some of them are. B&R take the view that

> if the only forces which shape cultural evolution are guided variation and directly biased transmission, [cultural transmission] would seem of little consequence; in the end, the only organizing force in cultural evolution would be natural selection acting on genetically transmitted predispositions . . . we would be able to predict cultural variation by asking what increases genetic fitness. (157)

It is possible that I have missed something in their argument, but this conclusion appears to be plainly wrong. Guided variation and direct bias will go their own way, producing some behaviors that are adaptive, others maladaptive, and others neutral (for the human individuals or for human-carried genes; human intelligence and rational choice may do better than randomly at making behavior 'adaptive' in the sense of serving human purposes, though this may well be hostile to genetic fitness). It would be quite easy to model the spread of tobacco-smoking, for example, by these mechanisms, and although smoking might, for all I know, be genetically adaptive, we cannot safely conclude that it is.

What led B&R astray? I think part of the answer is that they are trying to do two things at once: on the one hand, to explain that guided variation and direct bias will work, and what sorts of things they will do, and on the other, to account for the origin of the potential for guided variation and direct bias, i.e. to find under what circumstances natural selection would have yielded genes favoring guided variation and direct bias. This seems to be an unfortunate approach. It is easy to see that giraffes have long necks, much more speculative and risky trying to figure out how and why their long necks evolved. If there were a dispute about exactly how long their necks were, it would not be very helpful to decide the matter by conjectures about the optimal length favored by selection. This is like trying to decide whether a crime was committed by speculations about the identity of the criminal and his motive. In numerous cases the adaptive 'reason' for some feature of an organism, or even whether there is such a reason, remains mysterious or controversial. It should be possible to decide whether transmission by guided variation or direct bias does occur, and what its effects are, independently of speculation about how, or if, they could have been genetically advantageous.

Furthermore, most of the cultural evolution we are concerned with has taken place within the past ten thousand years or so, and we do not have to assume that the human genetic capacity for learning and invention has changed much during that period, though the social environment of the genes has changed greatly.

It may seem plausible that the great expansion of human population during the past several thousand years owes a lot to culture, but that may have no bearing on adaptiveness, which is a matter of frequencies of competing genes. A population can benefit from a trait which is reproductively harmful to each bearer of the trait. And if an individual makes a cultural innovation which enhances that individual's reproductive performance, but the innovation spreads sufficiently rapidly that numerous competing individuals soon benefit from it, then the innovation may have impaired the genetic fitness of the innovator.

Cumulative rational selection is made up of developments which help individuals to attain their goals. If we suppose that when the capacity for pursuing goals by rationally-understood methods first developed, it was adaptive, this is no guarantee that it will continue to be adaptive in new situations. With the development of culture, pursuit of individuals' goals might become increasingly irrelevant to genetic fitness, even if we supposed that the goals themselves were unchanged and genetically determined.

Once a species has developed some way along the rational-cultural path, it makes little sense to speculate about the possibility that a specific behavior could be selected for genetically. It is probably now impossible for a new specific behavior to become established in humans through genetic selection.

Individual and Cultural Learning

Cultural and individual learning are not as separable as B&R seem to think. Given certain plausible conditions, the capacity for individual learning will automatically become the capacity for cultural transmission. This fact casts doubt on B&R's discussion of genetic selection between cultural and individual learning, treated as simple alternatives governed by a pair of alleles. Given rationality, a certain degree of intelligence, and gregariousness, the great importance of culture will emerge almost automatically, because individuals will perceive it to be advantageous to copy practices with visibly advantageous outcomes, and to introduce changes in these imitated practices if the changes are thought to be improvements. If, as seems quite likely, rationality, intelligence, and gregariousness could each arise for reasons unconnected with the benefits of cultural transmission, then any further search for a biological origin of culture might be redundant; the genetic capacity for culture might have arisen without any selection for cultural transmission per se.

All learning is, of course, individual learning. However, following B&R in distinguishing 'cultural' from 'individual' learning (using 'individual' to mean 'non-cultural'), we can see that cultural learning can be advantageous only because what is learned culturally has a good chance of being advantageous. Yet this is the case only because past individual learning has been incorporated into the tradition of cultural learning, and this fact presupposes that the tradition admits some innovations derived from individual learning. Therefore, cultural learning is viable only as a supplement to individual learning; it cannot stand alone. Culture not guided by intelligent individual evaluation would just drift into senselessness.

B&R seem to think that any form of cultural transmission can itself become an object of genetic selection, but this is surely dubious where it implies selection of the conclusions individuals will draw as a result of rational processes. An individual who can learn either to hunt or to farm, to honor his neighbors with gifts or collect their heads to decorate his front door, can surely learn, alternatively, to copy the tallest man, the best hunter, or the majority, or to decide what to do in fireside discussions. If you can learn what to do, you can learn how to choose what to do. This is not to deny that there might be genes affecting cultural transmission; there might, for instance, be a 'conservative' allele making people more inclined to stick with tradition and less inclined to innovate, and a 'radical' allele. However, it is a truism that individuals or communities can change the way they make such choices, can change their decision-making rules in response to changes in circumstances or beliefs. A highly tradition-bound society may rapidly become more innovative after exposure to new ideas. Rules for making choices are themselves chosen. Rules for cultural transmission are themselves culturally modified. Furthermore, the extent to which a community is prepared to generate and accept innovations, and the kinds of innovations it will generate and accept, could be a purely rational strategy adjusted to recent experience of success or failure; in that case we would expect to find that 'innovative' societies are societies adjusted to conditions where a high rate of innovation pays, and 'tradition-bound' societies are societies adjusted to conditions where a low rate of innovation pays.

Providentialist Thinking

B&R seem to have imported from anthropology or from pop biology something of the functionalist or providentialist point of view. They tacitly assume that because something is prevalent and important to us, it exists for reasons intimately connected with that importance. But it may be that some human capacity which we value is just an incidental outcome of some other element which was selected for (along the lines of Williams's conjecture, in *Adaptation and Natural Selection,* about the origin of human genius). There could have been very strong selection for some feature of the human central nervous system, which then gave rise incidentally to greatly expanded possibilities for culture. It could be, for example, somehow highly advantageous for individuals to communicate by means of a conceptual language. Once in place, this would necessarily and immediately permit many kinds of behavior which might not be adaptive. The main genetic influences in cultural evolution could be remote and quite incidental, yet inevitable, consequences of some turn in genetic evolution taken for quite unrelated reasons. Similarly, many land animals can learn to swim if their environment changes to make this advantageous to them in pursuit of their goals, such as feeding or satisfying their curiosity. That a cat, a dog, or a monkey can learn to swim, and could under appropriate circumstances adjust to a life in which swimming was vitally important, does not require any theory that these animals have been selected in the past for the ability to swim. They just can swim. It's a stroke of luck, not an adaptation. Human culture is today greatly affected by literacy and electronic media, yet no one supposes (at least, I hope they don't) that print and broadcasting have appeared because they were selected for genetically. (It is possible, of course, that there may have recently been genetic selection for literacy, though this would have to be shown. It is just as likely on the face of it that there has been continuous selection against literacy since literacy began, if it has been the case that illiterates have had more kids, though I am afraid that this will not do as an excuse for state schooling.) What goes for books, radio, and TV may very well go for some cultural transmission processes which have been operative since before the dawn of history.

As an example of providentialist thinking, consider B&R's reference to celibate communities such as monasteries (202). If the celibacy rule is enforced, and if behavior is subject to selection solely for genetic fitness, it might seem that the appeal of the monastic life ought to have been eliminated, except on the wildly improbable theory that celibates are somehow able to help their close kin reproduce, to such a degree that this outweighs their own infertility—this has actually been proposed by one theorist (R.D. Alexander, quoted by B&R, 202)! B&R suggest that although living in a monastery is genetically maladaptive, it may be culturally adaptive, since monks are freed from the cares of family, and thus enabled to devote their energies to spreading their ideas. They make up for their lack of genetic offspring by begetting numerous cultural offspring. This is typical providentialism—looking for some way in which living like a monk is adaptive. Such ingenuity is wasted; there simply is no reason whatever why monasteries should be adaptive, genetically or culturally. Monasteries could keep going indefinitely even if their members were *less* able to spread their ideas, because monasteries are part of a wider religious culture, and in that religious culture monastic life is honored. If quarterbacks turned out to be below average in both fertility and persuasiveness, we would not deduce a trend toward ten-member football teams.

A determined search for adaptiveness is often misplaced, for example in the pursuit by some writers (not B&R) of an adaptive function for homosexuality. If you program something as subtle as mating behavior into a tiny bit of DNA there are liable to be glitches. If you design a pack of cards that will yield a variety of good hands, it will also probably yield some disappointing hands. (The fact that homosexuality is not adaptive should be suggested by the fact that it occurs in all mammals, and possibly in all sexually-reproducing animals. If it made some contribution to fitness by way of behavioral interaction, you would expect to find, given the great variety of behavior in different species, cases where homosexuality did not turn up, because in that particular context fitness did not result.) Genetically-favored behaviors may never have had any adaptiveness; it is not adaptive for a moth to fly into a flame. However, a genetically-determined behavior which may have been adaptive in the past may now be maladaptive or neutral. Sociobiologists are quite right to point out the enormous importance of genetically-favored behavior patterns among humans: sexual jealousy, aversion to incest, greater aggressiveness of males compared to females, greater ease of learning to form sentences than learning to do arithmetic (even though the latter is intrinsically much simpler than the former)—all these and many more genetically-favored tendencies help to shape human society. Where sociobiologists often err is in assuming that there must be some adaptive explanation for present institutions which result in part from these genetic influences. By "present" I mean any time within the past few thousand years. Since culture changes the situation in which genetic forces operate, the results may be quite unlike what they were in the past when these tendencies were selected for. In any case, there will always be incidental effects (just as the red color of blood is not in the least adaptive); a combination of genetically-favored behaviors will give rise incidentally to other behaviors, not themselves adaptive. So a genetic, or partly genetic, explanation of a cultural institution does not mean that the institution makes a contribution to genetic fitness; this is not even particularly likely.

Public Goods and Group Selection

B&R present an argument on public goods and group selection, discussed in terms of "rational, selfish individuals voluntarily cooperating to produce public goods" (227–29). They contend: 1. that there are serious public goods problems, such that certain important goods would not be produced at all by rational, selfish individuals; 2. that institutions actually exist to provide these public goods; 3. that this must require altruism; and 4. that general altruism (directed towards non-kin) requires to be explained by group se- lection. Every step of this argument is wrong.

First, real-life public goods problems are generally of the sort where a good will be underproduced, not totally unproduced. B&R give an example of two pastoralists who may choose to guard or not guard their jointly-pas- tured herd, but their example is unusual in that in it, externalities lead to no guarding at all: in this case, guarding is a pure public good. This is a pe- culiar and unlikely case: it is more realistic to suppose that there will be *some* guarding of herds, albeit less than the optimum quantity of guarding. But the peculiarity of their example is then assumed by B&R in all their subsequent discussion. Naturally, this leads them to suppose that something other than rational selfishness is causing so many vital public goods to be produced, when in fact it could well be that these goods are underproduced, just as the theory of rational selfish action would predict. They then tend to assume that altruism causes public goods to be produced, via such or- ganizations as cartels, labor unions, and the state. But cartels cannot be made to work except where it pays for each firm to participate and collusion can be policed effectively, so that it is in the rational selfish interest of all the individual firms. Successful cartels without government support are rare and short-lived for this very reason: they break down because of inter- nal cheating. Unions do provide an increased wage to their members (at the expense of other workers) and B&R make no attempt to show that the benefit the union provides the individual member is less than the cost of joining the union, and therefore that union-joining is altruistic.

B&R assume that where there is a gap left by selfish, rational action, this is *in fact* generally made up by some form of altruistic co-operation, and they puzzle over why this should be the case. But it can easily be shown that it is generally not the case—that is, there are numerous instances where the public good is undersupplied, just as the theory predicts. A simple example is over-fishing of commonly-owned fish populations, such as the now-extinct sardines which once kept in business the now-defunct cannery on Cannery Row. The public good of production of future fish through conservation of present stocks was undersupplied; no altruism prevented the competing fisheries from fishing the sardines to extinction, a manifestly inefficient outcome. Such examples of underproduction of a public good are commonplace.

There is a public good element in 'law and order', but also a large private good element. If I pay a security firm to watch my house, this will incidentally provide some relief from thieves to my neighbors; they will then free-ride on my provision of law and order, but notice that though this will diminish the amount they spend on law and order, it does not mean they will spend nothing. Generally, when the state takes over production of some service, output of that service tends to fall, and there is no reason to doubt that state provision of police protection is less than private provision would be. There may be someone who believes that the state altruistically makes up the difference between the law and order that would be provided by selfish, rational action and the social optimum, but I have never met him, and I'm quite sure he doesn't live on the south side of Chicago.

Group selection is like ESP; it shouldn't be appealed to until more mundane explanations have been tried. People are sometimes altruistic to strangers, and sometimes to thousands or millions of anonymous strangers, as when they donate to charities, vote in elections, or volunteer to stuff envelopes for world peace or the rights of animals. To place this in perspective, we should remind ourselves that most people, most of the time, do not behave like this. A Chicago economist once discovered empirically that people are ninety percent selfish, ten percent altruistic, and that sounds about right. There is a rhetorical sleight-of-hand by which B&R insinuate that "voluntary large-scale co-operation" is altruistic, but of course, most voluntary large-scale co-operation has no obviously altruistic component. The extraction, processing, and distribution of petroleum and petroleum products is a gigantic example of voluntary large-scale co-operation, mostly undertaken by individuals who seem to be in it for the money and other personal benefits. But why do some people some of the time (a few people a lot, a lot of people a little) do things out of a generalized altruism directed at large groups of non-kin? I don't see any great difficulty about this, because culture is an autonomous process not dictated by genes and rationality is an autonomous process not dictated by genes or culture.

Until Neolithic times, people lived in small groups composed largely of kin, and loyalty to these groups was justified by individual reproductive profitability. Since people can learn novel behaviors, and form theories which guide their actions, there doesn't seem to be any problem about loyalty to the small group being transferred to larger groups, once these larger groups emerged, and on balance, there is no reason to think such loyalty would be fiercely selected against. Altruism is further developed by an interpersonal chain reaction of individual rational calculations, which works roughly like this: 1. If other people mean me harm, they are a threat to me, and I will therefore punish any manifestation of harmful intent, and reward any manifestation of benevolent intent, especially if I can do it cheaply (e.g. by frowning or smiling); 2. 1 very much like other people to like me, e.g. to smile at me and speak softly rather than to glare at me and yell, so I will make it clear to people that I mean them well; 3. Since it is advantageous to me (in a presumptive, residual sense, when I have no over-riding personal interest in the contrary) to adopt a general policy of showing that I mean other people well, and encouraging other people to show that they mean me well, I can combine both goals by subscribing to an ideology that says everyone ought to mean everyone well.

No doubt there are other explanations, some of them cultural-selectionist. Thus, when various religions were in competition, there would be an advantage to those religions which had a universal message for all mankind: these religions would tend to win in competition with other religions which confined themselves to a particular group or locality.

There are formidable obstacles to group selection as a source of specific genetic adaptations, but even more difficulties arise when group selection is supposed to operate on the culture of human groups, for example: 1. Most groups are made up of smaller groups, and it is important for the welfare of a group that its sub-groups behave differently from each other.

This means that there may be sub-groups with differential fertility, yet the welfare of the sub-groups with higher fertility may be dependent on the behavior of the sub-groups with lower fertility; and 2. If there are two groups, one of which behaves more adaptively than the other, this will very likely be due to better rational choices by the individuals in the first group. In that case there will be no selective effect whatsoever, genetic or cultural, for any specific behavior. There will simply be selection for greater rationality or intelligence, whether genetically or culturally transmitted; superior rationality or intelligence leads to quite different behaviors on different occasions.

Sources of Human Action

In order to give satisfactory explanations of the development of human society, several different kinds of explanations, derived from different disciplines, must be drawn upon, notably: 1. genetic influences; 2. natural selection of culture; 3. rational pursuit of goals; and 4. interpersonal invisible-hand processes of the kind studied in economic theory. At present there seem to be a number of scholars actively trying to fit as much as possible into one or two of these categories, often with an audacious disregard for fairly obvious objections. This is probably more productive than aiming for an eclectic stew in the same cavalier spirit, but maybe people in these warring camps will eventually see the limitations of their monomaniacal approaches, and a soundly-based eclecticism will emerge. Even now, the ways in which these different kinds of explanations interact and limit each other is a fascinating field for critically-monitored speculation. For example, B&R discuss the implications of conformity for cultural transmission, but they do not touch upon the way in which trade encourages diversity of human groups because of the advantages of division of labor, and therefore stimulates nonconformity both within and among communities.

Aside from their argument on public goods, B&R generally do a very good job of spinning out the implications of their models. (A curious omission from their nearly exhaustive survey is what happens when two cultural traditions fuse. A well-documented case is the colonization of Pitcairn following the *Bounty* mutiny, producing a selective blend of English and Polynesian practices which was then perpetuated in isolation. Fusion might make people choose among traditions by out-of-the-ordinary methods, and although comparatively rare, might be of importance in global cultural evolution.) B&R are much more shaky when it comes to arguing for the applicability of their models. Empirical examples can be found which can be reconciled with their cultural transmission scenarios, but B&R apparently cannot supply a single clearly-established case of corroboration of a surprising or bold prediction, nor even a promising candidate for such a case.

When B&R's attention turns to doubts about the applicability of their models, they resort to facile remarks. Attacking "anti-adaptationists" who appeal to accidental evolutionary breakthroughs, B&R refer to "our understandable desire to see humans elevated somehow above the common run of beasts" and assert that "such hypotheses provide too convenient a way to rescue the assumption that humans have transcended nature" (282–83). Come now! Some of my best friends are beasts, but if humans transcending nature means that they operate according to novel principles way beyond the ken of other animals, then this is no "assumption" and it is never likely to need rescuing.

Critical Review: A Journal of Politics and Society, Winter 1988

19
THE MARKET SOCIALISTS' PREDICAMENT (1996)

There has recently been a remarkable proliferation of writing about "market socialism."[1] For the most part this literature has been produced by self-avowed "socialists" who earlier would not have added the qualification "market." These writers maintain that they have come to recognize the shortcomings of non-market socialism, while their passionate hostility to "capitalism" remains unassuaged. Some market socialists have not changed much in the kind of socialism they envision; it's just that the intellectual climate has changed so that they think it prudent to advertise more loudly the "market" dimension of their socialism. In other cases, the writers announce their conversion from classical or Soviet-style socialism to market socialism.

One explanation for this change of heart, or of verbal emphasis, is the abrupt demobilization of "the socialist camp"—Soviet Russia and its numerous colonies, both inside and outside the USSR. This regime was widely believed to practice state central planning, otherwise known as socialism. So the story goes: the end of the Soviet Union dealt a blow to the reputation of socialism. The remaining socialists need to distinguish their socialism sharply from the Soviet sort, while pursuing the struggle against capitalism. Hence the new emphasis on market socialism. Although this is undoubtedly the way in which many Western socialists experienced events, the whole episode looks different from a broader perspective.

The definitive end of Soviet-style socialism has had a serious impact upon the ruling ideas of our epoch, yet there are clear indications that

---

1   I am responding here especially to Bardhan and Roemer 1993, an excellent collection of consistently high-quality papers representing several points of view; Roosevelt and Belkin 1994, which contains some insightful contributions, and overall gives a vivid mosaic of the turmoil in recent socialist thinking; and Schweickart 1993, a fresh and forceful attempt to reformulate the case for socialism taking account of recent developments.

Marxism was in serious trouble before the point was reached when the imminent toppling of the Soviet regime could be expected with confidence. The growing recognition that the Soviet Union and China would be compelled to embark, somehow, upon the transition to capitalism, became quite marked in the 1980s. Among others, Andrei Amalrik, Steven N.S. Cheung, Harold Demsetz, Bernard Levin, Paul Craig Roberts, and Alexander Shtromas had all indicated as much by the mid-1980s or earlier. And there were those, like Marshall Goldman, Robert Kaiser, and Peter Rutland, who did not (as far as I know) predict a quick transition to capitalism, but did write convincingly about the desperate straits in which the Soviet Union found itself. Even some impeccable progressives had become aware that classical socialism was on its deathbed (see, for example, Howe 1994). Beginning in the early 1970s, a number of leading Marxists went public, so to speak, with the "crisis of Marxism," both as a movement and as a theoretical system (see Callinicos 1982, ch. 1), though naturally they always explained that a return to the essence of Marxism as they had identified it would be enough to put the patient back on his feet. The appearance and the reception of such works as Miller 1989, Nove 1983, and Schweickart 1980 confirm that a substantial "marketward" movement in socialist opinion predated the Soviet collapse. Meanwhile, a growing number of non-socialist observers had come to view socialist Russia as the world's sick man, immersed in a senescence not unlike that of the Ottoman empire a century earlier. If there had been a statesman of genius, instead of a Gorbachev, at the helm of the Soviet empire, it could have been kept afloat for several decades, but it might be that the prestige of Marxism would then have plummeted even more rapidly than it did.

A comparison of the trajectory of Marx's reputation with the trajectory of Freud's may be cautionary. Freud and the whole mythology of the unconscious mind were criticized quite tellingly from the inception of psychoanalysis. Again and again eloquent arguments were leveled against Freud that were never satisfactorily answered. Yet the general influence of Freud upon intellectuals and artists seems to have remained undiminished, except among empirically minded psychologists, until around the end of the 1980s, when attacks on Freud started being taken far more seriously than before.[2] Had there been a Freudist instead of a Marxist regime, and

---

2   As perhaps the most striking indication of the way things are going, see Crews 1995.

had this regime fallen at the same time as its real-world Marxist counterpart, we would doubtless be tempted to attribute the puncturing of Freudist credibility to that downfall alone, overlooking the autonomous movement of intellectual opinion.

The abrupt decline in socialism's intellectual appeal applied to all forms of socialism without exception, and to market socialism as much as any other. Soviet-style socialism, market socialism (whatever, precisely, that may mean), the planning of development usually favored by socialists as the best way to achieve economic growth in the poorer countries, workers' self-management, and the welfare state—all of these emerged from the 1980s with less credibility than they had entered that decade; it does not now look as if any of them will stage a comeback soon.

There is no need to repeat here what happened to Soviet socialism. In retrospect, however, the failure of market reforms of the Soviet economy may come to be seen as market socialism's last throw. Western socialist parties which had once promoted the incremental nationalization of industry turned decisively against it, as in France, Britain, and Greece. The notion that governments could design the path of development in poor countries was already being tacitly abandoned in the 1970s, when there began a wave of privatizations in both the Third and First worlds, often supported by nominally socialist parties who would earlier have fought them bitterly. Workers' self-management was an idea that might have been expected to flourish given the discrediting of other forms of socialism, but although it picked up some interest among erstwhile advocates of Soviet-style socialism, it made no headway politically.

The welfare state came increasingly under attack for generating excessive burdens and social pathologies, most especially in its model cases, Sweden, Norway, and New Zealand. The groundswell of disquiet anent the welfare state (to many people a form, if not the paradigm, of "socialism," but to Marxists a form of capitalism) is particularly striking, because the welfare state has yet to enter the mortal crisis so frequently predicted: underclass mayhem is but a tiny cloud on the horizon, and the actuarial collapse, as governments find themselves compelled to default upon entitlement payments, is not due for another twenty or thirty years (see, for example, Wolf 1996). If the critics of the world's welfare states are right, then the welfare state is now more attractive than it can ever be in the foreseeable future.

Markets and Socialism

The final attempts by socialists to rescue socialism in Russia took the form of greater accommodation with the market. As Janos Kornai has it, market socialism "is merely its predecessor, classical socialism, in the process of falling apart" (Kornai 1993, 47). Since we know from Marx that ideology is only the material world's distorted reflection in the human brain, we may extend Kornai's characterization to surmise that the new vogue for market socialism among Western academics is merely its predecessor, the leftist academics' faith in classical socialism, in the process of falling apart.

The original "socialism" was market socialism *avant la lettre*, at least in that it did not insist upon the elimination of all market relations. In early usage, "socialism" generally did not aim at the eradication of the market, whereas "communism" generally did. Marx the communist opposed Proudhon the socialist because Proudhon advanced a scheme to make the market conform to standards of justice, instead of seeking to abolish the market. At the end of Marx's life, however, Engels adopted the practice of employing the term "socialism" to mean Marxian communism. The old socialism, which did not insist upon the abolition of the market or even of private property, rapidly dwindled among both self-identified socialist intellectuals and socialist parties. The form of socialism which has dominated the minds of intellectuals in the twentieth century is therefore a set of doctrines that came into being, and defined itself from its inception, as a rejection of what had earlier been called "socialism," what might today be called "market socialism." "Socialism" became, at its core, communist: production for sale would be replaced by production for use, and the market ("commodity production") would be abolished. Yet simultaneously, Marxism incorporated elements of the market into its conception of socialism.[3] Doctrinally, this occurred by transforming Marx's first phase of communism, with its non-circulating labor-vouchers and complete absence of money, into a form of socialism in which money and wages would persist.

---

3   In Kautsky's 1902 pamphlet on the Erfurt Program, he insists on the need for money and wages in the early stages of socialism, and recognizes that this will come as a shock to some of his readers (Kautsky 1902, 129). In later works, Kautsky continued to move toward greater acceptance of elements in the organization of socialism which earlier Marxists would have considered purely capitalist.

This doctrinal shift was favored by the Marxist habit of supposing that the development of modern society was inherently driving toward the abolition of the market. It was considered Utopian to try and force the pace. Looking too far ahead could constitute a distraction from pressing practical tasks. More palpably, the rank and file memberships of the socialist-led mass working-class movements displayed no interest in abolishing the market. Capitalism, it was supposed, could be counted upon, in the fullness of time, to make these reformist-minded proletarians revolutionary in their praxis. In the meantime, the scientific revolutionist would not want to move too far ahead of the workers themselves.

The Marxists were misreading capitalism's laws of motion. Nothing in capitalism was tending toward the obsolescence of the market. While socialists endlessly debated how soon capitalism would reach its terminal crisis and how the socialization of production would be conducted, modern industry was becoming objectively more dependent upon the existence of a substantially free market. Marx's theory that "commodity production" (production for the market) had evolved into a fetter on the productive forces was exactly wrong. The reality, though few theorists could have explained why, was that the growth of the productive forces required the market's "anarchy of production." The tenacious dogma of a long-term tendency for competition to give rise to concentration and thereby to "monopoly" was at odds with reality (Steele 1992, 274–280). Neither was there any tendency for wage-workers as a class to be thrown into conflict with capitalists as a class (see ibid., 370–74).

The Bolsheviks seized power with the rationale that the bourgeois revolution had played itself out; socialism was "now gazing at us from all the windows of modern capitalism" (Lenin 1964, vol. 25, 363). Since it had become clear that the centralization of industry through competition was, at least, occurring with disappointing slowness, the new theory, extrapolating from German experience, was that central control of the banks plus wartime administrative controls—"state monopoly capitalism"—was the road to socialism. At first the Bolsheviks believed that they would be helped out by victorious revolutions in the West, but when this prospect receded, the Bolsheviks could see no reason why they could not begin moving to socialism alone. Their attempt to institute socialism had to be abandoned in 1921, but the rise of Stalin and the beginning of the first five-year plan signified the creation of a new and enigmatic system which would survive until the 1980s.

This system was already a kind of market socialism that used money both in personal consumption and in industrial allocation. At the same time it appeared, paradoxically, to be a comprehensive system of planning by material allocations.[4] The inefficiencies of this system were so bizarre that the Soviet Union was compelled to allow some freedom of discussion in the area of economic policy, with the result that wave after wave of talk about market-oriented reform rippled through the ruling circles from the 1960s on.[5]

The history of the Soviet bloc after the 1930s was, superficially, one of greater recognition of, and greater reliance on, the market. Although there were successive measures which eliminated various kinds of private or market economy that had constituted exceptions to the main form of industrial organization, that main form itself was increasingly firmly characterized as "commodity production." From time to time measures were even enacted to encourage enterprises to behave more like rivalrous competitors, although these measures failed to bring about that result. The system failed because the government could not find a way to make state industry behave like capitalist industry. Whether there is some way to do this—whether an economy dominated by "publicly owned" enterprises can ever match or even remotely approach the efficiency of an economy composed mainly of competitive private firms—is the issue on which the practical feasibility of market socialism turns.

What Is the New Market Socialism?

During the 1980s, Western socialist intellectuals who had inhabited a milieu in which some version of the Soviet system, modified by this or that reform,

4   The notion that the Soviet economy was ever centrally planned was called into question by such writers as Michael Polanyi, Paul Craig Roberts, Hillel Ticktin, and Eugene Zaleski. See Steele 1992, 266–68.

5   In the early 1960s the Western press was abuzz with talk about "Libermanism," the proposed introduction of more reliance on profits in guiding the performance of Soviet state firms. Was the Soviet Union going capitalist? Soviet ideologues replied that profit and loss had played a key role in the management of Soviet enterprise since the 1920s. There was, they maintained, no incongruity between socialism and profits.

was at least a respected option, found the climate changed: anything close to the Soviet system came to be beyond serious consideration.

But if classical socialism, or any adaptation thereof, is not the kind of socialism we want, what is socialism? And if, as socialists for the first time in eighty years agree almost unanimously, an acceptable socialism relies upon the market as a matter of principle, precisely how is it different from capitalism? Over the generations numerous socialists have wrestled with these questions, in successive waves of disappointment with Marxist theory or Soviet reality, so there is a ready supply of veterans who have been there already. But the latest wave of formerly classical socialists to be confronted with such questions may be the last wave, suspects itself to be the last, and is not greatly concerned with the thoughts of the earlier waves. The new market socialists rarely quote Eduard Bernstein, Anthony Crosland, or Sidney Hook.

The definition of socialism which seems to be the consensus, at least for the time being, is: 1. a market economy; 2. with some kind of public or noncapitalist ownership of much of industry; and 3. with workers' self-management (producers' co-operatives) in many enterprises. 1. is something socialism has in common with capitalism; its significance is that the new socialists renounce the goal of replacing the market with society-wide planning. 2. is the most controversial and the most vulnerable, because we have plenty of experience of state-run economies that endeavored to foster market competition among government enterprises, such as Hungary and Yugoslavia in the 1980s, and the results, while an improvement on classical socialism, were still markedly short of Western capitalism. There is now among socialists quite a lively awareness of the problem of the "soft budget constraint,"[6] for example, and this inclines them to believe that anything less than the autonomy of completely independent firms could be a serious

---

6   The problem of the "soft budget constraint" refers to an unintended but apparently inescapable consequence of any attempt to substitute vertical administrative commands for horizontal market relations in determining the total composition of output: the emergence of extensive vertical bargaining. In this context, such enterprise goals as profitability or cost reduction cannot stably be given the "hardness" they manifest under capitalism. The administration of "classical socialism" is unable to adopt a consistent stance of "sink or swim" with regard to the enterprises. See Kornai 1992, 140–44; Bardhan 1993.

problem for efficiency, while they are also uncomfortably aware that any such autonomy sadly renders the "public" character of the enterprises dubious. 3. refers to the internal organization of enterprises rather than the relations between enterprises as they constitute the whole economy.

Inevitably, then, the ambiguity, the equivocation, the search for new answers, is concentrated on 2., and especially on the problem of preserving 2. without abandoning 1. According to the older socialist wisdom, one of the great merits of socialism would be that all production units would conform to a common plan. They would not act at cross-purposes; they would not compete with each other; they would never have to close down and rudely move workers to other production units merely because financial results were negative. This view is now regarded by market socialists as naive, impracticable, and dangerous.

One alternative idea has been to give state-owned firms a great deal of competitive autonomy, but to allocate investment funds centrally. This is close to what was tried in Hungary for two decades. Some market socialists go even beyond this, however, and claim that capital markets can be incorporated within "socialism." David Belkin's survey of the course of recent socialist opinion concludes that "the use of markets in a planning framework shades into planning in a market framework, and social ownership shades into mixed ownership." He adds the question: "Does market socialism then simply shade into social democracy?" (Belkin 1994, 36).

Whereas John Roemer repudiates the notion that public ownership is a defining feature of socialism (Roemer 1993), Marc Fleurbaey describes his own proposal as neither capitalist nor market socialist, because there is no public ownership of production firms. Under Fleurbaey's scheme (which gives a good idea of the flavor of recent discussions of market socialism by its economically knowledgeable sympathizers), production enterprises would be owned by their workers. (Presumably there would be an inspectorate, to check up on firms and make sure they were practicing genuine self-management, penalizing workers who smuggled in departures from self-management. One can already hear the anonymous phone calls to this inspectorate from impeccably self-managed and unprofitable firms, setting the police onto their more successful competitors.) The stock and venture capital markets would be banned; the only type of external financing permitted would be for investors to deposit their savings with banks, which would then choose where to allocate credit. Fleurbaey argues that banks are better than securities markets at monitoring firms, which prompts the question why banks haven't already put the stock market out of business. To the objection that the restrictions imposed by his proposal "forbid mutually advantageous voluntary contracts of direct finance and wage labor, thus yielding a blatant inefficiency" (Fleurbaey 1993, 271), Fleurbaey responds that his proposed system achieves a public good effect, so there is a divergence between social and individual rationality; but it's not clear what public good he has in mind.

After listing some of the proposals for mitigating the efficiency problems associated with government ownership of industry, Thomas Weisskopf concedes that these cannot be expected to meet the "conventional efficiency criteria associated with a pure capitalist model," because the modified models restrict individuals' options for voluntary contracting. Weisskopf says that these inefficiencies are outweighed by "nonefficiency goals" and by "greater social rationality" (Weisskopf 1993, 120-21, 134). By greater social rationality, he means government action to correct for market imperfections, and by nonefficiency goals, he means greater equality, more democracy, and greater community. But it seems gratuitous to suppose that procedures which have been devised to rescue some workable form of "public ownership" after the classical form has been devastated by criticisms on efficiency grounds, will be especially well-suited to compensate for market imperfections (Putterman 1993, 165). And there is some obscurity about the ethical rationale for enforcing upon workers a tradeoff between real income and such values as equality, democracy, and community, different from the tradeoff those workers would arrive at by voluntary interaction. For the whole impetus of the new market socialism arises from the judgment that it is decidedly not legitimate to bring about a catastrophic fall in real income in pursuit of socialist goals, as necessitated by classical socialism.

The Predicament of the Market Socialist

The driving force of market socialism is a barely diminished moral revulsion against capitalism allied with the recognition that attempts to institute workable socialism on classical lines now appear hopeless. The market socialists find themselves under opposing pressures from two sides: from the side of feasibility (and also simple humanity, since like all of us they want to avoid the suffering caused by grandiose experiments with inefficient institutions), they are impelled to admit increasingly more elements of capitalism; from the side of moral sentiment, they are impelled to root out as many of these elements as they can.

Critics of market socialism have repeatedly pointed out (Hayek 1948, 186; Steele 1992, 192) that as socialism incorporates more scope for the market, it disappoints traditional socialist aspirations, while not incorporating enough of the market to approach the efficiency of capitalism. In his unusually clear-headed defense of market socialism, Weisskopf puts it this way: "Modifications of market socialist models designed to ameliorate their efficiency characteristics tend to bring those models into closer conformity with capitalism. In so doing, they tend to open up greater opportunities for the development of income inequalities and/or to reduce the scope of worker self-management" (Weisskopf 1993, 123–24).

The new market socialists' acceptance of the market makes it tricky to show that their socialism can offer much that is not equally available to the proponent of regulated capitalism. Market socialists often compare their own position with that of what they call "social democracy," a term they understand to mean regulated capitalism with state welfare provisions (Weisskopf 1994, 312–15; Belkin 1994, 36). The ideological geology here is ironic: the social democrats once travelled the same ground that the new market socialists now tread, but went a bit further. Social democracy as a movement used to be Marxist, it became by degrees market socialist, and now it is seen by the new market socialists as non-socialist by definition.

There is the question of whether an established market socialism could be a stable sociopolitical formation—whether it would be beset by crises of institutional instability, tending to push it either toward regulated capitalism or back toward classical socialism. But here I raise a different question: whether market socialism is stable as an ideology, whether it can endure to inspire future political movements. Let me appeal to a far-fetched analogy. There are Christian ministers who come to the conclusion that Jesus was never really born of a virgin, did not really change water into wine or wither the fig tree, and did not rise from the dead. As long as there are a good number of literalists who do believe all these stories, the freethinking ministers have some significance, but (it seems plausible) without the existence of a large body of believers who accept the Jesuine miracles literally, the freethinking ministers would not be able to maintain a substantial church for very long. They are always on a journey from Christian belief to its abandonment, even if most of them never quite reach that destination. Very roughly, we might say that this is so because the story of Jesus changing water into wine fits into a doctrine which has a power to convince, compel, and motivate. In Dawkinsian terms, it is a robust meme. The denial that this miracle occurred, however, draws most of its vigor as a meme from the fact that lots of people still believe the miracle did occur. The Marxist view of the world has also demonstrated a power to convince, compel, and motivate. But once certain crucial elements of this outlook have been abandoned, the result may be unstable, though its instability may be disguised as long as numerous individuals are making the transition from Marxism to the acceptance of capitalism.

Western academics who remain hostile to capitalism increasingly have recourse to technicalities of economic theory, to "externalities" and in particular to "public goods." We can understand this as a "socialism of the gaps," by analogy with the well-known "God of the Gaps," a derisory label for the intellectual phenomenon of theists basing their rationale for the theistic hypothesis on those things which science cannot yet explain satisfactorily. The contemporary academic socialist often proceeds by finding areas where the free market may not yield a theoretical optimum, and stakes out his case for socialism in these spots. Whatever we may think of the merits of such arguments, this kind of thinking emanates from a cast of mind alien to that of the traditional socialist, who holds 1. that markets are inherently irrational and wasteful; 2. that planning must always be superior to spontaneous human interaction; 3. that the existence of morally indefensible exploitation follows logically from the fact that individuals are permitted to receive interest on their savings; 4. that there is something demeaning and degrading in the fact that things are bought and sold; and 5. that inequalities of income and wealth are intrinsically bad. Of these propositions, the first two are factual ones, and now explicitly rejected by most socialists; the latter three are normative, and don't sit well with a wholehearted acceptance of the market.

A socialism of the gaps leads easily to regulated capitalism. Given the range of measures contemporary governments have implemented within a predominantly capitalist setting, it's not easy for market socialists to offer a plausible case that governments need to own enterprises in order to be able to correct some externality.

The Informational Role of Prices

Suddenly, it has become respectable to hold that Mises was right in his contention that centrally planned socialism cannot avoid immense inefficiencies because it lacks market prices for factors of production (Mises 1920). But the full purport of Mises's arguments against non-market socialism, and then against market socialism,[7] is often not grasped. Recent writers often point out, sometimes with evident puzzlement, that Nikolaas Pierson, Enrico Barone, Mises, and Hayek did not, in their arguments over the practical feasibility of market and nonmarket socialism, make much of the question of incentives. This was not, however, an oversight. It was a commonplace of discussions of socialism at the turn of the century that its feasibility turned upon questions of motivation. Socialists generally argued that people could be motivated to produce equally strongly by nonmonetary as by monetary motives, and that socialism would transform human nature, endowing people with different behavioral dispositions. Later, economists sympathetic to socialism (and even some quite unsympathetic) took the view that the strength of people's motives under different kinds of "material" or "moral" incentives was a matter on which economic theory per se could not pronounce.

Skeptics of the practical feasibility of socialism therefore had good reasons for seeking to establish that the calculational or informational objection to socialism stood by itself, independent of considerations of motivation.

---

7   Widespread use of the specific term "market socialism" (Marktsozialismus) arose at the beginning of the 1920s, with Eduard Heimann and Karl Polanyi. Mises responded to their proposals in Mises 1923; these arguments were incorporated into Mises 1936. His two main criticisms were that the proposals were unclear on whether industrial organization would be syndicalist or truly socialist, and that the market socialists focused exclusively on enterprise managers, ignoring the allocational role of capital and money markets.

Thus, Pierson, Barone, and Mises developed a genuinely new argument. The old argument was that modern industry required the market because only pecuniary motives would be strong enough to get individuals to do what was required. The new argument was that only market prices could effectively transmit certain kinds of information about costs, so modern industry required the market (and therefore it could not dispense with pecuniary motives, since without these the market would not function). In my criticism of Joseph Carens's simulated-market socialism (Steele 1992, 207–228; see Carens 1981) I have taken Mises's argument a little further: there are certain important kinds of information that cannot be accurately captured at all unless the individual experiences prices as directly relevant to personal consumption. Therefore, even powerfully motivated individuals determined to behave exactly as they would in a private property market, but without actual private property rights, could not do so, because they could not know how they would behave in that imaginary situation.

Self-Management: Oversold or Underbought?

Socialists have often been ambivalent about self-management (or industrial democracy, as it has more aptly been called). If firms produce for the market, then self-management does nothing to mitigate the typically capitalist phenomenon of competition. Independent, profit-seeking, self-managed firms will be just as inclined to subvert the great central plan as independent, profit-seeking, non-self-managed firms—perhaps more so, if the greater workplace solidarity that self-management proponents hope for does emerge. But once socialists abandon central planning and admit the need for competition, they often look more benignly on self-management.

Self-management in Yugoslavia has gone the way of Gosplan, and is just about as unlamented. Codetermination on the German pattern, which might be seen as a kind of halfway house to self-management, has never aroused much admiration among socialists outside Germany, presumably because it is too modest to possess any revolutionary glamour. Self-management proponents most often appeal to the example of the Mondragon co-operatives, but these are purely free-market entities which have achieved great things in non-belligerent co-existence with the capitalist environment. The Mondragon system could hardly have come about by any other route than that of being invented by individuals who had to justify every step according to financial results in a setting of voluntary transactions. A politically originated and imposed system would not have made the adjustments which now enable Mondragon to be recognized as successful. Yet we rarely encounter people who favor self-managed business enterprises on a purely voluntary basis without government involvement, or even those who favor legislation mandating that all enterprises be democratically managed, but then permit each enterprise to sink or swim according to ordinary business criteria.

Any consideration of self-management has to begin by recognizing that self-management is a legal and available option under capitalism; people are free to associate together in producers' co-ops, and they occasionally do. Thus, although the majority of arguments on the subject may give the impression that the topic under discussion is whether self-management is a good thing, we should bear in mind that the true topic is always distinct from that: it is whether self-management should be imposed on people who will not voluntarily opt for it.

I have elsewhere presented a case against the imposition of self-management in industry (Steele 1992, 328–346). First, the legal system typical of capitalist societies permits the establishment of producers' co-operatives. Second, producers' co-ops show no sign of ousting more conventional management forms in open competition. They are chiefly popular with intellectuals of above-average incomes, especially academics, who see self-management as beneficial chiefly for non-academics. The self-management movement is very much of a piece with the intellectual's wish that the proletariat would be less boorish, for example by preferring folk-dance to football. The third stage in my argument is to look at various claims that self-management is somehow unfairly discriminated against within capitalism. I have argued that such allegations are without merit: in some cases the discrimination does not appear to exist; in other cases, it would be fair.[8]

The real-life failure of self-management to out-compete other managerial forms requires some explanation, and is difficult to reconcile with

---

8 For example, it is not necessarily unfair when business enterprises do not get all the bank loans they want, and if banks discriminated against self-managed firms, this could be fair, if the banks believed that loans to self-managed firms were more risky. See Steele 1992, 338–342.

two assumptions often made by self-management proponents: that many workers would really love to have self-management where they work, and that self-management would lead to higher output. If workers like self-management, then they will be prepared to accept lower wages than they would accept in a non-self-managed enterprise. And if self-management made workers more productive, then it would yield a higher rate of return to investors, and investment funds would flow from non-self-managed to self-managed concerns. Notice that if either of these assumptions were true, and other relevant factors were neutral, the victory of self-management would be assured in a free market. Thus, observed reality suggests that workers either do not want self-management or want it so little that they are not prepared to pay (by accepting lower wages) what it costs (in reduced output).[9] If this is correct, then what justification could there be for imposing on workers a loss of welfare, by compelling them to accept self-management and lower living standards?[10]

Why Hate Capitalism?

Classical socialists hated capitalism in large part because it was unplanned; the haphazard, fetishistic character of allocations was perceived both as self-evidently inefficient, compared with conscious direction of the whole of industry, and as horribly demeaning to human dignity (Marx 1974, 76–84, 331–39; see Kornai 1992, 110–11). This Marxian revulsion against the reign of the commodity cannot be consistently maintained by market socialists. The market socialist has to accept that the composition of society's total output, while it may be pruned and modified by judicious central intervention (just as the proponent of regulated capitalism would maintain), is essentially an unplanned precipitate of an anarchic process. The consistent

---

9   My argument does not require that we can specify the reasons why self-management may be inefficient, and is independent of any such claims, or of their purported refutations. But there is, of course, no shortage of plausible suggestions. Some of the main reasons, according to economic theory, why self-managed firms will tend to be less efficient than more conventional firms are summarized in Arnold 1994, ch. 5.

10   In Steele 1992, 334–35, I go on to explain why it is intelligible that workers, in the great majority, don't buy self-management, and why, despite indefinitely rising real incomes, they may never buy it.

market socialist must accept that profit seeking and money making are wholesome and worthy; but not all market socialists have thoroughly internalized this view.

Once the Marxian hostility to "anarchy of production" and "commodity fetishism" has been abandoned, we can detect two main grounds for continued moral outrage against capitalism: inequality and exploitation. If the indispensability of a thoroughgoing market economy is accepted, it becomes easy to see that most of the inequalities in income and wealth that would arise under *laisser faire* can be suppressed only at the cost of a loss of efficiency. That there is a tradeoff between efficiency and equality is now very widely accepted among proponents of regulated capitalism (see Okun 1975). And a passion for equality runs counter to the socialist notion of exploitation, which rests upon the theory that some people are being systematically deprived of the income equivalent of part of their productive contribution. If we imagine that equality could be imposed without affecting anyone's output, then the less productive people would *ipso facto* be exploiting the more productive people.

Consider David Schweickart, a former Marxist, now a market socialist, who still thinks interest immorally exploitative, or at least lacking in any solid moral rationale. If there is a market economy, then individuals will be able to accumulate savings. If individuals are permitted to invest (in the everyday sense of the word) their savings, they may be able to get an interest return. According to the Marxian theory of surplus value, whose crucial assumptions Schweickart and many market socialists still seem to uphold, any such return can only be exploitative, in some ethically culpable sense. In Marx, this is based on the notion that interest (or "profit") comes at the expense of labor. Only labor creates value, therefore interest is a deduction from the laborer's product.

Here we need to distinguish between two contentions: the claim that the capital equipment made possible by saving and investment makes no contribution to the value of the product, and the claim that, whether or not capital equipment makes any contribution to the product, the owner of that equipment should not be entitled to receive any return from its provision, because (for example) merely owning a machine is purely passive, whereas working with the aid of that machine is active (and only "active" pursuits should be entitled to be paid); or (to take a quite different example) because the owner of the machine came by it illegitimately (he inherited it from his grandfather, who stole it). Marx's theory rests crucially on a version of the first contention. He took the view that capital equipment, as it is used up, can do no more than pass on its own value to the product; all new creation of value, and hence all "profit," comes only from labor. Though Marx also endorsed the second contention (Marx 1974, 667–693), this is peripheral to his account of exploitation. It is, however, the second contention that most readily appeals to gut socialists who have not read Marx.

Distinct from these two contentions, yet interacting with them, there is the issue of how, purely as a factual matter of price theory, the interest return to owners of capital is determined. Leaving aside all ethical questions, can we best explain the determination of interest by unpaid labor, as in Marx, or is interest the price of a productive contribution, as most non-Marxist economists maintain? If the latter, can the pricing of this productive contribution best be explained by pure "time preference," by some interaction of time preference and investment opportunities, by the productivity of capital, by "waiting," or by the capitalist as a supplier of "time"? Partisans of these various non-Marxist theories may disagree over important matters of theory, but most accept a common core of assumptions: that saving makes possible such things as machines, that machines make an objective contribution to production, that the owner of a machine may therefore be expected to get the market price of that contribution, that the amount of the contribution and therefore the amount of the payment can be explained by the theory of marginal productivity, and that there is a price differential for goods appearing at different times: people will pay more for something the sooner they take delivery of it. Unfortunately, Schweickart goes through parts of some of these alternative theories piecemeal, without isolating and confronting their common core.

The main drift of Schweickart's argument seems to owe a lot to his use of the term "productive activity." If only "productive activity" is to be considered to make a contribution to production, and if only labor is productive activity, then only labor makes a contribution to production, and (if only a contribution accords entitlement) the laborer is entitled to the whole of output. Some such argument seems to underly Schweickart's reasoning. For instance, Schweickart asks: "Suppose a government suddenly nationalizes the means of production, then does nothing else but charge workers a use tax. We wouldn't say, would we, that the government is engaging in productive activity, or that the tax is a return for the government's productive contribution?" (Schweickart 1993, 11).

Notice how this reasoning depends upon a term, "productive activity," which would not normally be employed here by a defender of the productive contribution of capital. Thus Schweickart's line of reasoning fails to address squarely the intuitively obvious point that capital makes a contribution to production, even if that contribution is not "activity." If A makes a spade, and B uses the spade to dig a trench, we wouldn't say, would we, that A makes no contribution to digging the trench? Obviously and indisputably, A does. (Schweickart does not, of course, explicitly deny this fact; he fails to address it explicitly.) But even more fundamentally, *the spade* makes a contribution. If the spade had fallen out of the sky, and B had picked it up, it would be B's good fortune, but there would be no doubt that the spade did make a contribution, in the sense that output would be higher than without it. In this case the contribution can be identified rather simply: it is the increase in the ease and speed with which B can dig the trench. If we ignore the effects on B's hands and frame of mind, the spade's contribution is a certain increment of trench dug per hour—physically equivalent to having another laborer doing some of the digging. In many cases, this simple comparison cannot be made, because the capital enables labor to produce something that could not be produced at all without that specific type of capital. In such cases, however, we can say that the product made possible by the specific type of capital is valued more highly by consumers than other products, and we can capture the notion of that specific capital's contribution by the marginal productivity theory.

It is a separate question whether A ought to be recompensed for his spade's contribution, and if so, how much, but the fact that the spade makes a contribution, in the plain sense that its presence affords an increase in output over its absence, can hardly be contested. The distinctiveness of these two issues is underscored by H.G. Johnson in a remark quoted by Schweickart, who taxes Johnson with tending to "mislead normative thought" (Schweickart 1993, 12). But it is Schweickart who is doing the misleading here. There is nothing normative about the statement that capital goods make a contribution to output; it is a generalization from a lot of facts, such as the fact that a spade makes a contribution to digging a trench. Nor is there anything normative about the claim that this contribution can be characterized by the theory of marginal productivity, or the further claim that under competition, your income, whether wages for your labor or interest on your savings, is the value of your marginal product. Whether true or false—and they seem to be true—these are all value-free, purely factual claims.

If capital makes a contribution to production, the question arises of who should in justice get the income which corresponds to that production. The answer traditionally given by libertarians is that this income should go to the rightful owner of the capital, or more strictly, that it is not contrary to justice if it does go to that owner. The rightful owner is defined as the person who acquired it by legitimate means: broadly, by voluntary sale or gift, or by making it out of materials he acquired by legitimate means. In practice, this most often translates into savings out of earnings. On this view, given an appropriate legal system, most of society's current stock of capital is owned by people who have worked and saved to accumulate it, or, in the case of widows and children, have received it by bequest from those who worked and saved. Of course, serious criticisms might be made of this kind of normative approach or of its practical applications, but Schweickart is hindered in making them here because of his muddling of the issues. He seems reluctant to grant that the volume of output owes something to capital equipment. Alternatively, he perhaps thinks that there is no connection between the present existence of this equipment and past voluntary acts of saving.

Pursuant to Schweickart's argument, then, the government "nationalizes" the means of production, confiscating them from their former possessors (who may be the rightful owners), and now pockets what would have been the former possessors' interest payment. Does this really demonstrate either that the means of production make no contribution or that no payment for this contribution should go to the former possessors, in large part the people whose savings made those means of production possible? If so, then a parallel argument proves that labor makes no contribution, or that the rightful owner of labor (the laborer) should not, in justice, be paid. For the government could own slaves and provide these to entrepreneurs, charging the entrepreneurs a "use tax."

Schweickart also conflates interest and entrepreneurial profit. Entrepreneurial profit comes from outguessing the market; an entrepreneur who does this reaps a portion of the gains he has conferred on society by moving resources to a hitherto overlooked superior allocation. Entrepreneurial profit or loss is conceptually distinct from interest. Schweickart gives an example of an entrepreneur who innovates and then reaps a perpetual gain (Schweickart 1993, 14–15). He asks: does the innovation justify the perpetual gain? In Schweickart's example, it's not really clear how the capitalist's *innovation* is connected with the perpetual gain, but if we suppose that she made a big entrepreneurial gain initially, because her new plow was such an improvement over prior technology that she sold a lot of corn by undercutting the prices charged by other farmers, then this would give her a temporary entrepreneurial profit. Like all entrepreneurial profit, this would be ephemeral under competition, since other producers would copy the innovator, but it might in a particular instance help an entrepreneur to accumulate a sum which might then yield income perpetually. No one claims that this income after the initial period is proximately due to innovation. It is (*ex hypothesi*) interest on capital, not a reward for innovation. The perpetual gain (after the initial innovation) comes from the stock of capital. Provided the capitalist keeps on maintaining or replacing the capital, refraining from spending it on her current consumption, this capital makes a contribution to output. The capitalist receives the equivalent of that contribution to output, a contribution her investment of her savings has made possible. This strikes me as eminently fair, and Schweickart offers nothing against it.

Schweickart does offer an argument apparently designed to show that someone who invests her savings in building machines does nothing to increase production (Schweickart 1993, 18). This is a form of an old socialist misconception about the relation between real and financial capital (Steele 1992, 195–200). Schweickart's claim is that if we look at what happens when an entrepreneur borrows money from someone with accumulated savings to buy a machine, we find that either the machine, or the means to make it, existed already, so the money savings are unnecessary. What this overlooks is that financial savings correspond to real savings: the more people save, the more it is possible to produce "for tomorrow" instead of "for today." The fact that the machine exists or can readily be made and the fact that someone has accumulated money savings are not unconnected. If the saver had instead blown the money on throwing lavish parties, society's stock of real capital ("machines") would now be smaller. If people suddenly became hugely less inclined to save, say because they believed the world was certain to end at midnight on December 31st, A.D. 2000, we would witness spectacular "capital consumption." Much capital equipment would cease to be replaced or maintained. There would be less equipment available to invest in future production, just because people would spend more of their incomes on current consumption.

Schweickart further argues that while the machine in his example could be purchased by the government printing money, instead of being purchased out of a capitalist's savings, we wouldn't say that printing money was productive. But inflating the currency does not, as a general rule, add to the stock of real capital. (If it did, we would not be so quick to grant that it wasn't productive.) Those most distant from the government's spending on that machine face higher prices as a result of the addition of printed currency; the machine has been purchased at their expense, much as if they had been taxed to pay for it. By contrast, the capitalist's saving is a deduction from her own current consumption, not from someone else's income.

Schweickart also attacks the legitimacy of interest as a manifestation of time preference. He states: "The jacket I wear today is the same jacket I shall wear next week" (Schweickart 1993, 22). Does this mean that Schweickart would be willing to pay the same sum for a jacket to be delivered one year or twenty years from now as for a similar jacket to be delivered this afternoon? Schweickart goes on to argue that time preference cannot be the explanation for interest because, when a capitalist lends to an entrepreneur, it cannot be true that the entrepreneur has a higher time preference than the capitalist, since the entrepreneur is not borrowing in order to consume. But Schweickart is mistaken in supposing that the time-preference theory requires the entrepreneur to have a higher time preference than the capitalist. It is a fact that no one, not even Professor Schweickart, in general views a good to be acquired in the remote future as equally valuable as an otherwise similar good to be acquired in the near future. If, instead of receiving wages a week or two after they started work, workers were asked to wait until their products had been sold before they got their pay, they would have to be paid a higher amount.

Another leading exponent of market socialism, John Roemer, suggests that the touchstone of socialism is that "profits" be equally divided among the population (Roemer 1993, 89ff). Roemer agrees that it would not be feasible to have complete equality of incomes. Thus, his market socialism would permit unequal wages, but would eliminate the possibility for individuals to accumulate savings yielding an income, and the possibility of a person's being able to "make a killing" by combining factors in a way which no one else had managed to perceive but which turned out to be highly productive. My point here is not to try to guess what peculiar view of modern industry allows someone to acknowledge that labor incomes have to be unequal, while insisting that incomes from saving and entrepreneurship be distributed equally. (Imposing either kind of equality seems to run the risk of a serious reduction in output.) What is relevant here is the continuity of moral outlook carried over from classical socialism: the fierce distaste for incomes earned by saving rather than by laboring.[11] This moral selectivity is all the more remarkable because in our economy nearly three quarters of the national income is payments for labor,[12] and of the remaining quarter, a very substantial portion at any one time has been saved fairly recently out of labor earnings. Differences in labor earnings, it would seem, have more weight in determining the actual pattern of income differences than do differences in wealth ownership. We might perhaps have expected to encounter some equalitarians, who, as a concession to practicality, would be prepared to permit unequal property incomes while insisting on equal wages for all and any

11   Pertinently enough, Arneson (1993, 289) raises the question of why the entire population, who receive these "profits" under some market socialist proposals, are not then culpable "exploiters." In a careful, extended analysis, Arnold 1994 shows that the organizational structures of market socialism would permit and encourage forms of exploitation normally precluded under capitalism.

12   U.S. Bureau of the Census 1994, 452. Table No. 692 shows that "Compensation of Employees" for 1993 was 73.38 percent of national income. Since morally charged socialist discussions often tacitly assume that "profits" typically go to "corporations," it's worth noting that the same table yields total pretax corporate profits at 9 percent, or just over 5 percent after tax. The point of bringing this up is not to belittle the ethical importance of corporate profits—if it's immoral to get a return on one's savings, then it's immoral to get a small return on one's savings—but to emphasize that the profits of corporations are not the biggest source of income inequalities.

occupations.[13] But we almost never do: the socialist conviction that present income from past saving is somehow morally tainted is very deeply rooted, though I know of no serious rationale for it.

There is a dissonance between the moral outlook that most commonly inspires people to be socialists and acceptance of a major role for the market. Because of this, the new market socialism is unlikely to endure as an ideological alternative in its present form. It is best seen as one route by which its proponents may gradually come to accept the optimality and the moral acceptability of some form of capitalism.

Critical Review, Summer 1996

References

Arneson, Richard J. 1993. Market Socialism and Egalitarian Ethics. In Bardhan and Roemer 1993.

Arnold, N. Scott. 1994. *The Philosophy and Economics of Market Socialism: A Critical Study*. New York: Oxford University Press.

Bardhan, Pranab K. 1993. On Tackling the Soft Budget Constraint in Market Socialism. In Bardhan and Roemer 1993.

Bardhan, Pranab K., and John E. Roemer, eds. 1993. *Market Socialism: The Current Debate*. New York: Oxford University Press.

Barone, Enrico. 1908. Il Ministerio della Produzione nello Stato Collectivista. *Giornale degli Economisti e Rivista di Statistica*. Translation in Hayek 1935.

Belkin, David. 1994. Why Market Socialism? From the Critique of Political Economy to Positive Political Economy. In Roosevelt and Belkin 1994.

Callinicos, Alex. 1982. *Is There a Future for Marxism?* Atlantic Highlands: Humanities Press.

---

13 Arneson remarks that market socialism "is liberally tolerant of inequalities of income stemming from the labor market but rigidly intolerant of inequalities of income stemming from differential ownership of capital by individuals" (Arneson 1993, 282). Arneson's paper acutely clarifies some of the different strands of moral thinking which combine uneasily in socialist discourse.

Carens, Joseph H. 1981. *Equality, Moral Incentives, and the Market: An Essay in Utopian Politico-Economic Theory*. Chicago: University of Chicago Press.

Crews, Frederick, et al. 1995. *The Memory Wars: Freud's Legacy in Dispute*. New York: NYRB.

Hayek, Friedrich A., ed. 1935. *Collectivist Economic Planning*. London: Routledge.

———. 1948. *Individualism and Economic Order*. Chicago: University of Chicago Press.

Howe, Irving. 1994. Thinking about Socialism: Achievements, Failures, and Possibilities. In Roosevelt and Belkin 1994.

Kautsky, Karl Johann. 1902. *The Social Revolution*. Chicago: Kerr.

Kornai, Janos. 1992. *The Socialist System: The Political Economy of Communism*. Princeton: Princeton University Press.

———. 1993. Market Socialism Revisited. In Bardhan and Roemer 1993.

Lenin, V.I. 1964. *Collected Works*. Moscow: Progress Publishers.

Marx, Karl. 1974. *Capital: A Critical Analysis of Capitalist Production*. Volume 1. Moscow: Progress.

Miller, David Leslie. 1989. *Market, State, and Community: Theoretical Foundations of Market Socialism*. Oxford: Clarendon Press.

Mises, Ludwig Edler von. 1920. Die Wirtschaftsrechnung im sozialistischen Gemeinwesen. *Archiv für Sozialwissenschaft und Sozialpolitik* 47:1. Translated in Hayek 1935.

———. 1923. Neue Beiträge zum Problem der sozialistischen Wirtschaftsrechnung. *Archiv für Sozialwissenschaft und Sozialpolitik* 51:2.

———. 1936. *Socialism: An Economic and Sociological Analysis*. London: Jonathan Cape.

Nove, Alec. 1983. *The Economics of Feasible Socialism*. New York: Allen and Unwin.

Okun, Arthur M. 1975. *Equality and Efficiency: The Big Tradeoff*. Washington, D.C.: Brookings Institution.

Pierson, Nikolaas. 1902. Het Waardeprobleem in een socialistische Maatschappij. *De Economist* 41. Translated in Hayek 1935.

Putterman, Louis. 1993. Incentive Problems Favoring Noncentralized Investment Fund Ownership. In Bardhan and Roemer 1993.

Roemer, John E. 1993. Can There Be Socialism after Communism? In Bardhan and Roemer 1993.

Roosevelt, Frank, and David Belkin, eds. 1994. *Why Market Socialism? Voices from Dissent*. Armonk: Sharpe.

Schweickart, David. 1980. *Capitalism or Worker Control? An Ethical and Economic Appraisal*. New York: Praeger.

———. 1993. *Against Capitalism*. Cambridge: Cambridge University Press.

Steele, David Ramsay. 1992. *From Marx to Mises: Post-Capitalist Society and the Challenge of Economic Calculation*. La Salle: Open Court.

U.S. Bureau of the Census. 1994. *Statistical Abstract of the United States 1994*. Washington, D.C.: U.S. Department of Commerce.

Weisskopf, Thomas E. 1993. A Democratic Enterprise-Based Market Socialism. In Bardhan and Roemer 1993.

———. 1994. Challenges to Market Socialism: A Response to Critics. In Roosevelt and Belkin 1994.

Wolf, Martin. 1996. Crisis of the Welfare State. *Financial Times* (23rd April).

20

NOZICK ON SUNK COSTS (1996)

Historical costs have powerful sway over untutored minds.[1]

I. Introduction

Robert Nozick challenges the view of sunk costs held by economists,[2] a view which has for about a century been considered an established part of economic theory. Nozick produces arguments which, he believes, show the untenability of "the economists' doctrine that sunk costs should be ignored" (p. 22). In this article I argue that Nozick's criticisms fail and that the economists' doctrine emerges unscathed.

II. The Economists' Doctrine of Sunk Costs

The sunk costs doctrine was for many years stated by economists without the words 'sunk costs'. The doctrine is one conclusion of the theory of opportunity costs and was understood as such from the early days of opportunity cost theory. Wicksteed's classic account, written in 1910, clearly explains and defends what we now call the doctrine of sunk costs.[3] According to the opportunity cost concept, the cost of an action is what is given up by taking that action. The only costs which should be weighed in making a decision are the avoidable and, hence, necessarily future costs entailed by that decision; these costs consist of the benefits which would have flowed from the next best option, had it been

---

1 George Stigler, *The Theory of Price*, 4th ed. (New York: Macmillan, 1987), p. 111.

2 Robert Nozick, *The Nature of Rationality* (Princeton: Princeton University Press, 1993), pp. 21–26. Where not otherwise stated, page and line references are to this work.

3 Philip H. Wicksteed, The Common *Sense of Political Economy and Selected Papers and Reviews on Economic Theory*, 2 vols. (London: Routledge, 1933), vol. 1, pp. 88–94, 373–91.

selected instead. The sunk costs doctrine follows: costs incurred in the past, historical costs, should not be counted as costs of present or future decisions.

For example, Bill decides to open a factory producing widgets. Bill's outlays include an expensive durable machine, for which he gets a loan to be repaid over several years. The machine (we stipulate) cannot be resold, and the loan repayments would still have to be kept up if the factory closed. The factory is built, and production starts. It turns out that the market had been misjudged, and the income statement shows a net loss, which is expected to continue as long as the loan payments have to be made. But if we subtract the loan repayments from expenses, the factory is making a profit.

The economist holds that, in deciding whether to keep the factory open, the loan repayments should be ignored (and, although this takes us beyond Nozick's discussion, will in fact, in a competitive market, generally be ignored). Since those repayments would still have to be made if the factory closed, they are not costs of continued operation.

In thinking about such issues, it is often helpful to consider hypothetical alternative scenarios by which the situation under discussion might have come about. We can compare the situation of Bill's widget factory, after production has commenced, with a scenario in which the machine had been donated as a free gift, and coincidentally Bill had an old, unrelated debt, amounting to the same as the loan repayments for the machine in the first scenario. According to economists, the two situations are alike in all relevant respects; therefore, the optimal decision in each case must be the same.

III. Nozick's First Argument: Using One Error to Counteract Another

I can distinguish five mutually independent arguments in Nozick's case against the sunk costs doctrine. I will label these 1 to 5 and follow Nozick in allocating the great majority of my space to his argument 1. I briefly discuss arguments 2 through 5 at the end of this article. Nozick's argument 1 is presented via the following example:

> If I think it would be good for me to see many plays or attend
> many concerts this year, and I know that when the evening of
> the performance arrives I frequently will not feel like rousing

myself at that moment to go out, then I can buy tickets to many of these events in advance. . . . Since I will not want to waste the money I have already spent on the tickets, I will attend more performances than I would if I left the decisions about attendance to each evening. (p. 22)

The protagonist of this story, whom I will call *N*, buys a ticket at time *A* because he can foresee that at the later time, *B*, he will feel too lethargic to go to the theater, and since at *A* he considers this "lethargy" undesirable, he wants to do something at *A* to make it more likely that at *B* he will override the lethargy. (This terminology of *A*, *B*, and a subsequent time, *C*, is employed by Nozick.) Since *N* knows that he is given to counting sunk costs, he uses this feature of his personality to manipulate his future decision. He knows at *A* that at *B* he will believe it to be an argument in favor of visiting the theater that he would otherwise have wasted the money he had spent, at *A*, on the ticket. Hence *N*'s propensity to count sunk costs can be used by *N* at *A* to make it more likely that at *B* he will do what he thinks at *A* that he should do. If *N*'s reasoning were along the lines envisaged by Nozick, *N* at *A* might turn down the opportunity of a free ticket and insist on paying $40 for it, or he might walk to the box office in the rain, which he detests, when he could just pick up the phone.

Nozick sees the counting of sunk costs as offering the possibility of a technique for overcoming temptation. If *N* at *A* knows that *N* at *B* will be prone to commit the sunk costs fallacy, *N* has one more technique with which he can act at *A* to change the way he will behave at *B*. "We can knowingly employ our tendency to take sunk costs seriously as a means of increasing our future rewards. If this tendency is irrational, it can be rationally utilized to check and overcome another irrationality" (p. 23).

The reference to future rewards arises because Nozick holds that frames of mind like that at *A* will recur at *C*, so that *N* will then look back on the whole sequence of events and prefer that he had gone to the theater at *B*.

IV. An Advantageous Error Is an Error

The most natural understanding of Nozick's argument 1 is that he accepts that *N* at *B* commits an error (an "irrationality") by counting sunk costs but that this error has an outcome which N at A regards as advantageous or beneficial, because it counteracts or cancels another error (or, more broadly, another deficiency or shortcoming), that of lethargy.

Insofar as Nozick asserts that we can imagine ways in which committing a certain kind of error might turn out to be advantageous, he does not contradict the economists' doctrine. It is not disputed that errors can turn out to be advantageous: two immediately obvious cases are (a) that in which the agent has incomplete knowledge, and by chance a decision relying on an error turns out to be best, and (b) the case where one error cancels out the effect of another error. Showing that an error may be beneficial or advantageous does not show that it is not an error. Drawing that conclusion would be an instance of the well-known fallacy of inferring the quality of a decision from its outcome.[4]

Nozick raises the possibility that an economist might say that according to Nozick's argument, the "irrationality" of counting sunk costs is desirable only for someone with another "irrationality" (p. 24). Nozick responds to this hypothetical objection by referring to his arguments 2 and 3 and then stating his argument 5. That is to say, Nozick pointedly does not contest the claim that his first and fourth arguments rely on one irrationality (error or deficiency) to counteract another. Yet it is misleading for Nozick to make his hypothetical economist appear to concede part of Nozick's argument and try to save a smaller area of validity for the sunk costs doctrine. Real economists do not say that counting sunk costs can never have a desirable

---

4   Ibid., vol. 1, pp. 72, 120-21; Stephen Nathanson, *The Ideal of Rationality: A Defense, within Reason* (Chicago: Open Court, 1994), pp. 49–51. Nathanson cites Rawls (*A Theory of Justice* [Cambridge, Mass.: Harvard University Press, 1971], p. 72), who calls it "subjectively rational" to do the best one can with the available information. I prefer to avoid such locutions by simply saying that counting sunk costs is an error. There may seem to be an air of paradox about the claim that a theory of successful action would classify a specific decision as wrong even though the outcome were successful. But this is superficial. The theory never recommends acting in a way known to be unsuccessful or failing to act in a way known to be successful. Erroneous actions with advantageous outcomes are either (a) flukes, like blowing the rent money on lottery tickets and winning $20 million, or (b) cases where a mistaken theory in the agent's mind leads to a pattern of successes. This latter is not always due to one error's counteracting another but would generally be susceptible to an explanation which would help in disentangling the successful outcomes of the mistakes from actual or possible unsuccessful outcomes.

outcome. Given that the agent's information is imperfect, any miscalculation, any folly, can turn out for the best. The economists' position is that counting sunk costs is an error: on the most obvious interpretation, this is confirmed rather than challenged by Nozick's argument 1. If Nozick denies that counting sunk costs is always an error, it seems to follow from his position that no type of error is always an error, for any type of error might be compensated for by some other error to yield a desirable outcome. We can equally well imagine some circumstance in which supposing that 2 + 2 = 5 would have a welcome outcome and then pronounce that this error is not always irrational, but only some of the time.

V. The Two Forms of the Sunk Costs Fallacy

Although economists sometimes speak of *the* fallacy of sunk costs, there are in fact two different forms of the fallacy, which tend to impel decisions in opposing directions. That form which takes up by far the greater attention and space in economics teaching I will call the "main form" of the fallacy; it is exemplified in the story of Bill and his widget factory. Here, according to economists, current operations should often be viewed as more profitable than uninstructed common sense would indicate, and current projects should often be continued where common sense might suggest that they should be terminated. The economist's rejection of the main form of the fallacy always, if it affects behavior at all, leads to the continued pursuit of projects which the fallacy would indicate should be abandoned. That is, the main form of the fallacy can never work in the direction required by Nozick's argument, but only in the opposite direction (if it affects behavior at all).[5] The other form of the fallacy, which most textbook treatments, for example, do not bother to mention,[6] is the

5   The fuller opportunity cost doctrine from which the sunk costs doctrine is derived might push in the opposite direction because of implicit costs. I follow Nozick in confining the discussion to those cases where a decision is made about whether to continue with some project. Some discussions of sunk costs relate instead to optimal pricing: whereas non-economists often suppose that what was paid in the past to produce or acquire something should influence what is charged for it now, economists say that this is immaterial.

6   I tested my impressions of what economists teach by looking at the relevant passages in forty introductory economics or intermediate price theory textbooks. Some failed

view that because expenditures have been made in the past and have not yet been recouped, therefore special attempts should be made to recoup those expenditures in the future. I will call this the "Concorde" form of the sunk costs fallacy.[7] Thus, if Hillary has paid to commence the building of a canal, which is now half completed, this is sometimes believed to provide a reason for Hillary to complete the canal, even if, in an alternative scenario, the half-completed canal existed as a natural geographical feature, and, knowing what Hillary now knows, she would not think it worthwhile to "complete" the canal. The economist says that these two scenarios are alike in all relevant respects: past expenditures do not justify future expenditures. The economist does not deny that, looking ahead, we ought to try to make income exceed costs. But we ought not to look back at costs irretrievably incurred in the past and make our behavior different from what it would have been if those past costs had not been incurred, in an attempt to recoup those costs in the future. Because those costs are now unavoidable, they are irrelevant, qua costs, to any current or future decisions.[8]

The second, or Concorde, form of the sunk costs doctrine is alone treated by Nozick. He does not mention the more commonly discussed main form of the doctrine and leaves the impression that the Concorde form (the rejection of the Concorde fallacy) is the whole doctrine. Only the Concorde form can help Nozick's argument.

to unambiguously mention sunk costs. Most that did do so mentioned only the main form, while others mentioned both forms. I found none where the Concorde form was given greater emphasis or where only the Concorde form was mentioned, except Stigler (pp. 111–12), which, however, gives a passing mention of the Concorde form and whose other examples are all about price setting rather than project continuation. I count as a "mention" an example which fits one or the other form- most texts don't explicitly distinguish them. Of the texts I looked at, only David Friedman's *Price Theory: An Intermediate Text* (Cincinnati: South-Western, 1986) clearly explains the distinction between the two forms, calling them "opposite mistakes" (pp. 279–280).

7   See Richard Dawkins, *The Selfish Gene*, 2d ed. (Oxford: Oxford University Press, 1989), p. 150.

8   On the economist's view of costs, see Wicksteed, pp. 373-91. For more recent accounts, see Armen Alchian, "Costs," in *International Encyclopedia of the Social Sciences*, ed. David L. Sills (New York: Macmillan, 1968), pp. 404–414; James M. Buchanan, *Cost and Choice: An Inquiry in Economic Theory* (Chicago: Markham, 1969).

VI. Why N Might Go to the Theater, Irrespective of Sunk Costs

People quite reasonably take steps to change their future circumstances in such a way that they will be more likely at some future time to choose to do one thing rather than another. It is not unusual for a person to buy exercise equipment in order to "make herself" exercise. This well-known stratagem doesn't necessarily involve counting sunk costs and may be free of error from the economist's standpoint. There are reasons not involving sunk costs why N, on the evening of the performance, might not go to the theater if he had not bought tickets, even though he would go if he had bought tickets. An unfocused awareness of these other motivations helps to make N's stratagem of committing himself by buying tickets in advance look plausible. This intuitive plausibility does not rest on counting sunk costs. The most obvious consideration—given a passing mention by Nozick (p. 22, lines 19–20)—is that if N has already bought a ticket, he does not have to pay for a ticket at B. Since the payment for the ticket has already been made and (we will suppose) cannot be unmade, the theater effectively has free admission for N at B. If he had not bought the ticket, on the other hand, admission would cost the price of the ticket, say, $40. There would additionally be a nonpecuniary cost, the time and effort spent making the purchase, which N might negatively value at $9. (Further, although Nozick assumes that N at B can costlessly be certain that seats of the relevant quality and price are not sold out, this is rarely the case.)[9]

N's plan at A makes sense without having N at B count sunk costs. N at A anticipates that N at B might not be sufficiently motivated to go to the theater, so N at A provides the motivation of a free ticket (free both monetarily and in terms of the nonpecuniary expense of the transaction of

---

9   Theater tickets are often cheaper when purchased in advance. From the standpoint of Nozick's argument, this is unfortunate, since it means that the anticipated sunk cost, and therefore the ability to manipulate one's own future behavior by incurring a cost, is lower. On the other hand, an individual might well think he shouldn't "waste" the theater ticket since its acquisition was such a bargain, and this erroneous thought might prompt him to go—another illustration of the fact that once we start relying on our intellectual confusion to get us to do things, any type of intellectual confusion may do just as well.

acquiring it) and in practice also dispels any uncertainty at B about availability and price of tickets by buying the ticket in advance.

This stratagem is most dependable where N at B does not fall for the sunk costs fallacy in its main form. If N at B is in the grip of this main form, then he will be inclined to rate the cost of going to the theater as $49 higher than he should (or perhaps some positive amount less than $49 higher, for the error exists if sunk costs are given any weight at all as present costs). N will fail to fully take on board the fact that the ticket, once paid for, is free.[10] And this error may dissuade him from going to the theater.

Not only does the above rationale offer an alternative to Nozick's reliance on sunk costs, but an understanding of this rationale makes the rational utilization of the Concorde fallacy appear far less promising. Suppose that N pays $40 for the ticket and would have paid up to $56 (a consumer's surplus of $16). When buying the ticket, N anticipates the visit to be worth $65 ($56 plus the nonpecuniary outlay valued at $9). Suppose that on the night, the visit is worth $5 to him. This is a considerable drop in N's valuation of the theater visit, a reduction of $60, yet N will still go to the theater—even if its value falls to one thousandth of a cent, he will go. (There are further costs of going, of course, but the valuation in question is already net of those costs.) Before there is any scope for the Concorde fallacy to make a difference, N's valuation of the theater visit must have fallen by at least $65.

There is another distinct motivation for N at B: he may not want to waste the ticket he has available at B. This is different from counting sunk costs, where N at B doesn't want to waste the money he paid at A for the ticket. If N at B possesses a ticket because he received it as a gift, there are no historical costs for N—he never bought the ticket—but he may still feel that he doesn't want to waste it. (No doubt this, too, is an error, but it is not an error of counting sunk costs.) N at A might buy the ticket to take advantage of this foreseen motivation on the part of N at B. In that case, there would be a sunk cost, but it would have nothing to do with N's reason at B for going to the theater or with N's reason at A for buying the ticket.

---

10   This assumes that the ticket has no other worthwhile employment. Suppose that, shortly before the performance, a friend offers N $2 for the ticket. Then at that point the cost to N of using the ticket to go to the theater is $2. Similarly, if the friend credibly offers $20,000 for the ticket, then $20,000 is the ticket cost (there are other costs) to N of going to the theater that night.

In Nozick's story, N buys a ticket to induce himself to behave in a certain way at a future time. This intrapersonal stratagem has an interpersonal counterpart: a person might buy someone else a ticket in order to change that other person's behavior. Notice that if this or any other ploy works interpersonally, it cannot be by utilizing a sunk cost error; hence, if it works intrapersonally for the same reason that it might work interpersonally, sunk costs are not intrinsic to that reason. Another possibility is that N at B intrinsically values the completion of projects already commenced or merely decided upon. (One of these projects might be attending the theater no less than eight times a year.) It is quite wrong to suppose, as Nozick sometimes seems to do, that this phenomenon in any way conflicts with the economists' view of sunk costs. I look at this further in Section XI below.

VII. The Switch in N's Goals

N at B has goals (and underlying preferences) that are not only different from those of N at A but opposed, so that frustrating N's pursuit of his goals at B can help N pursue his goals at A and vice versa. This feature, the mutual antagonism of N's goals on two different occasions, is essential to Nozick's first argument. The argument is therefore based on a sleight of hand, a virtual equivocation, for N's counting of sunk costs at B is held to help N pursue the goals he holds at A, when he does not count sunk costs (or is not required by the argument to count sunk costs). Counting sunk costs is not claimed to help N pursue the goals he pursues at B, when he counts sunk costs. N's goals have changed from A to B, so it is no surprise that an error he makes in pursuing his goals at one time, while this error does make him less effective at pursuing those goals, may very well help to make him more effective in pursuit of his goals at a different time, when he has contrary goals. At B, the point where it is claimed that N counts sunk costs, counting sunk costs does look like an error, since there is nothing to suggest that it helps N in effectively pursuing his goals at B, if we look at these goals in isolation from his goals at A.

Naturally, Nozick might dispute the "present aim" view of rationality implicit in the above discussion, but then there would be no need for Nozick's particular story. It would be enough for him to point out that a person may blunder in pursuit of (say) an objectively wrong goal, and, hence, a blunder may serve the agent's best interests. But it would then be evident that such a line of attack was pointless, for all that economists have claimed is that counting sunk costs is an error given the agent's actual goals at the time of the decision. Economists have not claimed that these goals were always wise.

But, it might possibly be said, N's counting sunk costs at B does effectively serve N's goals at A, and these are more important than N's goals at B, as they represent the authentic N, when he is in full command of his faculties, when his will is strong, and when he has a superior grasp of his own true interests. But this is evidently not persuasive enough to convince N at B. If counting sunk costs is an error, if it gives N at B a misleading picture of his alternatives, then N at A can be seen as trying to frustrate the actual wishes of N at B. This becomes instantly clear when we replace N at A and N at B with two different individuals (the interpersonal parallel). That individual P can thwart the desires of individual Q by capitalizing on Q's propensity to believe fallacies or commit errors is hardly surprising or interesting.

Counting sunk costs remains, in Nozick's example, an error, just as economists say. What Nozick has done is to identify a hypothetical case where the error of counting sunk costs can have welcome consequences— welcome to an outside observer or to the individual in a different, and contrary, frame of mind. The desirable quality of the consequences depends upon preferences contrary to those of the agent at the time of decision.

Nozick's discussion gives us no reason not to impute to him the following view: the economist's advice not to count sunk costs is unfortunate in some cases, because it is best in those cases for an individual to commit the error of counting sunk costs and thereby to be less effective at gratifying his preferences of the moment. If this is Nozick's view, it does not contradict the economist's doctrine.

Consider N at A, or at any other A-like, strong-willed time. It can never be to his advantage to count sunk costs while in this frame of mind, for any reason remotely like that in Nozick's example. ("Never" except in the oblique sense that it may be a concomitant of counting sunk costs at B that he also counts sunk costs at A.) Nozick's discussion in his argument 1 (and possibly his arguments 4 and 5) does not in the least go against the view that, relevant to a particular set of goals or preferences, counting sunk costs is always an error, in that it is not optimally conducive to attainment of those goals or satisfaction of those preferences. Nozick disapproves of N's goals and, hence, his preferences at B. Judged by a standard external to those goals, Nozick believes that we do not want people like N at B to be good at fulfilling their actual desires.

VIII. Privileging Strong-Willed Frames of Mind

Against my position, it might be contended that I am talking as though there were two agents, but there is truly only one. N really has the same preferences and goals all along: it's simply that, at B, his "real" preferences and goals are inoperative because of his weakness of will. (The terminology of strong and weak will is not employed by Nozick here, but it seems to be in the spirit of his discussion.)

Any such defense is foredoomed, since in the relevant sense, N's goals at B are real. N at B is both capable of counting sunk costs and of learning not to count sunk costs—precisely this is crucial to Nozick's account. It is only at B that N is stated to count sunk costs. If we are going to deny the reality of N's goals at B, then (aside from the implausibility of this denial) we must deny that N at B counts sunk costs and, hence, that N ever advantageously counts sunk costs.

We can be impartial with respect to the two sets of goals, A and B, or we can privilege one (Nozick would vote for A) at the expense of the other. In the first treatment, we simply observe that N wants different things at different times. We regard N's wants at B as every bit as legitimate, in every sense, as N's wants at A. In the second treatment, we side with A against B. Economic theory does not dispose us to either of these treatments; it is neutral on the matter (although no doubt economists often find the first more congenial).

Under the first treatment, it is uncontroversially evident that N at B is committing an error if he counts sunk costs: he will be poorer at gratifying his desires. It is not relevant that he has different and incompatible desires on other occasions. He just changes his mind from time to time. Under the second treatment, we side with N at A against N at B, and perhaps in some sense we suppose that N's goals at A are his true goals, his goals at B a betrayal of his true goals. But this merely means that we agree with N at A

that an error by N at B may be welcome, because we judge the goals of N at B to be reprehensible.

IX. Committing "Errors" on Principle

If an error leads to good results in some cases, we can, as it were, knowingly commit the error in order to get the good results. But then the "error" is no longer an error. It is a rule that superficially looks like an error when seen out of its proper context. An example is "With this rifle, you should aim to the right of the target." If the rifle has a bias to the left, and you shoot to the right to compensate for the bias, you are not thereby committing an error (even if you miss the target). If you know nothing of the left bias and shoot to the right because of poor aim, thereby unwittingly compensating for the left bias, you commit an error (even if you hit the bull's-eye).

Nozick writes of "rationally" utilizing "our tendency to take sunk costs seriously as a means of increasing our future rewards" (p. 23). But is it feasible for N at A to make N at B believe something fallacious, while N at A clearheadedly sees through the fallacy? N at B can hardly be expected to say to himself: "Ah, now it's time to start accepting a fallacy which will make me want to do what I wouldn't otherwise want to do." If N at B falls for the Concorde fallacy, then N at A must fall for it, too (if the occasion arises). So it's doubtful whether what Nozick seems to be recommending—that N at A rationally utilizes the proneness to error of N at B—could ever be accomplished.

X. Is the Concorde Error Advantageous?

Nozick holds that "taking sunk costs into account sometimes is desirable (so the economists' general condemnation is mistaken) and sometimes is not" (p. 23). As we have seen, this evades the question of whether counting sunk costs is always an error, as economists maintain, regardless of the desirability of the outcome. Nozick and the economists can agree that counting sunk costs will sometimes be advantageous and sometimes disadvantageous.

Does Nozick hold that it will so often be advantageous that the best policy is to count sunk costs rather than not? While this would not, as Nozick apparently supposes, refute the economists' doctrine, it would certainly form a fascinating rider to it, and one that perhaps ought to be mentioned in economics teaching. Nozick's view is unclear. At one point he seems to commit himself definitely to an agnostic position (p. 23, lines 34–36), but his assertion that the economists' rule "is not an appropriate general principle of decision" (p. 22) is troubling.

The citing of a hypothetical example where counting sunk costs turns out to be beneficial does not take us very far. Nozick makes no attempt to show that committing this kind of error will always, or typically, or more often than not, or in any appreciable proportion of instances be beneficial. We would scarcely be impressed by the demand that we reject the rule that you should not whimsically kill the next person you meet, because, after all, that person might secretly be a serial killer who not only richly deserves death but is getting ready to kill again; hence, the prohibition of random homicide is sometimes desirable and sometimes not. For that matter, in the theater example, almost any kind of error will do. If *N* is in the habit of losing his way, he might intend to go to a bar and end up by mistake at the theater. (Sometimes it's desirable to lose your way and sometimes not. And if you know that you are prone to lose your way, you can utilize this propensity by calculating in advance that you may be unable to find your way to the bar.)

Does Nozick perhaps hold that the agent can distinguish a subset of cases where counting sunk costs is likely to be advantageous, and count sunk costs on those occasions, failing to count them on all others? Nozick does not tell us of any general policy rule that he recommends in place of the economists' rule never to count sunk costs. If he recommends the rule always to count sunk costs, it seems immediately plausible that the disadvantageous applications will vastly outweigh the advantageous ones.

If, at the other extreme, he recommends that we count sunk costs only in those cases where doing so is likely to be advantageous, this presupposes that we have some way to distinguish these cases from others. In that event, to save his argument Nozick would have to avoid any mechanism by which the agent perceives the advantages and counts sunk costs because he sees the advantages. If he can do this, he does not need to count sunk costs at all: pursuit of the advantages would be sufficient.

Nozick cannot be recommending counting sunk costs as a general rule. He states that the economists' doctrine "may be a correct rule for the maximization of monetary profits" (p. 22). And, as we have seen, the main form of the sunk costs fallacy always tends to impel the agent in the opposite direction from that which Nozick finds desirable.

I have suggested that the persuasiveness of Nozick's theater ticket example derives from the assumption that N at B does not commit the main form of the sunk costs error. Nozick could take the position that he is referring only to the Concorde fallacy and that the main form of the fallacy is irrelevant to his argument. But it is doubtful that we could rely on an individual to be prone to the Concorde fallacy while immune to the main fallacy. The main fallacy can be quite subtle and may require protracted analysis to identify, whereas seeing through the Concorde fallacy makes no great demand on the intellect.

Even if we confine the recommended cases for counting sunk costs to the Concorde fallacy in noncommercial situations, counting sunk costs is going to lead to many disadvantageous outcomes. If N follows the rule at B, he is going to follow it at A. Furthermore, he is going to follow it at A-like times with respect to costs incurred at B-like times. And there is no reason to suppose even that following it at B-like times with respect to costs incurred at A-like times will always, or often, be advantageous.

In Nozick's example, N's lethargy explains his reduced inclination to go to the theater. But this reduced inclination might be a result of bad reviews, a tornado watch, N's being implored to help a niece with her homework, N's having a cough and being unwilling to distract other members of the audience, or N's receiving a free ticket for another show which is better in every way. Counting sunk costs must counteract these motives as effectively as it would counteract lethargy.

Even in the theater example, it's by no means clear that the Concorde fallacy will impel N to go to the theater. For N has expended resources on, say, comfortable furnishings in his home and has spent many an evening assiduously developing his human capital in the direction of becoming a virtuoso couch potato—every time he spends an evening away from home, he loses a chance to recoup some return on this past investment. Overeating or overdrinking can easily be facilitated by the erroneous thought that it would be a waste not to finish the bottle or what's in the fridge, because of the money or effort already expended in acquiring these. In such instances, proneness to the Concorde fallacy would make succumbing to temptation more likely.

XI. Wanting to Stay the Course Is Independent of Sunk Costs

The sunk costs doctrine doesn't prohibit any attention to historical costs or any guidance of present decisions by looking at past costs. For example, someone may examine the record of past costs and incomes to suggest what might happen in future analogous situations. Or, decisions taken and costs incurred in the past may have had repercussions which result in relevantly modifying the actual situation as it obtains later, at the moment of decision.

It is also possible that the agent may have a preference for finishing what she has started or for honoring her commitments. An individual may simply have a preference for making and honoring commitments; this may not, and generally does not, have anything to do with sunk costs.

At times Nozick seems to confound some such rationally impeccable motive with a sunk costs error (p. 22, lines 34–41), a tendency illustrated by his use of the grotesque phrase "honoring sunk costs" (p. 23). Costs qua costs cannot be honored, although commitments can. In honoring costs, if anyone would ever want to do anything so strange, one would be treating them as something other than costs, as, for example, in religiously venerating a recipe for Dundee cake, one would not be employing it as a recipe. As a matter of practical relevance, it will often be most important to maintain a commitment at an early stage when few costs may have been incurred.

If an agent has a preference or motivation inclining her to keep commitments or finish what she has started, this intrinsically has nothing to do with historical costs and may indeed occur where there are no historical costs. We should also be clear that even where someone is more inclined to persist with some course of action because of attention to historical costs, this is not necessarily an instance of what economists would identify as a sunk costs fallacy.

A person might imaginably (although somewhat bizarrely) have an independent preference for pursuing actions where there are sunk costs—

"independent" in the sense that this preference does not arise from a sunk cost fallacy but is one of the array of preferences with which the agent is endowed prior to any calculation of the benefits and costs of particular actions. The possibility of such an independent preference was recognized by Wicksteed, who remarks that a man setting his selling price by reference to past costs of production "is either allowing an irrelevant consideration to affect his judgment or else is deliberately taking a commercial risk to gratify a personal feeling."[11]

In the case of Bill's machine considered above, Bill might have promised his great-aunt, when she was on her deathbed, that he would close down the factory if it failed to recoup the cost of the machine. Any number of such motivations could be imagined. Perhaps in a stressful moment, Bill swore a vow to himself that he would recoup the cost of the machine or close the factory and now feels obliged to comply with that vow. Such cases are unusual—typically, Bill will not have sworn any such peculiar oath. However, even in those few cases where such a motive arises, the sunk costs doctrine is not contradicted. For in such cases, an additional goal of counting historical costs has been added to the conditions of the problem. As a result, a historical cost is used to derive a goal; in the stated conditions, the historical cost does not influence decisions because it is a cost but rather because it generates a goal. In such a case, the agent does not commit the mistake of supposing that the historical cost of the machine is a cost of keeping the factory running.

XII. Nozick's Fourth Argument

Nozick's fourth argument occupies the paragraph beginning near the bottom of page 23. As with argument 1, argument 4 has the agent deliberately incurring costs because he reckons that in the future he will count sunk costs and thus will be motivated to behave differently. But unlike argument 1, argument 4 relates not to a specific action (such as going to the theater on a particular night) but to the choice of a principle. Nozick conceives a principle as a rule for grouping actions so that they are treated uniformly (pp. 3–4, 17–18). For the most part, my criticisms of Nozick's argument 1

11   Wicksteed, p. 386.

also apply to his argument 4, but there are additional difficulties, of which I will mention two.

First, what is meant by choosing one principle rather than another? One would think that the only principle in question were that of not succumbing to temptation. I surmise that Nozick is implicitly referring back to his earlier discussion (p. 19, lines 13–17), and that the sort of thing he has in mind here is the desirability of a motive for preferring (a) the principle never to succumb to temptation to (b) the principle never to succumb to temptation except on a single imminent occasion. If this is Nozick's intention here, then it is mistaken. If past costs would afford a reason for maintaining principle (a), they would equally afford a reason for maintaining principle (b). The past costs provide no means of discriminating between the two alternative principles.

Second, the Concorde principle is irrelevant here, because it is in essence the notion that we should do something to recoup a past loss. In contrast, anyone can see that it is senseless to say: "I expended costs, yet these were amply compensated by the ensuing benefits; nonetheless, I must do something to recover those costs." Why should we suppose that the individual who has successfully resisted temptation on a number of occasions will now regard himself as being, so to speak, behind on the deal? Unless he does regard himself as being in a losing position so far, the Concorde fallacy is inapplicable.

Nozick's discussion of principles points to the possibility of a more straightforward and thoroughly rational approach: by grouping actions together, the agent attributes more significance to each action by virtue of its membership in the group. Thus, the agent derives more utility from an action because it belongs to the group,[12] and, hence, the cost of failing to perform that action is increased. This account is admittedly limited in that it leaves open the process by which the agent comes to ascribe enhanced significance to actions as members of a group, but some such method has decided advantages over relying on the Concorde approach, for example: (a)

---

12   But not as much utility as is derived from the entire group. Nozick claims that "the penalty for violating the principle this time becomes the disutility of violating it always" (p. 19). We do not, I take it, want to view getting drunk today as *equivalent* to getting drunk every remaining day of our lives.

it does not depend upon the inherently undesirable practice of relying on one's own muddleheadedness to make one do the right thing; (b) it has more direct relevance to the important notion of commitment, for the degree of commitment can vary independent of total past costs expended; (c) it avoids perverse consequences of the Concorde approach (such as abandoning continued pursuit of a goal because one discovers that it is turning out to be easier to achieve than one had believed, or deliberately incurring unnecessary costs only because they will affect one's later behavior through the Concorde fallacy); and (d) it avoids the indeterminacy of the Concorde approach (which urges one to keep allocating more resources to a losing project, without specifying at what point, if ever, this throwing of good resources after bad is to be discontinued).

XIII. Nozick's Second, Third, and Fifth Arguments

Nozick's second argument is framed thus: "We do not treat our past commitments to others as of no account except insofar as they affect our future returns" (p. 22). The immediate context shows that Nozick believes that this statement contradicts the sunk costs doctrine. But economists have never been in any doubt that individuals sometimes do erroneously count sunk costs.[13] And the mere fact of having a preference for keeping commitments to others does not entail any counting of sunk costs.

Nozick's third argument is that "we do not treat the past efforts we have devoted to ongoing projects of work or life as of no account (except insofar as this makes their continuance more likely to bring benefits than other freshly started projects would). Such projects help to define our sense of ourselves and of our lives" (p. 22). Here, too, what we do is not conclusive with respect to what we should, rationally or efficiently, do. And at the point of decision, defining her sense of herself and of her life is preferred by the agent to other desirabilia. This does not conflict with anything in

---

13   Wicksteed, pp. 91–94, 387; Robert H. Frank, *Microeconomics and Behavior* (New York: McGraw-Hill, 1991), pp. 13–14, 226–236. For a typical example of the way in which economists acknowledge that businesspeople are prone to count sunk costs and exhort them not to do so, see Thomas H. Nagle, *The Strategy and Tactics of Pricing: A Guide to Profitable Decision-Making* (Englewood Cliffs: Prentice Hall, 1987), pp. 21–23.

economic theory and has nothing to do with sunk costs. There is not even any claim here that the agent values defining her sense of herself and of her life just because she has expended resources on this in the past—although that would not amount to a sunk costs fallacy, as we have seen.

Nozick's fifth argument (p. 24, lines 34–40), draws upon a well-known argument by Thomas Schelling[14] that it may be useful to convince others that we will "irrationally" stick to our guns even in the face of threats which make it disadvantageous for us. The possibility that commitment to certain behaviors, a commitment that disregards momentary estimations of advantage, may be advantageous in the long term, because of the way in which awareness of such a commitment may modify the behaviors of other people, has been familiar to many economists for at least some decades.[15] It has nothing intrinsically to do with sunk costs, although there has been discussion of the advantages of behaving "irrationally,"[16] and if the propensity to maintain such commitments were made more likely because of a propensity to count sunk costs, this would be one more conceivable way in which an error could, on occasion, have advantageous consequences.

I conclude that of Nozick's five arguments against the economists' doctrine, arguments 1 and 4 are faulty in several fatal respects, while arguments 2, 3, and 5 embody simple mistakes. My narrow concern has been Nozick's claim that he has refuted the sunk costs doctrine as economists understand it, and my argument should not be taken to imply that there is nothing of value in Nozick's discussion or that parts of it could not profitably be reformulated to avoid the unwarranted allegation that the economists' doctrine is at fault.[17]

Ethics, April 1996

14   Thomas Schelling, *Arms and Influence* (New Haven: Yale University Press, 1966), pp. 35–91.

15   See Robert H. Frank, *Passions within Reason: The Strategic Role of the Emotions* (New York: Norton, 1988), pp. 47–70, and the references cited in p. 47n.

16   Schelling, *Arms and Influence*, and *The Strategy of Conflict* (Cambridge: Harvard University Press, 1960); Frank.

17   I thank N. Scott Arnold, David Barker, David Gordon, Barry Smith, and the editors of *Ethics* for helpful comments on drafts of this article.

21

The Atkins Diet as an Alternative Theory (2005)

The Atkins Diet has been condemned by the majority of qualified experts—nutritionists, dieticians, and physicians. Although the preponderance of hostile expert opinion has somewhat lessened since the publication, beginning in 2002, of studies which seem to vindicate Atkins,[1] the majority of established authorities still denounce the Atkins Diet and warn sternly against its conjectured dangerous consequences.

The American Cancer Society, American Heart Association, American Dietetic Association, and American Kidney Fund have all issued official statements strongly discouraging the Atkins Diet. And a number of eminent dieticians such as Dean Ornish have vilified all low-carb diets in colorful terms. The venom of the hostility to Atkins can be gauged from the title of one of the leading anti-Atkins books, *Killer Diets*.[2]

At the same time, there are some experts who support the Atkins Diet, or in some cases deliver a mixed verdict, saying that the Atkins Diet is, if not perfect, an improvement on the typical American diet. Advocates of the Atkins Diet sometimes have letters after their names, including "M.D." and "Ph.D.", and often argue in detail that the reigning dietary doctrine is wrong, citing research and questioning the interpretation of research findings by the dominant anti-Atkins propagandists.

What's the ordinary person, someone with no qualifications in nutritional science, to make of this? Should we automatically trust the experts?

---

1 Among many such studies, see Eric C. Westman *et al.*, *American Journal of Medicine* (July 2002); F.F. Samaha *et al.*, *New England Journal of Medicine* (22nd May, 2003); Gary D. Foster *et al.*, *New England Journal of Medicine* (22nd May, 2003); William S. Yancy Jr. *et al.*, *Annals of Internal Medicine* (18th May, 2004).

2 Laura Muha, *Killer Diets: Are Low-Carb Diets High Risk?* (New York: Chamberlain, 2004).

And if the experts are divided, should we always go with the majority and turn a deaf ear to dissenting voices?

Sixty years ago, George Orwell became troubled by the fact that he accepted many scientific opinions without knowing the reasoning behind them. Orwell asserted that he, like most non-scientists of above-average education, would not be able to mount very effective arguments against the Earth being flat.[3] He personally did not doubt that the Earth is round, yet he was bothered by the fact that he seemed to be accepting this scientific consensus with the same uncritical trust as the member of a preliterate tribe might accept the pronouncements of its witchdoctor—or the same blind faith as a loyal subject of a totalitarian regime.

When Orwell wrote, most of Europe was dominated by National Socialist Germany and Soviet Russia. In both parts of Europe, the views of the dominant scientific experts were taught in schools, and most experts seemed to accept them.

In the German dominated area, the official Nazi line prevailed. Not only were some races claimed to be inferior to others, but many theories originated by Jews, such as Einstein's Relativity, were dismissed as pseudoscience.

Meanwhile, in Soviet Russia, a sixth of the world's population were taught that all of genetics was pseudoscience, and that the theories of Stalin's favored biologist, Trofim Lysenko, were correct. Even eminent scientists in Britain and America, if they were politically sympathetic to Communism, defended Lysenko's theories against Mendel's genetics, while all Western biologists not sympathetic to Communism (more than ninety percent of them) favored Mendel, and held that Lysenko was a wretched mountebank.[4] These developments made it clear that there can be a large element of ideological bias in the determination of the expert consensus on various issues.

Dominant Theories and Alternative Theories

The Atkins Diet is an example of an unorthodox doctrine or a dissident school of thought. In this chapter I will call it an "alternative theory." It's a

---

3   George Orwell, *Complete Works* (London: Secker and Warburg, 1998) Volume XVIII, pp. 521–22.

4   See David Joravsky, *The Lysenko Affair* (Cambridge: Harvard University Press, 1970).

rival system of ideas, in opposition to the ideas held by most experts in the field, as found in college courses, especially textbooks, and in the public opinions of the most eminent qualified people. Here are a few other examples of alternative theories:

- Advocacy of megadoses of vitamins by Linus Pauling and others;[5]

- Chiropractic;[6]

- Homeopathy (an unorthodox form of medical treatment which recommends as remedies minute doses of substances that in larger doses would actually cause the symptoms of the ailment);[7]

- The conspiracy theory of the killing of President Kennedy;[8]

- Creation Science;[9]

- Noam Chomsky's account of U.S. foreign policy;[10]

5   Ewan Cameron and Linus Pauling, *Cancer and Vitamin C* (Philadelphia: Camino, 1993). The dominant experts are not as dismissive of large doses of vitamins as they were twenty years ago, but they still reject the complete Pauling argument.

6   Michael Lenarz, *The Chiropractic Way* (New York: Bantam, 2003).

7   Bill Gray, *Homeopathy: Science or Myth?* (Berkeley: North Atlantic, 2000). Homeopathy, chiropractic, and numerous other unorthodox doctrines are all outlined in The Burton Goldberg Group, *Alternative Medicine: The Definitive Guide* (Tiburon: Future Medicine, 1993).

8   James H. Fetzer, ed., *Murder in Dealey Plaza: What We Know Now that We Didn't Know Then about the Death of JFK* (Chicago: Catfeet Press, 2000); Noel Twyman, *Bloody Treason: On Solving History's Greatest Murder Mystery, the Assassination of John F. Kennedy* (Rancho Santa Fe: Laurel, 1997).

9   Duane Gish, *The Amazing Story of Creation: From Science and the Bible* (Green Forest: Master Books, 1996). A more sophisticated statement of a Creationist position by a number of qualified professionals is William A. Dembski, ed., *Mere Creation: Science, Faith, and Intelligent Design* (Downer's Grove: InterVarsity Press, 1998).

10   Noam Chomsky, *Hegemony or Survival: America's Quest for Global Dominance* (New York: Holt, 2003).

- The theory that someone other than Shakespeare wrote the known "works of Shakespeare";[11]

- An alternative reconstruction of Christian history, popularized in Dan Brown's novel, *The Da Vinci Code*, according to which a secret group within the Church is suppressing the fact that descendants of Jesus and his wife Mary Magdalene are alive today.[12]

- The Orgone Therapy of Wilhelm Reich;[13]

- Climatologists who reject the currently fashionable theory of Global Warming;[14]

- Marxist economists, who reject the dominant neoclassical theory of marginal productivity, in favor of the labor theory of value;[15]

- The theory that the U.S. government is concealing a contact with alien spacecraft at Roswell, New Mexico, in 1947, and the related theory that many thousands of people have been abducted by aliens and experimented upon by these aliens in their spaceships.[16]

---

11 Among leading candidates are Christopher Marlowe (whose early death must have been faked), Francis Bacon, and the Earl of Oxford. For a survey of different views, see John Michell, *Who Wrote Shakespeare?* (New York: Thames and Hudson, 1996).

12 Michael Baigent, Richard Leigh, and Henry Lincoln, *Holy Blood, Holy Grail* (New York: Dell, 1983 [1982]).

13 Wilhelm Reich, *The Function of the Orgasm* (New York: Farrar, Straus, and Giroux, 1973).

14 Patrick J. Michaels and Robert C. Balling, Jr., *The Satanic Gases: Clearing the Air about Global Warming* (Washington, D.C.: Cato Institute, 2000).

15 Ernest Mandel, *Introduction to Marxist Economic Theory* (New York: Pathfinder, 1974); Michael Charles Howard and J.E. King, *The Political Economy of Marx*, second edition (New York: New York University Press, 1988).

16 Philip J. Corso, *The Day After Roswell* (New York: Simon and Schuster, 1997); David M. Jacobs, *Secret Life: First-hand Documented Accounts of UFO Abductions* (New York: Simon and Schuster, 1992).

● Thomas Gold's theory that petroleum is not a fossil fuel, but is part of the primordial substance out of which the Earth was formed, and exists at deep levels in superabundant quantities.[17]

These are just a handful of examples plucked at random from thousands of "alternative theories." We could also mention numerous alternative diets, less famous than the Atkins diet and equally out of favor with the dominant dietetic doctrine. Some of these diets, like the Gaylord Hauser, Protein Power, NeanderThin, or Sugar Busters diets, have affinities with Atkins, while some, like the Macrobiotic or Pritikin diets, are virtually the opposite of Atkins.

Dominant Theories Change

The consensus of qualified experts at any one time is very often reversed later. "Crackpot" theories have become scientific orthodoxy. One of many examples is the movement of continents. People have often noticed that, on a map of the world, the coast of South America seems to fit the coast of Africa, as if these were pieces of a jigsaw puzzle. At one time, anyone suggesting that this had some significance, as showing that the continents had broken apart, was ridiculed as a simpleton or a crackpot. Yet today this breaking apart and movement of continents is the established scientific consensus. It's called Plate Tectonics—and you're now an ignoramus or a crackpot if you question it. Another example is the existence of meteorites. At one time, reports of rocks falling from the sky were viewed much as reports of alien abductions are viewed today. Yet all scientists now acknowledge that rocks do indeed fall from the sky.

The reverse has also occurred. The view, maintained in the Bible, that God deliberately and separately created all the various kinds of living things, and did so about six thousand years ago, was widely accepted among biologists until the nineteenth century. In this case what was once scientific orthodoxy has now become heterodox and "crackpot."

17   Thomas Gold, *The Deep Hot Biosphere: The Myth of Fossil Fuels* (New York: Copernicus, 2001 [1998]).

It's reasonable to suppose that some of today's important conclusions of established experts are wrong and will in time be dropped. If we were to list all the hundreds of currently accepted scientific theories, we could be pretty sure that many of these will be rejected within the next fifty years. This has happened in every fifty-year period over the last few centuries, and no one believes that this process has just now stopped. We expect that many of today's most respected scientific theories (now accepted as "scientific fact") will be discarded by science, though we don't know which ones.

There's a scene in the Woody Allen movie *Sleeper*, where the awakening Sleeper is plied with cigarettes and chocolates by physicians in attendance. Viewers instantly get Allen's point: the reigning opinion among experts has often changed and will probably therefore change again. Expert opinion is fallible and revisable. What they tell you today is dangerous, they will probably tell you tomorrow is lifesaving. The fact that most or all experts favor some view certainly does not mean that it is true, or even that it will continue to be the expert consensus for very much longer. So why should we place any reliance on it?

The Problem of Induction

This brings us right up against one of the classic philosophical problems, the problem of Induction.[18] The word "induction" has a number of different meanings. In the Atkins Diet, the beginning phase, where a person first adjusts her eating patterns, is called "Induction." In electronics, there is a process called "induction" which refers to what happens when you move a magnet inside a coil.

We're going to look at a different sense of induction. In philosophy, "induction" refers to a procedure by which we arrive at conclusions that go beyond our experience. For example, having seen thousands of white swans, and none of any other color, can we conclude that all swans are white? Having witnessed a new period of daylight after every night of our lives, can we be confident that the Sun will rise tomorrow? If all the vegetarians we have ever known have been untrustworthy, can we reasonably infer that all vegetarians are untrustworthy?

18 See Bertrand Russell, *The Problems of Philosophy* (Oxford: Oxford University Press, 1959 [1912]), pp. 60–69.

Questions like these arise in everyday life and they also arise in science. Much of the philosophical discussion of induction has been about induction as a scientific method, but the conclusions apply to all other kinds of knowledge too, including such common-sense conceptions as the theory that water never runs uphill or that a red sunset indicates fine weather the next day.

Induction has often been described as "going from the particular to the general (or the universal)," as opposed to "going from the general (or the universal) to the particular." The problem of induction is a matter of logic. Logic is the discipline which examines *what follows from what*. Logic is not concerned with whether statements are true or false, but with what other statements have to be true, *if* a specific statement is true. For instance, if we accept that "all Atkins dieters eat beef" and that "Bill Irwin is an Atkins dieter," it certainly follows that Bill Irwin eats beef. Logic is not interested in whether it's true or false that all Atkins dieters eat beef or that Bill Irwin is an Atkins dieter. Logic is concerned with whether, *if* it's true that all Atkins dieters eat beef, and *if* it's also true that Bill Irwin is an Atkins dieter, it *must follow* that Bill Irwin eats beef.

And it must indeed follow! Logicians agree that if all Atkins dieters eat beef and Bill Irwin is an Atkins dieter, then Bill Irwin eats beef. In the terminology of logic, this is a valid inference: it really does follow. By the way, this particular kind of inference is called a syllogism, and was identified by Aristotle over two thousand years ago. It has been described as going from the general, or the universal (all Atkins dieters eat beef) to the particular (if Bill Irwin is an Atkins dieter, then he eats beef).

The problem of induction arises because science (and everyday reasoning) seems to require going in the reverse direction, from the particular to the universal. Science is concerned to find "laws," universal generalizations which admit of no exception. Of course, there's much more to science than universal laws, yet such laws are crucial to science.

How does science arrive at its universal laws? Traditionally, the answer has been: by observation. But now the problem of induction rears its grinning head. Observation is always of a limited number of cases, not of all cases. How can we get from observation of some cases to conclusions about all cases?

Induction—forming universal conclusions from a limited number of observations—has been discussed by many philosophers, notably Aristotle (fourth century B.C.) and Sextus Empiricus (third century A.D.), but its difficulties were raised most sharply by David Hume in the eighteenth century A.D. Hume pointed out that no amount of observations of one type of thing could ever justify us in concluding that what we observed would be true of all cases of that type of thing. Nor, as Hume also shrewdly pointed out, could it ever justify us in concluding that the general law was even "probably" true.

Hume was convinced that we do derive universal laws from repeated observations, and yet he believed that this was a logically indefensible thing to do. He therefore reluctantly concluded that our habit of coming up with general laws, though unavoidable, was unreasonable. This conclusion was unwelcome to Hume, who had hoped to find a method for discriminating between what he thought would be justified beliefs (science) and what he thought would be unjustified ones (Christianity and other forms of contemptible superstition). Although Hume did go on to describe ways in which this discrimination could be made, he felt himself to be defeated by what he took to be something illogical, and therefore unreasonable, at the heart of the way we all necessarily think.

After Hume, many philosophers wrestled with this problem. Their solutions mostly fall into two categories. One view is that since we cannot logically arrive at universal conclusions from particular observations, the universal conclusions must already be in our minds. We do not find universal laws in nature, but impose them on nature. This approach, developed by Kant, was taken up by philosophers like Fichte, Schelling, and Hegel, known as "idealists."

The alternative and much more common view, traceable in the writings of philosophers like Francis Bacon and John Stuart Mill, is that as we obviously do learn by experience and observation, we must therefore somehow reason by induction, from the particular to the general. Since logic shows this to be impossible, logic must be incomplete. Logic is therefore renamed "deductive logic," and it is supposed that there is some other logic called "inductive logic," which somehow enables us to get from particular observations to universal conclusions. Unfortunately, no such logic has been discovered—or at least, none which commands the general assent of logicians, philosophers, or scientists.[19]

---

19   From now on, I follow the Popperian or Critical Rationalist view that there is no such thing as inductive logic. For a different approach, which argues that there is a way to

Popper's Solution to the Problem of Induction

Early in the twentieth century, Karl Popper came up with a new solution to the problem of induction.[20] Popper accepted Hume's conclusion that nothing could ever justify us in going from "the particular to the general," or in other words, from a limited number of observations to a universal law. But he did not accept that there was anything unreasonable about science.

Popper pointed out that while a proposed scientific "law" could never be *proved* or *established* by any number of observed instances (no matter how many Atkins dieters we find who do eat beef, this can never prove that all Atkins dieters, at all times and places, will eat beef), a proposed scientific law could possibly be "disproved" or *falsified* (just one case of an Atkins dieter who does not eat beef proves that it is false that all Atkins dieters eat beef).

This apparently trivial logical point actually has tremendous repercussions. What it means is this: although no amount of observation can show any theory to be true, observation can sometimes show a theory to be false. And this means that, despite the total absence of positive "proof" for any universal theory, not all such theories are equal. It's entirely reasonable to prefer one theory to another, if one theory has not been falsified and another theory has been falsified.

So, where we have to choose between two theories, we should try to think of cases where they contradict one another in what they claim will be observed. We can then try to set up a test, some experiment which will show one theory to be false without showing the other theory to be false. What was striking, and to many quite shocking, about the studies like those cited above in note 1 was that they indicated, not only that the Atkins Diet leads to rapid loss of weight, but also that it causes a significant improvement in blood lipid profiles, superior to the effects of low-fat, low-cholesterol diets. This was a result the advocates of a low-fat, low-cholesterol diet

---

arrive at a logic of induction, in this case on Bayesian lines, see Colin Howson and Peter Urbach, *Scientific Reasoning: The Bayesian Approach*, third edition (Chicago: Open Court, 2005).

20 Expounded in his *Logic of Scientific Discovery*, which first appeared in German in 1934. A good straightforward account is Popper, *Realism and the Aim of Science* (Totowa: Rowman and Littlefield, 1983), pp. 31–88.

had not expected and could not account for—eating more fat and cholesterol (while cutting carbs) lowers your body fat and your blood cholesterol—though it was predicted by Atkins.

The result of Popper's solution is that Hume was quite right to point out that scientific induction is logically indefensible, but quite wrong to conclude that acceptance of a scientific theory entails an unreasonable kind of thinking. The thinking required is entirely reasonable, it conforms to deductive logic, and there is no need to hanker for any other kind of logic.[21]

This Popperian or Critical Rationalist view implies that no theory ever becomes "final." We always have to leave open the possibility that any theory might have to be discarded. But this turns out to be a realistic view of science, for we know that in the history of science some very firmly entrenched scientific theories have been abandoned and replaced by new theories. The most staggeringly successful scientific theory of all time, Newton's theory of space, time, and gravitation, was eventually falsified and replaced by Einstein's theory—though Einstein did not believe his own theory to be true, and predicted that it would in its turn eventually be replaced by a better theory.[22]

The fact that no theory is finally established does not mean that "anything goes." One theory is replaced by another because the new theory survives the collected observations so far, which the old theory could not survive. Unless some of these observations turn out to be mistakes, hoaxes, or hallucinations, a third theory which will replace the second theory must do better than the second theory *and* the first theory. We are not free to go back to the first theory at our whim—if our aim is to get on the track of the truth.

Popper's Critical Rationalism explains how one theory, perhaps false, can be an improvement over another false theory. If a theory has been well tested and has survived, it makes sense to prefer this theory to others. And even though the theory may turn out to be false, it may yet approximate to

---

21 It's now fashionable to distinguish deduction from induction by the criterion that deduction is certain while induction is probable. However, conclusions stating probabilities can be derived purely deductively from statistical premises: this has no bearing on the problem of induction.

22 Newton's theory survives as a special case within Einstein's theory: Newton's theory remains a good approximation for a wide range of phenomena.

the truth in many cases. A false theory can be extremely useful, if it is a good approximation to the truth across a certain range of possibilities. Even though we cannot know that the current theory is true, we can know that it appears closer to the truth than its predecessors.

Kuhn's Paradigms

If observations can test theories and show which theories are best, you might think that there would always be complete agreement on which is the best theory. The real situation is much more messy. A good theory often has troubling anomalies, cases where some observations (or conclusions of some other currently accepted theories) seem to go against the theory, even though, taken as a whole, this theory appears to make the best sense of all the observations. Scientists may disagree on just how troubling those anomalies are. They may, in effect, bet on a promising-looking theory being successful, feeling confident that further research will eventually show that the theory does not really conflict with observations.

Inspired by Popper's solution to the problem of induction,[23] Thomas Kuhn made a close study of "scientific revolutions," historical examples where one firmly established theory was overthrown and replaced by a new theory. He found that in many cases, the existing scientists were not converted to belief in the new theories. They went to their graves defending the old theories. New recruits, young scientists, accepted the new theories, which therefore became dominant as the old guard died off.

Kuhn applied the term "paradigm" to the totality of scientific theories, rules, and traditions in operation in a particular discipline at a given time. He claimed that when a great "scientific revolution" occurs, the majority of existing specialists are so wedded to the old paradigm that they cannot fully understand the new theory. Adherents of the old and the new paradigms "talk past each other," seeing things so differently that they do not identify the same strengths and weaknesses in the two rival viewpoints. Young

---

23　Although Popper and Kuhn had sharp disagreements and are usually cast as opponents, Kuhn accepted Popper's solution to the induction problem, and Popper broadly accepted Kuhn's account of the history of physics. See Kuhn's comparison of his views with Popper's, and Popper's reply to Kuhn, in Paul A. Schilpp, ed., *The Philosophy of Karl Popper* (La Salle: Open Court, 1974), pp. 798–819, 1144–48.

scientists or scientists from other disciplines are usually better situated to switch to the new paradigm and therefore more fully appreciate the merits of the new theory. (It's notable that a high proportion of low-carb advocates, like Atkins and Agatston, are cardiologists, not dieticians, by background.)

First Question: Does It Ever Make Sense to "Trust the Experts"?

How should a non-expert person make up her mind about what the scientific experts are saying? Right off the bat, one precaution we should take is to check up on whether the supposed "experts" really are the appropriate experts. For example, a doctor, an ordinary practicing physician, may be no more of an expert on the science of human diet than you would be if you spent a couple of hours on the Internet. The doctor may just be repeating the fashionable or official line, without drawing upon any special knowledge. Individuals who have been through medical school and come out with an M.D. have often received very little training in the proper ways to conduct research, and a busy family doctor may not have kept up with the latest research by reading current journals of human nutrition.[24] It's also far from clear that the U.S. Department of Agriculture is an appropriate body to be laying down guidelines on what we should eat.

Assuming we're dealing with genuine experts in the relevant field, our first question is: does it ever make sense to rely upon expert opinion when we don't know what the experts know? Why is it any more reasonable for us to accept what astronomers tell us about the phases of the Moon or what the USDA tells us about the optimal diet than it is for the member of a preliterate tribe to accept the witch doctor's recommendation that he kill his child in order to ensure the rebirth of the sun?

Here the answer depends upon a theory we hold about the way this group of experts arrives at its preferred theories. If we think that they do this by proposing theories and trying hard to falsify them, subsequently preferring the theories which survive such tests, it will make sense for us to accept the theories currently preferred by this group of experts.

---

24 Medical experts have a notorious history of scaring people with bogus "health risks." The classic account is Alex Comfort, *The Anxiety Makers* (New York: Dell, 1969).

This involves a theory of our own, a theory about the way the group of experts operates. This theory of ours can be tested, and might be falsified. For example, if this group of experts is susceptible to pressure from interest groups, or is prone to make ideological statements about "social responsibility," that would be a sign that they are perhaps not subjecting their theories to severe tests. Their views might then quite properly be disregarded, just as the views of National Socialist "racial scientists" and Soviet Lysenkoists should have been disregarded (and were disregarded by most scientists and laypeople in non-totalitarian countries).

It's not the holding of strong opinions that puts a question mark over a community of scientists. It doesn't matter much if scientists are "biased," in the sense of firmly believing in a theory and ardently hoping that it will be vindicated. On balance, this kind of intense commitment to a point of view is probably helpful, though it obviously has its dangers. What matters is the possibility that a community of scientists may be more concerned to defend some theory than to subject it to severe tests. There is no guarantee that a professional community of scientists will not become transformed into a cultlike priesthood, their minds closed to views they classify as heresy. The best protection against such a transformation is open debate. The more politically or ideologically involved a group of experts is, the more what they say should be looked at closely, for possible signs of dogmatism and blindness to problems in their favored theory.

The more they depend upon government money, or money from business interests concerned with the area of their research, the more they should be viewed with suspicion, especially if what they say is welcome to the purveyors of current policies. The Department of Agriculture's experts are unlikely to start a campaign against the near-ubiquity of high-fructose corn syrup. Yet this is a matter of degree, and we should not be perfectionist. Scientific communities have always been subject to ideological and political pressures, and just because they are not pure as driven snow does not mean that everything they say is worthless.

So the answer to our first question, the question that troubled Orwell, is: yes, it does make sense to accept what is currently said by scientific experts in a given field. This is not because of any blind faith in science, or any guarantee that their current theories will not be falsified tomorrow. It makes sense for us to accept—provisionally and tentatively—what scientists say for the same reason that it makes sense for them to accept—provisionally and tentatively—the theory which has done better than its rivals at surviving attempts to prove it wrong. This theory may not be true, it is definitely not the final word of some infallible oracle, but it is preferable to any known alternative, and even if it turns out to be wrong, it will very likely be at least approximately true in many circumstances.

As for the tribal witchdoctor, it may not be entirely unreasonable to accept his recommendations too, in the absence of strong indications to the contrary. But this will be a better bet if there is rivalry among competing witchdoctors and free debate between them, and if they are observed to occasionally revise their "theories" in the light of both observation and argument.

Second Question: Does It Ever Make Sense to Go Against the Dominant Experts?

Science is often presented to children as a triumph of obvious truth over obvious falsehood. The merits of the triumphant view are pointed out, but the merits of the defeated view, and the difficulties which seemed to lie in the later triumphant view, are often not mentioned. While this provides a story that is easy to understand, it can be highly misleading. For example, the theory that the Earth spins and orbits the sun was rejected by no less a hardheaded enemy of superstition than Francis Bacon, for reasons which seemed to him very persuasive.[25] The great early astronomer Tycho Brahe also refused to swallow the moving Earth. Galileo rejected the theory that the Moon causes the tides, partly because he considered it an astrological theory of occult forces.

Science progresses by debate and disputation. It is typically untidy and often acrimonious. Significant scientific advances are usually highly controversial. Arguments, even bitter quarrels, between different opinions are therefore not alien to science, and we should never seek to rise above them by appealing to "the established facts," meaning the current consensus of scientists' opinions.

---

25   See Peter Urbach, *Francis Bacon's Philosophy of Science* (La Salle: Open Court, 1987), pp. 125–134.

What should the ordinary person do about these scientific debates? So far I have been assuming that there is a clear line separating "the ordinary person" from "the expert scientist." In fact, the division is not so clearcut. Science is a specialized occupation, just as plumbing or crime prevention are specialized occupations. But some non-plumbers may fix their own dripping pipes, and some non-police officers may shoot a rapist or a burglar. Specialization is only a matter of convenience. Scientists, like plumbers and police officers, are doing something for the rest of us, just because each of us can't do everything.

In fact, many contributions to science have been made by unqualified amateurs or people on the fringes of a scientific profession, and there is some evidence that specialized disciplines sealed off from interaction with the general public become hidebound and sterile.[26] There are also valuable contributions by scholars in disciplines other than their own narrow specialty. Kuhn, as we have seen, claimed that major innovations are more likely to be made by outsiders, and many historians of science agree with Kuhn. Experts in specialized disciplines often find that explaining their theories to the general public helps them to develop those very theories, and in some cases, genuine new contributions are made by works aimed at a broad popular audience, a good example being the best-selling books of Richard Dawkins on evolutionary biology.[27]

The progress of science is a social process, involving the interaction of many individuals, and it is an inherently controversial process, advancing by debate, disputation, criticism, and the clash of competing theories. In this process of argumentative exploration, privileging specific groups as uniquely qualified to pronounce on various topics can be harmful. Debate, persuasive advocacy, and confrontation of rival views are not imperfections, but necessary aspects of the growth of knowledge.

When a dominant theory is challenged by an alternative theory, the result may be the revolutionary overthrow of the dominant theory or it may be the continuation of the dominant theory. But it's also possible that

---

26   See W.W. Bartley III, *Unfathomed Knowledge, Unmeasured Wealth: On Universities and the Wealth of Nations* (La Salle: Open Court, 1990), pp. 120–142.

27   Dawkins's concept of the "meme" has now been adopted in several social-science disciplines. It was first propounded in his popular work, *The Selfish Gene* (Oxford: Oxford University Press, 1976).

the dominant theory becomes modified by its responses to the alternative theory. We see this in the case of the Atkins Diet.

Twenty years ago opponents of the Atkins Diet generally claimed that it was not an effective way to lose weight. Few people claim this now: most critics concede that Atkins does work. Defenders of the dominant theory fall back on four assertions: 1. that the Atkins Diet works by cutting calorie intake, and not in the way that Robert Atkins contended; 2. that Atkins's opposition to soda, potato chips, and other refined carbohydrates is correct, but not his strict limitation of unrefined carbohydrates; 3. that there may possibly be long-term injurious effects from a high-protein diet (the most commonly cited of these so far uncorroborated surmises is kidney damage); and 4. that the studies conducted to date have involved small numbers of subjects, and their findings may not be borne out by studies on a bigger scale.

Don't Leave It to the Experts

Should we accept the recommendations of most dietary experts or should we adopt the Atkins Diet or some other alternative diet? I have not tried to answer this question here.

What I have claimed is that there is nothing necessarily foolish or wrongheaded about accepting the recommendations of experts in a field about which you know very little. And neither is there anything necessarily foolish or wrong-headed about taking the side of an alternative theory against the established consensus of experts.

Which of these you do in this particular case I leave to you. Read some of the controversy and you will automatically come up with a point of view. This will be tentative and revisable in the light of further information, but so are all theories and all conclusions, expert or non-expert. Jump right into the ongoing debate: what else is your mind for? Human Knowledge is too important to be left to experts.

The Atkins Diet and Philosophy: Chewing the Fat with Kant and Nietzsche
(2005)

22

WILL EMERGING MEDIA
CREATE A COLLECTIVE MIND? (2016)

From time to time throughout the modern history of the West, various writers have proposed that human beings united by communications might (possibly inadvertently) create a collective entity possessing its own intelligence and consciousness. This so far hypothetical new entity has been called a global brain, a super-brain, a world brain, a collective consciousness, or most recently by Michael Chorost, a world wide mind.

A character in Hawthorne's *The House of the Seven Gables* (1851) demands:

> Is it a fact—or have I dreamt it—that, by means of electricity, the world of matter has become a great nerve, vibrating thousands of miles in a breathless point of time? Rather the round globe is a vast head, a brain, instinct with intelligence! (Quoted in Chorost 2011, 177)

Hawthorne envisioned the possibility of a "global brain" emerging from the transmission of messages by telegraph. A century later the Catholic thinker Teilhard de Chardin thought he saw the emergence from the global network of communication of "a harmonized collectivity of consciousness, the equivalent of a sort of super-consciousness" (Quoted in Heylighen 2011, 280). Peter Russell's widely acclaimed book also forecast the appearance of the "global brain" (Russell 1995).

Michael Chorost looks forward to the emergence of what he calls the "world wide mind," by which he means a system of human interaction which is itself conscious, even self-conscious, and capable of purposive action (Chorost 2011, 177–78). He sees this super-mind or collective mind emerging from the Internet, or as he puts it, "the Internet plus humanity". (I will omit this qualification, because I see the Internet as a human social institution, albeit one that makes use of various physical artifacts.) However, a novelty of Chorost's work is that he attaches the appearance of the world wide mind to the emergence of what he calls "brain-to-brain communications technology" (27), which, if Chorost is right, is about to become an exciting "emerging medium." More broadly, Chorost's ideas are similar to those of earlier writers such as Francis Heylighen, but he does not cite those writers. Heylighen's discussion is presented in an academic context, Chorost's in that of a popular trade book, but Chorost's is in no way inferior to Heylighen's, and goes into some of the issues more deeply, though very unsystematically.

The Twofold Message of Chorost's Book

Chorost has two things to tell us, which in his view go together, but which can be considered separately. One is that we are on the threshold of many practical applications of "brain-to-brain" communication, the other is that this new medium, combined with the Internet, will lead to a great collective consciousness, what he calls a "world wide mind."

What Chorost calls "brain-to-brain communication" is more commonly called brain-brain interfacing (BBI), and I will from now on refer to it as BBI. To give a flavor of Chorost's discussion of BBI, we can look at two of his examples. First, there is the case of the future drug bust conducted by a team of cops who are linked to each other by BBI. Each police officer is aware of the position of each of the other cops, just as effortlessly as he is aware of the position of his own limbs. When one of the cops is hit in the chest by a bullet, all of the other cops feel it too, and know which one has been hit. (The assumption here seems to be that they will not feel the full agony of the one who was hit; their awareness will be something like that of a vivid memory of having been hit.) Each officer is immediately aware of things that each of the other cops can perceive, and with this knowledge is able to adjust to the likely reactions of the drug gang (19–22).

A second example is the scenario in which "a far-flung group of physicists" are all working on the unification of quantum mechanics and general relativity (any other unsolved theoretical problem would do equally well).

One of them has the germ of an "aha!" idea, "but it's just a teasing sensation rather than a verbally articulated thought" (173). However, this sense of excitement at the possibility of a breakthrough is picked up by the rig in her brain and transmitted to all the other physicists, together with enough fragmentary ideas to convey the occasion for her sense of excitement. Other physicists respond by looking at this cluster of ideas, and have further "aha!" ideas, which are also transmitted, and thus by a chain reaction of these thoughts and transmissions, members of the group quickly focus on a promising solution. Chorost comments: "This is brainstorming, but it's facilitated by the direct exchange of emotions and associations within the group, and it can happen at any moment" (174)

Chorost envisages BBI as occurring by modifying neurons so that they become sensitive to light, then using tubular nanowires reaching into various locations in the brain, to transmit light signals. Less invasively, light or electrical impulses can be directed onto parts of the brain from points between the skull and the brain, without the use of nanowires. Chorost himself emphasizes how rapidly research is moving in this area and it is possible that, in a few years' time, Chorosts's outline of specific techniques will seem like a flying steam-engine. In August 2013 (more than a year after the publication of Chorost's book) it was announced that, in an experiment conducted by Rajesh Rao, one person, his brain linked to another person's, was able, by thinking about moving his finger (but not actually moving it) to make the other person's finger move (Armstrong and Ma 2013). Essentially the same thing had been done earlier with the brains of two rats, and then with the brain of a human and the brain of a rat. To get one brain, by having a thought about something, to cause a motor response in another brain, is a lot easier than getting one brain, by having a thought about something, to cause a thought about the same thing to arise in another brain, but rapid progress is expected. The Rao human-to-human BBI experiment did not use optogenetics or nanowires, but simply electro-encephalography and transcranial magnetic stimulation. Back in 2009, researchers at the University of Southampton, England, had already accomplished transmission of thoughts from one brain to another using similar technology, though this was confined to 'thoughts' expressed in a binary code (University of Southampton 2009).

BBI is an extension of brain-computer interfacing (BCI), in which we have traditionally been concerned with just one brain interacting with a computer (Rao 2013; Graimann, Allison, and Pfurtscheller 2010). The most urgent applications of BCI (and perhaps, to begin with, BBI) lie in the medical area, in helping people overcome certain disabilities. The most straightforward examples of BCI merely replace some missing bodily function. The subject of Chorost's first book was his own experience with cochlear implants (Chorost 2005). Cochlear implants replace the natural mechanism of hearing. People with cochlear implants can usually hear quite well, though they have to work at it to achieve this ability, and the way the implant works is completely different from the natural process of hearing.

BCI is also employed to help paralyzed people do what non-paralyzed people do routinely—use their thoughts to move parts of their body. Thought-controlled prosthetics are already a commonplace, along with the ability to thought-control the movement of a cursor on a computer screen. Those of us who enjoyed the Clint Eastwood movie *Firefox* (1982), with its "thought-controlled weapons," were somewhat skeptical at the time (Clint, you will recall, had to remind himself to "think in Russian") but we can already view this as pretty ho-hum.

Two Minds with But a Single Thought

Before moving on, I should mention one conceptual point which always seems to come up in discussions of this topic, and which tends to cloud the issue. News coverage of Rao's breakthrough described it as "telepathy," the researchers themselves referred to it in jest as a "Vulcan mind meld," and in my experience, philosophers who hear about BBI for the first time always want to talk about how you can have the same thought in two different minds. Although Chorost's mode of presentation is entertainingly unsystematic and anecdotal, he does shrewdly cover a number of key points, and here, he points out that literal telepathy or mind reading is and always will be impossible (18–19). When a 'thought' is 'transmitted' from one brain to another because the brains are modified and linked by an apparatus, what we have here is a thought in one brain causing the production of a thought (another, different thought, of course, in the sense that two people's thoughts are always different brain-events) with similar content in another brain. In other words, it is no more telepathy than is conveying a thought by spoken language; it's just that the transmission is quicker and perhaps that the mechanism of transmission may be more easily overlooked. Furthermore, most BBI transmissions of thoughts, and any of substantial precision, will involve words, so the utility of the whole method will draw upon the elements of verbal communication.

When we employ the expression 'two minds with but a single thought' we mean 'two minds, each with a token of but a single thought-type'. This will continue to be true with BBI. Nor can we even assume that the thought as transmitted by BBI will be more accurately reproduced in the receiving brain than it would be by spoken or written language. The tendency to assume that it will be a more accurate reproduction because it is quicker and subjectively more direct may be a hazardous prejudice that we will have to guard against.

Many people who excitedly discuss these new developments say things like 'Now we actually have brain-to-brain communication!' However, all communication between humans is and always has been brain-to-brain. When you read "Where the bee sucks, there suck I," the brain of Shakespeare (or whoever really wrote it) has communicated with your brain. Sometimes people will qualify these new media by calling them '*direct* brain to brain communication'. But there is a complicated piece of electronic equipment attached to your skull, and another complicated piece of equipment attached to the receiver's skull, and the first piece of equipment transmits something by phone (perhaps by Internet) to the second piece of equipment. This is an extremely roundabout way of communicating, compared with just talking! What's meant, of course, is that the sender simply has a thought and this causes a similar thought in someone else's mind. It seems 'direct' to the sender and the receiver because they don't have to do anything except think.

If Chorost is right about the imminent appearance of practical applications of BBI, this is certainly a topic for a book in itself. However, Chorost repeatedly indicates (even in the very title of his book) that for him the true importance of BBI lies in the emergence of the global brain or world wide mind. My impression, from reading reviews and other discussions of Chorost's book online, is that a few people are skeptical about the future of BBI, but almost no one exhibits any skepticism about the world wide mind, or about the assumption that if BBI were to become an everyday reality, it would somehow favor the emergence of a world wide mind. I am not going to discuss the likely practical applications of BBI. Instead, I am going to oppose the notion that a global brain or world wide mind could ever emerge from the interaction of many individual human minds, *with or without BBI*. My view is that BBI is just the latest in a series of technologies (including the telegraph in the Hawthorne example), hailed as harbingers of a collective mind, but actually nothing of the kind.

Collective Consciousness

Claims of a collective consciousness are often advanced as metaphor. There are two main forms of this metaphor. First, we may see a group or team of individuals so well-co-ordinated in their behavior that we're inclined to say 'It's as if they were a single organism'. A football team in action, or a pack of wolves or lionesses bringing down an ungulate, may seem to fit the separate individual actions together so well that we may say the individuals appear to act 'as one'. In the case of the football team there may actually be one mind (the coach's) which has formulated the co-ordinated plan, though the players may not need to fully understand the plan. If the individual players do all understand the plan, then that is an understanding in the minds of each member of the team; there is no 'remainder' of understanding the plan which is not accounted for by summing the individual understandings. In this supposition, the coach and the players each understand the plan; no other entity does. The collaboration of the members may have properties of which they are all unaware, but these properties do not constitute consciousness. In the case of the predators, there was never an overall plan for the pack; the individuals act each in such a way that, interacting with the way the other individuals act, leads to a combined result from which they all benefit. This might be because natural selection, acting on the genes of individual animals which habitually hunt in packs, has led to certain individual behaviors under certain conditions, or it might be because the aggregate outcome of individual animals doing what they would tend to do anyway, is an ordered complexity of group behavior.

The other form of the metaphor appears in such entities as rallies, party conferences, committee meetings, or religious meetings. We may speak of any such collectivity as though it were an individual with its own consciousness—'the committee agonized, then reluctantly decided to reject the motion'. We also observe that sometimes participants in such meetings will say things like 'We all felt as one; the speaker voiced our thoughts'. Sometimes the individuals may themselves believe there is a supra-consciousness, as when members of a religious group believe that they are all simultaneously being inspired by a spirit, but in such cases it is at least possible to offer an explanation in terms of discrete individuals with particular beliefs. As in the case of hunting packs, the interaction of several people may have properties the individuals don't know about, but this doesn't betoken an added consciousness.

There may genuinely be interactions among the individuals, even unconscious interactions, which modify the individual functioning of each of them, so that the existence of the collectivity generates outcomes that could not be achieved simply by summing the behaviors of isolated individuals. That this is a possibility does not contradict the general perspective that the interactions of individual consciousnesses do not create a new and distinct consciousness for the collectivity in addition to the consciousness of each individual.

Individuals may affect the behavior of the collectivity in various ways: 1. The individuals may behave in particular ways, and the collectivity may aggregate those behaviors; 2. The individuals may take part in a decision-making process, such as voting, or deciding by lot, which influences the decisions of the leadership of the collectivity; 3. the individuals by their interactions may incidentally generate outcomes which they didn't intend. There are myriads of such influences, which generally do not tempt us to attribute the outcomes to a super-brain or collective mind, except as admitted metaphor.

Chorost's account, at least some of the time, clearly signals that he sees the need to go beyond this figurative description of collective intentionality, if he is to validate any serious claim to a world-wide mind (176–183). Chorost gives us a clear discussion of the conditions which might have to be fulfilled for the Internet to become conscious. However, in the course of answering this question, he sometimes confounds certain different categories. First, he confounds consciousness and self-consciousness. In my view this is not a serious problem and we can ignore it. Consciousness and self-consciousness are definitionally distinct, though it is a reasonable position to maintain that consciousness cannot actually occur without some element of self-consciousness. If anything, Chorost's references to self-consciousness render substantiation of his claims about a world wide mind somewhat more demanding. If we imagine how we might determine that the Internet had become conscious or self-conscious, the latter attainment would presumably require stronger evidence.

Chorost uses the word 'intelligence' in a specific way, which I am uneasy about, but which I will accept within this paper. Chorost implicitly defines intelligence as any ability to respond adaptively, or at least, any such ability if the response is above some level of complexity. There is one point in his argument where he confounds intelligence, so defined, and consciousness, though most of the time he recognizes an important distinction between them. Chorost maintains that, in addition to the intelligence or consciousness that may or may not be possessed by an individual ant, an ant colony is intelligent *and therefore conscious*, because it performs complex tasks. Chorost writes that in a colony of leafcutter ants, all an individual ant can do is follow its simple rules. "But out of these rules a clear collective awareness of the world emerges" (185). This is surely mistaken, the ant colony has no awareness of anything. "Scientists," writes Chorost, "already know that collective 'minds' like ant colonies do things that can reasonably be called 'conscious', such as finding food and consuming it" (178). Here the adverb is unhappy: "picturesquely," perhaps, but not "reasonably." The ant colony certainly behaves in some respects as if it were aware, but so do many other entities in nature, where we are not tempted to impute awareness, for example a plant bending its shoots so that it grows towards the light. Chorost's only evidence for the colony's awareness is that it performs complex tasks, but as he says, it does this because each individual ant is impelled to follow rules. The individual ant may or may not be aware it is following the rules (we don't have to decide that question) but the fact that the resultant of the ant's rule-following interactions leads to adaptive consequences does not imply that the colony is aware of anything. The behavior of the colony is fully explained by the individual ants following the rules, so there is no need to posit colony 'awareness', which if it did arise would have nothing to do, no object to occupy its attention. The complex tasks are conceived and attributed by us, not by the ants, either individually or collectively, much as we might say that it is the task of electric storms to equilibrate electrical charges between the clouds and the ground, or the task of the surf to make sure that the bigger pebbles are higher up the beach than the smaller pebbles. Whether or not an individual ant is conscious (this is an open question, though I incline to the view that an ant is a little robot, bereft of any flicker of consciousness), the ant colony is not conscious.

If the ant colony were indeed aware, then most of Chorost's discussion here would be pointless: we need look no further for the Internet's awareness, and therefore consciousness, since the Internet certainly performs complex tasks, and would therefore, prima facie, already be vastly more 'aware' than the ant colony. In fact a ten-dollar pocket calculator is far more 'intelligent' (according to this way of talking) than an ant colony, without being aware. Chorost fully accepts that the Internet is not, or probably not, already conscious, and holds that further developments are required before it can become so (180–83), and therefore we can view his equation of intelligence with consciousness in the ant colony example as a momentary lapse from the assumptions of his main line of argument.

More than once, however, Chorost confounds the consciousness of the collective entity with the consciousness of its component parts. The existence of a collective consciousness is distinct from the question of the consciousness of the individuals whose interaction gives rise to that collective entity. If a group of conscious individuals communicate with each other, and thereby 'share' some of the contents of their consciousness, this in itself does not automatically create a collective consciousness. Something additional would be required before the collective entity itself became conscious. At times, Chorost explicitly recognizes this, but at other times he tends to slide from one to the other.

Complexity and Functions

In pursuit of the question whether the Internet could ever become conscious, Chorost begins by looking at sheer numerical complexity as the possible key to consciousness. He points out that the Internet has far fewer components than the human brain, with two billion computers rather than a hundred billion neurons (178). However, the Internet could conceivably grow to the point where it had an equivalent number of components as the brain, yet it doesn't follow that this would do anything to give the Internet consciousness. Nor is it clear that the Internet could not acquire consciousness with its present level of complexity, or a lower level. We just do not yet know how the human brain produces consciousness, and when we do find out, we may find that it could produce consciousness with a far smaller number of neurons than it currently possesses (which might have implications for the possibility of consciousness in animals with simpler brains).

Having begun by discussing the sheer number of components or the connections between them, Chorost then introduces other factors, such as variation in the types of components (corresponding to variations in the types of neurons), and he looks for possible similarities, present or future, between the structure of the Internet and the structure of the human brain (181–82). This approach acknowledges that sheer complexity is not necessarily the point. But a similar problem arises. We do not yet know which aspects of brain structure are necessary or sufficient for the production of consciousness, and if we did know this, we might be able to see that a different structure, perhaps a far simpler one, would also create consciousness. This seems especially likely because we know that the brain controls many unconscious bodily functions, so possibly some aspects of brain structure are there because of those automatic functions and would not be needed if we were concerned only with the production of consciousness.

Chorost argues, following Elkhonon Goldberg (2009) that Google and Wikipedia play a role in the Internet analogous to that of the frontal lobe in the brain (Goldberg 2009). Here is one attempt to guess at the relevance for consciousness of aspects of the brain's structure, and look for a counterpart in the Internet, but the assumptions are very uncertain. We do not really yet know whether anything like the frontal lobe is required for the production of consciousness.

'Intelligent' Systems of Human Interaction

According to Chorost's usage, intelligence may not betoken consciousness: a fishnet is intelligent (not just the designer or user of the fishnet). An intelligent entity may be a physical object, such as a fishnet, or it may be a system of human interaction, such as a game of musical chairs.

There are innumerable systems of human interaction which are intelligent in Chorost's sense. We live out our lives immersed in them. A simple example, pointed out by Michael Polanyi, is the way people distribute themselves in a theater with open seating (Polanyi 1951, 155). The result is one person per seat, and if the theater is not filled, the least desirable seats left empty. People who arrive early get better seats, and the seats become occupied according to a definite pattern, not randomly. Here individuals interact, following rules, and the orderly result is something they don't need to aim for. We may say that the group has an additional intelligence unknown to the individual members, but we would be in error to say that the group were conscious.

Another example arises from the finding that if a large number of non-experts are asked to make an estimate of, say, the number of beans in a jar, or the market value of a cow, and their answers are averaged, the result will be closer to the truth than the estimate of any single expert. (Surowiecki 2004). We may say that if this system is employed, the whole system is 'more intelligent than the experts' in the sense that it out-performs them. But we don't mean that the system knows what it is doing or is aware of anything, much less aware of itself.

The adversarial system in a law court would be another example. There are two sides, each striving to produce a convincing case to the detriment of the other side. The result is that various outcomes occur which could not have been reached by any non-adversarial method. Again, we might say that the system has some measure of intelligence beyond that of the individuals, but we don't want to say that the system is conscious.

We're surrounded by these systems of human interaction which are 'intelligent' in the same sense that the ant colony is intelligent. We might call them 'social gadgets'. They are computational devices made up of human interactions. The pre-eminent example is the world market economy. In this system, as understood by Léon Walras, numerous pieces of information are transformed into signals which lead to modifications of behavior tending toward an optimal allocation. For example, the discovery of a new way to extract some mineral, m, from lower-grade natural reserves, leads to a fall in the price of m, which leads to greater use of m in many different applications, each change in the rate of use being governed by thousands of different precise (though usually unformulated) elasticities of substitution. The prices of thousands of other inputs also change as a direct result, the price of complements of m rising, and of substitutes for m falling, in each case by a uniquely determined magnitude, and accompanied by an associated magnitude in the quantity of that input employed, each change having many thousands, and normally millions, of ripple effects upon the pricing structure, encouraging the output of some goods and discouraging that of others, favoring some productive techniques over others, and signaling to ultimate consumers the real cost of resources used in the production of the goods they consume, and all this happens in a way which makes the most efficient use of all the resources available to society. As a result of this system, for example, the consumer can tell by a glance at supermarket shelves that orange juice extracted and then transported unprocessed has required more of the world's resources than orange juice which has been concentrated, then transported, then rehydrated, which has in turn required more resources than orange juice concentrated then transported and sold as frozen concentrate—and not only this ranking, but the precise amount by which the rankings are separated—all this where 'more' means bringing about a greater reduction in production of millions of other possible consumer goods (Walras 2010; see Hayek 1948).

Here we have a highly intricate and intelligent device—far more intricate and far more intelligent than the Internet, and far more intricate than could ever be catalogued in full detail by an observer. Not only is the market a vast computer consisting of human interactions, but it is marked by division into components of many different types—capital and money markets, futures markets, commodities markets, real estate markets, and so on—just the kind of specialization Chorost sees as a mark of mind (179). Yet historically, the market has often been perceived as notable for its lack of consciousness. Karl Marx considered the market outmoded and looked forward to its abolition, primarily because it was a manifestation of "anarchy", and was not under conscious direction (Marx 1970, 336–37, 472, 496). I do not know of anyone who has speculated that the market economy itself could acquire consciousness. Ironically, the twenty-first-century prophets of artificial intelligence might suppose they could have set Marx straight: by analogy with some of their other reasoning, we might say that the market is conscious, even self-aware, as shown by the indisputable fact that it is intelligent (if we define intelligence as intricately adaptive behavior). Yet on this point Marx was surely right: the market is not conscious and cannot be subordinated to conscious control, because it is by its very nature an automatic, anarchic, and mindless system.

Three Models of Collective Consciousness

Could some system of human interaction, such as the market or the Internet, ever evolve to the point where it developed its own consciousness? Just what form would we expect this to take, and how would we know it was occurring? Just what would the entity be conscious of? (More loosely, what would it be thinking about?)

We can imagine three possible models for such a development:

1. The Borg. Individual humans are deprived of their individuality and become like mechanisms in a large unit, a collective, controlling mind. This is something like The Borg in *Star Trek: The Next Generation*, like the mysterious controlling intelligence in Frank Herbert's *The Santaroga Barrier*, or like the relation between the Hive Queens and their subordinate Formic organisms (the Buggers) in the Ender saga. In this model, the collective mind supplants the minds of its component parts. They cease to be true minds and their consciousness is that of the central controller. They may have some autonomy, just as parts of our body can perform automatic tasks and respond to stimuli. In this model, any consciousness displayed by the individual components is simply that of the central mind, and each component has lost the consciousness it formerly possessed.

2. Humans as neurons in the super-brain. We continue to have our own consciousnesses, and our own individual intentionalities. Our lives continue to be our own; we continue to give personal meaning to our actions, and we continue to interact with other individuals, each with their own intentionalities and consciousnesses. And on top, so to speak, of this human society of interacting individual minds, there arises a new, additional super-mind, with thoughts, values, and intentions of its own,

quite distinguishable from and additional to the thoughts, values, and intentions of the millions of individual humans.

3. The 'I' finds an outlet in the 'we'. We each continue to pursue our own goals in our own way, as individuals, but our desires and intentions express themselves through the group mind. The group mind facilitates and amplifies our ability to do what we want to do. This model literalizes the metaphor of participatory democracy. We really can express and fulfill our individuality through the group and in doing so we become parts of a single group consciousness.

The crucial difference between model #3 and model #2 is that in model #2 the contents of the collective consciousness are in principle completely separate from the contents of the component consciousnesses.

The Three Models Considered

Chorost distinguishes between what I have called model #1 and an alternative, but in this alternative he does not clearly distinguish between #2 and #3. His references to the alternative vacillate between characterizations appropriate to #3 and to #2.

If we consider these three models, we see that #3 is more attractive than #2, which is more attractive than #1, and that #3 is more obviously impracticable than #2, which is more obviously impracticable than #1.

Model #1 is similar to what we know, in many folklore traditions and other stories, as 'possession' of one mind by another, for example the possession of the king Théoden by the mind of Saruman in *The Two Towers*. Empirical psychology has found no trace of possession of one mind by another, but the concept is very familiar to us from stories. It is nearly always considered undesirable, usually quite frightening. The nineteenth century gave us a new conduit for possession: hypnosis. The most popular novels at the end of the nineteenth century were *Trilby* and *Dracula*, both taking the notion of possession of one personality by another to extreme and terrifying lengths. Empirical psychology has not been able to corroborate the feats of Svengali or the Transylvanian Count, but the possibilities remain worrisome to many people. Naturally, one person may strongly influence another by persuasion, and if we meet someone who has been recruited by a religious, political, or therapeutic cult, we may think that they have been 'possessed', but this usage is purely figurative.

Model #1 seems intuitively more plausible than the other two, I suggest, because of our gut belief that *consciousness is inherently personal and unitary*. Model #1 is a super-brain which deprives the component parts of their individuality. That we, as individuals should be fully in possession of ourselves and our minds and at the same time components of another mind—not metaphorically, an association of persons with minds, but literally, another mind—appears almost incomprehensible.

It is now a simple matter for an experimenter, by directly stimulating a person's brain, or by sending a signal to a person's brain as in the experiment by Rao, to cause a part of the person's body to move. In all the accounts I have read, the person whose body moves perceives this movement as involuntary. The subject will sometimes say to the experimenter: 'I didn't do that. You did that.' To the extent that the experimenter is in control, the subject loses control, and this is what we would expect. Extrapolating, if the experimenter had complete control, the subject would have no control at all. The subject would either be an unconscious mannequin or a helpless spectator of his body.

Models #2 and #3 have in common that the individuals comprising the collective mind do not lose their distinctively individual consciousnesses. But in #2, the individual consciousness has no necessary relation to the collective mind. In thinking about cases like these, it may help to pose three questions:

1. What new mental content is added by the collective mind?

2. What is the relation between the mental content of the collective mind and that of the individual components?

3. Does the collective mind initiate action?

These questions help us to avoid confusing the 'thoughts' of the collective mind with the thoughts of the individuals 'composing' it. The third question can also be rendered: Does the collective mind exhibit purposive behavior, and if so, how? Again, this purposive behavior has to be distinguished from the purposive behavior of the component individuals.

In both models #2 and #3, individuals retain their own consciousnesses (presumably their own thoughts and purposes), unlike in #1, and the individuals do not automatically or necessarily know that the thoughts and purposes of the collective mind exist. In model #2 it is conceivable that the collective mind might be thinking thoughts and pursuing goals, the existence of which are not even suspected by any of the component individuals. In model #3 we have to assume that the thoughts and goals of the collective mind are somehow identifiable with the thoughts and goals of the component individuals. And so in model #3, which is the most attractive model and the one often envisioned by Chorost and other writers, we have to suppose that the collective mind operates by a process of feedback from many component minds to each component mind. But of course, the mere existence of such feedback is not sufficient to prove the existence of a collective mind. Such feedback is familiar and entirely commonplace and does not by itself require us to postulate a collective mind.

Some of Chorost's discussion might be compatible with model #2, but mostly he seems to assume that the content of the collective mind will have something to do with the content of the individual minds. There is a conceptual sleight of hand going on here. We know that several consciousnesses may communicate, and may each gain something from their mutual communication. We also know that this gain to each consciousness does not generally amount to the creation of a new, additional, collective consciousness. Yet we may be lulled by Chorost's treatment into supposing that the collective consciousness is an extension of this more familiar process. If we are concerned with stamp-collecting, and gain something from our mutual communication with other individual philatelists, which enhances our awareness of stamp-collecting, we tend to assume that if a collective consciousness springs into existence, it too will have philately on its mind and will somehow be like an echo chamber for the social intercourse of philatelists. But why assume any such thing? The conscious brain does not share the preoccupations of the neurons, because neurons do not have any preoccupations, but if we are to treat individual human consciousnesses as analogous to neurons in the collective entity, why assume that the collective consciousness will be thinking about anything to do with what the individual consciousnesses are thinking? Vague association may lead us to suppose that this would be likely, but more careful attention discloses that it is, at the very least, an added complication, another hurdle to be overcome if collective consciousness is to be considered possible.

Chorost often writes as if any attributes of the consciousnesses of the components might somehow seep into the collective consciousness. Consider this passage:

> Online newspapers could be seen as sensory organs. Blogs and newspaper columnists could be seen as collective amygdala, in that they respond emotionally to events and thus signal their importance to the rest of the system. . . . Facebook can be seen as the beginning of an oxytocin/vasopressin/serotonin system. Dating websites are pure testosterone and estrogen, facilitating mating displays and pair-bonding. (Chorost, 182–83)

Bloggers and online newspaper columnists do respond emotionally, but there is no emotion in blogs or newspapers, any more than there is any smell of the salt sea in a manuscript of *The Thousand Nights and One Night*. The emotion is confined within the bodies of individual humans and cannot leak out of them into their communications, except figuratively. Testosterone and estrogen affect the moods and the actions of people who patronize dating websites, but there is no testosterone or estrogen in the websites themselves.

Model #3 is less realistically imaginable than model #2. A collective mind that thinks similar thoughts and has similar feelings as the individuals whose interactions compose it faces extraordinary hurdles beyond those faced by a collective mind which does not share the subjectivities of its components. Furthermore, if consciousness requires emotion, and emotion is generated by substances like oxytocin and serotonin, then the emergence of Internet consciousness confronts an obstacle, because these substances are confined within the bodies of the individual humans. The fact that one's person's emotion may affect other people's emotions, even by BBI, does not give the Internet its own emotions, or anything analogous.

Chorost tends to suppose that a collective mind would share all the knowledge of its components and thus put all this knowledge together to arrive at a high degree of wisdom. But the possibility can be entertained that a collective mind would be rather stupid. We may be distracted from such a possibility by Chorost's employment of the term 'intelligence'. If the collective mind has a high degree of intelligence, how could it be stupid? Quite easily, because of Chorost's special usage of the term 'intelligence'. Applying this conception of intelligence, we would judge the brain of a human being with an IQ of 55 to be highly intelligent. For after all, that brain controls such functions as his heartbeat and his entire autonomic system, and these are intricately adaptive and therefore 'intelligent' accomplishments. So the fact that the Internet might one day arrive at the level of 'intelligence' of the human brain does not rule out the possibility that it might be not very bright, judged by more colloquial criteria of intelligence. In this case, an Internet consciousness might be nothing more than a source of inefficiencies, supposing that the rather dull-witted Internet consciousness could start meddling in the affairs of the less dull-witted humans.

What our consideration of the three models helps to bring out is the problematic nature of the concept of a consciousness of which the component parts are each themselves conscious. We have never observed any such entity, and as we try to imagine it, we have a hard time understanding the relations between the content of the individual consciousnesses and the content of the collective consciousness. Do we suppose that (for instance) while the individuals believe Newton's theory, the collective mind has arrived at Einstein's theory? And if so, is the collective mind at some point going to get around to informing the individuals about the superiority of Einstein's theory? Or is it going to stealthily rig things so that the individuals are induced to stumble upon Einstein's theory? Or perhaps the collective mind will use Einstein's theory to modify calculations about the trajectories of spaceships, so that the individuals just find themselves getting better results out of their computers without knowing why?

Or will the proponents of the super-brain respond that any such scenarios are ridiculous, that the collective mind only works through the individual minds, only has the thoughts that the individual minds have? In that case, how do we distinguish the literal collective mind from a purely metaphorical collective mind, merely one more social gadget, one more computing device comprising human interactions?

Chorost gives a number of intriguing and provocative examples of possible future applications of brain-to-brain communication. What is striking, however, is that on close examination, all of these examples without exception definitely do not involve any literal collective mind, but only the metaphorical collective mind: groups of human individuals communicating and co-operating. No actual example is ever supplied of a future scenario in which a collective mind is demonstrably involved, unless we count his presumably semi-serious reference to the possibility that an unexplained financial crisis might be due to the intervention of the world wide mind (188)—but here no hint is offered as to how anything like that could happen. And given the still speculative and controversial nature of the causation of financial crises, it is doubtful that we could ever have a crisis where anyone would be able to say, 'Since all other explanations fail, this must be a case where the collective consciousness has been meddling, damn it.' They could just as easily have said that in 2008 or in 1929. In Chorosts's descriptions of both the drug bust and the theoretical physics brainstorming, there is no indication that a new consciousness has sprung into existence in addition to the consciousness of the individual humans. Quick awareness of where someone else is and how he's feeling is still just awareness of where he is and how he's feeling. Speeded up brainstorming may turn out to be very useful but is still brainstorming. The collective mind is still strictly metaphorical.

The Unity of Consciousness

Phenomenologically, consciousness possesses unity. Everything of which one is simultaneously conscious forms part of a single experience. We do not have any evidence of a consciousness made up of discrete conscious parts. It is conceivable that this unity is just inseparable from consciousness. We might adapt Searle's phrase that consciousness has a first-person ontology (Searle 1992, 20–21) to read that it has a first-person-singular ontology. Ever since Kant identified what he called "the transcendental unity of apperception," writers on consciousness have concerned themselves with the unity of consciousness. That consciousness always has some kind of unity is well-nigh unanimous among philosophical writers on conscious-ness, though there is room for disagreement about the scope of this unity (Bayne and Chalmers 2003).

A challenge to the unity of consciousness appeared to come from the famous split-brain research by Sperry and Gazzaniga (Gazzaniga 1970; 1987). Chorost appeals to this phenomenon to argue for the coming to-gether of multiple consciousnesses to make one global mind (8–9, 49, 55). When the connection between the two hemispheres of the brain is surgi-cally severed, various odd phenomena occur in which a person seems to be simultaneously aware and unaware of something, according to which half of the brain is 'consulted'. Bayne has argued, however, that the results are best interpreted, not as evidence of the co-existence of two separate con-sciousnesses in the same body, but as a 'switching' phenomenon in which a single consciousness alternates between access to different areas.

The significance of the split-brain challenge is not that two conscious-nesses might co-exist in the same body, for two consciousnesses might still be two separate consciousnesses, each one unified. Its significance lies in the possibility that two consciousnesses might be able to complement each other, coming together to form a unified consciousness, while each continues to keep some kind of independence. This is required by model #2 or model #3. So far, nothing has been observed of the nature of a new consciousness emerging from the coming together of two or more consciousnesses. Chorost suggests that it might happen, but the purposes of the combined consciousness might be so alien to our thinking that we would not be able to understand it (177–78)—which does raise the question of why he is so en-thusiastic for it to happen. If the split brain shows the creation of an addi-tional consciousness from the inter-communication of two consciousnesses, this would at least be one example of such a phenomenon. However, it would still be a big leap to the emergence of collective consciousness in a system of human social interaction. The two hemispheres of the brain evolved to-gether and are adapted to work with each other—their separation is artificial and inherently pathological—whereas individual humans are not adapted to merge their consciousnesses with each other, except metaphorically in social co-operation. Furthermore, it is dubious to say that each hemisphere, when collaborating with the other, retains its own independent consciousness. And, of course, there are only two hemispheres, not millions.

Conditions for Consciousness

What general conditions have to obtain for some entity to become conscious? We don't know, but I will mention three possibilities.

1. Complexity of information processing produces consciousness.

This theory is quite popular among journalists, and a few AI zealots, who predict that at some point in the next hundred years, computers will automatically acquire consciousness because they have become so complex. It may no doubt turn out that some level of complexity is a precondition for consciousness, but mere increase in *any* kind of complexity is not going to yield consciousness, any more than it will yield photosynthesis. Consciousness is a matter of subjective experience and involves ascription of meaning. It is arbitrary to suppose that some amount of unqualified complexity is going to produce, as a sort of incidental by-product, a computer that can think and feel or that finds meaning in the world, though of course more computing power might enable a computer to do better at simulating consciousness without actually possessing it—a very different matter. If this is correct then, by analogy, we have no basis for supposing that the ever-growing complexity of the Internet could make the Internet itself conscious.

2. Specific physical conditions that some specific physical (for instance, electro-chemical) conditions are necessary and perhaps sufficient for consciousness.

Consciousness is produced inside brains and this suggests the possibility that some definite physical conditions might be necessary or sufficient to produce consciousness. At the simplest level, perhaps the existence of a specific group of molecules might produce consciousness. This seems more likely to be a necessary than a sufficient condition. Presumably this physical complex would have to be linked up in some specific way with some broader structure. Could this physical complex be duplicated and somehow placed in the appropriate relationship with the Internet?

If there were some such group of molecules, we might imagine that we could purchase a consciousness plug-in for our laptops. We plug it in and the laptop becomes conscious. Now supposing some such plug-in has been developed, how would we plug it in to the Internet? How would we make it confer consciousness on the Internet rather than on some specific piece of hardware being utilized by the Internet? Bear in mind that if some such plug-in were marketed, and everyone had them on their computers, this would confer consciousness on each computer, but would do nothing to confer consciousness on the Internet, or on any system of interaction of several computers, just as everyone in this room is now (I hope) conscious but the collectivity of all of us is certainly not conscious.

3. Consciousness arises in the context of self-organizing systems capable of purposive action.

For my third possibility I am going to consider the theory formulated by Ellis and Newton in *How the Mind Uses the Brain* (Ellis and Newton 2010). I do this partly because I view this theory as more persuasive than most, but also because it shares much with several other respectable theories, and so may be used to illustrate the general difficulties in conceiving of a collective consciousness with individual humans, or human interactions, as components.

The Ellis-Newton theory, a type of enactivism, has roots in both phenomenology and neuroscience. "Conscious beings understand the world either by acting in relation to it, or by imagining how we would act relative to it" (vii). The fact that mechanical gadgets are not conscious while some animals are conscious is associated with the fact that mechanical gadgets only react whereas animals act. The most fundamental way of understanding objects and concepts is in terms of their affordances—the possible opportunities they afford for action. Unlike some theorists who hold that action is what matters and that representations in the brain can be dispensed with, understanding begins, for Ellis and Newton, with imagining how we might act in relation to the world. The main way in which this occurs is by actually instigating efferent action commands which are then inhibited (x–xi). A curious phenomenon corroborating this analysis is the rare behavioral disorder known as 'utilization behavior', in which the patient is unable to perceive a thing without acting in relation to it (cannot perceive a cup without attempting to drink from it, for instance); this patient has the command to act but his brain lacks the capacity to create inhibitory neurotransmitters (xv). The motivation of action is always emotional, so emotion is essential for the creation of consciousness, and emotion helps to account for the 'what it's like' quality of conscious states (xiv). The possibility of thought-controlled prosthetic devices and other appliances arises because the brain activity involved in imagining an action is fundamentally the same as the brain activity involved in executing the action (xvii). To avoid circularity, the Ellis-Newton theory requires that there be some form of preconscious action imaging, and that the brain's capacity to accomplish this is a necessary condition for moving beyond mere unconscious information-processing to consciousness.

We do have to make room for the fact that consciousness can exist without action, or without any action other than purely mental action. A totally paralyzed person can be conscious, and can compose a poem or solve a math problem (though unable to transmit these results to anyone else). This fact can be accommodated by acknowledging that there is no necessary connection between consciousness and behavior, while still retaining the idea that being able to imagine how to act in relation to a thing is the evolutionary and to some extent even the phenomenological condition for thinking about that thing (xix–xxi).

Assuming that the Ellis-Newton theory, or some theory like it, is a correct account of the genesis of consciousness, it points to difficulties with the supposition that the Internet could ever become conscious. As far as we know, consciousness has only ever arisen in the brains of animals which needed to act quickly in relation to an ever-changing and complex environment in order to survive and reproduce. Given that we know (from the paralyzed person example) that this context of action is not essential to consciousness, there is the logical possibility that consciousness could arise in some different way, but at least we can say that the evolutionary impulse to consciousness is absent in the case of the Internet. It's not clear that the Internet or any other entity could be said to benefit from the acquisition of consciousness, as Chorost himself observes (Chorost, 179). An acting animal is a self-organizing system whose reproduction chances are influenced by moment-to-moment events over which it has some control. The Internet, by contrast, is an artifact which serves the purposes of millions of individual humans, and does not have to do anything to survive, any more than church polyphony or plays in blank verse had to do anything of their own volition to survive; the Internet could go the way of both of those types of activities if individual humans ever ceased to find it useful.

The Internet is not governed by any impulse to *do* anything, in the sense that an elephant or a human is so governed. In fact, if we turn to Model #2, the Internet would encounter an obstacle to doing anything: whatever it might decide to do might make it less efficient at serving individual human purposes. Instead of the Internet, we could consider a different social institution: language. We cannot even take seriously the suggestion that language itself might become conscious, and I suggest that is because we understand enough about language to know that it does not do anything, in the sense of purposively acting to pursue its own goals.

Chorost supposes that the super-brain will emerge from various spontaneous developments in the Internet, but some of the difficulties in this conception may be highlighted by supposing that we wanted to design the Internet to be conscious. As we think of eventually finding out enough about the production of consciousness to be able to design conscious robots or conscious computers, we similarly might see the present Internet as a robot or computer, albeit one made up of human interactions mediated through computers. But whereas we surmise that conscious robots might be better able to watch the kids or walk the dog, and would be designed with such abilities in mind, what would we expect the conscious Internet to do for us that the present unconscious Internet, or a future much augmented but still unconscious Internet, cannot do?

Conclusion

My view is that a community of conversing individuals, even one enhanced by brain-to-brain signals, is not going to develop its own consciousness in addition to the consciousness of the separate individuals. More generally, the Internet is a human social institution, and human social institutions do not literally acquire consciousness. I do not claim to have demonstrated this. My approach has been to show that if we think specifically about what is entailed in the notion of a collective consciousness, we become more acutely aware of its vagueness and of some of the problems with it. We have yet to be given a coherent picture of what a world wide mind could possibly be like.

Philosophy of Emerging Media, 2016

References

Armstrong, Doree, and Michelle Ma. 2013. Researcher Controls Colleague's Motions in 1st Human Brain-to-Brain Interface. Seattle: University of Washington (August 27th).

Bayne, Tim. 2008. The Unity of Consciousness and the Split-Brain Syndrome. *Journal of Philosophy* 105:6, 277–300.

———. 2010. *The Unity of Consciousness*. New York: Oxford University Press.

Bayne, Tim, and David J. Chalmers. 2003. What Is the Unity of Consciousness? In Cleeremans 2003.

Chorost, Michael. 2005. *Rebuilt: How Becoming Part Computer Made Me More Human*. New York: Houghton Mifflin.

———. 2011. *World Wide Mind: The Coming Integration of Humanity, Machines, and the Internet*. New York: Free Press.

Cleeremans, Axel, ed. 2003. *The Unity of Consciousness: Binding, Integration, Dissociation*. Oxford: Oxford University Press.

Ellis, Ralph D., and Natika Newton. 2010. *How the Mind Uses the Brain: To Move the Body and Image the Universe*. Chicago: Open Court.

Gazzaniga, Michael. 1970. *The Bisected Brain*. New York: Appleton.

———. 1987. *Social Brain: Discovering the Networks of the Mind*. New York: Basic Books.

Goldberg, Elkhonon. 2009. *The New Executive Brain: Frontal Lobes in a Complex World*. New York: Oxford University Press.

Graimann, Bernhard, Brendon Allison, and Gert Pfurtscheller, eds. 2010. *Brain-Computer Interfaces: Revolutionizing Human-Computer Interaction*. Heidelberg: Springer.

Grinin, Leonid, Robert L. Carneiro, Andrey V. Korotayev, and Fred Spier. 2011. *Evolution: Cosmic, Biological, Social*. Volgograd: Uchitel.

Hayek, F.A. 1948. The Use of Knowledge in Society. In F.A. Hayek, *Individualism and Economic Order*. Chicago: University of Chicago Press.

Heylighen, Francis. 2011. Conceptions of a Global Brain: A Historical Review. In Grinin et al. 2011.

Marx, Karl. 1970 [1867]. *Capital: A Critical Analysis of Capitalist Production*, Volume I. Moscow: Progress.

Polanyi, Michael. 1951. *The Logic of Liberty: Reflections and Rejoinders*. London: Routledge.

Rao, Rajesh P.N. 2013. *Brain-Computer Interfacing: An Introduction*. Cambridge: Cambridge University Press.

Russell, Peter. 1995 [1983]. *The Global Brain Awakens: Our Next Evolutionary Leap*. Palo Alto: Global Brain Inc.

Searle, John R. 1992. *The Rediscovery of the Mind*. Cambridge: MIT Press.

Surowiecki, Joseph. 2004. *The Wisdom of Crowds: Why the Many Are Smarter than the Few and How Collective Wisdom Shapes Business, Economies, Societies, and Nations*. New York: Doubleday.

University of Southampton. 2009. Brain-Computer Interface Allows Person-to-Person Communication through Power of Thought. ScienceDaily, at <www.sciencedaily.com/releases/2009/10/091006102647.htm>.

Walras, Léon. 2010 [1874]. *Elements of Pure Economics*. New York: Routledge.

23

WHAT FOLLOWS FROM THE NONEXISTENCE
OF MENTAL ILLNESS? (2017)

Does Thomas Szasz's opposition to psychiatric coercion follow from his denial of the existence of mental illness? My question isn't whether either or
both of these Szasz positions are correct, but whether one implies the other.

In 1961 Szasz published *The Myth of Mental Illness* (amplifying an article
with the same title, from a year earlier). His subsequent books, nearly forty
of them, would all preach the same message. Szasz maintained that there
is literally no such thing as 'mental illness'. Illness is a condition of the body,
and mental illness is no more than a metaphor (Szasz 1991, 23; 2007, 3–4;
2010, 267). "Because the mind is not a bodily organ, it can be diseased only
in a metaphorical sense" (Szasz 2001, 13).

Equally consistently, Szasz held that treating people against their will
is unwarranted and immoral. He argued and actively campaigned against
all coercion by the state in the name of mental health. He opposed involuntary commitment of the 'mentally ill', all compulsory treatment of adults,
and all legal restrictions on voluntary ingestion of chemical substances,
from tobacco to crystal meth (Szasz 2001, 127–165).

Szasz evidently believed that there is a tight connection between the
proposition that there is literally no such thing as mental illness and the
proposition that all psychiatric coercion is wrong, or at least unjustified.
Again and again he reveals that he assumes some such tight connection
(1976, 189; 2010, 267–68), but he never spells out an argument demonstrating this connection.

It might seem at first blush that, since the case for psychiatric coercion
is usually made in terms of the reality of mental illness, to refute the existence of mental illness would automatically destroy the case for psychiatric
coercion. But since proponents of psychiatric coercion generally view the

reality of mental illness as uncontentious, they naturally talk in terms of mental illness. This doesn't demonstrate that the literal existence of mental illness is crucial to their support for coercion. We can imagine people convinced by Szasz's arguments that there is no literal mental illness continuing to hold that people exhibiting certain types of behaviors ought to be coerced. And we can imagine people holding that mental illness does exist and at the same time holding that some or all of currently practiced psychiatric coercion is unwarranted. Why should the existence of literal mental illness be considered—either by Szasz or by his opponents—as decisive, or even relevant, for the policy issue of psychiatric coercion?

What Szasz Does Not Dispute

Szasz does not dispute the existence of the forms of behavior customarily classified as mental illness (Szasz 2001, 114–15). He does not deny, for instance, that people sometimes become very sad or anxious for no apparently commensurate reason, or that they sometimes believe very fanciful things, or that their speech and other behavior sometimes takes on baffling non-standard forms, or that they sometimes seriously injure themselves from what look like bizarre motives. Szasz insists that these are not illnesses or symptoms of illnesses, any more than they are examples of possession by evil spirits. Szasz calls them "problems in living" (Szasz 1991, 19).

Szasz also does not deny the existence of brain conditions, including brain diseases, which affect people's behavior and emotions, sometimes for the worse. Iodine deficiency, syphilis of the brain, epilepsy, head injury, ingestion of toxic substances, Alzheimer's dementia, are some uncontentious examples of medical conditions which may have harmful consequences in people's emotions and behavior. It is uncontroversial that brain conditions may have emotional and behavioral symptoms, or in other words, mental symptoms.

Szasz points out that many of these mental symptoms used to be viewed as purely psychological in origin because the underlying physical conditions of the brain were not known. And when these underlying conditions did become known, these patterns of behavior and feeling were then taken away from psychiatry:

. . . as soon as a disease thought to be mental is proven to be physical, it is removed from the domain of psychiatry and placed in that of medicine, to be treated henceforth by internists, neurologists, or neurosurgeons. This is what happened with paresis, pellagra, epilepsy, and brain tumors. (Szasz 1997, 70)

Since Szasz accepts the common-sense medical view that many patterns of behavior and feeling were once observed and discussed (and even treated) without their neurological causes being known, and that these causes were later identified, he has to acknowledge that there are very likely some present-day patterns where the neurological cause is unknown, but where this cause will probably be discovered in the future (Szasz 1997, 52).

The Metamorphosis of Metaphor

The crucial point disputed by Szasz is not the existence of physical illnesses with mental consequences, but the description of these illnesses as literally mental. In his view, only the body can be literally sick, ill, or diseased. To say that the mind is sick is to employ a metaphor, like saying that the economy is sick or that the condition of the contemporary novel is sick.

Szasz's claim that literal mental illness doesn't exist is, I think, true, with a couple of big qualifications.

The first qualification is that the line between literal and metaphorical is not always sharp. For example, when we set a trap for someone in a poker game, do we view the expression 'setting a trap' as literal or metaphorical? This kind of usage no doubt arose as an analogy with preparing a mechanical snare or a concealed pit for an animal (or human) victim, but what was once a metaphor has become so commonplace over many centuries that we hardly think of it as a metaphor. Someone might learn the use of this term in competitive games or in espionage without even knowing about the original meaning.

Or again, the first person to talk about a 'virus' that infects a computer was no doubt employing a metaphor, but it's not so clear that it remains a metaphor today. It may be that the use of the word 'virus' in the computer context is now so well established that it is no longer a metaphor. If biologists replaced 'virus' with a new term and the use of the old term was completely forgotten in its biological context, this might have no effect on the use of the term 'virus' in the computer context.

In some cases, a word usage evolves so that people don't even know about the original meaning. Most people who use the expression 'plain sailing' don't know that it was once spelled 'plane sailing' and referred to the assumption that the surface of the sea was flat rather than curved, which greatly simplified the calculation of a ship's position at the cost of introducing a slight inaccuracy. Here the metaphor has broken completely free of its origins, and people who employ the phrase can hardly be said to be using a metaphor, because they have never known what was once the literal meaning.

It's a matter for judgment whether this has occurred yet with 'mental illness'. I accept that it has not. However in this case, the more general (or as we would now tend to suppose 'metaphorical') usage was the original one. In old-fashioned but still comprehensible expressions like 'It's an ill wind that blows no one any good', or 'Don't think ill of me', we see the ancient usage of 'ill' to apply to anything wrong, unfortunate, or amiss. If English speakers six centuries ago had had any notion of an entity called 'the economy,' they would have had no hesitation in saying 'Something is ill with the economy' or perhaps even 'We have an ill economy this year', and they would have meant it literally. Indeed Szasz does say that the modern, scientific meaning of illness or disease, which he contrasts with its metaphorical sense in the phrase 'mental illness', is less than two centuries old (Szasz 2001, 12–15).

The Nonexistence of Literal Mental Illness

Szasz is right to say that mental illness is no literal illness, because the word 'illness' in its strictly medical context has acquired a very precise meaning, and this is the only meaning that most people immediately think of when they encounter the word 'illness'. Furthermore, many proponents of 'mental' illness make their non-metaphorical position more difficult to defend by insisting that mental illness is illness 'just like any other illness'.

Szasz accepts that there are (or might easily be) as yet unidentified brain diseases with characteristic patterns of emotional and behavioral effects. (From now on, for brevity, I will use the expression 'brain diseases with mental symptoms'.) It follows that people, such as psychiatrists, might notice the same pattern of mental effects recurring in a number of people, and *surmise* or *conjecture* that these were due to some as yet unidentified brain disease. And they might, in any particular case, be right. Or, of course, they might be wrong.

We see, then, that Szasz and conventional psychiatry are in one respect much closer together than we might think. Both accept that patterns of emotions and behavior may be caused by a brain disease, including the possibility of a brain disease that we haven't identified, and perhaps don't even know how to look for.

So exactly where do Szasz and conventional psychiatry differ? One answer might be that they differ because conventional psychiatrists persist in using the term 'mental illness'. But Szasz can have no objection to the term 'brain disease with mental symptoms', and if, when psychiatrists say 'mental illness', they actually mean 'brain disease with mental symptoms', then Szasz's objection becomes a somewhat trivial and purely semantic point.

We still speak of 'sunrise' and 'sunset', even though we know that these terms are literally incorrect. Provided we understand that the sun does not really rise or set, but becomes observable or unobservable because the Earth is spinning, no harm is done by continuing with the traditional terminology, which taken strictly literally might be misleading. Similarly, if psychiatrists say 'mental illness' and mean 'brain disease with mental symptoms', provided they do understand that minds cannot strictly be sick, there can be no objection that they are mistaking a metaphor for literal truth. They might be making a different mistake, such as thinking there is a brain disease when there really isn't, but they can't be accused of taking a metaphor literally.

So this is my second big qualification. Just as it would be excessively pedantic to object to the word 'sunset' in most routine contexts, so it may be excessively pedantic to object to 'mental illness', if it is taken to mean 'brain disease with mental symptoms'. Such an understanding of the phrase seems to be very prevalent today, perhaps more prevalent than ever before. Although the claim that mental illnesses are brain diseases goes back centuries, it is certainly more popular today than fifty years ago. What this development means is that it would not be very difficult for psychiatrists to agree that mental illness is a metaphor and to switch to the term 'brain disease with mental symptoms', leaving their other views intact and continuing to favor psychiatric coercion. Szasz does not welcome this trend in psychiatry, but generally tends to give the impression that he dismisses the claim that brain diseases can be attributed to those diagnosed as mentally ill (Szasz 1997, 49–52, 344–46).

The Virchowian Definition of Disease

If someone observes a pattern of emotion and behavior—what I'm calling a mental pattern—and surmises that these might be caused by a brain disease, Szasz evidently supposes that they are doing something illegitimate. Why would this be illegitimate? The only answer we can extract from Szasz's writings is that this would contradict the Virchowian conception of what qualifies as a disease.

According to this view, associated with Rudolf Virchow (1821–1902), a disease can't be identified unless there is some observable bodily lesion (structural injury or deformity). Thus, nothing can be a disease unless it can be observed by a pathologist. If it can't be identified in a cadaver, it is not a disease. A corpse can have atherosclerosis or bunions, therefore these are diseases. A corpse cannot have bipolar disorder or Internet addiction, therefore these are not diseases (Szasz 1997, 71–73).

Some argue that the Virchowian conception is overly restrictive. A corpse can't have a susceptibility to migraine, for example. (In some cases migraines are caused by something observable in the brain, such as a tumor, but most migraines have no such observable bodily correlate.) But aside from that, there are historical cases where the specific physical correlate of a disease was at first unknown, and later became known. (I use the term 'correlate' to avoid taking a position on whether the Virchowian theory holds that the physical lesion is the *cause* of the disease or *is* the disease. Szasz seems to think it is the latter, but it is not clear that this was what Virchow held.)

The physical abnormality does not *become* a disease or the physical correlate of a disease when it is discovered. If it were a disease after discovery, then it must have been a disease before discovery. We therefore have to accept that there can be diseases where the physical correlate is not known.

What this means is that we have to bear in mind the distinction between qualifying as a disease by some medical convention and actually being a disease. Virchow's rule is a rule of method for physicians, not a rule of philosophical ontology. It is the adoption of a convention for accrediting diseases, not a claim about the possible existence of diseases. It might conceivably be a good rule for physicians to recognize only such diseases as can be associated with a known lesion, but this cannot alter the fact that there are real diseases which cannot be associated with a known lesion. To suppose otherwise would be to consider that epilepsy *became* a disease only when the responsible brain condition was identified, or that bubonic plague *became* a disease only when the *Yersinia pestis* bacterium was found.

Szasz might want to insist that Virchow's rule is a correct rule of method, and ought to be applied in all cases of putative disease. That would rule out all cases of so-called mental illness—we would not be able to call them 'brain diseases with mental symptoms' because Virchow's rule doesn't permit us to call anything a disease until we have identified the specific physical condition which defines the disease. But if we observe a characteristic cluster of symptoms, why shouldn't we conjecture that it is the result of a physical condition, such as a brain illness, even though we can't yet identify that physical condition? There is no good reason why we should not entertain some such hypothesis—which is different, of course, from uncritically taking it to be true once we have thought of it.

Szasz's equivocal interpretation of Virchow runs all through his many statements of his position, sometimes rendering these statements self-contradictory. For example:

> Diseases are demonstrable anatomical or physiological lesions that may occur naturally or be caused by human agents. Although diseases may not be recognized or understood, they "exist." People "have" hypertension or malaria, regardless of whether or not they know it or physicians diagnose it. (Szasz 2010, 276)

The first two sentences contradict each other. If the lesion has to be demonstrable, then people cannot have the disease before the lesion is even suspected. And where is the lesion in hypertension (high blood pressure)?

There is no lesion, and pathologists cannot discover hypertension in a corpse.

The Virchowian definition does not really help Szasz make his case. Szasz has not come up with some reasoning which prevents us from saying: 'We observe certain emotional and behavioral peculiarities. We conjecture that they are symptoms of a disease, whose physical nature has yet to be discovered'. No argument has been offered to show that such a way of thinking is illegitimate or wrong-headed.

The conclusion we have arrived at (a conclusion Szasz occasionally seem to dispute but at other times seems to accept, and a conclusion which is in any case practically indisputable) is that there is not necessarily anything wrong with observing mental symptoms, and conjecturing that these might be caused by, and therefore might be symptoms of, a brain condition. This conclusion doesn't mean that any such conjectured condition has actually been accurately specified for any of the currently accepted 'mental illnesses'. It merely means that no such conjecture can be ruled out a priori. It is up to psychiatrists or others to make a case for the existence of each putative brain disease.

However, the general possibility that there might be as yet unidentified brain diseases with mental symptoms is hardly outlandish, because, for example, we know that intake of some drugs or toxic substances can cause mental symptoms—such as hallucinations, unusual euphoria, intense fearfulness, or difficulty in concentrating one's thoughts—and if such mental symptoms can be caused by ingested chemicals, it is no great leap to suppose that they might also be sometimes caused by other physical changes in the body.

Szasz's Denials of Factual Propositions about Brain Diseases

When discussing various putative psychiatric illnesses—notably schizophrenia, about which Szasz has written more than any other alleged psychiatric disease—Szasz alternates between denying that there is an 'it' there at all—that some definite pattern of mental features has been identified—and accepting that there is an 'it' while denying that it represents a disease. This alternation can perhaps be defended by saying that Szasz wants to test out both claims of psychiatry independently.

Szasz makes some substantive factual claims about the possibility of brain diseases, which do not follow from his basic insight into the metaphorical nature of mental illness. The crucial point here (for my argument) is not whether Szasz is right or wrong in these claims, but the fact that these claims cannot be logically derived from his fundamental claim about mental illness.

Many psychiatrists now say that various mental illnesses, such as schizophrenia or bipolar disorder, are caused by a chemical imbalance in the brain. Szasz points out that no one has ever observed or detected any such supposed chemical imbalance, which is correct (Valenstein 1998; Wyatt and Midkiff 2006; Wyatt and Midkiff 2007), and well worth bearing in mind, but not relevant to the main point, which is that a chemical imbalance in the brain is one hypothesis to account for a pattern of mental manifestations, and there can be no reason to dismiss this hypothesis out of hand.

Szasz not only states that this supposed chemical imbalance has not been detected, which is true, but also on occasion seems to be implying that there is no such chemical imbalance accounting for, say, schizophrenia. Often, however, we find on close examination of his text that he literally asserts only that there is no *proven* chemical imbalance (1997, 346–49), which is merely another way of saying that the supposed chemical imbalance has not been detected. So what of the possibility that there might be a suspected or conjectured chemical imbalance, which might be a good working hypothesis because other explanations for the observed mental patterns seem inadequate? It is just here that the debate should be focused, but Szasz's approach tends to ignore it.

Szasz's evident claim that there is no chemical imbalance (not just that there is no proven chemical imbalance), emerges most clearly in aphoristic passages like the following:

> If you believe that you are Jesus or that the Communists are after you (and they are not)—then your belief is likely to be regarded as a symptom of schizophrenia. But if you believe that Jesus is the Son of God or that Communism is the only scientifically and morally correct form of government—then your belief is likely to be regarded as a reflection of who you are: Christian or Communist. That is why I think that we will

discover the chemical cause of schizophrenia when we discover the chemical cause of Christianity and Communism. No sooner and no later. (Szasz 1990, 215–16)

The reasoning here seems to be that if one belief is caused by a chemical imbalance, then so must another belief be similarly caused. Now, we know that if you're a Christian or a Communist, you most likely became an adherent of one or another of these doctrinal systems because you were persuaded, as a result of hearing people talk about them, that their essential propositions are true. That's how we know that you did *not* become a Christian or a Communist because of a chemical imbalance in your brain. In contrast, if you came to believe that you are Jesus or that the Communists are after you, this was not because of anyone trying to persuade you of these beliefs. Your adoption of such beliefs showed more originality and independence of thought than the typical Christian or Communist. If it's possible for any beliefs to be the result of chemical imbalances in the brain, the beliefs that you are Jesus or that the Communists are after you do indeed look like better candidates for such causation.

Just to be clear, I suppose we all take it for granted—Szasz evidently did (Szasz 2010, 101)—that if you are a Christian or a Communist this will have some consequences for events going on in your brain. (Because it is not necessary in this context, I do not here explore the question of whether being a Christian or a Communist *is* a matter of events going on in your brain, though that is what I believe.) But in complex systems there can be explanations at different levels, and there can be 'downward causation' from higher levels to lower levels, as well as 'upward causation' from lower levels to higher (Campbell 1974; Campbell 1990). Szasz's assumption of the equivalent causation of different beliefs is not as self-evident as he supposed. It is not entirely preposterous that there could be a chemical-imbalance explanation of paranoid thought-patterns and no chemical-imbalance explanation for the adoption of conventional belief-systems.

Szasz's Non-Sequitur

Because of the eloquent, pithy, and somewhat oracular manner in which Szasz often presents his argument, there is a tendency for readers to suppose that if literal mental illness is an incoherent notion, then schizophrenia cannot be caused by a chemical imbalance. But Szasz doesn't produce any argument to this effect. There is actually no logical connection at all between these two assertions. The hypothetical causation of schizophrenia by a chemical imbalance may turn out to be true or false. (Since decades of research, generously assisted by the pharmaceutical companies, have so far failed to find it, we may be inclined to speculate that its long-term chances, as a scientific hypothesis, do not look promising). But it is not disallowed by the contention that there are no literal mental illnesses. Szasz might be right on both counts, but his second claim is not derivable from his first, and needs to be investigated, tested, and evaluated with different arguments, which must be mainly empirical rather than semantic or conceptual.

Consider this typical assertion by Szasz:

> If we accept the proposition that X is not an illness unless there are *defining, objective, anatomical criteria for it*, in other words, that X is not an illness unless it can be diagnosed by examining some part of the patient's body, then it is absurd to call a condition that lacks precisely that characteristic a "real illness." (Szasz 2001, 83; italics in original)

Szasz is forgetting that we already know that "the proposition" must be false, because we know that people have had illnesses before anyone had found their anatomical criteria. Leave aside the point that not everyone agrees with that definition of an illness—some people would say that a person who experiences migraine attacks actually has an illness. Still, we recall that Szasz himself accepts that people throughout history were really ill long before the "defining, objective, anatomical criteria" of their illnesses were discovered. The absurdity Szasz points to does not arise if someone says: 'I admit that we can't yet establish the anatomical signs of this illness, but I conjecture that there is such an illness'.

This thought naturally occurred to Szasz, who, immediately after the above, writes "It may happen in medicine that we do not yet know whether a problematic condition is or is not illness" (tacitly conceding again that X may be an illness when we have no anatomical criteria for it). He goes on to say that in criminal justice, it is considered better to let a thousand guilty persons go free than to convict a single innocent person, whereas "our medical maxim is that it is better to falsely diagnose and unnecessarily treat a thousand healthy persons than to mistakenly declare a single sick person healthy and thus deprive him of treatment."

Here Szasz has quietly dropped his immediately preceding claim of absurdity. It may be mistaken policy, it may even be an appalling scandal, to treat a thousand people unnecessarily to be sure of helping the one who really benefits from treatment, but there's nothing absurd about it. The problem in Szasz's presentation of his argument arises from his tendency not to make a sharp distinction between someone actually having an illness and that person's complying with the practical requirement we may have adopted to recognize him as having an accredited illness.

Where did Szasz get the thousand-to-one ratio from? In the immediate context of Szasz's remarks we can infer that if a person or his family insist that there is something wrong with him, and medical tests can discover nothing wrong with him, Szasz says that under current arrangements he will always be 'given treatment' for a 'mental illness', and Szasz's estimate of the likelihood that he will actually have something medically wrong with him is one in a thousand-and-one.

Szasz's position, then, is that people see psychiatrists because of problems they have or problems other people have with them. These problems may possibly be due to brain diseases which have not yet been physically identified, but this (in Szasz's judgment) can only be true in a tiny minority of cases at most. Szasz assumes that the great majority of people (picturesquely, one thousand out of every 1,001) who see psychiatrists don't have any unidentified brain disease. What this amounts to is the proposition that 'mental illnesses' (brain diseases with mental symptoms) are at the very least hugely over-diagnosed. This may well be true (I think it very likely is) but it has no logical relation to the claim that there are no literal mental illnesses.

Many psychiatrists and other mental health professionals talk as if all problems in living are diseases. Notice, however, that there is a distinction between the claim that some apparent problems in living, referred to by psychiatry as diseases, are not diseases—that there is an area of human behavior, choice, emotion, and suffering which does not belong to the domain of psychiatry or medicine—and the claim that all such problems in living are not diseases (or caused by diseases). The first claim, one with which I agree, makes up the topic of much of Szasz's writing—his trenchant and witty exposure of the follies of mental-health imperialism. As to the second claim, I'm more inclined to doubt it. But in any case, the two claims are not the same claim.

In correspondence with Szasz about *The Myth of Mental Illness*, Sir Karl Popper stated that he believed Szasz was "95% right" but did not accept the total nonexistence of mental illness. The published extracts from the correspondence (Schaler 2004, 136) do not make absolutely clear what Popper meant here, but I think it's reasonable to surmise that he meant that something like ninety-five percent of what is labeled mental illness is no illness at all, as Szasz maintained, whereas the other five percent of it is (contrary to Szasz) due to brain disease. My impression is that this is what a lot of thoughtful people, dubious about the pretensions of psychiatric imperialism, do believe. Naturally, there's no significance in the precise figure of five percent. It might be one percent or it might be twenty percent.

Psychiatry has moved both closer to Szasz's position and further away from it. Fifty years ago, psychiatrists would be more likely to adhere to psychoanalytic notions of the causation of mental diseases/problems in living. Now they are more likely to insist that such problems must be due to a purely physical cause, such as chemical imbalance in the brain. This is closer to Szasz's position in that it harmonizes better with the view that if something is a disease, it can only be a disease of the body. But it is further away from Szasz's view because it views as medical problems states of affairs which in his judgment we should not regard as medical at all. The early Szasz was decidedly an adherent of psychoanalysis in its then fashionable incarnations of ego psychology, object-relations theory, and interpersonal psychology (Szasz 2010, 95–101, 213–225). The later Szasz no longer expressed any support for psychoanalytic theory, and perhaps had become disillusioned with it. But Szasz always held that people with problems in living can be helped by psychotherapy, which consists in talking with them about their subjective mental life—including their assumptions, goals, and values. And psychotherapy falls within a liberal definition of 'psychoanalysis'. From Szasz's point of view, psychoanalysis, broadly defined, was at least attempting to treat people as human beings, while the medical approach tends to dehumanize them by converting their real personal and ethical problems into diseases. However, this stance ignores the question: are some of these people's real human problems due to disorders of their brains? As we have seen, despite superficial appearance, Szasz has never offered us any reason to discount this possibility a priori.

Consider Szasz's famous and moving essay, "What Psychiatry Can and Cannot Do." (Szasz 1991, 79–86). In the first page or two, Szasz briefly mentions and criticizes the concept of mental illness. Then, he presents a number of pseudonymous case histories which display, in heart-rending fashion, the disgraceful horrors routinely perpetrated by modern psychiatry. However, these case histories would be just as effective in calling psychiatric practice into question if they were not preceded by his dismissive mention of 'mental illness'. We could delete the reference to mental illness, and then a believer in the existence of some brain diseases with mental symptoms could easily respond to these case histories by saying, 'Yes, isn't it sad the damage psychiatry can do when it becomes corrupt and is allowed to stray outside its proper area of competence? We should be much more careful about defining the area in which psychiatry can operate, and repudiating its pretensions outside this circumscribed area.'

Although he often seems to be rejecting the possibility that mental symptoms might be due to an as yet unidentified brain disease, Szasz also expresses the view that it would make little or no difference if brain correlates for putative diseases such as schizophrenia were to be discovered (1990, 222–24). And he has also asserted that such a discovery would actually strengthen his own argument against coercive psychiatry (Szasz 1997, 347).

What Would Justify Psychiatric Coercion?

Szasz has given us no reason to rule out a priori the possibility that we can conjecture, from observing someone's behavior, that they have a brain disease with mental symptoms, though we don't yet know (and may never know) what physical condition in their brain constitutes the disease.

The fact that this conjecture makes sense and can't be ruled out doesn't imply that any claim as to the existence of any such brain disease is true. What would incline us to suppose it might be true in any particular instance?

First, we would need clear evidence that there is an 'it' there at all. What this means in practice is that if a large number of psychiatrists were to 'examine' (talk to) a person, a very high percentage of them (close to one hundred percent) should agree on whether this person has or does not have a mental illness (a brain disease with mental symptoms), and if so, precisely what that mental illness is. We expect this from doctors deciding whether someone has cancer or atherosclerosis, and we expect something analogous from accountants auditing a company's financial records. We should certainly never take these opinions very seriously if we think there is frequent disagreement on actual cases among these accredited experts.

It is particularly important to insist on this minimum condition because there are no physical tests for these hypothesized brain diseases. The supposed diseases are only surmised to account for the patient's behavior or mental state. There has never been a case, and with current knowledge never could be a case, where the psychiatrist says to the patient: "The test results have come back from the lab and I'm happy to inform you that you do not have schizophrenia." (Or: "Your family say you're an asshole, but unfortunately for them, science says you're a sane asshole.") There are no lab tests for schizophrenia or depression, and if in the future such tests were ever to be developed, these conditions would, as Szasz often reminds us, become recognized as neurological diseases, not the province of psychiatry.

Unanimity or near-unanimity of diagnosis by numerous psychiatrists of the same patient would be an essential requirement for allowing the hypothesis that the patient has a brain disease to affect policy, but it would still not prove that he had a brain disease. People's behavior often falls into regularly recurring patterns for reasons other than that they all have a chemical imbalance in their brains. It might be that the psychiatrists are indeed detecting a common pattern—that there really is an 'it' there—but that this pattern is not due to a brain disease. So before we accepted that a person's behavior were accounted for by a brain disease, we would have to see arguments, based on the peculiar nature of his particular behavior, that it was not better explained by some alternative hypothesis.

Suppose then, that the cluster of symptoms is unanimously identified and that alternative explanations don't look very convincing. In a particular instance, we decide that a good case has been made that we're dealing with a brain disease. This is still a long way from justifying coercion. If we look at those brain diseases where the physical cause in the brain has actually been found—epilepsy, Alzheimer's, or stroke—the sufferers are not normally locked up and no one thinks they should be. Contrary to Virchow's rule, I think that migraine (or susceptibility to migraine) is obviously a brain disease where the brain defect has not (in most cases) been discovered. And yet no one thinks migraine sufferers should be locked up. In fact, there is no legal provision for committing anyone with a known brain disease, and the moment a physical cause for schizophrenia were established, the immediate effect might be that schizophrenics *qua* schizophrenics could not be committed. Judges or juries routinely commit or acquit people on the basis of testimony by psychiatrists, almost never on the basis of testimony by neurologists. To save the situation (and an important portion of their income) psychiatrists would probably maintain that these patients had something wrong with them in addition to the newly identified brain condition, something which, in turn, would be attributed to an additional and still-unknown brain condition. This response becomes even more likely because the newly discovered physical cause for schizophrenia would almost certainly not apply to some diagnosed cases of schizophrenia, and a way would have to be found for continuing to deprive those patients of their normal legal protections.

The general rule of the medical profession is that individuals may not be treated against their will, no matter how imperative this may seem to the physician and no matter how foolish the individual may be in refusing treatment. This holds just as much for brain disease as for lung disease.

Two reasons are suggested for why 'the mentally ill' should be consigned to a mental hospital against their wishes. One is that they are dangerous to the public or to themselves. Another is that due to their disease, their judgment is impaired, so that they cannot seek the treatment they would seek if their judgment were not impaired—a veritable Catch-22.

Both these rationales for coercion are, on the face of it, not overwhelmingly convincing. Do people diagnosed as schizophrenic or bipolar attack other people more frequently than random members of the general population? And if they do, do they do so by a greater percentage than Ethnic Group A, Religious Group X, or Occupational Group Q (take your choice)?

In practice, most discussion of involuntary commitment could easily be detached from any psychiatric input. If someone says 'Charles Manson should be locked up for life', this has obvious common-sense appeal, whether we think that Manson is a schizophrenic (and schizophrenia is a brain disease), a schizophrenic (and schizophrenia is not a brain disease), a demon, a human possessed by a demon, a vampire, a zombie, a golem, a space alien, or a very wicked person with fanciful beliefs. Psychiatrists do not know of any technique which could reliably convert Manson into a competent yet non-threatening individual. So the only serious practical question here is whether the public can be protected from Manson by methods which do not contravene the rights and liberties Manson has in common with everyone else.

Next consider the notion that someone cannot be allowed to choose whether he will have treatment or not, because he suffers from a brain disease that impairs his judgment.

The mere fact that someone's judgment is not very good is not normally considered sufficient to justify their coercive treatment. Many individuals not diagnosed as mentally ill may show poor judgment, while many individuals diagnosed as mentally ill may show excellent judgment. Poor judgment comes with the territory of being human, and individuals must to some extent take the consequences of their poor judgment. We don't, for example, coercively set aside a person's decision to seek a divorce, sell their house, buy a car, donate organs to medical research, join the Moonies, raise all-in on the flop, or make a will, merely because their judgment is poor. (They may be ruled incompetent, but that is generally a matter of whether they understand what's going on, something in principle distinct from any diagnosis of brain disease.) In all walks of life except psychiatry, we acknowledge that individuals are perfectly entitled to act upon their poor judgment. Someone who 'hears voices' may be distracted, and may therefore make poor decisions, but so may someone else be distracted by a painful back condition, rowdy neighbors, or a spouse's nagging.

All kinds of 'mentally ill' people do voluntarily seek treatment, so it cannot be a general rule that a symptom of some mental illness is unwillingness to be treated. Persons with no diagnosis of mental illness often decline to seek treatment for a disease, and physicians cannot compel them, no matter how strongly they feel that these persons are being foolish.

As a background to this discussion, there is the research material indicating that people classified as seriously mentally ill can in general be relied upon to make rational choices. Studies of the most hopeless cases of psychosis show that the psychotics act rationally: they respond to incentives. Given rewards for behaving in particular ways, they adapt their behavior to comply (Battalio et al. 1973; Winkler 1970; Winkler 1972). The same applies to addicts (addiction is still often labeled a mental illness): studies invariably show that even the most hardened and recalcitrant addicts will adjust their drug consumption. For example, the most hopeless institutionalized cases of extreme alcoholism, if given free access to alcohol along with rewards for moderating their alcohol consumption, will moderate. There is similar evidence for conscious control exercised by heroin and cocaine addicts (Schaler 2000, 21–32).

The usual joke here is that "they may be crazy but they're not stupid." However, non-stupidity sets a limit to craziness. People diagnosed as seriously mentally ill generally make intelligible choices. As for always making the best choices, that's not something we're entitled to demand of any group of people on pain of their being incarcerated without trial.

Szasz has attacked psychiatry on many different grounds. Some of these grounds are effective, quite independently of his pedantic denial of the literal existence of mental illness, and may even lose some of their impact by being associated with it.

One of the most persuasive reasons offered by Szasz for viewing psychiatric theory as a pseudoscience is that it changes its diagnostic categories by a process of political horse-trading among interest groups and advocacy groups. Some examples are well-known. Until 1973, American psychiatry classified homosexuality as a disease. Since 1973, homosexuality has not been a disease. This switch was not indicated by any research or any theoretical developments. No findings had been published with the remotest bearing on the question of whether homosexuality is a disease. The switch was made in response to pressure from gay rights groups. When an APA "working group" was revising the DSM and proposing to identify rape (or "rapism") as a mental disease, feminists were concerned that this diagnosis might get rapists off, so the psychiatrists caved to the feminists. They similarly abandoned the labeling as "masochism" of women who remain in abusive relationships (Szasz 1997, 79–80).

What are we to make of this? Obviously, that the theory of psychiatry is largely pseudoscience, not genuine science, and certainly not a genuine branch of medicine. No other branch of medicine would behave like this; it would be a scandal if they did. Yet we have no guarantee that even pseudoscience may not stumble upon the truth in particular instances. So again, we cannot conclude that there is no such thing as an unidentified brain disease with mental symptoms, just because this forms part of a currently thriving pseudoscience.

Szasz and the Mind-Body Problem

Why did Szasz lay such emphasis on the mythical nature of mental illness, and continue to do so over the decades, leading to widespread misunderstanding of his arguments against coercive psychiatry? I don't know the answer, but I suspect that it is related to an odd feature of Szasz's thinking—his unsatisfactory conception of the relation between mind and brain. It is, at the very least, clear that events in the mind can affect events in the brain and vice versa, and so we would expect someone who has spent a lifetime discussing mental illness, with a large part of that concerned with the possibility that what is called mental illness is due to brain disease, to take a position on the relation of mind and brain, or at least to disclose some interesting views on the topic.

To consider such matters as the causation of mental symptoms by brain diseases, it helps to have some conception of what philosophers traditionally call the mind-body problem, which given modern knowledge of the brain, means the relation between mind and brain. This relation between mind and brain is an area where Szasz seems to have very definite views, and yet simultaneously is strangely reticent.

As we read most of Szasz's work, we become conscious of an odd lacuna: he repeatedly draws a bright line between consciousness and physiology, as though these are independent realms. He discusses mental events as though they generally happen independently of brain events. This is the more remarkable because he is an atheist with no theological commitments. We wonder what he thinks about the relation of mind and brain. With *The Meaning of Mind* (1996), we find out that he has no coherent view of the relation between mind and brain and (while the book does have a sprinkling of keen insights here and there) his uninformed comments on those who have carefully elaborated various philosophical theories often miss the point.

Szasz briskly reviews a number of writers, whom he presents as adherents of a "new cult" (Szasz 1996, 81) he calls "neurophilosophy"—Daniel Dennett, Patricia Churchland, Paul Churchland, John Searle, Karl Popper and John Eccles, Francis Crick, and Julian Jaynes. If he had merely pointed out that some of these (such as the Churchlands) have erroneous beliefs about psychiatry, Szasz would have been on safer ground. He pays almost no attention to the differences between these thinkers. It is hard to imagine philosophers more different in their fundamental mind-body theories than Dennett, Searle, and Popper, and it would be helpful to know what Szasz thought about these differences, but Szasz writes as though he knows nothing of them. Some of Szasz's remarks seem to suggest he would be closest to Popper's interactionism, but he is so determinedly reticent on the mind-body relation that we can't be sure. Jaynes is a psychologist and popular writer whom almost all philosophers would dismiss as a fanciful proponent of a demonstrably false historical thesis.

What seems to concern Szasz is that all the writers he mentions here acknowledge a close association of mind and brain, and even go so far as to equate the two. He fastens on this aspect of their thinking (usually just turning up a quotation where they assert the equivalence of mind and brain) and does not pursue any other aspect of their thinking. Szasz attributes the denial of personal responsibility to all of those mentioned (76), dubious in several cases and an egregious blunder when applied to Searle or Popper (Searle 2007; Popper 1972). His unfamiliarity with the area is indicated by his not knowing that 'intentionality' has a specialized meaning in philosophy of mind—he assumes it refers to intentions (82).

I can find no more than three things we can be sure of in Szasz's view of the mind-brain relation: that the mind cannot exist without the body (Szasz 1996, 76) (agreed by almost everyone); that the mind is not the brain; and that the mind is not defined by consciousness (Szasz 1996, 81). Szasz thinks that mind and brain cannot be the same because we have two different words for them (75) which likewise shows that the Morning Star is not the Evening Star and that heat is not molecular motion. Szasz maintains that "equating mind with brain implies a denial of the distinctively human activities called 'minding', 'talking to oneself', and 'being responsible'" (75), but offers no reason for this claim, which most of the writers he is discussing would reject. (I take it for granted that the equivalence of mind and brain is a kind of hyperbole, if only because the brain controls autonomic functions like heartbeat which are not part of the mind. A stricter formulation would be that the mind consists of a class of brain events.)

A general theme of Szasz's remarks here (75–80) is that persons are not brains and that no "materialist account" can be given of persons. But then, where is the person located? It has to be 1. the brain; 2. some other part of the body; 3. somewhere other than the body; or 4. nowhere at all. Which? Szasz doesn't give us any hint as to what his answer would be. It seems clear to me that the person is inside the skull, but I accept that there are other views which can be defended. When it comes to the relation of mind and brain as a philosophical topic, Szasz does not offer us anything which would help us understand his conception of the mind-brain relation.

In Conclusion

Szasz advances two claims, which he evidently supposes are tightly connected. These claims are that there is no such thing as literal mental illness and that psychiatric coercion is wrong. These claims may both be correct (I think they are), but they are not tightly connected. Szasz's denial of the literal existence of mental illness is an interesting conceptual insight, but contrary to his own apparent view, it has few implications for policy.

Szasz has developed some effective arguments against psychiatric coercion, and against the pretensions of psychiatry generally, but these arguments are strictly independent of his conceptual thesis about mental illness, and might have been more persuasive if they had been elaborated without the distraction of that conceptual analysis.

If I am right, then arguing that there is no literal mental illness is neither necessary nor particularly effective in making a case against psychiatric coercion. It's quite correct as a piece of conceptual analysis—"a mind diseased" is indeed an incoherent notion, as the doctor hinted (but was too tactful to state explicitly) in response to Macbeth (*Macbeth*, Act V, Scene 3). There can literally be no such thing as a mental illness. But this is a pedantic point, like the literal nonexistence of sunrise and sunset.

Today the most popular unpacking of 'mental illness' by far is 'unidentified brain illness with mental symptoms', and there is nothing incoherent about that. Attempts to deny outright that such things exist are misplaced, because there is every reason to surmise that such things could exist. On the other hand, psychiatry's claims to have identified such entities, constructed from mental symptoms alone, are often dubious in particular cases, and even the definite acceptance of such psychiatric diagnoses would not take us very far towards justifying psychiatric coercion.

Critics of psychiatric theory and psychiatric coercion should not lay too much emphasis on the literal nonexistence of mental illness, but should do what Szasz in fact did much of the time: criticize both the foundations of specific psychiatric diagnoses and the arguments for withholding from those diagnosed as 'mentally ill' the usual civil liberties and legal protections enjoyed by all other competent adults.

Thomas S. Szasz: The Man and His Ideas (2017)

References

Battalio, R.C., John H. Kagel, Robin C. Winkler, Edwin B. Fisher, Jr., Robert L. Basmann, and Leonard Krasner. 1973. A Test of Consumer Demand Theory Using Observations of Individual Consumer Purchases. *Economic Inquiry* 11: 4 (December).

Campbell, Donald T. 1974. Downward Causation in Hierarchically Organised Biological Systems. In Francisco Jose Ayala and Theodosius Dobzhansky, eds., *Studies in the Philosophy of Biology: Reduction and Related Problems*. London: Macmillan.

———. 1990. Levels of Organization, Downward Causation, and the Selection-Theory Approach to Evolutionary Epistemology. In Gary Greenberg and Ethel Tobach, eds., *Theories of the Evolution of Knowing*. Hillsdale: Erlbaum.

Popper, Karl R. 1972. *Objective Knowledge: An Evolutionary Approach*. Oxford: Oxford University Press.

Schaler, Jeffrey A. 2000. *Addiction Is a Choice*. Chicago: Open Court.

———, ed. 2004. *Szasz Under Fire: The Psychiatric Abolitionist Faces His Critics*. Chicago: Open Court.

Searle, John R. 2007. *Freedom and Neurobiology: Reflections on Free Will, Language, and Political Power*. New York: Columbia University Press.

Szasz, Thomas S. 1960. The Myth of Mental Illness. *American Psychologist* 15: 113.

——. 1976. *Schizophrenia: The Sacred Symbol of Psychiatry*. New York: Basic Books.

——. 1990. *The Untamed Tongue: A Dissenting Dictionary*. La Salle: Open Court.

——. 1991 [1970]. *Ideology and Insanity: Essays on the Psychiatric Dehumanization of Man*. Syracuse: Syracuse University Press.

——. 1997 [1987]. *Insanity: The Idea and Its Consequences*. Syracuse: Syracuse University Press.

——. 2001. *Pharmacracy: Medicine and Politics in America*. Westport: Praeger.

——. 2002 [1996]. *The Meaning of Mind: Language, Morality, and Neuroscience*. Syracuse: Syracuse University Press.

——. 2007. *The Medicalization of Everyday Life: Selected Essays*. Syracuse: Syracuse University Press.

——. 2010 [1961]. *The Myth of Mental Illness: Foundations of a Theory of Personal Conduct*. New York: Harper Perennial.

Valenstein, Elliot S. 1998. *Blaming the Brain: The Truth about Drugs and Mental Health*. New York: The Free Press.

Winkler, Robin C. 1970. Management of Chronic Psychiatric Patients by a Token Reinforcement System. *Journal of Applied Behavior Analysis* 3 (Spring).

——. 1972. An Experimental Analysis of Economic Balance: Savings and Wages in a Token Economy. *Behavior Therapy* 4:1 (December)

Wyatt, W. Joseph, and Donna M. Midkiff. 2006. Biological Psychiatry: A Practice in Search of a Science. *Behavior and Social Issues* 15.

——. 2007. Psychiatry's Thirty-Five-Year, Non-Empirical Reach for Biological Explanations. *Behavior and Social Issues* 16.

Publication Histories

The pieces in this collection are all substantially the same as originally written or published. Slight differences are often due to my reversing editorial alterations made by the original publishers. In some cases, I have used here the original file as submitted, so I may not even be aware of some small differences from the published form. In a few cases, where it did not unduly interrupt the flow of the main text, I have moved what was originally a footnote into the main text. Quite rarely, I changed a sentence to improve the style, but I have not modified everything which now makes me wince a little. I have recently read through all these pieces and I still agree with all the main points, though I wouldn't always give them exactly the same emphasis today.

Chapter 1. 'Alice in Wonderland' appeared in *Free Life*, journal of the Libertarian Alliance, 5:1–2 (probably 1987), and then in *Liberty* (May 1988).

Both publications received my original file, and the version in *Free Life* introduced numerous errors, some quite serious, consequently the version in *Liberty* is closer to what I wrote and is almost identical to what's reproduced here.

Chapter 2. 'Partial Recall' appeared in *Liberty* 7:3 (March 1994).

In my subsequent reading and thinking, I have become steadily more convinced that there is no such thing as a repressed memory (and no such thing as the unconscious mind). For a closer look at some related ideas, see the book I wrote with Michael Edelstein and Richard Kujoth, *Therapy Breakthrough: Why Some Psychotherapies Work Better than Others* (Open Court, 2013). There is still a lot of pseudoscience even in mainstream psychology, but it seems to be slowly diminishing. A good sign is the appearance of a book like *50 Great Myths of Popular Psychology: Shattering Widespread Misconceptions about Human Behavior*, by Scott O. Lilienfeld, Steven J. Lynn, John Ruscio, and Barry L. Beyerstein (Blackwell, 2010).

Chapter 3. 'Why Stop at Term Limits?' appeared in *National Review*, September 11th 1995.

A government chosen by lot from the entire adult population is not my first preference (that would be a very sophisticated form of anarchy of the sort expounded by J.C. Lester in his *Escape from Leviathan* and envisioned by David Barker in his *Welcome to Free America*). But I do suspect it would be an improvement on what we have now.

Chapter 4. 'Yes, Gambling Is Productive and Rational' first appeared in *Liberty* 11:1 (September 1997).

I wrote it with the intention that it would be reprinted in condensed form in *Legalized Gambling: For and Against*, edited by Rod Evans and Irwin Berent (Open Court, 1998), and it was. It has also been reprinted in various other places, but there is still a deficiency of popular understanding of the powerful case for fully legal gambling.

Chapter 5. 'The Mystery of Fascism' appeared in *Liberty* 15:11 (November 2001).

In the late 1960s, knowing nothing about fascism (but thinking I knew something), I was surprised to hear my then socialist comrade Adam Buick casually remark that up to 1914 Benito Mussolini was the Che Guevara of his day. Over succeeding years I read quite a bit on the subject. Some time in 2000, the late Bill Bradford asked me what I could write for an upcoming issue of *Liberty*, and when I mentioned this possibility, expressed keen interest.

'The Mystery of Fascism' gives its name to this collection because it's so often cited and hailed as a classic. It's the greatest of my greatest hits, and though it's very far from the best thing I've written, I'm quite fond of it.

Chapter 6. 'An Unexpected Discovery' appeared in *Liberty* 16:7 (July 2002).

This is a personal memoir which includes an account of how it came to be written.

Chapter 7. 'Taking the JFK Assassination Conspiracy Theory Seriously' appeared in *Liberty* 17:11 (November 2003).

The founder and editor of *Liberty*, the late Bill Bradford, gave this piece the silly title 'Wasn't It a Little Crowded on That Grassy Knoll?' Okay, my original title, restored here, is somewhat dry, but it does capture the distinctive point: that instead of only looking for flaws in the 'official' account of the murder of Kennedy, we should *also* look for flaws in the various conspiracy theories, by seriously asking ourselves the question, 'What else would have to be true for this conspiracy theory to be true?' I take the same approach to the unofficial theories of '9/11 Truth', where I think the flaws are even more embarrassing than in the unofficial theories of the Kennedy assassination. Having said that, I suppose I ought to add that each conspiracy theory should be evaluated on its merits, and I have no doubt that some conspiracy theories are true.

Chapter 8. 'The Sacred Element' first appeared in *Liberty* 17:3 (March 2003).

Until around 1991 I believed in the global warming theory because I had heard so many people, some of them apparently qualified, assert it. Then I happened to hear a presentation by Fred Singer putting the contrary view, and I decided to read up on it. It took me several years to become thoroughly convinced of the skeptical position on this matter (which, we unfortunately have to keep repeating, is not that there is no human-caused global warming, but that this is slight compared with natural fluctuations and is on balance probably beneficial).

Chapter 9. 'Life, Liberty, and the Treadmill'. Since this piece appeared in *Liberty* 19:2 (February 2005), research continues to substantiate 1. that happiness rises with income (though at a low and declining rate once a level of modest comfort is reached) and 2. that economic freedom (free-market capitalism) is most conducive to happiness—both indirectly, because it raises income more than any alternative, and directly, because people are happier in a freer economy, independent of their level of income.

Chapter 10. 'Is God Coming or Going?' appeared in *Philosophy Now* 78 (April–May 2010).

When I wrote this, it was quite fashionable to say that the US was an exception to secularization, that American religion was in great shape, that there was a God Gene, and all the rest of it. You don't hear so much of this uninformed prattle any more, but it still occasionally crops up, so maybe this brief refutation is still worth reading.

Chapter 11. 'Safe Dex'. This is one of two chapters I wrote for *Dexter and Philosophy: Mind over Spatter*, edited by Richard Greene, George A. Reisch, and Rachel Robison-Greene (Open Court, 2011).

I haven't watched every TV show ever made, but of those I have watched, I consider *Dexter* as second only to *Breaking Bad*. Like a child, I wish that *Dexter* could have gone on forever, and I still catch myself wondering about a future season in which Hannah and Harrison, living in a heavenly, leafy suburb of Buenos Aires, are menaced by a horrific villain who somehow knows all about their past, but then a watchful figure emerges from the shadows and discreetly disposes of the villain . . . not before encountering major surprises and life-threatening setbacks. I'm available to write the script. Or to be the script-writer's very humble assistant. I'll drop everything else.

Chapter 12. 'The Bigotry of the New Atheism' was first published in 2014 but written in 2008 or 2009, which accounts for its not mentioning some relevant recent events.

I wrote it, under the title 'An Old Atheist's Qualms about the New Atheism', as a companion piece to 'Is God Coming or Going?' and submitted both to *Philosophy Now*, which did quickly print 'Is God Coming or Going?' but held on to this piece for some years before telling me they would not be using it. I then adapted it very slightly and put it on the London Libertarian blog (April 12th 2014) under the title 'The Bigotry of the New Atheism (by an Old Atheist)'.

Chapter 13. 'The Fallacy of Sheer Bulk'. The London Libertarian (February 24th 2014).

Chapter 14. 'A Moral Defense of Meat-Eating'. The London Libertarian (May 6th 2014).

Chapter 15. 'How I Could Have Made Hillary President' was posted in the London Libertarian (February 22nd 2018) and reprinted in *Scott Adams and Philosophy: A Hole in the Fabric of Reality* (2018). The present version has a few differences from the original, including the correction of two factual slips.

Chapter 16. 'Scott Adams and the Pinocchio Fallacy' first appeared in *Scott Adams and Philosophy: A Hole in the Fabric of Reality*, edited by Daniel Yim, Galen Foresman, and Robert Arp (Open Court, 2018).

Chapter 17. Hayek's Theory of Cultural Group Selection'. *Journal of Libertarian Studies* VIII:2 (Summer 1987).

It appeared with the following author's note: "This paper was presented at the Midwestern Libertarian Scholars' Conference, Chicago, April 13–14, 1984. (A few minor revisions were made in April 1986.) The paper is a reworking of part of 'Spontaneous Order and Traditionalism in Hayek', which, in turn, was an expanded version of a paper first delivered to the Colloquium on Austrian Philosophy and Austrian Politics, London, April 26–27, 1980." Until I put this collection together, I had completely forgotten all of this.

Chapter 18. 'How We Got Here' appeared in *Critical Review: A Journal of Politics and Society* 2:1 (Winter 1988).

I give the journal's full title because there have been other journals called *Critical Review*. As I re-read the piece now, it strikes me as remarkably sensible and completely persuasive. Indeed, it brings back the twinge of a haunting fear I routinely experience anent things I have written—that everything in it is so obviously true that no one could possibly disagree, and that therefore it must be a waste of time saying it.

Chapter 19. 'The Market Socialists' Predicament' appeared under the title 'Between Immorality and Unfeasibility: The Market Socialist Predicament' in *Critical Review: A Journal of Politics and Society* 10:3 (Summer 1996).

This piece spotlights the plight of those who feel they have to accept that the government owning everything and trying to plan the economy has been a total failure, while they still want to go on hating capitalism.

Chapter 20. 'Nozick on Sunk Costs' appeared in *Ethics* 106 (April 1996).

Since scholarship has never been my day job, I have usually not made an effort to publish in the more prestigious journals. Most of the other pieces in this collection were sent to more or less anyone (no disrespect intended) in response to ad hoc opportunities and requests—with a strong bias toward places which I hoped I could trust not to make any editorial changes, especially not without my consent. When I read Nozick's book *The Nature of Rationality*, I was shocked by his dreadfully muddled treatment of the sunk costs theory, and quickly wrote the first draft of this piece, taking his argument apart. I then found I had produced something too closely reasoned for any popular publication and it had to go in a scholarly journal. I decided I might as well start at the top, for once, with *Ethics* ('the top' of journals which would view this kind of paper as within their subject area), and submitted it to *Ethics*, thinking it likely this would just be the first of several rejections. But the people at *Ethics* liked it and made various suggestions for changes, which I accepted. I've lost the original draft and the correspondence, but I know I didn't feel that the final version in any way betrayed my real intentions. I recall that some of the changes they asked for were even improvements (you won't often catch me saying that). At this time, I knew quite a number of mostly young libertarians who like me had interests in scholarly issues but no academic position and who assured me that it was impossible to publish in a top-flight journal without 'connections'. I viewed publication of this piece as refuting those libertarian comrades, as well as refuting Nozick on sunk costs.

Chapter 21. 'The Atkins Diet as an Alternative Theory' appeared as 'Why and When Should We Rely on Scientific Experts? The Atkins Diet as an Alternative Theory' in *The Atkins Diet and Philosophy: Chewing the Fat with Kant and Nietzsche*, edited by Lisa Heldke, Kerri Mommer, and Cynthia Pineo (Open Court, 2005).

This was before the days when we had all heard of the Paleo Diet, before Gary Taubes, before Abel James's *Fat Burning Man* podcasts, before David Perlmutter, and long before the whole sorry story of the rise and fall of the low-fat diet had been so perceptively charted by Nina Teicholz. Now we know that Dr. Robert Atkins was indeed onto something.

Chapter 22. 'Will Emerging Media Create a Collective Mind?' appeared in the collection, *Philosophy of Emerging Media: Understanding, Appreciation,*

Application, edited by Juliet Floyd and James Katz and published by Oxford University Press in 2016.

Out of the blue I was invited by Professor James Katz to a conference at Boston University in 2015 on 'Philosophy of Emerging Media'. The organizers may have assumed that, as Editorial Director of a book publishing company, I would have something to say about the future of books. I hope they weren't too disappointed by what I gave them instead. The presentations from the conference were written up and included (along with some additional commissioned papers) in the collection as published.

23. 'What Follows from the Non-Existence of Mental Illness?' appeared in the collection, *Thomas S. Szasz: The Man and His Ideas*, edited by Jeffrey A. Schaler, Henry Zvi Lothane, and Richard E. Vatz (Routledge, 2017).

I had various contacts with the late Tom Szasz by phone and email but never met him in the flesh. He expressed admiration for some of my writings, including the pieces which are now Chapters 5 and 6 of this book. I have known Jeffrey Schaler for some years, and I'm proud to say I was the in-house editor at Open Court for his classic work, *Addiction Is a Choice* (Open Court, 2000). Jeff asked me to write something for a proposed collection on Thomas Szasz, to be likely published by Transaction. Knowing that Jeff is more of a card-carrying Szaszian than I am, I felt that he might object to my criticisms of Szasz's ideas, but he liked the piece and accepted it gladly, expressing his regret that Tom hadn't lived to read it. A few of the ideas in this article were anticipated in a little piece I posted on the London Libertarian blog ('Remembering Tom Szasz', August 7th 2014). While the volume was in preparation, the Transaction publishing firm was swallowed, digested, and assimilated by Taylor and Francis, and the book appeared in their Routledge imprint.

INDEX